Here Is Wisdom

Here Is Wisdom

*Wisdom Motifs and Their Function
in the Book of Revelation*

∽

JIN WOOK KIM

WIPF & STOCK • Eugene, Oregon

HERE IS WISDOM
Wisdom Motifs and Their Function in the Book of Revelation

Copyright © 2026 Jin Wook Kim. All rights reserved. Except for brief quotations in critical publications or reviews, no part of this book may be reproduced in any manner without prior written permission from the publisher. Write: Permissions, Wipf and Stock Publishers, 199 W. 8th Ave., Suite 3, Eugene, OR 97401.

Wipf & Stock
An Imprint of Wipf and Stock Publishers
199 W. 8th Ave., Suite 3
Eugene, OR 97401

www.wipfandstock.com

PAPERBACK ISBN: 979-8-3852-6598-5
HARDCOVER ISBN: 979-8-3852-6599-2
EBOOK ISBN: 979-8-3852-6600-5

"Unless otherwise indicated, all Scripture quotations are from The ESV® Bible (The Holy Bible, English Standard Version®), © 2001 by Crossway, a publishing ministry of Good News Publishers. Used by permission. All rights reserved."

To my Savior and Lord, whom I want to serve until He comes.

Contents

Preface | ix
List of Abbreviations | xi

Chapter 1: Introduction | 1
    Thesis | 3
    History of Research | 8
    Methodology | 30
    Conclusion | 32

Chapter 2: Σοφία in Revelation as Divine Wisdom | 34
    First and Second Instances: Revelation 5:12 and 7:12 | 35
        Revelation 5:12 | 35
        Revelation 7:12 | 49
    Summary and Conclusion | 61

Chapter 3: Σοφία in Revelation as Wisdom for God's Faithful People | 63
    Third and Fourth Instances: Revelation 13:18 and 17:9 | 63
        Revelation 13:18 | 64
        Revelation 17:9 | 82
    Summary and Conclusion | | 108

Chapter 4: Two-Women Motif outside of Revelation | 110
    Extrabiblical Background | 112
        Graeco-Roman Literature | 112
        Second Temple Jewish Literature | 123
    Biblical Background: Proverbs 1–9 | 133
    Summary and Conclusion | 139

Chapter 5: Two-Women Motif in Revelation | 140
    The Evil Woman Babylon | 140
        Babylon's Portrayal as the Evil Woman | 142

Babylon's Demise as the Evil Woman | 149
The Ethical Choice: "Come Out" | 153
The Virtuous Woman New Jerusalem | 155
New Jerusalem's Portrayal as the Virtuous Woman | 156
New Jerusalem's Rise as the Virtuous Woman | 162
The Ethical Choice: "Come" | 172
Conclusion: Babylon and New Jerusalem | 174
Two Other Women Figures in Revelation | 176
The Woman Jezebel | 176
The Radiant Woman | 181
Summary and Conclusion | 186

Chapter 6: Blessings and Vice Lists in Revelation | 188
Macarisms in Revelation | 189
Macarism 1 and 6: Revelation 1:3 and 22:7 | 190
Macarism 2: Revelation 14:13 | 190
Macarism 3: Revelation 16:15 | 196
Macarism 4: Revelation 19:9 | 198
Macarism 5: Revelation 20:6 | 200
Macarism 7: Revelation 22:14 | 204
Conclusion: Macarisms as a Whole | 206
Vice Lists in Revelation | 207
Vice List 1: Revelation 9:20–21 | 208
Vice List 2: Revelation 21:8 | 212
Vice List 3: Revelation 21:27 | 216
Vice List 4: Revelation 22:15 | 221
Conclusion: Vice Lists as a Whole | 225
Summary and Conclusion | 226

Chapter 7: Conclusion | 227
Summary and Synthesis | 227
Possibilities for Future Research | 234
Implications for the Church Today | 235

Bibliography | 239

Preface

I HAVE ALWAYS BEEN fascinated by the world John paints in the book of Revelation. The more I read it, the more I wanted to study what Revelation is all about. I loved figuring out the theological meanings of the passages in Revelation and gaining new insights from various theological perspectives, like a detective who gets excited when new evidence comes to the fore. In short, I loved to gain new information regarding the book of Revelation. But then, it dawned on me. Knowing what Revelation teaches is one thing, but knowing why Revelation teaches what it teaches is a whole new other, but just as important. This dawning gained momentum as I learned about literary critical methods such as rhetorical criticism and discourse analysis in one of the PhD seminars taught by Dr. Mark Taylor at Southwestern Baptist Theological Seminary. It was concretized as I discussed the importance of ethics and the significance of the use of wisdom literature for Revelation with Dr. Paul Hoskins, whom I worked for as a grading assistant. The current study is a fruition of that dawning, hopefully one among many others to come. A heartfelt gratitude goes to Drs. Taylor and Hoskins for their vigilant guidance, both academic and spiritual.

I must also express my sincere gratitude to my doctoral supervisor, James R. Wicker. His positive support, careful attention even to the minute details, and pastoral encouragement have been tremendous. This work would not have been possible without his academic and pastoral guidance. Finally, words cannot express how much I am thankful to my family. My wife Kyung Hyun has been a constant beacon of support. She was firm in love when I was fragile. She was there to pray for me and to reassure me of God's purpose when I could not see a way forward. My son Joel's consistent roars of "you can do it" have also been the perfect boost that I needed to complete this project. Thank you all, and thank you my family, from the bottom of my heart.

Jin Wook Kim
Fort Worth, Texas
2024

Abbreviations

ANES	Ancient Near Eastern Studies
AUSS	Andrews University Seminary Studies
BBR	Bulletin for Biblical Research
BDAG	W. Baur, F. W. Danker, W. F. Arndt, F. W. Gingrich, A Greek-English Lexicon of the New Testament and other Early Christian Literature, 3rd ed.
BETL	Bibliotheca Ephemeridum Theologicarum Lovaniensium
BJRL	Bulletin of the John Rylands Library
BR	Biblical Research
BZNW	Beihefte zur Zeitschrift für die Neutestamentliche Wissenschaft
CBR	Currents in Biblical Research
CBQ	The Catholic Biblical Quarterly
CCSS	Catholic Commentary on Sacred Scripture
CTQ	Concordia Theological Quarterly
DSD	Dead Sea Discoveries
EDNT	Exegetical Dictionary of the New Testament
HALOT	The Hebrew and Aramaic Lexicon of the Old Testament
JBL	Journal of Biblical Literature
JBT	Journal of Biblical Theology
JECH	Journal of Early Christian History
JETS	Journal of the Evangelical Theological Society

JGRChJ	Journal of Greco-Roman Christianity and Judaism
JSNT	Journal for the Study of the New Testament
JSNTSup	Journal for the Study of the New Testament Supplement Series
JSOT	Journal for the Study of the Old Testament
JSOTSup	Journal for the Study of the Old Testament Supplement Series
JSP	Journal for the Study of the Pseudepigrapha
JSPSup	Journal for the Study of the Pseudepigrapha Supplement Series
KJOTS	The Korean Journal of Old Testament Studies
LCL	The Loeb Classical Library
LNTS	Library of New Testament Studies
MSJ	The Master's Seminary Journal
NCBC	New Cambridge Bible Commentary
NICNT	The New International Commentary on the New Testament
NICOT	The New International Commentary on the Old Testament
NovT	Novum Testamentum
NSBT	New Studies in Biblical Theology
NTS	New Testament Studies
NTT	New Testament Theology
OTS	Oudtestamentische Studiën
PIBA	Proceedings of the Irish Biblical Association
PNTC	Pillar New Testament Commentary
RevistB	Revista Bíblica
RTR	The Reformed Theological Review
SBL	Society of Biblical Literature
SCJ	Stone-Campbell Journal
ThStKr	Theologische Studien und Kritiken

TrinJ	Trinity Journal
WTJ	The Westminster Theological Journal
WUNT	Wissenschaftliche Untersuchungen zum Neuen Testament

CHAPTER 1

Introduction

APOCALYPSES DO NOT SIMPLY present otherworldly views of history and reality or information about the end times. They intend to do something—to teach and to exhort their readers by showing them a view of reality that is beyond this world. In other words, ethics is just as essential to apocalypses as history or eschatology. As Patrick A. Tiller states, "Moral exhortation (how one ought to live in this world) has probably always been one of the functions of apocalyptic literature."[1]

However, past scholarship has not always stressed the significance ethics plays in apocalyptic literature. The reason for this is arguably twofold: (1) scholars have largely focused on the question of setting and origin of the apocalypses and (2) scholars likewise have largely focused on eschatological aspects of this literature.[2] This lack has been somewhat remedied due to the rise of literary criticism and subsequent studies that deal with the literary function of apocalyptic literature, but more work needs to be done. The book of Revelation is no exception.

One way the author of Revelation exhorts his readers is through the use of wisdom motifs.[3] Wisdom, by its nature, has a strong paraenetic

1. Tiller, "Rich and Poor," 178.

2. For example, J. A. T. Robinson's understanding had become quite standard, namely that in late Judaism, apocalyptic writers went one way, and the scribal writers went the other way, the former concerned with the future and did not take any interest in how people should live in the present, and the latter developing rabbinic teachings to be codified in Mishnah and Talmud. Robinson, *Jesus and His Coming*, 94–95. See also, Barton, "Ethics in Apocalyptic," 37–51.

3. Wisdom motif can be defined as a smallest meaning-bearing unit within a text that often recurs and that has to do with sapiential themes. See Arweiler, "Thematics," accessed August 5, 2022, http://dx.doi.org/10.1163/1574-9347_bnp_e15303920.

function, and it is thus not a surprise when one encounters sapiential materials in the biblical writings, let alone the book of Revelation.[4] Unfortunately, however, most of New Testament scholarship on the subject of wisdom traditions in relation to the apocalyptic has been spent on the teachings of Jesus as found in the Gospels, especially on the issue of the elusive Q source,[5] or on the genre studies.[6] Again, the main focus has been on the issue of origin or source, namely the effort to trace the origin of Jesus's sayings,[7] as well as to trace the origin of the apocalyptic genre, whereas the question of function is sidelined.

With specific regards to the book of Revelation, wisdom motifs in relation to the function and ethics of the book have rarely been tackled.[8] This is surprising, especially when ethics is an essential feature of apocalyptic literature and wisdom motifs play a significant role in promoting ethical behavior. More importantly, works that treat wisdom motifs and their functions in the book of Revelation in a systematic and coherent fashion are virtually non-existent, a scholarly gap the present study seeks to address.[9] A comprehensive study on the wisdom motifs and their func-

---

4. This is because biblical authors not only want to impart information to the readers, but also want to affect the thinking and the behavior of the readers. This understanding has been especially clarified by the speech-act theory. See, for instance, Osborne, *Hermeneutical Spiral*, 23, 379 and Vanhoozer, *Is There a Meaning*.

5. The debate has been centered around the makeup of Q, whether it was essentially a collection of wisdom sayings or whether it included apocalyptic predictions. For a quick and helpful summary of the debate, see Collins, *Seers, Sibyls and Sages*, 385–86. The same summary by Collins is also found in Perdue et al., *In Search of Wisdom*, 165–85.

6. The relationship between wisdom as a genre and apocalyptic as a genre has been subject to much debate. See the section below entitled "History of Research."

7. Pauline studies face a similar trend. Paul's apocalypticism is also assessed in terms of where Paul would have gotten the idea, whether it be from a Jewish tradition, Hellenistic tradition, some other ancient tradition, or some combination of these traditions. Further, the main focus of Paul and his apocalyptic thinking seems to be epistemological, namely how apocalypticism has affected Paul's worldview and theology, rather than how apocalypticism is functioning in Paul's arguments. For a quick summary of apocalyptic studies in Pauline scholarship, see Blackwell et al., *Paul and the Apocalyptic Imagination*, 3–21. For a rare and good example of a study that focuses on how apocalyptic traditions are functioning in Paul's arguments, see Johnson, *Function of Apocalyptic*.

8. See the section below entitled "History of Research" for works that do treat wisdom motifs and their functions in the book of Revelation.

9. Although a number of commentaries do make observations on how certain wisdom motifs are functioning in the book of Revelation, these observations, however, are brief treatments and are not systematic or coherent interpretations.

tions in the book of Revelation will in turn also contribute to a clearer understanding of the purpose and the ethics found in Revelation.

THESIS

The present study seeks to analyze the wisdom motifs found in the book of Revelation in order to present their rhetorical function. The thesis of the present study is that Revelation uses wisdom motifs strategically to exhort the readers toward a certain ethical behavior, a life of unwavering fidelity to Christ.[10] To put it differently, the saints are called to live a life of loyalty or faithfulness to Christ in a world where allures to disloyalty or unfaithfulness abound. The one who has "wisdom" will be able to recognize the true and gruesome reality of this world and choose not to be influenced by it. Scholars frequently note that the book of Revelation has strong paraenetic emphasis.[11] However, not everyone agrees on which paraenetic emphasis constitutes the primary purpose of Revelation as a whole. While this theme of loyalty and disloyalty may seem generalized and not specific enough, it is broad enough to encompass various purposes proposed by others and works well for the purpose of the present study which is to understand the reason and function of wisdom motifs found in Revelation.[12] As this study hopes to show, the most likely intent of the author in utilizing wisdom motifs is to promote a life of unwavering fidelity to Christ on the part of the readers.[13] These wisdom motifs include: (1) σοφία passages, (2) a two-women topos, and (3) blessings and vice lists.

---

10. This study follows the line of thinking as exemplified by Rodney Thomas, who, in tracing the magical motifs found in Revelation, understands the author to be claiming that those who rely upon things that do not come from God are committing disloyalty to God. Thomas, *Magical Motifs*.

11. In fact, scholars often note that Revelation differs from the Jewish apocalypses in having a much stronger paraenetic emphasis. See Fiorenza, "Phenomenon of Early Christian Apocalyptic," 302 and Collins, *Seers, Sibyls and Sages*, 118.

12. This study's purpose is not to decide which scholar's proposal regarding the purpose of the book of Revelation is the right one. Thus, the various purposes of Revelation as proposed by various scholars will not be recounted and be pitted against each other here. However, one can find a succinct chart of the various proposals regarding the purpose of Revelation in appendix 3 of Robinson, "Sexual Immorality Language," 229–30.

13. This study thus goes against the postmodernist approach that understands authorial intent to be unnecessary. This writer concurs with Yarbro Collins' declaration that there is something "inhumane and immoral" about not looking for authorial intent when using a text. See Yarbro Collins, *Cosmology and Eschatology*, 1.

Σοφία Passages

First, there are four instances in the book of Revelation where the specific word σοφία occurs.[14] The first instance occurs at a pivotal point in Revelation where Christ, who is the Lion and the Lamb, is claimed as the only one worthy enough to open the scroll with the seven seals which contains the judgments that will ensue throughout Revelation.[15] Christ who was slain is worthy to receive wisdom (Rev 5:12), and with that wisdom he will regulate the judgments that will follow.[16] The second instance occurs right after the sealing of God's people and is another throne room vision where God is worshipped as one to whom wisdom belongs in eternity (Rev 7:12).

The third instance is a riddle or a challenge to the readers—to calculate the number of the beast (Rev 13:18). Revelation 13 is another important junction in the storyline of Revelation, since it describes how the dragon, through the beast and the false prophet, persecutes God's people and deceives the world into idolatry. No matter what "calculating the number" may entail, the challenge to the readers is significant and clear: those with wisdom should understand the reality of how the beast operates in the world. The fourth instance occurs in the description of Babylon the Great and of the beast (Rev 17:9). Similar to the third instance, those with wisdom are once again challenged to understand the reality of the beast in relation to Babylon the Great.

Thus, the first two instances claim that σοφία belongs only to the Lamb and to God. The last two instances challenge the readers by claiming that those who have wisdom should be able to understand the reality that the author is presenting. In short, the author has placed the word σοφία and the call to this σοφία at key points in the narrative of Revelation so that the people of God would see the reality of the kingdom of the beast and not align their fidelity to this kingdom.[17] Like σοφία that

---

14. Rev 5:12; 7:12; 13:18; 17:9.

15. That the scroll contains judgments is clear from Revelation 6 where Christ begins to open the scroll and the judgments follow.

16. Rev 5:12 also states that Christ is worthy to receive wealth, which is another important theme found in Revelation.

17. Thus, σοφία involves not only understanding the true reality of the world, but also the demand for right response. Stuckenbruck, "Disclosure of Wisdom," 359. Similarly, Richard Bauckham argues that Revelation, as a prophecy, involves both a prophetic discernment of the situation and a prophetic demand for right response. Bauckham, "Approaching the Apocalypse," 94.

belongs only to God and to the Lamb, the people who exhibit this σοφία should also belong only to God and to the Lamb.

Two-Women Topos

Second, the book of Revelation invokes what Barbara Rossing has termed "the two-women topos."[18] As exemplified in Proverbs 1–9, the two-women topos utilizes two types of women, one evil and one virtuous, who call the readers to follow after them. This has the rhetorical effect of challenging the readers to make the obvious and right choice: to ignore the evil woman but to follow the virtuous woman. Revelation also personifies two cities, Babylon and the New Jerusalem, and contrasts them (Rev 17–22). By portraying the two cities as two different women, John exhorts the readers to make the right choice in following the New Jerusalem the bride and to not be enticed by Babylon the harlot. Furthermore, Revelation also introduces two other women: Jezebel in Revelation 2 and a woman clothed with the sun in Revelation 12. The present study will also connect these women with the harlot and the bride to give a fuller picture of the two-women topos and how it functions in the book of Revelation, something Rossing did not adequately cover in her work.

Blessings and Vice Lists

Third, Revelation employs macarisms and vice lists to define acceptable and unacceptable behaviors. Analyzing both elements together thus can provide valuable insight into Revelation's ethics. In fact, macarisms of the book of Revelation occur strategically to challenge the readers for an appropriate behavior, that is, unwavering fidelity to Christ.[19] There are seven μακάριος (or μακάριοι) sayings in Revelation that appear throughout the

---

18. Rossing, *Two Cities*.

19. Collins notes that virtue and vice lists are likely from wisdom origin, rather than prophecy, as seen from *1 Enoch*, Sir 2:12–14; 41:8–9, and *2 Enoch*. See Collins, *Seers, Sibyls and Sages*, 395–96. As for the blessing sayings (macarisms), they also figure quite prominently in wisdom literatures and genres and is a literary form closely tied with wisdom tradition. See Job 5:17; Prov 3:13; 3:18; 8:32, 34; 14:21; 16:20; 20:7; 28:14; 29:18; Jas 1:12. See also the Beatitudes of Jesus in Matthew 5:3–11. The Psalter also has a high number of blessing saying occurrences, with many of them being closely tied to wisdom themes or topics. See especially Ps 1:1; 34:8; 40:4; 94:12; 106:3; 112:1; 119:1–2; 128:1.

book.[20] Structurally, the first one (Rev 1:3) and the last two (Rev 22:7, 14) serve as bookends and promote the importance of keeping (τηρέω) the words contained in Revelation.[21] The second one (Rev 14:13) occurs near the end of an important interlude (Rev 12–14) that is situated in between the vision of the seventh trumpet and that describes the nature of the dragon, the beast, and the false prophet. The second macarism is also fronted with the command to write (γράψον), which in turn shows the importance of the saying. Ironically, the blessed ones here are the ones who die in the Lord, not those who live and succeed in the world by following the beast (Rev 13:16–17), and they are described as ones whose deeds follow them, again showing the importance of right behavior.

The third macarism (Rev 16:15) is found in the vision of the sixth bowl, where the eschatological battle of the Armageddon is described. This saying stands out, because it occurs quite abruptly in the middle of the vision of the Armageddon; the vision actually will flow naturally if the saying was not there. The blessing saying itself is also fronted with a familiar proverbial saying about Jesus coming like a thief (cf. Matt 24:42–44; 1 Thess 5:2–4; 2 Pet 3:10; Rev 3:3). When compared with Revelation 3:3–4 where another "thief" saying is found, it seems most likely that the idea of keeping one's garments on and staying awake has to do with hearing and keeping the Lord's commands in repentance, as it is the case with Revelation 22:14.

The fourth macarism (Rev 19:9) is also fronted with the command to write like the second saying and occurs after the fall of the harlot and immediately after the introduction of the bride. In this case, the blessed are those who are invited to the marriage supper of the Lamb, and this challenges the readers to align themselves with the bride, not with the harlot. Not surprisingly, the bride is characterized as one who is clothed with fine linen (βύσσινον), and this fine linen (βύσσινον) is identified

---

20. Rev 1:3; 14:13; 16:15; 19:9; 20:6; 22:7; 22:14.

21. Revelation 22:14 literally states, "Blessed are those who wash their robes." The metaphor of washing robes refers to the saints' participation in true faith, perseverance, and obedience to God's commands (cf. Rev 7:14; 19:7–9). See Hoskins, *Revelation*, 474–75. Thus, the μακάριος saying of Revelation 22:14 also stresses the importance of obedience and fidelity to God and to Christ. This is further confirmed in other manuscripts where the phrase "those who wash their robes" has been changed to "those who do his commands" (ποιοῦντες τὰς ἐντολὰς αὐτοῦ), probably reflecting the understanding that the metaphor of washing robes should be comprehended as obeying God's commands. See Beale, *Revelation*, 1140.

to be the righteous acts (τὰ δικαιώματα) of the saints (Rev 19:8).²² The fifth macarism (Rev 20:6) occurs right after the description of the first resurrection in the vision of the millennial kingdom. Those who showed fidelity to God and to Christ, those who did not worship the beast and who did not receive its mark (Rev 20:4), are the blessed ones who partake in the first resurrection.

A related term to μακάριος also appears in the book of Revelation, namely εὐλογία.²³ Similar to the instances of σοφία, the term εὐλογία occurs in the throne room visions where God and the Lamb are praised. In these exaltations, blessing (εὐλογία) is proclaimed to belong to God and to the Lamb, just as σοφία is proclaimed to belong to them. Thus, it becomes fitting that God and the Lamb, who are the source of blessing (εὐλογία), can address blessings (μακάριοι) to their people. Just as those with true σοφία should belong to God since true σοφία is only found in God, those with true μακάριος should also belong to God since God is the true source of εὐλογία. While those who are of the world are deceived into thinking that blessings can be gained when they follow the ways of the beast (e.g., Rev 13), the truly blessed are the ones who follow the ways of God and of the Lamb.

On the other hand, there are three proper vice lists in the book of Revelation.²⁴ The first vice list appears at the end of the sixth trumpet.²⁵ In effect, Rev 9:20–21 provides important information regarding the nature and purpose of the three series of judgments. By this point in Revelation, the readers would wonder why God would allow these series of judgments upon the world. The first vice list answers that question. It is because the people of the world have an idolatrous nature and sins which make them unrepentant, even with experiencing these severe judgments. The people refuse to repent because they remain faithful to the beast, whose kingdom will begin to be described in Revelation 12–18.²⁶

---

22. The motif of dress and undress occurs frequently in the prophetic and wisdom literatures of the Old Testament. The description of dress or undress not only provides character information, but also gives insights as to the nature or identity of that character. See Parrott, "Apparel Oft Proclaims the (Jerusale)man." This motif of dress and undress shall be discussed in more detail in a subsequent chapter of this present study.

23. Rev 5:12, 13; 7:12.

24. Rev 9:20–21; 21:8; 22:15.

25. Cf. Rev 11:14. After the interlude in Rev 10:1—11:13, the author picks up the very ending of the sixth trumpet (also called the second woe) again in Rev 11:14 in order to continue the vision of the seven trumpets that he left off in Rev 9:21.

26. Hoskins, *Revelation*, 181.

The second vice list (Rev 21:8) occurs at the end of the vision of the new heaven and new earth, and just before the introduction of the New Jerusalem. In Revelation 21:5–8, it is God himself, not any other spokesperson, who proclaims that those contained in the vice list will face the second death, namely the lake of fire.[27] In this list, cowards (τοῖς δειλοῖς) appear first in the catalogue, which is an unusual way of identifying sinners. But this seems to be intentional; John wants to remind his readers that those who do not persevere in faith but cower away will not enjoy the blessings of the New Jerusalem.[28] The third vice list (Rev 22:15) occurs near the end of the book, right after the last blessing saying (Rev 22:14). Similar to the second vice list, the third list also has the effect of reminding the readers that they really do not want to be found outside God's city.

In addition to these three vice lists, Revelation has one other ethical list (Rev 21:27). This list contains two vices and one virtue and occurs near the end of the vision of the New Jerusalem. Although it is not a vice list proper, it is an ethical catalogue nonetheless, and since it has a connection with the third vice list proper, this study will take the opportunity to group and to treat this ethical list with the other vice lists of Revelation.

HISTORY OF RESEARCH

In order to understand the need for the present study, it is now necessary to assess what the scholarly contribution, as well as its trend, has been in the areas of apocalyptic studies in general and of the book of Revelation in particular. This will envisage the scholarly lacuna that currently exists in Revelation studies regarding wisdom motifs and ethics. This section will look at two main areas: apocalyptic studies in general and studies regarding sapiential elements in the book of Revelation in particular.

---

27. Revelation 1:8 and 21:5–8 are the only times in Revelation where God himself is explicitly identified as the speaker.

28. There is a considerable debate surrounding the authorship of Revelation. Whereas the early church almost unanimously identified Revelation's author to be the Apostle John, modern scholarship has posited various arguments against this traditional notion (Hoskins, *Revelation*, 13–21). However, since there is no consensus among modern scholars as to who the author might be, and since both the external evidence and internal evidence can be argued for the Apostle John being the author, this study will follow Mounce's advice in accepting the author of Revelation as John the apostle. Mounce, *Revelation*, 15. Nonetheless, authorship has no bearing on the course of this study, for what matters is the authenticity and trustworthiness of Revelation's claims.

Apocalyptic Studies

In modern apocalyptic studies, there are two related developments that are pertinent for the present study which must be looked at. The first is the debate regarding the origin of the apocalypse, which has to do with the relationship between wisdom and apocalyptic, and the second is the debate regarding the genre of the apocalypse.[29]

The Origin of the Apocalypse

Since this debate has been summarized numerous times elsewhere,[30] the present study will only recount the salient points and persons involved. As older biblical research began to pave the road to Wellhausen and higher criticism, scholarly focus also began to shift to reconstructing the original setting or the *Sitz im Leben* of biblical texts. Apocalyptic studies also followed this trend, and scholars began to posit how Jewish apocalyptic literature came to be and from where.[31] For many scholars, it was the thought that the decline of prophecy during the postexilic era must be related to the rise of apocalypticism during the same era which in turn made them understand that apocalypticism must have come out of the prophetic tradition.[32]

---

29. This study uses the term "apocalypse" to denote a specific corpus of literature, not a movement nor a worldview. Although apocalypse as a literature and apocalypticism as a movement or worldview may be related, careful distinguishment between them is helpful for the purpose of this study. See Hanson, "Apocalypticism," 28–34 and Collins, *Daniel*, 2–5.

30. For instance, see Collins, *Seers, Sibyls and Sages*; chapter 2 of Johnson, *Function of Apocalyptic*; Johnson, "Wisdom and Apocalyptic in Paul," 263–83; Johnson, "From Where Should Apocalyptic Be Found?," 215–32; Morray-Jones, "Opening of Heaven," 10–36.

31. Thus, even before Wellhausen, scholars such as Friedrich Lücke and Eduard Reuss argued that the apocalyptic developed out of prophecy. For a succinct and comprehensive review of past scholarship on Jewish apocalyptic, see Hanson, "Prolegomena," 389–413. Bousset went a different route, arguing that the apocalyptic is to be traced to Persian Dualism, but this suggestion did not have the appeal as it did with prophecy. Bousset, *Religion des Judentums*, 506–16.

32. Finitsis, *Visions and Eschatology*, 5–6. Finitsis notes that R. H. Charles was the first scholar who explicitly stated that apocalypticism replaced prophecy when it died. He also notes H. H. Rowley's famous statement, namely that "apocalyptic is the child of prophecy," which definitively changed the direction of scholarship towards looking at the relationship between prophecy and apocalyptic. See Charles, *Religious Development*, 32–33 and Rowley, *Relevance of Apocalyptic*, 15.

However, while most scholars surmised that apocalypticism arose from prophecy, it was with von Rad that a viable alternative began to circulate. For von Rad, it is not prophecy that is the most likely source from which apocalypticism arose, but rather wisdom tradition.[33] In other words, wisdom literature is not simply a distant cousin to the apocalyptic, a notion most scholars were willing to accept,[34] but a direct mother, a notion most scholars will come to reject.

There are two main reasons why von Rad wished to connect apocalypses with wisdom and not with prophecy. First, there is an incompatibility between the apocalyptic view of history and the prophetic view of history.[35] Prophetic literature places high importance on Israel's saving history, but apocalyptic literature diminishes its importance and emphasizes the deterministic nature of world history, and for von Rad, this was a key stumbling block as to why prophecy could not be the predecessor of the apocalypse.[36] If apocalyptic tradition really came out of the prophetic tradition, then there should not be this sharp scale of discontinuity regarding the importance of the history of Israel between the two. Second, for von Rad, the rise of apocalyptic literature must be traced back to OT wisdom tradition, not prophecy, since apocalyptic literature exhibits a quest for knowledge, much like wisdom literature.[37] This quest for knowledge found in apocalyptic literatures is claimed by von Rad to be the "nerve center" of the apocalypse, which in turn meant that wisdom is the likely source for the apocalypse.[38] Apocalyptic literatures' constant plea for understanding, instead of direct moral imperatives found in prophecy, was another important factor to von Rad in disconnecting the origin of apocalypse from prophecy.[39]

33. It was actually Gustav Hölscher who seems to have first proposed the idea that apocalyptic thinking owed a debt to OT wisdom corpus, but Gerhard von Rad is the one who expanded Hölscher's theory and who popularized the notion that wisdom is the source of apocalypticism, not prophecy. Hölscher, "Die Entstehung des Buches Daniel," 113–38.

34. See Johnson, "Apocalypticism, Apocalyptic Literature."

35. Von Rad, *Old Testament Theology*, vol. 2, 303–4.

36. Johnson, "From Where Should Apocalyptic Be Found?," 215. See also Hartman, *Prophecy Interpreted*, 23–26.

37. Von Rad, *Old Testament Theology*, vol. 2, 306–8.

38. Von Rad, *Old Testament Theology*, vol. 2, 306.

39. Cf. Collins, *Seers, Sibyls and Sages*, 332–33. Collins also identifies the emphasis for understanding found in apocalyptic literatures to be of fundamental difference between prophecy and apocalyptic. However, this difference does not impede upon the book of Revelation, since Revelation's author identifies the work to be prophecy (Rev

Therefore, by emphasizing the discontinuities between prophecy and apocalypse and by identifying the quest for knowledge as an important feature of the apocalypse, von Rad was able to propose wisdom as the sole candidate responsible for the rise of the apocalypse. But what of eschatology that is so prevalent in both prophecy and apocalypse but lacking in wisdom? According to von Rad, while eschatology may be lacking in Hebrew wisdom books, which is a specific feature (sicherste Spezifikum) of apocalypticism, one can nonetheless conjecture that wisdom's encyclopedic interest for all things could have gradually come to be preoccupied with the last things in the later periods.[40] Thus, it is true that the OT wisdom books lack eschatological insights, but this lack would have been remedied as wisdom grew, especially during the postexilic era.[41] After all, Daniel, Baruch, Ezra, and Enoch were all claimed to be sages and not prophets.[42] The charge of wisdom's lack of eschatology, therefore, is not strong enough for von Rad to dismantle his proposition that the apocalypse grew out of wisdom.

There is no doubt that von Rad made an impact in apocalyptic studies with his research. For one, he sought to address scholarship's one-sided emphasis on eschatology when dealing with the origin of the apocalypse and pointed out the unfair neglect of the cosmological and speculative concerns found in the apocalypses, as well as their sapiential character.[43]

1:3) and since Revelation has numerous moral imperatives (esp. Rev 2–3; 18:4).

40. Von Rad, *Theologie des Alten Testaments*, vol. 2, 328–29. See also, Von Rad, *Weisheit in Israel*, 357–58.

41. Von Rad understands the development of wisdom in two major stages. The first stage developed during the period of monarchy and is characterized as wisdom from everyday experience, as exemplified in OT wisdom books. The second stage developed during the postexilic period and is characterized as theological wisdom, with God being the mediator of Revelation and the teacher of wisdom. It is this second stage that von Rad believes to have provided the eschatological link to apocalypticism. Von Rad, *Old Testament Theology*, vol. 1, 418–53 and von Rad, *Wisdom in Israel*, 15–23, 54–65. See also, Perdue, *Wisdom & Creation*, 41–42. As support to his case, von Rad mentions Wisdom of Solomon as an example exhibiting the "eschatologisierung der Weisheit," but notes it very briefly. See von Rad, *Theologie des Alten Testaments*, vol. 2, 329. Nonetheless, Wisdom of Solomon is dated to be around the turn of the era (first century BC to first century AD), too late to give any definitive answer to the question of origin of the apocalyptic, although it does provide the case for the presence of explicit eschatology in a wisdom literature. Needless to say, von Rad's overdependence on postbiblical wisdom literature in making his case but not so much on biblical wisdom has been widely questioned and refuted. For a succinct summary of weaknesses to von Rad's approach to wisdom, see Telfer, "Gerhard von Rad (1901–1971)," 198–99.

42. Von Rad, *Old Testament Theology*, vol. 2, 306.

43. Collins, *Apocalyptic Imagination*, 27; Sæbø, "Old Testament Apocalyptic," 86.

Nevertheless, most scholars remain unconvinced that wisdom is the direct source of the apocalypse despite numerous revisions to von Rad's thesis in subsequent editions of his *Theology*. What von Rad regarded as a minor setback, namely wisdom's apparent lack of eschatology, is still the lynchpin of protest to von Rad's thesis.[44]

Moreover, the comparative methodology used by von Rad and other scholars of his time steeped in historical-critical approach has also been proven to be flawed. Paul D. Hanson, for one, calls the comparative method utilized by biblical scholarship of the first half of the twentieth century on the origin of the apocalypse "faulty," and states, "The origins of apocalyptic cannot be explained by a method which juxtaposes seventh- and second-century compositions and then proceeds to account for the features of the latter by reference to its immediate environment."[45] In other words, those who employ the comparative method usually take the rise of the apocalypse as a postexilic phenomenon with little to no ties to prophetic Yahwism, and thereby proceed to link the cause to outside influences such as Persian dualism or Hellenistic influences.[46] This has the adverse effect of misconstruing the source of the apocalypse.[47] In effect, Paul Hanson is one among many who, instead of emphasizing the dissimilarities or discontinuities apocalypses have against the biblical corpus, has sought to see essential continuities apocalypses have with the biblical corpus and Israelite religion in general.[48] It is safe to say that, since the second half of the twentieth century, biblical scholarship on the origin of the apocalypse has taken Hanson's advice in seeing more of the

---

44. For instance, Matthew Goff rejects von Rad because he believes eschatology is prevalent in both postexilic prophetic and apocalyptic literatures, but not so in wisdom literature. Goff, "Wisdom and Apocalypticism," 52, 59–60.

45. Hanson, *The Dawn of Apocalyptic*, 6.

46. Although von Rad sought to link the rise of the apocalypse to Israelite wisdom and not so much to an influence outside of Israelite religion, he is still attacked by Hanson for not seeing the primary connection to pre-exilic Israelite religion. Hanson, *The Dawn of Apocalyptic*, 5.

47. Hanson, *The Dawn of Apocalyptic*, 7.

48. To be clear, Paul Hanson does seek to tie the origin of the apocalypse to pre-exilic prophecy because he understands a line of continuity between prophetic eschatology and apocalyptic eschatology. In fact, Hanson argues that apocalyptic eschatology began to dawn from within the Israelite prophetic tradition during sixth to fifth centuries BC, as the prophetic optimism in the restoration of God's nation began to erode in the exilic and postexilic communities. Hanson, *The Dawn of Apocalyptic*, 6–29. In so doing, Hanson is obviously understanding eschatology to be of essential feature that connects the apocalypse with prophecy (contra von Rad).

continuities apocalypses have with centuries-old Jewish traditions rather than simply crediting the origin to outside factors, although outside influences should not be too quickly dismissed.

Yet, this does not mean that von Rad's theory regarding the apocalypses arising from wisdom roots has completely vanished. Others, such as Hans-Peter Müller, have sought to refine von Rad's theory. Building upon von Rad, Müller makes the case that the rise of the apocalyptic can be credited to mantic wisdom.[49] Von Rad's mistake was in not making a clear distinction between *Bildungsweisheit* and *mantische Weisheit*, and this made him struggle with the question of perceived lack of eschatology in biblical wisdom books.[50] On the other hand, Müller argues that a specific type of wisdom known as mantic wisdom, which was concerned with dreams and omens, existed in Israel since ancient times, and it is precisely this mantic wisdom that is responsible for the rise of Jewish apocalyptic.[51] Israel probably got to know mantic wisdom better once the nation went into exile, into close contact with the pagan environment, and the grim political situation of exilic and postexilic Israel made the transition from mantic wisdom to apocalyptic all the more welcome.[52] In the end, it is from this connection between mantic wisdom and apocalyptic that the gradual inclusion of elements from the neighboring *Bildungsweisheit* occurred in Jewish apocalyptic.[53]

A recent example of a scholar who probes the relationship between wisdom and apocalypse is Timothy Johnson.[54] Observing that von Rad

49. Müller, "Mantische Weisheit und Apokalyptik," 268–93. John J. Collins also has made the same claim. Collins, "Court-Tales in Daniel," 218–34.

50. Müller, "Mantische Weisheit und Apokalyptik," 271.

51. Müller provides several evidence from the Old Testament that may prove the existence of mantic wisdom in Israel. First, he believes that the use of the Hebrew noun חָכָם in certain contexts such as Genesis 41:8 and Isaiah 44:25 refer to the official designation of mantics whom Israel knew from its pagan environment. Second, Müller claims that two figures of the Old Testament, namely Joseph and Daniel, were mantic sages. Müller, "Mantische Weisheit und Apokalyptik," 271–80.

52. Müller, "Mantische Weisheit und Apokalyptik," 274, 291. To be clear, Müller does not believe that mantic wisdom is solely responsible for the rise of the apocalyptic. Jewish apocalyptic is a product of multiple factors, including prophecy. However, he nonetheless believes mantic wisdom to be an integral, if not the most important, factor.

53. Müller, "Mantische Weisheit und Apokalyptik," 292. "Sodann wird gerade der Zusammenhang von mantischer Weisheit und Apokalyptik Anlaß gegeben haben, nach und nach auch Elemente der benachbarten Bildungsweisheit in die Apokalyptik eingehen zu lassen, insbesondere protowissenschaftliche Stoffe aus den Bereichen der Kosmologie, Astronomie, Meteorologie, Medizin u.s.w."

54. Johnson, "From Where Should Apocalyptic Be Found?," 215–32.

utilized postbiblical materials to support his theory and not the biblical corpus, Johnson seeks to test von Rad's proposal using biblical material. Thus, he analyzes the book of Job to see whether it can serve to support von Rad's theory, and he indeed believes that Job is a plausible canonical candidate that may evidence the transition from wisdom to apocalypse.[55] This is because Job's quasi-wisdom status, its postexilic dating, and its literary and thematic factors likely suggest Job's governing genre as an apocalypse that is in its early stage of development.[56]

Another important milestone in biblical scholarship concerning the relationship between wisdom and apocalypse is the Wisdom and Apocalypticism in Early Judaism and Early Christianity Consultation of SBL, which was later renamed as the Wisdom and Apocalypticism Group. The group was inaugurated in 1994 with the aim of bringing together two categories often held distinct in biblical scholarship, namely wisdom and apocalypse.[57] What the group wanted to do, in short, was to analyze the interrelationships between these categories instead of precisely differentiating them. The group's basic premise was that scholarship has needlessly divided wisdom and apocalypse as two separate categories, that this is indeed problematic, and that reexamination of the boundaries between the two categories is now needed.[58] Thus, the scholars involved used a "both-and" approach of analyzing texts that were deemed either wisdom or apocalypse not in terms of categories, but in terms of how the texts utilized both modes of discourse.[59] The group also believed that, by identifying and reconstructing the social contexts of these texts, albeit an insurmountable task, one could arrive at a more precise recognition of the relationship between sapiential and apocalyptic modes of discourse.[60] The result and progress of the group's work, according to those involved, are seen as positive: "What the Group has accomplished successfully, . . . is to show that wisdom and apocalypticism are *indeed* related both in many of their literary aspects and in their social contexts."[61]

All in all, it is true that origin studies since the time of von Rad have contributed to apocalyptic studies. However, what is important to note at

---

55. Johnson, "From Where Should Apocalyptic Be Found?," 230.
56. Johnson, "From Where Should Apocalyptic Be Found?," 216–17.
57. Wright and Wills, "Introduction," 1.
58. Wright and Wills, "Introduction," 2.
59. Wright and Wills, "Introduction," 2.
60. Wright and Wills, "Introduction," 3, 9.
61. Wright and Wills, "Introduction," 3.

this point is that, despite numerous studies that have been put forward since von Rad, there is currently no consensus regarding the origin of Jewish and Christian apocalypses. While there are indeed indications of wisdom traditions in early Jewish and Christian apocalypses, the question regarding the exact relationship between wisdom and apocalypse still remains open.[62] Johann M. Schmidt's positive assertion that by thoroughly investigating how the apocalyptic adopted and adapted tradition, scholars will be able to answer all the questions concerning the origin of the apocalyptic has not yet been proven true.[63]

Instead, the current trend in apocalyptic studies is one that has largely moved away from the comparative methodology that was once popular during the nineteenth century. As the methodology of the Wisdom and Apocalypticism Group of SBL well attests, the present trend is focused more on studying the interrelationships between wisdom, prophecy, and apocalypse than on distinguishing and separating these categories.[64] There are even voices that argue strongly against doing origin studies. For instance, Eibert Tigchelaar claims that origin studies suffer from a major misconception, namely that drawing sharp distinctions between genre, theology, and worldview led to the assumption that there was only one origin.[65] Rather, in a culture, several realities, whether theological, sociological, religious, or literary, are all intermingled; they do not have clear dividing lines. This means that a genre such as apocalypse could not have risen from a single source, whether it be wisdom or prophecy, but from a myriad of coalesced causes.[66] The origin studies' misconception makes this complex cultural reality far too simplistic and in turn is flawed. Tigchelaar thus concludes:

> Genres, modes of thought and world views can be regarded as cultural fabrics. Origins, being no more than the warp, only explain these fabrics partly. Real understanding can only be

---

62. Johnson, *Function of Apocalyptic*, 58.
63. Schmidt, *Die jüdische Apokalyptik*.
64. See also, Collins, "Wisdom, Apocalypticism," 165–85.
65. Tigchelaar, *Prophets of Old*, 10.
66. John Collins concurs with this assessment. Collins, *Daniel*, 40. Thus, Collins is another scholar who also cautions against tracing the general relationship between the categories of wisdom, apocalypse, and prophecy as this endeavor is severely problematic and counterproductive. See Collins, *Seers, Sibyls and Sages*, 369–70 and Collins, *Apocalyptic Imagination*, 26–28.

obtained by studying why and how features from different origins came to be put together.⁶⁷

In keeping with the current trend then, this study will not seek to prove from where exactly Revelation's author might have gotten his traditions or motifs. While it is clear that apocalypse has affinities with wisdom, this study will move beyond the general origin issues and deal more specifically with the literary function of these wisdom motifs in Revelation.⁶⁸ If indeed wisdom has close connections with apocalypses, then it is worthwhile to see how apocalypses use wisdom elements.⁶⁹ Numerous studies on wisdom and apocalypse in Jewish writings, especially the Dead Sea Scrolls, have been done.⁷⁰ The present study will extend the study field to the only apocalypse in the New Testament, namely the book of Revelation, and will seek to analyze the function of wisdom elements in this specific work.

The Genre of the Apocalypse

A related but distinct development in apocalyptic studies involves the study of genre. Whereas origin studies primarily have to do with historical questions, genre studies are chiefly concerned with literary questions. As this section will show, the study of the genre of the apocalypse has a close correlation to the matter of ethics or paraenesis found in the genre.

67. Tigchelaar, *Prophets of Old*, 11.

68. This writer agrees with Elizabeth Johnson's statement. "Although the religio-historical question of apocalypticism's ancestry will continue to provoke important research, what is necessary for the present study is an analysis of the *function* of such intersections of these diverse traditions in specific documents." Johnson, *Function of Apocalyptic*, 71.

69. The direction of influence could be opposite as well. While it is customary to think that wisdom has influenced apocalyptic writings, it is also possible that apocalyptic traditions have influenced sapiential writings. For scholars who argue for the possibility of the latter, see Collins, *Jewish Wisdom*, 117 and Knibb, "The Book of Enoch," 210. But as Knibb further notes, the parallels between apocalypse and wisdom more likely point to a shared thought world. Rather than seeing the direction of influence in an overly simplified manner, it may be better to see it as being complex and multifaceted. This is again the reason why this study avoids doing origin studies as much as possible and will merely identify wisdom motifs in Revelation where they are found and ask why the author has utilized those motifs.

70. For instance, see Tov, *Discoveries in the Judaean Desert*, volumes 20 and 34. John Collins even remarked that "The Sapiential Work from Qumran should give pause to those who take wisdom and apocalypticism as mutually incompatible forms of discourse." Collins, *Jewish Wisdom*, 228.

As apocalyptic studies continued to advance, so did the unfortunate confusion surrounding what exactly scholars mean by the term apocalypse.[71] Coupled with this confusion was the debate regarding what apocalypses are and what writings should constitute this particular corpus. To provide a headway out of this complication, Robert W. Funk launched what is known as the Forms and Genres project in the Society of Biblical Literature.[72] The project was to be led by John J. Collins with the objective of providing a preliminary definition of the genre of apocalypse and of seeking mutual agreement on what texts should belong to this genre. Regarding the former objective, those involved with the project agreed upon the following definition of the genre of apocalypse:

> "Apocalypse" is a genre of revelatory literature with a narrative framework, in which a revelation is mediated by an otherworldly being to a human recipient, disclosing a transcendent reality which is both temporal, insofar as it envisages eschatological salvation, and spatial insofar as it involves another, supernatural world.[73]

Regarding the latter, the group found many works, both Greco-Roman and Jewish, as well as Christian, to belong to the genre of apocalypse according to the above definition. The group further categorized the genre into six distinct types: (1) historical apocalypses with no otherworldly journey, (2) apocalypses with cosmic and/or political eschatology (which have neither historical review nor otherworldly journey), (3) apocalypses with only personal eschatology (and no otherworldly journey),

---

71. Thus, scholars began to see the need for distinguishing between apocalypse as a genre, as a worldview, or as a movement. See Hanson, "Apocalypticism," 28–34.

72. The findings of the Forms and Genres project were published in 1979 in the fourteenth volume of *Semeia*. See Collins, *Apocalypse*.

73. Collins, "Introduction," 9. Carmignac also came to a similar definition of the genre apocalypse as the Forms and Genres project, despite having worked autonomously. Carmignac asserts that apocalypse should be defined as a literary genre of revelatory type that presents a transcendent reality. Thus, Carmignac also emphasizes transcendence as a key feature of the genre apocalypse like Collins. In his own words, apocalypse is a "genre littéraire qui présente, à travers des symboles typiques, des révélations soit sur Dieu, soit sur les anges ou les démons, soit sur leurs partisans, soit sur les instruments de leur action." Carmignac, "L'Apocalyptique?," 20. See also Carmignac, "Description," 165. The difference between Collins and Carmignac would be that the former acknowledges the presence of an otherworldly mediator as an essential feature of the genre, whereas the latter would not. Still, Carmignac himself has noted Collins' definition as being quite similar to his own definition. See Carmignac, "L'Apocalyptique?," 33.

(4) historical apocalypses with an otherworldly journey, (5) otherworldly journeys with cosmic and/or political eschatology, and (6) otherworldly journeys with only personal eschatology.[74] According to the group, no Greco-Roman or Jewish works belong to the second type except for certain Christian works, most notably the book of Revelation.[75]

The effort in delineating what apocalypses are by the Forms and Genres project has been heralded as providing an important bedrock for the genre discussion.[76] It provided initial classification and characterization as to what scholars mean when they speak about the genre of apocalypse. The project also provided a clear distinction between apocalypse as a genre and apocalypticism as a sociological movement or apocalyptic eschatology as a religious view (hence a distinction between form and genre).[77] Nonetheless, there have been voices that argue against the definition proposed by Collins and his team.[78] On one hand, the definition by Collins and his team emphasized both form and content. Apocalypse's form is unique in that it involves revelation announced by an otherworldly mediator; its content has a dual aspect of eschatology and revelation of heavenly mysteries.[79] On the other hand, there were those such as Christopher Rowland who did not want eschatology to be part of the definition. For Rowland, the genre of apocalypse should be defined simply as a revelation of heavenly mysteries and nothing more should be added to the definition.[80] Most recently, Benjamin Reynolds

---

74. Collins, "Introduction," 13–15.
75. Collins, "Introduction," 14.
76. Yarbro Collins, "Apocalypse Now," 449.
77. Sanders, "The Genre," 450–51, 453.
78. There have also been those who argued against the methodology used by Collins and the team as well, especially regarding the issue of genre itself. For instance, Richard Horsley disagrees that there is such a thing as a genre of apocalypse and argues that " . . . there were no defined boundaries between texts and other cultural expressions previously categorized as either apocalyptic or sapiential." Horsley, *Scribes*, 4 and Horsley, *Revolt of the Scribes*, 193–207. However, Collins claims that while genres have fuzzy edges and can participate in other genres, there is still an implicit notion of genre that every interpreter works with when trying to understand a given text. Thus, the role of genre is essential in interpretation. See Collins, *Apocalyptic Imagination*, 12–42, for Collins' full discussion on the genre debate, especially pages 17 to 19. See also, Collins, "The Genre Apocalypse Reconsidered," 21–40, for Collins' more up-to-date discussion and defense on genre.
79. Collins, "Apocalypse Now," 448–49.
80. Rowland, *The Open Heaven*, 14. Rowland saw the overemphasizing of eschatology in the apocalypses and wanted to disassociate from this one-sidedness. However, as Collins notes, trying to disconnect eschatology with apocalypses is also an overreaction

and Loren Stuckenbruck produced a volume in which the contributors focus on how a revelatory understanding of Jewish apocalyptic traditions can help in understanding the thought of the New Testament, rather than looking specifically at apocalyptic eschatology.[81] According to Reynolds and Stuckenbruck, Collins made the mistake of equating eschatology with the entirety of Jewish apocalyptic tradition, and the renewed focus on the revelatory nature of these writings sheds new light on what can be considered apocalyptic.[82]

Yet others promoted their own opinions on how apocalypses should be defined. Meeting in the same year when the Forms and Genres Project announced its findings, the Uppsala international colloquium of 1979 displayed exactly this tendency by evidencing just how different and variegated scholars' understanding of the genre apocalypse can be.[83] Jean Carmignac, while similar to Collins, nonetheless communicated his difference by endorsing that the genre of apocalypse must be defined as heavenly revelations containing symbolic frescoes.[84] Lars Hartman even wondered whether talking about genre is helpful at all, although he did argue that communication aspects between the author and the reader are important to consider if scholars were to talk about genre.[85] Criticizing both the traditional definitions which observed lists of traits that are supposedly found in apocalypses and the work done by the Forms and Genres Project, E. P. Sanders argued for a return to an essentialist definition of Jewish apocalypses, namely a revelation that deals with the themes of restoration and reversal.[86] Still, George Nickelsburg wanted a renewed attention to the social and cultural factors that gave rise to the apocalyptic writings rather than focusing on genre and content.[87] In the end, no consensus was reached for a definition of apocalypse despite

---

and is itself one-sided. No matter how abused, eschatology is an essential part of the genre apocalypse. See Collins, *Apocalyptic Imagination*, 19.

81. Reynolds and Stuckenbruck, *The Jewish Apocalyptic Tradition*.

82. Reynolds and Stuckenbruck, *The Jewish Apocalyptic Tradition*, 6–9. See also, Reynolds, "Jewish Apocalyptic Tradition."

83. Papers presented during the 1979 Uppsala conference can be found at Hellholm, *Apocalypticism in the Mediterranean World*.

84. Carmignac, "Description," 163–70.

85. Hartman, "Survey of the Problem," 329–44.

86. Sanders, "The Genre," 447–59, esp. 448 and 454–58.

87. Nickelsburg, "Social Aspects," 641–54.

several attempts to do so.[88] Describing the apocalypses, instead of defining them, was the optimistic agreement reached at the colloquium.[89]

Despite these hurdles, the consultation on the Early Christian Apocalypticism at the Society of Biblical Literature continued to work on and to refine the initial work done by Collins and his team of scholars. The program unit's continued endeavor on the genre of apocalypse was published in 1986 in the thirty-sixth volume of *Semeia*.[90] One significant development, in relation to the purpose of present study, was in the area of paraenesis. Collins' initial definition did not reserve a place for paraenesis, and he simply remarked that "Paraenesis occurs somewhat more frequently in Christian apocalypses although it is rare even there."[91] To be sure, Collins did believe that paraenesis is an important element in apocalyptic literature, but nonetheless relegated it as a minor feature of the genre.[92] The Uppsala international colloquium of 1979 also noticed this shortcoming.[93]

The Early Christian Apocalypticism group at the Society of Biblical Literature sought to rightly remedy this problem by proposing to emend the definition of the genre to provide a more prominent place for paraenesis. David Hellholm, on one hand, claimed that Collins' initial definition of the genre apocalypse dealt only with two aspects, namely form and content, when any genre discussion should involve three aspects, namely form, content, and function.[94] Thus, Hellholm proposed to add a functional dimension to the definition, namely that the genre of apocalypse is *"intended for a group in crisis with the purpose of exhortation and/or consolation by means of divine authority."*[95] David E. Aune,

88. Hellholm, "Introduction," 2.
89. Yarbro Collins, "Apocalypse Now," 449.
90. Yarbro Collins, *Early Christian Apocalypticism*.
91. Collins, "Introduction," 13.
92. Cf. Collins, "The Genre Apocalypse Reconsidered," 25.
93. For instance, Elisabeth Schüssler Fiorenza argued that Collins' definition can only map out cross-cultural characteristics of the genre apocalypse and is unable to highlight the unique characteristics of individual apocalypses and text units, especially the unique nature of explicit paraenesis found in early Christian apocalyptic texts. See Fiorenza, "Phenomenon of Early Christian Apocalyptic," 295–316. Also, Lars Hartman acknowledged Collins' work but argued for more investigation on the illocution and sociolinguistic function of the apocalyptic texts on the propositional level. Hartman, "Survey of the Problem," 329–44.
94. Hellholm, "Problem of Apocalyptic Genre," 13–64.
95. Hellholm, "Problem of Apocalyptic Genre," 27. Emphasis his.

on the other hand, while agreeing with Hellholm's analysis of the three aspects to the genre, nonetheless rejected Hellholm's proposal of adding "exhortation and/or consolation" to Collins' definition because he understood Hellholm's proposal to be too specific and not comprehensive enough to cover all the apocalypses.[96] For Aune, a more abstract notion of function was understood to work better for the definition of the genre apocalypse, and he gave a much lengthier formulation than the one offered by Hellholm.[97] By taking both Hellholm's and Aune's advices into account then, the working group agreed that the following addition was to be made to the definition of apocalypse in *Semeia 14*: "*intended to interpret present, earthly circumstances in light of the supernatural world and of the future, and to influence both the understanding and the behavior of the audience by means of divine authority.*"[98]

The efforts in defining the genre of apocalypse by the two working groups of the Society of Biblical Literature have surely impacted how scholars approach apocalypses. The biggest impact, as alluded above, is in the area of function. Apocalyptic literature intends to influence, to teach, and to exhort its readers, and thus does not solely provide history or eschatology, although they too are important elements of the genre. In keeping with this proposal, John Collins has now articulated his position clearer by acknowledging that all apocalypses do indeed address problems faced by the original audiences and that "The function of the apocalyptic literature is to shape one's imaginative perception of a situation and so lay the basis for whatever course of action it exhorts."[99] There have now been numerous studies since *Semeia 36* that deal with the functions of apocalyptic literatures.

For instance, David L. Barr has more recently argued in a similar fashion by proposing to modify the current definition of the genre of apocalypse to include the effect of the writing on the audience.[100] Ac-

96. Aune, "The Apocalypse of John," 65–96, especially page 91.

97. Aune, "The Apocalypse of John," 87. According to Aune, apocalypse functions in three ways: (1) to legitimate the transcendent authorization of the message, (2) to conceal the message which the text reveals through literary devices, structures, and imagery, and (3) to encourage the recipients of the message to modify their cognitive and behavioral stance in conformity with transcendent perspectives.

98. Yarbro Collins, "Introduction," 7. Emphasis original. See also, Yarbro Collins, "Apocalypse Now," 450.

99. Collins, *The Apocalyptic Imagination*, 42. See also, Collins, *Seers, Sibyls and Sages*, 25–38.

100. Barr, "Beyond Genre," 71–89.

cording to Barr, apocalypses function to encourage a life-change on the part of the audience, to live rightly in light of the transcendent reality.[101] Thomas Sappington has categorized Jewish apocalypses according to their literary functions.[102] Others have followed Yarbro Collins' suggestion of tackling the functions of individual apocalyptic writings, even apocalyptic units within individual works, rather than working on the definition of the genre of apocalypse per se.[103] For example, Loren Stuckenbruck has explored the function of *1 Enoch* 10 where the unit's motif of the nations' eventual worship of Yahweh functions to reinvoke the supremacy of Israel's faith and to give hope for a reversal of Israel's gloomy condition of subjugation.[104]

With specific regards to the function of the book of Revelation, there have also been numerous studies. Yarbro Collins herself has contributed early in this area by suggesting that Revelation has a cathartic function of evoking strong feelings on the part of the readers who are experiencing a perceived crisis under the Roman rule in order that they may not compromise with the Roman culture.[105] Others have focused on Revelation's liturgical function or missional function.[106] Of particular importance is Michelle Lee's work on understanding the function of Revelation as a combination of both method and message.[107] According to Lee, scholars have tended to concentrate on either Revelation's message (what it teaches, such as heavenly knowledge or eschatology) or method (how it communicates through hortatory or motivational means) when

101. Barr, "Beyond Genre," 89. Thus, Barr argues that he is different from Aune. Aune suggests that apocalypses aim to interpret the present in light of the supernatural, whereas Barr understands that apocalypses go further in actually producing a life-changing effect on the audience in light of the supernatural.

102. Sappington, "The Factor of Function," 83–123. Sappington argues that the literary functions of consolation, exhortation, and admonition are all present in each of the Jewish apocalypses, and thus should become definitional to the genre.

103. Yarbro Collins' suggestion in her own words is as follows. "Since consensus has not yet been reached on the definition of the literary genre of apocalypse or the phenomenon of apocalypticism, generalizations about the function of apocalypticism would be premature at this stage of the discussion. The most appropriate approach for the present seems to be the investigation of the function of particular apocalyptic writings in their historical settings." See, Yarbro Collins, "Persecution and Vengeance," 729.

104. Stuckenbruck, "Early Enochic Tradition," 225–41.

105. Yarbro Collins, *Crisis and Catharsis*.

106. For an example of the former, see Nakhro, "The Worship of God." See also Nakhro, "The Meaning of Worship," 75–85. and Nakhro, "The Manner of Worship," 165–80. For the latter, see Peters, *The Mandate of the Church*.

107. Lee, "A Call to Martyrdom," 164–94.

dealing with the function of Revelation.[108] Rather, Lee argues that both the message and the method should be combined to understand more fully the function of the book, and proceeds to unpack Revelation's chiastic structure in order to understand its central message and in turn its function.[109]

In turn, this study will follow Lee's advice in understanding Revelation in terms of both method and message. Specifically, this study will seek to analyze Revelation's method of employing wisdom motifs throughout the book and to examine how they function in communicating the book's message. Various works on understanding the function of Revelation have been put forward since *Semeia* 36, but none exists that comprehensively inspect wisdom motifs in Revelation to see how they are employed by the author in promoting its message. The present study will thus extend scholarship's work on the genre of the apocalypse and the function of the genre to the book of Revelation in consideration of its wisdom motifs.

Revelation Studies

Regarding specific studies on wisdom motifs in the book of Revelation, only a few works exist. Barbara Rossing's work examines the familiar two-women tradition or topos of the wisdom tradition and how it functions in the visionary rhetoric of Revelation. Two works by Tina Pippin and Loren Stuckenbruck examine the occurrence of the word "wisdom" in Revelation.

First, Rossing's work assesses extensively the two-women topos found in the two city visions of Revelation. Rossing argues that John introduced the two cities in Revelation as contrasting feminine figures in order to invoke a familiar ethical teaching of two women, a teaching well known to the original readers from sapiential traditions of both biblical wisdom and the non-biblical story of Heracles.[110] Nonetheless, Rossing's

---

108. Lee, "A Call to Martyrdom," 164.

109. Lee, "A Call to Martyrdom," 164, 174–92. For Lee, Revelation's author structured his writing using chiasm to exhort his readers to follow Christ's example to martyrdom in order to obtain the eternal reward. As the readers participate in understanding the visions by following the chiasm, Revelation functions to compel them to make the right decision.

110. Rossing, *Two Cities*, 14. Rossing summarizes the two-women topos as having two basic elements: (1) visual contrast of two women, one evil and one good, and (2) exhortation to choose between the two. See Rossing, *Two Cities*, 37–38.

claim is that Revelation's author directly borrowed the two-women topos from biblical wisdom traditions, Proverbs 1–9 in particular, and not from Xenophon's retelling of the story of Heracles, since the language world of Revelation is primarily Jewish.[111] Using the two-women topos then, John was able to present ethical alternatives: for the audience to shun the evil woman and to embrace the good woman.[112] Yet John did not stop here but actually transformed the two women figures into cities or empires. The evil woman is transformed into Babylon or Rome, whereas the good woman, God's bride, is transformed into New Jerusalem.[113] In doing so, John thereby is able to turn the general two-women topos into a political critique and exhortation; the audience is exhorted to come out of Rome in order to participate in God's new city.[114]

Rossing's thesis thus builds upon the work by Elisabeth Schüssler Fiorenza who claimed that Revelation employs deliberative rhetoric, namely exhorting the audience to right course of action.[115] However, unlike Fiorenza who saw the feminine personification of the two cities cautiously as gender stereotyping, Rossing believes that the personification contributes positively to Revelation's rhetoric when viewed in light of the two-women topos.[116] In fact, Rossing understands the two-women topos as having a substantial role in Revelation's portrayal of the two cities, a role that goes conjointly with the prophetic tradition. She makes a convincing argument regarding Babylon's appearance and condemnation in Revelation 17–18. Not only is Babylon regarded as a "woman" (γυνή) twice in Revelation 17:3–4, but the description of her adornment also does not have a full parallel in the prophetic books of the Bible.[117] Furthermore, whereas most scholars who see prophetic allusions in Revelation's Babylon readily point to Ezekiel or Jeremiah as the source, the actual city that gets condemned for its prostitution in these prophetic books is Jerusalem, not Babylon.[118] Finally, the purpose of indictment

---

111. Rossing, *Two Cities*, 41.
112. Rossing, *Two Cities*, 14.
113. Rossing, *Two Cities*, 14–15, 59.
114. Rossing, *Two Cities*, 15.
115. See Fiorenza, *Revelation*, 21, 129–30.
116. Rossing, *Two Cities*, 16.
117. Rossing, *Two Cities*, 72–76.
118. Rossing, *Two Cities*, 74–75. Jan Fekkes understood this problem and thus argued that the source is not Ezekiel or Jeremiah but comes exclusively from prophetic oracles against Babylon. See Fekkes, *Isaiah*, 102–3, 210. Rossing mentions Fekkes'

in these prophetic books is different from Revelation. Whereas Ezekiel's purpose is to inform Jerusalem of its sins and to vindicate God's judgment against her, Revelation's purpose is more hortatory: to convince the readers to dissociate from Babylon.[119] This rhetorical appeal is much more in line with Proverbs' warning against the evil woman than it is with the prophetic tradition.[120]

Nonetheless, there are clear indications of prophetic traditions in the portrayal of Babylon, especially regarding the imagery of wrath and judgment. What then is the exact relationship between the sapiential and prophetic traditions in Revelation 17–18? Rossing argues that once John has used the evil woman imagery of the wisdom traditions to invoke the two-women topos, he quickly merges it with the city imagery of the prophetic traditions to bring about a political critique. Thus, John moves the two-women topos from the realm of wisdom and personal ethics to the political realm with the aid of the OT prophetic traditions.[121] The transformation is seamless, since the two-women topos itself was frequently used in wisdom and apocalyptic writings with a variety of uses including that of the political and since the OT prophetic traditions also frequently personified cities as female figures.[122] The same is true for the portrayal of the bride. Here again, the good woman imagery functions to invoke the two-women topos and then is quickly transformed into God's new city.[123] All in all, by using the two-women topos of the sapiential traditions, John is able to convince the audience more effectively in choosing the good woman (God's New Jerusalem) and not the evil woman (Babylon/Rome). Here is Rossing's conclusion in her own words:

> The author of Revelation constructs New Jerusalem as an alternative to Babylon and calls for a choice between the two cities. New Jerusalem is a contrasting political economy, an alternative

---

argument but still understands it to be incomplete; anti-Babylon oracles alone cannot account for the description of Babylon in Revelation 17–18. Rossing, *Two Cities*, 75.

119. Rossing, *Two Cities*, 76.
120. Rossing, *Two Cities*, 76–77.
121. Rossing, *Two Cities*, 59, 82, 99.
122. Rossing, *Two Cities*, 18, 25, 41, 53, 59. Rossing argues that a variety of Jewish authors expanded the two-women topos originally found in wisdom setting into other settings such as the apocalyptic, and this is evidenced by writings from Qumran. This means that the existence of the wisdom topos in Revelation is likely, for the evidence from Qumran and other writings show that there was not a clear separation between apocalyptic and sapiential genres in Hellenistic Judaism. See Rossing, *Two Cities*, 53–54.
123. Rossing, *Two Cities*, 141–47.

vision of the world and of God's liberating purpose. The audience must undertake an exodus out of Babylon in order to participate in God's city, the New Jerusalem.[124]

Rossing's work is very helpful in seeing wisdom traditions at work in Revelation. She laments the fact that scholarship has recognized wisdom influence only for a few passages in Revelation.[125] Rossing is certainly correct to claim that ethical appeals run throughout Revelation and that wisdom motifs such as macarisms and vice lists serve an important role in those appeals.[126] However, Rossing focuses too narrowly on the two-women topos and its function in invoking an ethical either-or choice. She primarily sees the two women in terms of rhetorical style or device devoid of textual meaning.[127] Not only does Rossing pay little attention to the significance of the woman imagery, she also does not see the multivalence of the two women/cities. Thus, she limits the woman imagery to only a few verses in Revelation and does not wish to connect the two women of Revelation 17–22 to earlier occurrences of female figures in Revelation. For instance, Rossing is unwilling to see the bride as the church but only as God's eschatological city and does not connect the bride to the woman of Revelation 12.[128] In turn, this study will build upon the salient points made by Rossing regarding the sapiential two-women topos and discuss more meaningfully the significance of all woman imagery found in Revelation.

Second, Tina Pippin and Loren Stuckenbruck have both produced articles on the occurrence of the word σοφία in Revelation. Similar to Rossing, Pippin understands Revelation to be invoking an ethical dualism, but one that results from the book's seeming tension between chaos and creation.[129] The author of Revelation is showing the readers what the ethical choices are and how to play by the rules so that they will triumph and reach God's utopia.[130] On the other hand, anyone who disrupts God's order of creation such as Jezebel and the harlot will meet their ultimate crisis of the abyss and be destroyed.[131] The author is able to show the

---

124. Rossing, *Two Cities*, 161.
125. Rossing, *Two Cities*, 56.
126. Rossing, *Two Cities*, 55–59.
127. Huber, *Like a Bride Adorned*, 41.
128. See Rossing, *Two Cities*, 12, 137, and 160–61.
129. Pippin, "Wisdom and Apocalyptic," 285–95.
130. Pippin, "Wisdom and Apocalyptic," 287.
131. Pippin, "Wisdom and Apocalyptic," 287.

readers the right way because he has the wisdom of the end time (Rev 22:18–19).¹³²

This tension between chaos and creation, as well as the resulting ethical motivation, can be especially seen in the four passages in Revelation where the word σοφία occurs. The first two passages where σοφία appears (Rev 5:12; 7:12) specifically locate σοφία to be dwelling with God. God and the Lamb possess wisdom and those who are near the throne such as the twenty-four elders also have this wisdom because they are the ones who "know" (οἶδα; Rev 7:14), and if one wants to receive this wisdom then one must imitate the wise ones near the throne.¹³³ The third instance where σοφία occurs is Revelation 13:18, and Pippin argues that the use of the word in this case is in reference to esoteric knowledge of the Christian apocalyptic sense.¹³⁴ This means that those who have this esoteric knowledge will understand the mystery of the beast, namely that the beast is representing the threat of the earthly political and economic power, that this imperial power will be overthrown, and that the threat of this beast is nothing compared to God's threat of chaos to those who follow this beast.¹³⁵ In this way, Revelation becomes motivational rhetoric; those who understand the mysteries will choose rightly by not associating with the beast and in so doing, will find God's utopia of wisdom.¹³⁶ Finally, Pippin's feminist interpretation comes to the fore with the fourth occurrence of the word σοφία in Revelation. According to Pippin, Revelation 17:9 shows that the true lady σοφία is displaced and disempowered on earth in Revelation.¹³⁷ She also has antitheses, namely Jezebel and the harlot, and John makes it so that the female threat is great in Revelation; those who follow these women will end up in the abyss, the ultimate chaos.¹³⁸ Thus, Revelation encourages readers to gain true σοφία to make the right choice in not associating with the beast or the dangerous women.

Pippin's work utilizes the occurrence of the word σοφία in Revelation well to show that Revelation presents a strong ethical appeal. However, rather than developing the argument for an expanded role of

132. Pippin, "Wisdom and Apocalyptic," 285.
133. Pippin, "Wisdom and Apocalyptic," 288–89.
134. Pippin, "Wisdom and Apocalyptic," 290.
135. Pippin, "Wisdom and Apocalyptic," 291.
136. Pippin, "Wisdom and Apocalyptic," 291.
137. Pippin, "Wisdom and Apocalyptic," 292–93.
138. Pippin, "Wisdom and Apocalyptic," 293.

wisdom tradition in Revelation, Pippin focuses on the ways the personified Sophia figure is disempowered in Revelation. She emphasizes how the other female figures in Revelation are negatively portrayed and harassed, and in the case of the harlot in Revelation 17:16, how a woman could be sexually raped and murdered.[139] This is indeed problematic for Pippin since women are treated poorly in Revelation. Yet, as noted above, Rossing's two-women topos can help in mitigating this problem. Furthermore, when viewed in light of the two-women motif, Revelation does have more to say regarding Sophia or the good woman than Pippin allows. This study will go further than Pippin in dealing with Revelation's female figures in light of the wisdom tradition and in discussing more extensively how the four occurrences of the word σοφία are functioning in the context of Revelation.

More helpful is Loren Stuckenbruck's treatment of the word σοφία in Revelation. Crucial to Stuckenbruck's argument is that, though the word σοφία occurs only four times in Revelation, it has been placed strategically to tell the readers that the book is not to be read only as a disclosure of future knowledge but also as a call to discern John's visions.[140] Stuckenbruck first notes that the first two occurrences of σοφία can be distinguished from the second pair since they function to claim that true σοφία belongs only to God and to the Lamb.[141] The first wisdom occurs in the third place among the list of seven attributes ascribed to the Lamb by the heavenly cohort in Revelation 5:12. Interestingly, in Revelation 5:13, another list of attributes follows, but this time it is ascribed both to God and to the Lamb by all creation and only includes the last four elements just attributed to the Lamb in 5:12.[142] For Stuckenbruck, this strategy allows to present the Lamb to be additionally worthy of power, wealth, and wisdom, the three elements only mentioned in 5:12 but not in 5:13, and for the Lamb to represent a redefinition of meaning, namely that it is only through the Lamb that one can discern what true power, wealth, and wisdom are.[143] The second wisdom also appears in an acclamation of worship by the heavenly cohort where the focus of worship is especially toward God in Revelation 7:12. This again serves to show

---

139. Cf. Pippin, *Death and Desire*, 164.
140. Stuckenbruck, "Disclosure of Wisdom," 347–59.
141. Stuckenbruck, "Disclosure of Wisdom," 349.
142. Stuckenbruck, "Disclosure of Wisdom," 349.
143. Stuckenbruck, "Disclosure of Wisdom," 349–50.

that real wisdom belongs to God and stands in sharp contrast to another earthly reality John will start to unpack in Revelation 8 onward.[144]

Unlike the first two occurrences of σοφία, the last two serves to challenge the readers to gain insight.[145] The third wisdom in Revelation 13:18 occurs in the middle of a long section of a series of interludes (Rev 11:19—15:4), flanked on either end by the trumpet and bowl judgments.[146] This long section describes, in Stuckenbruck's words, the mythical vision of powers that threaten the faithful and stand opposite to the vision of unhindered worship in Revelation 5 and 7.[147] In the middle of this vision is the call for wisdom that is twofold; the saints are to identify the number of the beast and, in knowing the beast's reality, to position themselves with the Lamb despite the threat.[148] The fourth wisdom in Revelation 17:9 is analogous to the third and calls the readers to perceive once again the reality of the beast. Yet, it adds a further dimension; even John the seer must correct his mistake in his marveling of Babylon and in extension, the readers as well, in continuing to correct one's perception of reality through wisdom and to be loyal to God and to the Lamb.[149]

In turn, Stuckenbruck shows much more effectively than Pippin how the four occurrences of the word σοφία are functioning in the context of Revelation. He proves convincingly that epistemology plays an essential role in Revelation; the readers are to have a wise mind in discerning reality as portrayed by the author's visions and to act accordingly.[150] Nonetheless, Stuckenbruck did not provide a detailed and comprehensive analysis of the immediate and broader contexts in which the four occurrences of σοφία are found, especially for the latter two, since the length of the article (only thirteen pages) is too short to cover all aspects. A fuller discussion of the nature of the beast's kingdom and of Babylon in association with the call for wisdom in the literary contexts they are found in will bring out more meaningfully the ethical appeals these wisdom motifs make in Revelation. This study will thus build upon Stuckenbruck's analysis and examine more extensively the context and function of the four σοφία occurrences.

144. Stuckenbruck, "Disclosure of Wisdom," 350–51.
145. Stuckenbruck, "Disclosure of Wisdom," 351.
146. Stuckenbruck, "Disclosure of Wisdom," 351.
147. Stuckenbruck, "Disclosure of Wisdom," 353.
148. Stuckenbruck, "Disclosure of Wisdom," 352–56.
149. Stuckenbruck, "Disclosure of Wisdom," 358–59.
150. Stuckenbruck, "Disclosure of Wisdom," 359.

METHODOLOGY

The primary aim of this study is to ascertain the intended rhetorical function of wisdom motifs in the book of Revelation in relation to the book's ethics.[151] This study presupposes that authorial intent is behind every text and that the author or authors have written his or her text in order to achieve a particular effect upon the audience.[152] In order to achieve this aim, this study employs a grammatical-historical approach to the study of wisdom motifs in Revelation so as to analyze the text at hand more closely. More specifically, this study analyzes what Cotterell and Turner called "discourse meaning," namely looking at how the author has shaped the literary contexts where wisdom motifs appear.[153] A "discourse" is any coherent section of language written or oral.[154] In the case of this study, any coherent unit of text where a wisdom motif appears would constitute a discourse to be analyzed.

To do so, the immediate contexts in which the wisdom motifs are present in Revelation will first be examined. Second, the wisdom motifs will be examined in light of one another in the overall context of Revelation. Interpretation of the text will also be made where necessary to bring out the intended meaning and significance of the discourses that contain wisdom motifs. Furthermore, since discourses and contexts do not occur in a vacuum, this study will need to discuss one wisdom motif in connection with a different one at certain points.[155] Finally, this study will rarely be reading Revelation in context of other Jewish apocalypses but will focus largely on the text of Revelation at hand.

---

151. Rhetoric can be defined as the author's literary artistry and argument in convincing others. See Black, "Rhetorical Criticism," 166. Thus, ascertaining the rhetorical function of wisdom motifs has to do with understanding how the author has employed the motifs in the argument for persuading the readers.

152. Patrick and Scult further argue that a discourse incorporates a whole range of linguistic instrumentalities to construct "a particular relationship with an audience in order to communicate a message." Patrick and Scult, *Rhetoric and Biblical Interpretation*, 12. Similarly, Tull claims, "Arising out of a writer's desire to communicate a particular viewpoint in relation to other relevant viewpoints, a text is designed to maximize its persuasive powers." Tull, "Rhetorical Criticism and Intertextuality," 175. This study contends that one of the linguistic instrumentalities the author of Revelation uses to persuade the audience is wisdom motifs.

153. Cotterell and Turner, *Linguistics & Biblical Interpretation*.

154. Cotterell and Turner, *Linguistics & Biblical Interpretation*, 53, 230.

155. For instance, treatment of the fourth occurrence of the word σοφία will be made in connection with the two-women motif since both motifs occur in the larger context of Babylon the harlot.

Also important for this study is the need for outlining what constitutes wisdom motifs. Like apocalypse, perhaps even more, defining what the wisdom corpus and tradition is remains difficult. On one hand, more traditional scholars such as Crenshaw attempted to limit wisdom texts as distinct from those of the prophets by providing a list of traits peculiar to wisdom in form and content.[156] On the other hand, modern scholars such as Sneed want to delimit wisdom to the point of espousing pan-sapientialism, to show that wisdom tradition is behind all of Hebrew canon.[157] Thus, the issue here, as it was in apocalyptic genre studies, is whether it is possible to define wisdom genre narrowly and distinctively using the traditional criteria of form, content, and context or not.

There is a truth to the claim that the genre of wisdom is a modern category and not one given by the biblical writers.[158] However, it is also true that readers' previous experiences of literature, its style, subject matter, and choice of words do aid in the understanding of the types of literature that are in front of them.[159] This study, in turn, does not presume to settle the genre debate once and for all, but is one that acknowledges that such genre categories are nonetheless helpful in the understanding of biblical texts, that different genres and sub-genres can appear together in a given work, and that analyzing how these genres and their motifs are functioning can be a fruitful research.[160] Thus, in order to be as descriptive as possible in understanding the function of wisdom motifs in Revelation, the present study shall apply the following three criteria for detecting the presence of wisdom motifs in John's Apocalypse.

First, language representative of the wisdom genre should appear in a given context. The word "wisdom" (Hebrew *ḥokmâ* and Greek σοφία)

156. See Crenshaw, *Old Testament Wisdom*, 11, 24–27.

157. See Sneed, "Is the 'Wisdom Tradition' a Tradition?," 50–71. Sneed argues that there is a wisdom mode (not a genre, but a much more abstract category) prevalent in the Hebrew canon and that this is because the same scribal scholars or wisdom writers were behind the composition and preservation of all of Hebrew biblical texts. To be sure, Sneed himself does not seem to wish to promote pan-sapientialism since he distinguishes wisdom mode from other modes of biblical texts. However, he still exhibits pan-sapiential tendency by arguing that wisdom tradition is behind all biblical tradition and is itself not a separate tradition. For more information and discussion of the history of research on wisdom tradition, see Kynes, "Modern Scholarly Wisdom Tradition," 11–38.

158. Weeks, *An Introduction*, 142.

159. Weeks, "Wisdom, Form and Genre," 161.

160. For the solid argument supporting the concept of wisdom literature as a genre, see especially Fox, "Three Theses on Wisdom," 75–83.

and its cognates and synonyms (knowledge, understanding, discretion, mind) would be a good indication.[161] Second, forms representative of the wisdom genre will indicate the likely presence of wisdom elements. Such forms would include, but not be limited to, praise/vice lists, wisdom sayings, exhortation/admonitions, riddles, and proverbs.[162] Third, themes and ideas representative of the wisdom genre should also appear. Theodicean matters, origin of wisdom, and correct human behavior can be indicative of wisdom influence.[163] Of course, comparison or contrast between alternative ways or entities is also a well-known device of sapiential literature, especially in Revelation.[164]

The first two criteria then have to do with language and form, the third criteria with content. These criteria are not unique to wisdom genre alone, but the presence of several of them in a given context will indicate the presence of wisdom motif in that context. Again, this study's approach as noted above will further substantiate that wisdom motifs are employed deliberately in Revelation to invoke a certain ethical appeal to the audience.

CONCLUSION

Based on the criteria above, this study shall proceed to analyze three major wisdom motifs that are present in Revelation. Chapter 2 will analyze the first two instances of the word "wisdom" in Revelation (Rev 5:12; 7:12), and chapter 3 will analyze the latter two instances (Rev 13:18; 17:9). In keeping with the methodology outlined in the previous section, the immediate contexts of each instance shall first be assessed and then the larger context of how they function together in the book will follow. In the end, a summary and synthesis of how the four instances of the word "wisdom" are operating will be provided.

Chapters 4 and 5 will examine the two-women motif. Using Proverbs 1–9 as well as other sources that contain the two-women motif, its function and significance will first be ascertained in chapter 4. This earlier

---

161. For a list of vocabulary characteristic of wisdom literature, see Whybray, *The Intellectual Tradition*, 74–76, 142–49. See also, Coughenour, "Enoch and Wisdom," 30–31.

162. For a list of forms characteristic of wisdom literature, see Crenshaw, "Wisdom," 229–62. See also, Gammie, "Paraenetic Literature," 41–77.

163. Johnson, *Function of Apocalyptic*, 65.

164. Gammie, "Paraenetic Literature," 56.

conclusion will then be used to establish the meaning and function of the two-women motif in Revelation in its immediate and larger context in chapter 5. Chapter 5 will not only look at the contrasting city visions of Babylon the harlot (Rev 17–18) and New Jerusalem the bride (Rev 19, 21–22), but also Revelation's other mentions of female figures (the Thyatira letter's Jezebel and the woman clothed with the sun in Revelation 12) to understand more fully how the two-women motif is functioning in Revelation. A synthesis on the significance of the two-women motif in Revelation will conclude the chapter.

Chapter 6 will deal with the macarisms and vice lists that are found within Revelation. These ethical catalogues and sayings will be examined in their immediate and larger contexts to ascertain their literary function. Finally, a synthesis will be offered regarding the meaning and significance of the macarisms and vice lists in Revelation.

Chapter 7 will conclude this study. It will summarize all the findings from the previous chapters and provide a synthesis of the function and significance of wisdom motifs in the book of Revelation. Chapter 7 will end with implications the present study has for the church today and for future study.

CHAPTER 2

Σοφία in Revelation as Divine Wisdom

THE WORD σοφία APPEARS in four places in the book of Revelation.[1] The first two instances testify that σοφία belongs solely to God and to the Lamb. The last two instances invite the readers to exhibit σοφία and to understand the reality the author is portraying. This study shall show that these occurrences are not random. John has strategically placed the word σοφία in the narrative of Revelation to promote the idea that true wisdom belongs to God and also to the Lamb, and that those who belong to God's kingdom should in turn display this wisdom in recognizing the deception of the beast's kingdom. In seeing this deceptive reality of the beast's kingdom through wisdom, God's people must turn away from it, not aligning their fidelity to this dishonest kingdom.

Also interesting is the fact that John never associates σοφία and its cognates to his characterization of the beast and its followers. It is as if the beast and its followers have no wisdom or are unable to display wisdom (true wisdom that is), although they might live luxuriously on this earth.[2] On the other hand, it is Christ's followers who are specifically called upon to display wisdom and understanding, even though they

---

1. The four places are Revelation 5:12, 7:12, 13:18, and 17:9.

2. The notion of luxurious living by beast's followers are especially emphasized in Revelation 18. John uses the noun στρῆνος and the verb στρηνιάω to describe the luxurious living that was spent by the harlot Babylon and her cooperators in Revelation 18:3, 18:7, and 18:9. The merchants who associated themselves with the harlot are also described to have gained wealth (πλουτέω) from her in Revelation 18:3, 18:15, and 18:19. The truth that Babylon herself is an ally of the beast is clear from the fact that she is portrayed as riding the beast in Revelation 17:3.

do not get to live luxuriously as the beast's followers do.³ It is apparent that for John, being wise has less to do with the condition of one's living standards on this earth and more to do with seeing the true reality of this world.

Wisdom then, is a key and necessary feature that characterizes those who belong to God. John knows that his readers should already possess this wisdom if they are God's people and wants them to exercise this wisdom in understanding the reality of the world. This chapter will look at the first two instances where the word σοφία occurs in detail and then the next chapter will analyze the last two instances. Together, the two chapters will seek to apprehend how the passages are functioning in promoting the kind of ethics John envisions.

FIRST AND SECOND INSTANCES: REVELATION 5:12 AND 7:12

As noted earlier, John employs the first two occurrences of the word σοφία to show that wisdom belongs to God and to the Lamb exclusively. Furthermore, this section will show that John wants his readers to realize that there is indeed a redefinition of what true wisdom is. This true wisdom is one that is closely tied to Christ's work of sacrifice.

Revelation 5:12

The first occurrence of the word σοφία takes place in Revelation 5:12. Here, Christ the Lamb is praised to be worthy to receive seven things, the third item being σοφία. Revelation 5:12 stands at a crucial point in the narrative of Revelation. John has just finished his letters to the seven churches by the end of chapter 3 of Revelation.⁴ Starting with chapter 4,

---

3. The fact that believers are in a disadvantageous position in regard to the world's wealth is clear from Revelation 13:15–18 where believers who do not follow the beast nor take its mark are not allowed to buy or sell.

4. Revelation 2–3 is in fact Christ's words to the seven churches that John communicates. Taken together, Revelation 2–3 is commonly referred to as seven letters to the seven churches in Asia Minor. Whether one takes the seven churches literally or symbolically is not a matter relevant to this study. However, scholars agree that Revelation 2–3 forms a distinct unit in the narrative of Revelation. Nevertheless, this does not mean that Revelation 2–3 is a letter, but the rest of Revelation is not. Revelation, from its beginning to the end, maintains a framework of a letter with an extended introduction (chs. 1–3) and benediction (22:20–21). See Beale, *Revelation*, 223. This fact makes Beale

the narrative takes a dramatic turn as the same voice that commanded John to write (1:10) now calls him to come up to heaven so that he can see "what must happen after these things" (4:1).[5] What John right away sees, moreover, is not what will happen on the earth, but rather a majestic view of the heavenly throne.

Indeed, Revelation 4–5, where the first occurrence of the word σοφία takes place, is a literary unit that is vitally important for the theological worldview of Revelation.[6] Troubles, misconducts, and rebukes occupied most of the messages to the seven churches in Revelation 2–3. Starting with Revelation 4, however, John is moved up to heaven where there is "an atmosphere of perfect assurance and peace."[7] The theological message for this dramatic shift seems to be clear: while imperfections and finiteness abound on this earth, God is still on his throne in absolute sovereignty and transcendence.[8] Before John prophesies what will happen on the earth, he wants his readers to understand first and foremost that God still reigns in absolute power. As he is about to show, imperfect power flourishes on this earth, vying for people's allegiance. Yet, believers must remember the cosmic sovereignty of God and Christ and give them glory and fidelity just like those around the heavenly throne, despite the alluring calls of things or beings that are finite such as human empires or the beast.[9]

Moreover, this strategic placement of the throne room vision before John's actual pronouncement of the future events indicates that

---

to conclude thus: "It is in this sense that we can call the letters the literary microcosm of the entire book's macrocosmic structure." Beale, *Revelation*, 224.

5. Unless otherwise noted, the English translation is the author's own.

6. The reasons why Revelation 4 and 5 should be taken as unified and not separated are aptly captured in Stuckenbruck, "Revelation 4–5," 235–48. According to Stuckenbruck, the main reason why Revelation 4–5 is one vision is because Revelation 4 contains many Christological details that are later picked up throughout Revelation, including Revelation 5. This means that Revelation 4 should not be taken as standing alone, devoid of "Christian" character. Stuckenbruck thus states, " . . . perhaps Revelation 4 and 5 should not be considered two separate or contrasting visions; instead, perhaps consider how they may be essentially *one* vision, that is, a drama that unfolds in two stages." Stuckenbruck, "Revelation 4–5," 246. Emphasis original.

7. Charles, *Revelation*, vol. 1, 102–3. Thus, Charles notes that "The dramatic contrast [between chapter 4 and chapters 1–3, on the one hand, and chapter 4 and chapter 5, on the other] could not be greater." Charles, *Revelation*, vol. 1, 102.

8. Bauckham, *Theology*, 43–47.

9. Bauckham, *Theology*, 44–45. See also Butler, "The Politics of Worship," 7–23 and Morton, "Glory to God," 90.

John's primary concern is not eschatology but epistemology.¹⁰ To be sure, larger portions of the book of Revelation do contain information about the future, but fundamental for John is for his readers to understand the future in light of what has been revealed, namely that God and Christ are in control of all things. Eschatology is not the only feature important in apocalyptic genre, but also the disclosure of heavenly knowledge. In this manner, Revelation is akin to other Jewish apocalypses that have the notion of the disclosure of the cosmos and of wisdom as one of their prominent features.¹¹ Apocalypses such as *1 Enoch*, *2 Enoch*, and *3 Baruch* include the experience of the ascension to heaven and the revelation of heavenly mysteries, and the same is true of Revelation.¹² As noted in chapter 1, this feature of the disclosure of heavenly knowledge or wisdom is one that is quite in line with sapiential literature. In any case, this disclosure of knowledge of the throne room serves as the basis for comprehending the rest of the book of Revelation. Hence, it must be deliberate on John's part that the word σοφία appears during the throne room vision, to let his readers recognize that understanding this vision is vital for their discernment.

Consequently, worship dominates the scene in Revelation 4. God, with an appearance of jasper and carnelian, is sitting on his throne which is encircled by an emerald-like rainbow (4:2–3). Twenty-four thrones with twenty-four elders surround the throne (4:4). Before the throne are seven torches of fire, identified as the seven spirits of God (4:5). Four living creatures that look like lion, ox, man, and eagle are around the throne (4:6–7). The four living creatures and the twenty-four elders then perform a crescendo of worship to God (4:8–11). The entire scenery is majestic and wonderous.

Yet, for John at least, it seems not all things are well in heaven. The atmosphere of the throne room vision changes from "the uninterrupted praise of God into a sense of panic" as John is unable to find anyone in all of creation worthy to open the scroll that is in God's right hand (5:1–4).¹³

10. Stuckenbruck, "Disclosure of Wisdom," 348. Stuckenbruck defines epistemology as "a way of construing the world that is shaped by what has been revealed."

11. Reynolds and Stuckenbruck, "Introduction," 7–8.

12. Reynolds and Stuckenbruck, "Introduction," 8.

13. Stuckenbruck, "Revelation 4–5," 238. The various arguments as to the identity of the scroll that is in God's right hand have been succinctly summarized by Beale. See Beale, *Revelation*, 339–48. No matter what the exact identity of the scroll may be, Beale makes a valid point that its contents likely have to do with God's plan of the future in light of Revelation 5:9 and Daniel 12:4 (cf. Rev 4:1). Beale, *Revelation*, 347–48.

This sense of panic, however, seems to be reserved for John alone, for one of the elders assures him that there is indeed someone worthy, namely the Lion who is also Lamb (5:5–6). This introduction of Christ in Revelation 5 is very important for the theology of the book. John hears that Christ who is the Lion and the Root of David "has conquered" (ἐνίκησεν) and thus can open the scroll (5:5). But who John actually sees is the Lamb, standing as though he had been slain (5:6).

The image of Lion and of David evokes royal and messianic connotations.[14] Thus, action befitting of the messianic king, Jesus is testified to have conquered, which in turn enables him to be the only one who can open the scroll.[15] But this act of conquering by Jesus likely refers to his defeat of Satan, sin, and death at the cross.[16] This is why when John sees Jesus, he does not see the expected Lion but rather a slain Lamb. Osborne succinctly captures the irony in this way:

> Thus far it seems Jesus will destroy the nations, certainly a theme of this book. However, the next verse will clarify this and give the great Christian paradox—Jesus has "conquered" primarily not through military might, though that is to come, but through his sacrificial death (5:6, 9, 12) . . . . As the royal Messiah, Jesus wages a messianic war against evil, and the major weapon that defeats the enemies of God is the cross.[17]

---

14. The title of "Lion" goes back to Genesis 49:9, where Jacob prophesied over Judah that he is a "lion's whelp." Genesis 49:9 has long been understood to carry a messianic connotation. This is attested, for example, in 2 Esdras 12:31–32 where the messiah is clearly associated with the title of "Lion." This connotation is complimented by Jesus's second title in Revelation 5:5, the title of "the Root of David." Although there is a debate whether "the Root of David" title refers to Jesus being a descendent of David (Jesus came from David's root/line) or to Jesus being the creator/ancestor of David (Jesus is the root from which David came), the very mention of the name David alone strongly recalls messianic overtones. For the arguments surrounding the phrase "the Root of David," see Aune, *Revelation 1–5*, 350–51; Beale, *Revelation*, 349, 1146; Boxall, *Revelation*, 97; Caird, *Revelation*, 74; Mounce, *Revelation*, 131 fn. 15; Osborne, *Revelation*, 254; Swete, *Apocalypse*, 77. For those who argue specifically that the title refers to Jesus being David's creator, see Hughes, *Revelation*, 79 and MacLeod, "The Lion," 333–34. In any case, the two titles of "Lion" and "the Root of David" together introduces Jesus as the messianic king who shall reign.

15. The infinitive ἀνοῖξαι (to open) expresses purpose or result. Beale, *Revelation*, 349. Either way, it is the act of conquering that enables Jesus to open the scroll.

16. Ladd, *Revelation*, 84. Ladd mentions Hebrews 2:14–15, Matthew 12:29, Luke 10:18, John 12:31, 16:11, Colossians 2:15, and 2 Timothy 1:10 as other New Testament passages where Christ's defeat of Satan, sin, and death are captured.

17. Osborne, *Revelation*, 254.

Therefore, there is a redefinition of what it means "to conquer" in Revelation. One does not simply "conquer" by might. In fact, this is what the beast attempts to do against God's people. The beast conquers the two witnesses in Revelation 11:7 and the saints in 13:7.[18] On the other hand, God's people are also called to conquer. At the end of all seven letters to the seven churches in Revelation 2–3, Christ calls the believers to conquer. In fact, Christ's last call to conquer in his letter to Laodicea in 3:21 hints that the believers must conquer as Christ himself has conquered.

But the specific details of what to conquer and how to do so are conspicuously missing in the seven letters of Revelation 2–3. By Revelation 5:5–6, what and how the believers should conquer become clearer: it is to conquer Satan by sacrificial death just like Christ. But does this mean that all believers need to become martyrs in order to conquer? Μὴ γένοιτο! The Gospel of John, as well as the rest of Revelation, furnishes a qualification as to what it means to conquer by sacrificial death.[19]

In the Fourth Gospel, Jesus claims that every work he performs are done in the obedience to the Father and thus reflect the Father's will (John 5:19–20, 36; 17:4). Jesus does not do anything out of his own accord (8:42) and even what he says is given by the Father who sent him (12:49–50). More importantly, Jesus knew that his work on the cross was included in the task commanded by the Father (12:27; 19:28, 30). While it might be that through his specific work on the cross, Jesus defeated Satan (12:31–33) and can claim, "I have conquered (νενίκηκα) the world" (16:33), but it is essential to remember that Jesus's work on the cross is part of the work the Father gave him to do. Therefore, in the Gospel of John, it is not simply Jesus's death that is the basis for his conquering; it is Jesus staying faithful to the Father in complete obedience in all the work

18. While there are debates as to the specific identity of the two witnesses in Revelation 11, it is clear that they are God's people.

19. This writer understands all Johannine corpus (John, 1–3 John, and Revelation) to be written by the Apostle John. But whether one recognizes the Gospel of John and Revelation to be authored by John the apostle or not, it is credible that both books are connected very closely in theology. For scholars who argue for the similarities between the Gospel of John and Revelation, see Frey, "Erwägungen," 326–429 and Rainbow, *Johannine Theology*, 9–10, 39–51. The similarities lead Frey to conclude that both books are connected to John at least in part. Frey, "Erwägungen," 428. Whereas most monographs on Johannine theology utilize the Fourth Gospel and the Johannine Epistles only, the similarities lead Rainbow to further incorporate the book of Revelation into his discussion of Johannine theology. For the position that the Gospel of John and Revelation were written by different authors other than the Apostle John, see Bauckham, *Jesus and the Eyewitnesses*, 412–37, 550–89; Eurell, "Reconsidering the John of Revelation," 505–18; Koester, *The End*, 47–48.

that he did, including his work on the cross, which becomes the basis for his conquering.[20]

This line of thought clearly continues in the book of Revelation. In Revelation 12:11, the believers are said to "have conquered" (ἐνίκησαν) Satan by the blood of the Lamb and by the word of their testimony. Here, the object of the believers' conquering is made crystal clear: Satan and his powers.[21] The method with which the believers conquer Satan is also specified.[22] First, God's people conquer Satan by the blood of the Lamb. Through Christ's death on the cross, Satan's accusations are no longer effective on God's people for whom Christ's blood makes atonement and cleanses from sin.[23] As Christ overcame Satan through his resurrection, so do the believers overcome Satan's guilty verdict of the second death (2:11; 20:6).[24]

Second, God's people also conquer Satan "by the word of their testimony" (διὰ τὸν λόγον τῆς μαρτυρίας αὐτῶν). The exact meaning of the phrase "by the word of their testimony" is debated. On one hand, one could take αὐτῶν as objective genitive, thus rendering the phrase as "by

---

20. This in turn is the reason why the cross is also connected to the theme of glory in the Gospel of John. Jesus gave the Father glory by doing the works the Father gave him to do and expects that the Father will also glorify him (John 17:4–5). That the cross is part of the work the Father gave him to do is clearly reflected in John 13:31, where Jesus claims that "now" (νῦν) he is glorified, because Judas Iscariot just left to betray him. Furthermore, John uses the verb "to lift up" (ὑψόω) in reference to Jesus going up on the cross, and this verb is closely tied to the verb "to glorify" (δοξάζω) in the Gospel (3:14–15; 7:39; 8:28; 12:16, 32–34; cf. Isa 52:13 LXX). Therefore, the cross is the first step in Jesus's glorification, not his shame, in the Gospel of John. For more discussion on the theme of glory and the cross in John, see Bauckham, *Gospel of Glory*, 43–62.

21. Likewise, Revelation 15:2 mentions that the believers have conquered the beast, its image, and the number of its name. Satan exerts his powerful influence through the beast on this earth according to Revelation 13. Hence, it is when the believers conquer the beast by rejecting the beast and its tempting ways while on this earth, they also conquer Satan. "The victors are the faithful people of God who did not serve the Beast or his image." Hoskins, *Revelation*, 286.

22. The two διά with the accusative constructions in Revelation 12:11 likely take on the idea of means. See Beckwith, *Apocalypse*, 627. Fanning, however, understands the two constructions to denote a causal sense, not means. Fanning, *Revelation*, 358. But the same construction also occurs in Revelation 13:14, and it is very likely to denote means or instrument there. Either way, the nuance is subtle.

23. Hoskins, *Revelation*, 219. The idea of Christ's blood cleansing the believers from sin is visibly captured in Revelation 7:13–14. There, the believers are said to have washed their robes and made them white in the blood of the Lamb. In all normality, a robe soaked in blood should turn red. But the robes in fact turn white, a clear symbolism that shows the purifying effect of Christ's blood upon the believer.

24. Beale, *Revelation*, 664.

the word of [God's or the Lamb's] testimony to them."[25] Taken this way, the meaning becomes that God or the Lamb is responsible for the believers' conquering; the believers' role in the conquering is minimal or nonexistent. On the other hand, one could take αὐτῶν as subjective genitive, making the phrase to mean "by the word of their testimony."[26] Thus, the believers have a role in the conquering—they are to live as faithful witnesses who testify to others about their Lord. While both nuances are possible, the latter nuance seems emphasized, especially since Revelation 12:17 further describes the believers as ones who keep the commandments of God and who hold the testimony of Jesus.[27] To keep and to hold are clearly roles the believers are to act upon. Revelation thereby ascribes responsibilities on the believers' part in how they ought to live and to conquer in this world.

Therefore, in Revelation, there is in fact a twofold redefinition of what it truly means to conquer. First, one conquers by the Lamb's blood. God's people are covered by the blood Christ shed on the cross, and they are freed from Satan's accusations, sin, and death. Second, one also conquers by the word of one's testimony. As Christ stayed faithful to the Father in obedience while on the earth, even to death on the cross, and thereby conquered, God's people are called to conquer in like manner by staying faithful to God in obedience, even to death by martyrdom (cf. Rev 2:10, 13; 6:11; 11:7; 13:10). It is when the believers conquer Satan and his powers on this earth in this manner, they will inherit the blessings of eternal life (21:7).[28] Their conquering of Satan is so intricately connected to the Lamb's work and testimony.[29]

---

25. Lohmeyer takes this view. See Lohmeyer, *Offenbarung*, 103.

26. Smalley takes this view. See Smalley, *Revelation*, 328.

27. So also Beale concurs. Beale, *Revelation*, 664.

28. See also, Tabb, *All Things New*, 108–10. The blessing of eternal life promised to the one who conquers in Revelation 21:7 is a covenantal promise. This is seen clearly with the use of the covenantal formula, "I will be to him God and he will be to me son" (ἔσομαι αὐτῷ θεὸς καὶ αὐτὸς ἔσται μοι υἱός), which echoes the covenant language of Exodus 6:7. See Keener, *Revelation*, 488–89. Harker further argues that the covenant motif continues through Revelation 21:9—22:5 in order to call the believers into faithful discipleship that is anchored in the hope of covenant renewal. Harker, "Intertextuality," 45–73. In a similar vein, Decker demonstrates that the Old Testament allusions in Revelation 2–3 reflect covenant motif in encouraging the seven churches to remain faithful to Christ who is their covenant king. Decker, "Covenant Fidelity," 165–93. Thus, the covenant motifs in Revelation also function in promoting fidelity to God and Christ.

29. The same idea regarding the believers' conquering is also found in 1 John. In 1 John 2:13, the elder testifies that the young men have conquered the evil one. Likewise

This is why John focuses on the fact that Christ's worthiness to open the scroll is due to his conquering in Revelation 5.[30] Before his vision gets fully underway starting in Revelation 6, John wants to assure his readers that God and the Lamb are in absolute control. Whatever happens or will happen on the earth, God is still on his throne. In fact, the events that occur on the earth are going to be initiated by the Lamb as he opens the seals on the scroll.[31] God's plan of redemption and judgment is thus under the Lamb's sovereign control who has conquered and is worthy.[32] Christ is at the crux of everything, and even the meaning of victorious life is redefined in him. The believers must follow suit in knowing this transcendent truth.

Hence Christ can approach God who sits on the heavenly throne and take the scroll from God's right hand (Rev 5:6–7). Christ also receives the same kind of worship that God received in Revelation 4. When the Lamb takes the scroll, the four living creatures and the twenty-four elders first fall down before him and sing a new song (ᾠδὴν καινὴν) of worship to him (5:8–10).[33] In line with the Old Testament where the phrase "new song" is mentioned, the content of the new song has to do with God's redemptive work.[34] But in Revelation, it is specifically God's redemptive work through the Lamb who was slain and who has purchased people by

---

in 1 John 4:4, the elder claims that the believers have conquered the false prophets (also called antichrists in 1 John) because God who is in them is greater than the one who is in the world. In 1 John 5:4–5, the elder further states that God's people who believe in Christ have conquered the world through their faith. Thus, 1 John also communicates the truth that the believers can conquer Satan and his powers through Christ and through their faith in Christ.

30. Mathewson even notes that the perfect tenses are utilized in the actual appearance of the Lamb in Revelation 5:6–7 (ἑστηκὸς, ἐσφαγμένον, ἀπεσταλμένοι, and εἴληφεν) so that the main character can stand out within the visionary narrative. This "frontgrounds" or focuses attention on the important features of the Lamb, namely his standing as though slain, his authority to send forth the seven spirits, and his reception of the scroll. Yet, this Lamb's actual appearance is "backgrounded" or supported by the aorist tenses in Revelation 5:5 (ἐνίκησεν and ἀνοῖξαι), namely the reason that the Lamb is worthy to open the scroll is due to his conquering. Mathewson, "Verbal Aspect," 65–74.

31. Hoskins, *Revelation*, 136.

32. Beale, *Revelation*, 350.

33. For OT passages where the phrase "new song" is used, see Pss 33:3; 40:3; 96:1; 98:1; 144:9; 149:1; Isa 42:10.

34. Patterson has compared four psalms where the phrase "new song" occurs and has found that one of the common themes that exhibit all the psalms is the theme of God's saving power and acts. See Patterson, "Singing the New Song," 430.

his blood that causes the four living creatures and the twenty-four elders to worship.[35] The song also testifies that those who were purchased by Christ were made a kingdom and priests who shall reign on the earth, a clear allusion to Exodus 19:6. This further clarifies that the Lamb's sacrificial work is also the work of the paschal lamb, and Isbell has convincingly argued that even the content of the song itself follows the basic order of events of the original Exodus.[36] Thus, Christ is worthy to take the scroll and to open its seals precisely because he has effected a re-creation for the redeemed; like Israel in the past, those who have associated themselves with the blood of the Lamb and who have been redeemed from bondage have become God's chosen people, his kingdom of priests.[37] The believers' identity is forever redefined by Christ.

Following the lead of the four living creatures and of the twenty-four elders, the angels, numbered to be myriads of myriads and thousands of thousands, join in the worship (5:11–12).[38] Much like the acclamation given to God in Revelation 4:11, the Lamb now receives full honor with seven qualities.[39] Three of those qualities (glory, honor, and power) appeared in 4:11 in reverse order. Scholars have also noted that this ascription of virtues to the Lamb in 5:12 is a doxology, and the angels are not bestowing these virtues to the Lamb but are simply acknowledging them.[40] All of this mounts up to one message: the Lamb is worshipped with divine qualities that belong properly to God.[41]

---

35. MacLeod notes three things about Christ's death in this worship. First, Christ's death was a sacrificial death. Second, it was a redemptive death. Third, it was a universal death in its benefits. MacLeod, "The Adoration of God," 463–64.

36. Isbell, "The Past Is Yet to Come," 137–42. See also Charles, "Apocalyptic Tribute," 467–68.

37. Isbell, "Exodus Typology," 142.

38. Osborne notes that a myriad was the highest number known in the Greco-Roman world. Osborne, *Revelation*, 262. Thus, John sees and hears the worship of innumerable host of angels, which is also often mentioned in the OT (i.e., Deut 33:2; Job 25:3; Ps 68:17; 89:7; Dan 7:10).

39. Ian Paul observes that the seven qualities signify completeness or totality of affirmation. Paul, *Revelation*, 137. So also Hoskins, *Revelation*, 136.

40. Fanning, *Revelation*, 228. For a more detailed analysis on the doxological form, see Aune, *Revelation 1–5*, 43–45.

41. Aune, *Revelation 1–5*, 365. Aune further notes that, not only are the items in the list of virtues qualities that belong properly to God, but they can also be bestowed on the king by God. So also Smalley, *Revelation*, 139. This observation leads to confirm that as the divine king, Christ alone is to be worshipped; any other worship of earthly political realities is idolatry.

Once more in Revelation 5:12, the Lamb who is slain (ἐσφαγμένον) is testified to be worthy (ἄξιόν) to receive this doxology.[42] John wants to strongly emphasize the Lamb's worthiness and the truth that this worthiness is summed up in his work of sacrifice.[43] As he is about to show, there is an ongoing conflict of sovereignties and of ideologies on this earth. The beast deceives the people of this earth to follow and to worship him (Rev 13; 20:3, 8). Those who do not submit to the beast's rule are persecuted (Rev 2:10, 13; 11:7; 12:17; 13:7, 15–17; 17:6). Yet, Revelation 16:6 expresses that the only thing the beast and its followers are worthy (ἄξιοί) of is God's judgment, not worship. True and explicit worship, on the other hand, belongs to God and to the Lamb who are worthy (4:11; 5:12). Moreover, it is those who stay faithful to God, who do not submit to the beast's rule, are the ones worthy to remain with Christ (3:4).[44]

Thus, not only is Revelation 4–5 intended to assure the readers of the absolute sovereignty of God and of the Lamb, the pericope of the throne room vision also functions to challenge the readers to admit that this absolute sovereignty is the only sovereignty worthy of their compliance. Hence John associates the reality of one's allegiance with whom one worships in Revelation. In other words, the object of people's worship shows which sovereignty they are submitting themselves under, whether God's or the beast's.[45] Revelation 5:12 gives a clear answer and stresses that the

---

42. Fanning observes that this time, John uses the perfect tense of σφάζω to draw attention to the ongoing effect of Christ's redemptive accomplishment through the cross. Fanning, *Revelation*, 227 fn. 88.

43. Osborne, *Revelation*, 262.

44. It is those who do not soil their garments who are promised to walk with Christ in white because of their worthiness in Revelation 3:4. Revelation 3:5 further clarifies that the promise of walking with Christ in white garments has to do with eternal life for those who conquer. Based on Revelation 3:1–3, not soiling one's garments has to do with one's works that are acceptable to God, namely keeping what one has received and heard. Thus, the Sardis letter in Revelation 3:1–6 testifies that it is those who submit to God's rule, who stay faithful to God, are the ones who are worthy to receive eternal life.

45. This insight comes from Richard Bauckham. Bauckham understands that the conflict of sovereignties is often portrayed in Revelation in terms of worship. In Revelation 13, the universal worship of the beast indicates the rejection of divine rule by the world, Rome in particular. In Revelation 15 and 19, on the other hand, the universal worship of God indicates the coming of God's kingdom. According to Bauckham, Revelation thus draws a clear line between those who worship the beast and those who worship God, and worship in heaven follows every stage of God's victory in Revelation. Bauckham, *Theology*, 34–35. J. Daryl Charles also concurs. Charles, "Apocalyptic Tribute," 464.

Lamb is the only sovereign worthy to receive worship.[46] Once again, it is because of his sacrifice that the Lamb is deemed worthy. Bauckham has stated this emphasized truth in this manner: "... Christ's sacrificial death *belongs to the way God rules the world.*"[47] Christ has redefined not only the meaning of conquering life (5:5–6), but also the meaning of reigning life (5:10). Taken together, this must be life in the fullest and perfect sense, and Revelation makes it clear that it is only found in Christ and his ways.

Now this section of the study has arrived at the heart of the matter. The third item on the list of the ascribed virtues to Christ in Revelation 5:12 is "wisdom" (σοφία). That the word σοφία occurs in the third place on the list does not seem to matter much. More important is to notice that this is the first time the word σοφία appears in Revelation. While the ascription of virtues in 5:12 is akin to that ascribed to the Father in 4:11, the word σοφία noticeably does not occur in 4:11.[48] This obviously does not mean that wisdom only belongs to Christ and not to the Father, since wisdom does get ascribed to the Father in 7:12. Nevertheless, it is interesting that John ascribes wisdom specifically to Christ first rather than to the Father, and this is likely intentional. If so, then the reason must be connected to how John introduced the Lamb in Revelation 5.

As noted above, the Lamb has been introduced as one who is at the crux of everything.[49] The Lamb lives a victorious, conquering life precisely because he was slain. His slain nature is also what proves him worthy to be a true sovereign. As such, he is the only one who can take the scroll from God's right hand and unleash its contents. Only the Lamb has absolute control over the fate of the world and its people. The people's

---

46. Of course, both God and the Lamb are to be worshipped, not just the Lamb in Revelation. "It is important to notice how the scene is so structured that the worship of the Lamb (5:8–12) leads to the worship of God and the Lamb together (5:13)." Bauckham, *Theology*, 60. See also, Schedtler, "Praising Christ the King," 164.

47. Bauckham, *Theology*, 64. Emphasis original.

48. While there are other words in the list of Revelation 5:12 that do not appear in the list of 4:11, this work is concerned only with σοφία. However, especially interesting is the occurrence of the word πλοῦτον in 5:12 that does not appear in 4:11 nor in 7:12 where another ascription of virtues to the Father occurs. It is almost as if John wants to emphasize that true wealth is only found and redefined in Christ.

49. The focus in Revelation 1–3 was on Christ being the Lord over the church. Revelation 4–5 expands this focus to show that Christ is not only Lord over the church, but the entire creation. Hence, not only does Christ hold the seven stars and stand in the midst of the lampstands, which represent his lordship over his church (1:20), but he also has seven horns and seven eyes that are sent out into all the earth, which represent his lordship over entire world (5:6).

identity rests squarely on him. It necessarily follows then that the Lamb is the one who redefines the meaning of life, and Revelation 5 testifies that this redefinition comes from the Lamb's own example, namely that true life is one that is lived out in full obedience to the Father, even to the point of death.

Now, John testifies that the same slain Lamb is worthy to receive wisdom, which means that even the meaning of wisdom is redefined in Christ and by Christ.[50] John is about to show in Revelation that false notions of power, wealth, and wisdom are rampant on the earth, and he wants the readers to understand first and foremost that true notions of power, wealth, and wisdom are in stark contrast and can be discerned only through the Lamb.[51] That this is John's intention is evident from comparing Revelation 5:12 with 5:13. In 5:13, all creation now give one final worship to both God and the Lamb, and the doxology in 5:13 repeats the last four items from the doxology in 5:12. This makes the first three items from the doxology in 5:12, namely power, wealth, and wisdom, stand out by communicating that they especially belong to the Lamb. One can argue that power, wealth, and wisdom are those things that the world considers what successful life entails, and John is revealing that the Lamb has them and knows them. Especially, John wants to show that the Lamb knows and redefines what true wise living is, and this must be why John ascribes wisdom to Christ first rather than to the Father.

Scholars have also noted that the background to the doxology in Revelation 5:12 can be traced back to 1 Chronicles 29 and Daniel 2.[52] In 1 Chronicles 29:10–12, David, at the end of his reign as king of Israel, praises God in front of all assembly and ascribes power, wealth, might, and glory to God. Since 1 Chronicles 29:10 states that David "blessed" (εὐλόγησεν) God when giving him the doxology, it would mean that five items out of seven in Revelation 5:12 appear in 1 Chronicles 29, namely power, wealth, might, glory, and blessing. The reason why David ascribes

---

50. Stuckenbruck, "Disclosure of Wisdom," 349.

51. Stuckenbruck, "Disclosure of Wisdom," 349–50.

52. An example of a scholar who argues for 1 Chronicles 29 being the most relevant for Revelation 5:12 is Buist Fanning. Fanning, *Revelation*, 228. For an example of a scholar who believes Daniel 2 is the most relevant, see Aune, *Revelation 1–5*, 364. Beale seems to give the most balanced view. He argues that the combination of power, wealth, might, and glory comes from 1 Chronicles 29, while the use of wisdom is from Daniel 2. Beale, *Revelation*, 364. In any case, Daniel 2 clearly stands behind the use of wisdom in the doxology of Revelation 5:12, for the word does not appear in 1 Chronicles 29:10–12.

σοφία IN REVELATION AS DIVINE WISDOM   47

these virtues to God is relevant for Revelation 5:12. It is because the whole world is God's kingdom, and God rules over all things (1 Chr 29:11–12).

Similarly, in Daniel 2:20, Daniel ascribes to God wisdom and greatness because God rules over the kings of the earth (Dan 2:21) and because God has revealed the mystery of Nebuchadnezzar's dream to Daniel (2:22–23). In Daniel 2:37, it would seem strange for Daniel to ascribe kingdom, might, honor, and glory to king Nebuchadnezzar and not to God, but the context makes it clear that this is because God has given these things to Nebuchadnezzar. In fact, Nebuchadnezzar's dream itself has to do with God controlling the kingdoms of the earth, of which Nebuchadnezzar's is but a small picture. Thus, the context of Daniel 2 shows that the two doxologies in Daniel 2:20 and 2:37 have to do with one truth: God's sovereignty over the kingdoms of the earth.[53]

In keeping with these two Old Testament backgrounds, the doxology in Revelation 5:12 also has to do with God's sovereignty over all the earth, but gives it an added dimension, namely that it is indeed the Lamb who has this absolute sovereignty. Other sovereignties that exist on this earth pale in comparison. Even the authority of the beast exists only because it is allowed by God (and the Lamb) for a time.[54] The Lamb rules over all creation and knows the true ways of this world.[55] Christ who is the wisdom of God (1 Cor 1:24, 30) and in whom all wisdom and knowledge are hidden (Col 2:3) is thus fitting to be acknowledged with true wisdom in Revelation 5:12. The Lamb, together with God, are the only absolute sovereignties, to whom all creation must give allegiance in worship (Rev 5:13–14).

Furthermore, Daniel 2's connection of wisdom with the revelation of heavenly mysteries is quite relevant to Revelation 5's use of the word wisdom. As noted earlier, Revelation, along with other Jewish apocalypses,

---

53. Beale notes that the combination of terms for might, honor, and glory also appears in Job 37:22–23 and 40:10, but argues that Daniel is the likely candidate for the background of these terms in Revelation 5:12 and not Job, since both in Daniel and in Revelation, the terms occur in the same order and refer to kingship. Beale, *Revelation*, 365.

54. Cf. Rev 13:5, 7, 14, 15; 17:12. The prominent recurrence of the divine passive ἐδόθη in Revelation 13 strongly suggests that God is the ultimate source of the beast's authority. So also Hoskins, *Revelation*, 236, Osborne, *Revelation*, 498, and Prigent, *L'Apocalypse*, 204.

55. Unlike the dragon and his associates that are known for deceit (Rev 12:9; 13:14; 18:23; 20:2–3, 7–8), Revelation portrays the Lamb and his followers to be entirely without deceit (3:14; 14:5). The Lamb is true in all his ways, and his followers are to be also true in all their ways. Bauckham, *Theology*, 91.

makes the ascension to heaven and the revelation of heavenly mysteries its prominent features. *1 Enoch*, as it is the case with Daniel, especially calls this revelatory experience "wisdom." In the *Book of the Watchers*, Enoch calls his revelation "wisdom," which the chosen will receive and live (*1 En.* 5:8), and in the *Book of the Luminaries*, Enoch calls once again the revelation given to him by the angel Uriel "wisdom," which he now passes down to his children (*1 En.* 82:2; cf. 92:1). Thus, the allusion to Daniel 2 in Revelation 5:12 and Revelation's affinities to Jewish apocalypses such as *1 Enoch* suggest the likelihood of Revelation also communicating the idea that the disclosure of the knowledge of the heavenly throne room itself is wisdom. Additionally, by ascribing intentionally this wisdom to the Lamb in Revelation 5:12, John conveys that this revelation of the throne room is in fact a disclosure of true wisdom which has the Lamb at its core.[56] This, in turn, is why John can call on his readers to exercise wisdom later in Revelation (13:18; 17:9), since wisdom has already been disclosed. All of John's words in Revelation hinges on the true wisdom of the throne room vision which has the Lamb at the center and must be understood in light of it.

In conclusion, Revelation 4–5 testifies that God reigns in absolute sovereignty and that this sovereignty is shared by Christ. As the sovereign king, the Lamb has full authority to govern the world. Further, this is the king who has wisdom, and with that wisdom he shall execute proper judgments. This means that wisdom is an attribute with which one can discern the true nature of reality. After all, the Lamb can only judge accordingly if he knows the true nature of all things. Indeed, Revelation testifies that Christ will judge the world justly as the one and only wise and sovereign king.[57]

But John wants the readers to also know that this wisdom the Lamb has is redefined wisdom; it is not the wisdom of the world. One needs to remember that it is the slain Lamb who is worthy to receive this wisdom. Christ's slain nature has revised the true essence of conquering life. His slainness has also redefined the true essence of wisdom. Revelation's readers are to realize that living victoriously and wisely is intimately tied to Christ's way of living, namely life that is in full obedience to the Father even to the point of death. Wise living is not about following the ways of

---

56. This must be why John begins Revelation by stating that it is the revelation of Jesus Christ (1:1).

57. Cf. Rev 11:18; 16:6; 19:2; 20:11–15. One does not have to reiterate that in Revelation, God's judgments and the Lamb's judgments are one and the same.

σοφία IN REVELATION AS DIVINE WISDOM 49

the world in allying with the beast to reap his benefits (cf. Rev 13). Rather, true wise living is following the ways of Christ in full allegiance to God despite the threats of death from the beast. The Lamb who has wisdom to discern the true nature of reality will see each person's path of allegiance and judge accordingly. Therefore, before John's visions get fully underway, he makes sure to set down the rules for proper Christian living, and he does so strategically by introducing the slain Lamb in Revelation 5 as one who has conquered, as one who has wisdom, and to whom people's allegiance and worship belong. In fact, knowing this revelation about the Lamb is itself wisdom, with which God's people must discern all realities.

Revelation 7:12

The second instance of the word σοφία occurs in another throne room vision in Revelation 7:12. The throne room vision of Revelation 7 shares many affinities with the throne room vision of Revelation 4–5. There are also differences such as the presence of those clothed in white robes before the throne, and their identity in turn becomes very important for the message Revelation 7 is trying to communicate. Also, this time, God is the one who is directly credited with σοφία by the angels, the elders, and the four living creatures, although the Lamb is not far from the picture.[58]

Most scholars agree that Revelation 7 is the book's first interlude.[59] As such, Revelation 7 breaks the flow of the narrative and gives it a necessary pause. In Revelation 5, Christ was seen to take the scroll with seven seals from God's right hand. Then, as Christ began to take off the seals one by one, judgments ensued in Revelation 6. The narrative of the seal judgments seemed to have reached its climax with the opening of the sixth seal and the description of the subsequent apocalyptic events (Rev 6:12–17).[60] The anticipation of what will happen when Christ opens the

---

58. In the same way, although the Lamb was directly credited with σοφία in Revelation 5:12, God was not far from the picture since, in Revelation 5:13, both God and the Lamb are worshipped.

59. Other interludes in Revelation include, but not limited to, Revelation 10:1—11:13 and 12:1—14:20. Nonetheless, the interludes of Revelation 7, 10:1—11:13, and 12–14 seem to be the most significant, for they occur in between the sixth and seventh seals (Rev 7), the sixth and seventh trumpets (Rev 10:1—11:13), and the seventh trumpet itself (Rev 12–14). In short, these interludes break the important sequence of the series of judgments, which give a significant pause in the narrative.

60. There are indeed different positions on how to understand the sequence and time of Revelation's 21 judgments. There is neither space nor incentive to rehearse the

final seventh seal is great. Yet, John upsets this anticipation as he breaks the narrative by inserting an interlude before the account of the seventh seal (Rev 8:1–5).

There must be a special reason why John does this, for the interlude of Revelation 7 interrupts an otherwise smooth narrative of the seven seals. Rhetorically, it may be because the sudden interruption of an interlude seizes the attention of the audience. But more importantly, it is because there is an important message that the author wants to communicate as he continues his presentation of the 21 judgments which shall span a large portion of the book of Revelation (Rev 6–16).[61] By this point in the narrative, the audience has been left to wonder what their fate will be during these judgments. The especially shocking apocalyptic imagery of the sixth seal and its consequence has left them all the more vulnerable. John anticipates these difficulties and assures the audience with a clear answer, namely that the faithful believers shall be protected from the judgments and that their eternal fate shall be secure before God. This is the message of the interlude of Revelation 7.

Hence in Revelation 7, John begins the interlude by giving a vision of the four angels standing at the four corners of the earth. The four angels are seen to be holding back the four winds so that no winds might blow on the earth (Rev 7:1). The repeated notion of the number "four" signals that this vision is one that affects the entire world.[62] The idea of holding back the four winds refers to the postponing of God's divine judgment which the Lamb executes.[63] The reason for this delay is so that God's

---

varying positions in this study. For a succinct summary of the various views, see Jones, "Sequential Interpretation," 9–31. Nevertheless, this writer is in the position that the first four seal judgments are currently ongoing, the fifth seal is transitional, and the last two seals occur at the time of the end. One can notice this since, starting with the sixth seal, John's language changes to be fully apocalyptic. In this manner, although this writer is a historic premillennialist, this writer concurs with Beale in understanding the timing of the seven seal judgments. Beale, *Revelation*, 370–71, 390, 396–402, 445–46.

61. Hoskins observes that the interludes of Revelation provide a needed perspective or clarification for interpreting the 21 judgments. Hoskins, *Revelation*, 147.

62. According to Yarbro Collins, numerical symbolism is used in apocalyptic literatures to order two things, namely the experience of time and the experience of space. Yarbro Collins, *Cosmology and Eschatology*, 56 and 135–37. In the case of Revelation 7:1, the number four is used to order the experience of space, namely one's perception of the entire world. Beale lists various passages from biblical and extrabiblical literatures as compelling evidence for the number four symbolizing the entire world. Beale, *Revelation*, 406.

63. Wind, standing in reference for divine judgment, is frequent in the book of Jeremiah (Jer 4:11–13; 49:36; 51:1–2). What is more, Jeremiah 49:36 specifically

servants can be sealed on their foreheads before the four angels with the four winds can harm the world (7:2–3). This sealing of God's servants shows that the ultimate object of the judgment must be people, for those who are not sealed will have to take on the full effect of God's judgment. But God's servants are sealed, and since sealing on the forehead signifies ownership and protection (cf. Ezek 9), the vision of the four angels with the four winds is intended to assure John's audience that true believers shall be protected from God's judgment.[64]

But as soon as the audience is comforted with the news of the sealing, they are confronted with a seeming dilemma. John does not give a description of the actual sealing but instead testifies that he simply heard (ἤκουσα) the number of those sealed, 144,000 from every tribe of the sons of Israel (Rev 7:4–8). Revelation's original readers must not have been all Jews; they were from the seven churches in Asia Minor. Hence, it is conceivable that this sealing would have come as a discomfort especially to those believers who were not Jews, for it seems as if they will not be protected by God from the coming judgment. But for all probability, although the audience may initially have been shocked to hear that the sealing was the sealing of God's servants from Israel, they would have recognized themselves to somehow all belong to the 144,000. After all, they are all God's servants (cf. Rev 1:1; 2:20) who are intended to receive the seal of the living God (7:3).[65]

---

mentions the four winds which will completely destroy Elam. See Hoskins, *Revelation*, 148; Osborne, *Revelation*, 306. Beale, Beasley-Murray, Morris, and a few other scholars also make a connection to Zechariah 6:1–8, where the four horsemen or chariots are associated with the four winds of heaven. See Beale, *Revelation*, 406; Beasley-Murray, *Revelation*, 142; Morris, *Revelation*, 112. If so, then it is likely that the four horsemen of the Apocalypse (Rev 6:1–8) are also connected with the four horsemen of Zechariah. For the connection between Zechariah 6:1–8 and Revelation 6:1–8, see Allen, "Zechariah's Horse Visions," 222–39 (esp. 230–33). In any case, it is clear that the four winds mentioned in Revelation 7 have to do with God's judgment.

64. Istrate, "Sealing the Slaves of God," 96 and 123. Escaffre has studied the use of the word forehead in the OT and has found that "Dans la Bible hébraïque, le front est donc la partie du corps visible par tous qui peut témoigner de l'identité de la personne, de sa consécration au Seigneur ou de son infidélité." Escaffre, "Un signe sur le front," 15.

65. Istrate, "Sealing the Slaves of God," 127–28. Hoskins also notes that, in Revelation 14:1–4 where the 144,000 reappears, they are said to have been "purchased from among men" (14:4). Since the only other "purchased" people mentioned in Revelation are those purchased from every tribe, tongue, people, and nation" (5:9), it makes strong sense to understand that the 144,000 are not comprised of only Jews, but Jews and Gentiles alike. Hoskins, *Revelation*, 152.

This strongly suggests that the 144,000 from the tribes of Israel is not to be read literally but symbolically.[66] This symbolic reading of the 144,000 is amplified when examining John's listing of the twelve tribes in Revelation 7:5-8. Bauckham has aptly noted that John's list is without precedent, with the greatest difficulty being John's unique rendition of omitting Dan and Ephraim and yet including Joseph and Manasseh.[67] To answer this difficulty, however, Bauckham entertains the possibility of carelessness on the writer's part, namely that he did not care how he ordered the tribes.[68] But this is unlikely, for Revelation is intricately composed with rich OT traditions. It would be far better to understand that John has masterfully composed his list with specific intentions.[69]

As many have noted, the tribe of Judah heads the list, and this must be because the Messiah is from this tribe (cf. Rev 5:5). John has likely omitted Dan and Ephraim from the list because these two tribes were notoriously known for their association with idolatry (cf. Judg 18:14-31; 1 Kgs 12:25-30; Hos 4:17—5:9).[70] Revelation takes seriously the issue of idolatry (Rev 2:14, 20; 9:20), and it makes sense that Dan and Ephraim

---

66. This study thus goes against those exegetes such as Feuillet who argue that the list in Revelation 7:4-8 refers only to Jewish Christians whereas the innumerable multitude mentioned in Revelation 7:9-17 refers to the church, thereby understanding Revelation 7:4-8 and 7:9-17 to represent two distinct groups of people. See Feuillet, "Les 144,000 Israélites," 191-224. See also, Fanning, *Revelation*, 261-64; Patterson, *Revelation*, 194-99; Thomas, *Revelation 1-7*, 476; Walvoord, *Revelation*, 141-43.

67. Bauckham, "List of the Tribes," 99-115.

68. Bauckham, "List of the Tribes," 113. Aune also follows Bauckham and thinks that the most likely explanation is that Dan is dropped from the list to simply keep the total number of tribes to twelve. Aune, *Revelation 6-16*, 463.

69. Christopher Smith has also argued the same. Smith, "Tribes of Revelation 7," 213-18.

70. Scholars have also posited the reason for the omission of Dan to the tribe's apostasy, citing *T. Dan* 5:4-8, or to the tradition that the antichrist would originate from the tribe, citing Irenaeus' *Adversus Haereses* 5.30.2 and Hippolytus' *De Antichristo*, 14.5-6. See Kraft, *Offenbarung*, 127. For a succinct summary of these arguments, see Aune, *Revelation 6-16*, 462-63 and Beale, *Revelation*, 420-21. These arguments seem unconvincing, for as Bauckham has noted, *T. Dan* 5:9-13 envisions the subsequent restoration of Dan and its eschatological salvation, and the tradition of the antichrist originating from Dan is not found in any Jewish text and is very likely to be a Christian interpolation dating later than Revelation. Bauckham, "List of the Tribes," 100-1. Winkle furthermore made an interesting case that the omission of Dan should be attributed to the tribe's connection with Judas Iscariot. Winkle, "Another Look," 53-67. While interesting, it must be observed that much of Winkle's case is an implicit conjecture, and thereby should be understood with caution.

would thus be omitted from the list.[71] After all, no idolators can enter the New Jerusalem (21:8; 22:15). In any case, the fact that Dan is not omitted in any of the lists of the twelve tribes in early Jewish literature but is omitted in Revelation 7 strongly contends that Revelation's list should be viewed symbolically rather than literally.[72] If so, then the 144,000 sealed from the tribes of Israel refers not to ethnic Jews, but to the people of God in its fullness, the new Israel.[73]

It is also important to recognize that the 144,000 who are sealed are an army. Bauckham again is helpful in this matter in noting that the numbering of those sealed from the tribes of Israel is that of a census.[74] In the OT, a census was always done in estimating the military strength of the nation.[75] This notion is enhanced when considering the reappearance of the 144,000 in Revelation 14. There, the 144,000 are pictured to stand alongside the Lamb on Mount Zion (14:1), the place of divine deliverance and victory.[76] That the 144,000 have the Lamb's name and the Father's name on their foreheads invokes a clear connection with the 144,000 of Revelation 7 who were sealed on their foreheads; they are same people.[77] The scenery of Revelation 14:1–5 is that of a victorious messianic king and his army. It necessarily follows then that the 144,000 of Revelation 7 are the messianic army of the Lamb, who is also the Lion of Judah.

As the messianic army, the people of God follow the Lamb wherever he goes (14:4). This means that as an army, they conquer like the Lamb conquers.[78] As it was shown in Revelation 5, the Lamb had conquered

---

71. So Osborne, *Revelation*, 314.

72. Pseudo-Philo *Bib. Ant.* 25:4 does omit Dan from its list, but this is certainly due to corrupt transmission. See Aune, *Revelation 6–16*, 462.

73. So also Yarbro Collins, *Cosmology and Eschatology*, 130. Yarbro Collins states that "The use of the twelve tribes evokes a sense of chosenness; these tribes, this people is chosen from among all people. The twelve thousand from each tribe intensifies the impression of chosenness, or exclusivity."

74. Bauckham, *Theology*, 77.

75. Bauckham, *Theology*, 77.

76. Mounce, *Revelation*, 264.

77. Revelation 14:3–4 goes on to state that the 144,000 were redeemed from the earth and from mankind, which is further evidence that they consist of all people and not just ethnic Jews. Furthermore, the 144,000 of Revelation 14 are in clear contrast to the people who worship the beast in Revelation 13. Since the people who follow the beast in Revelation 13 consist of people from all the earth (13:3, 12, 14, 16), it stands to reason that the 144,000 who follow the Lamb in Revelation 14 should also consist of people from all the earth.

78. Osborne argues that this army motif shows that the people of God will be

via sacrificial death. This ultimately meant that the Lamb conquered by living a life of faithfulness to the Father, even to the point of death on the cross. The same is true of Christ's army. The people of God do not conquer by military victory, but rather by living a life of faithfulness to the Lamb and to the Father.

Thus Revelation 14:4 also states that the 144,000 are those who have not been defiled with women (ἐμολύνθησαν), for they are virgins (παρθένοι). In Revelation, the issue of idolatry is closely tied with the notion of sexual immorality or harlotry. People commit idolatry when they engage in sexual immorality (2:14, 20–23; 14:8; 17:2; 18:3, 9; 19:2).[79] This is because unfaithfulness lies in the roots of both, and when people worship the beast along with the harlots of Revelation such as Jezebel and Babylon, they engage in unfaithfulness to God.[80] But Revelation 14:4 does not only refer to spiritual purity but also to moral purity. It is not simply the case that the 144,000 are those who have not committed sexual immorality, but who have in fact refrained from all sexual relations.[81] This is a language that speaks of ritual purity that was demanded for those in the Lord's army (Deut 23:9–14; 1 Sam 21:4–5; 2 Sam 11:9–13).[82] The army of God is consecrated to the Lord, and they are to keep themselves pure and holy by abstaining from all sexual relations. In Revelation, this certainly works as a metaphor—God's people are to exhibit an extraordinary consecration to the Lamb by keeping themselves pure morally.[83] In short, the people of God, who are also the Lamb's army engaged in the holy war, must display faithfulness that is above and beyond to the Lord in their lives just like the Lamb.

So John communicates in Revelation 7:1–8 that the true and faithful believers shall be protected from God's judgment the Lamb executes and that those protected are indeed the Lord's army, consecrated to the Lord in all faithfulness. John also gives the answer as to the duration of the

---

militant in their witness of the gospel, will be willing to achieve victory by means of martyrdom, and will conquer the army of the beast in the end. Osborne, *Revelation*, 313.

79. Revelation follows the line of Jeremiah and Ezekiel where worshipping idols is expressed as committing adultery. See, for example, Jeremiah 3:6–10 and Ezekiel 23:37.

80. Hoskins, *Revelation*, 265.

81. Fanning, *Revelation*, 390–91.

82. Bauckham, *Climax*, 230–31.

83. Bauckham, *Climax*, 231.

protection in Revelation 7:9–17; it is from now until the end.[84] In Revelation 7:9–17, John transitions to another vision which he testifies that he saw (εἶδον). What he sees is an innumerable multitude from the whole world standing before the throne and before the Lamb (7:9). In turn, this effectively becomes another throne room vision comparable to the one in Revelation 4–5.

Scholars have long debated whether this innumerable multitude is the same group as the 144,000 or not. This study does not intend to solve this debate once and for all but does submit to the prospect that they are one and the same. First, as noted above, the 144,000 refers not to ethnic Jews only, but to all faithful believers who are God's servants. Since the innumerable multitude are from every nation, tribes, peoples, and tongues (7:9), and since they can stand before the throne and before the Lamb, it is reasonable to contend that they are those who were sealed, the 144,000.[85] This fourfold phrase of referring to all people from the world first occurred in Revelation 5:9–10, where the four living creatures and the twenty-four elders worshipped the Lamb confessing that by his blood, the Lamb has ransomed people from every tribe, tongue, people, and nation, and has made them a kingdom (βασιλείαν; singular) and priests to God.[86] Not only does this evidence that the two throne room visions of Revelation 4–5 and Revelation 7 are connected, it also shows that what the four living creatures and the elders were worshipping about in Revelation 5:9–10 has come to pass in Revelation 7:9. This in turn signals that the vision of the innumerable multitude lies in the future, at the time of the end. More importantly, the worship confessed that the Lamb has brought all people from the world and has made them one kingdom, God's kingdom. This kingdom has one army, the 144,000, and if this reasoning is correct, then it means that the 144,000 are made up of all people from the world just like the innumerable multitude.

---

84. This study argues that the vision in Revelation 7:1–8 refers to what is happening "in the now," whereas the vision in Revelation 7:9–17 refers to what will happen "in the end." See Beale, *Revelation*, 405–6; Hoskins, *Revelation*, 147; Osborne, *Revelation*, 303; Smalley, *Revelation*, 201–2.

85. The fourfold phrase "nation, tribe, people, and tongue" occurs 7 times in Revelation, though never exactly in the same form (5:9; 7:9; 10:11; 11:9; 13:7; 14:6; 17:15), and refers to all people/nations from the world. See Bauckham, *Climax*, 326–37 and Paul, *Revelation*, 136.

86. Although there is a variant where the text reads βασιλεῖς instead of βασιλείαν, the latter is likely the original reading, for it is a more difficult reading and since it has a stronger manuscript evidence.

Second, the same rhetorical technique of "hearing and seeing" is used in Revelation 7 that John used in Revelation 5. By juxtaposing "hearing" and "seeing" to refer to the same entity, John makes it so that the readers understand and interpret one in light of the other and vice versa. In Revelation 5:2, an angel asked a question, "Who is worthy to open the scroll and to loosen its seals?" The answer came in 5:5 where John first heard that it would be the Lion from the tribe of Judah, the root of David. But who John actually saw was the Lamb standing as though slain (5:6). This is clearly paralleled in Revelation 7. In Revelation 6:17, a question was put forward: "the great day of their (God's and the Lamb's) wrath has come, and who is able to stand?" The answer comes in 7:4 where John hears that it would be the sealed 144,000. But who John actually sees is the innumerable multitude (7:9). Just as the Lion proved to be the Lamb, the army of the 144,000 who are ready for battle proves to be a countless, international crowd who celebrates the victory already won.[87]

At this point, it would be apt to address one challenge that those who understand the 144,000 and the innumerable multitude to be two distinct groups frequently raise, namely the fact that the 144,000 as a group is clearly numbered in 7:4–8 whereas the innumerable multitude is explicitly stated by John to be a group "which no one is able to number" (ὃν ἀριθμῆσαι αὐτὸν οὐδεὶς ἐδύνατο) in 7:9. The argument is that if one group can be precisely numbered and the other cannot, then John is likely talking about two different kinds of groups. However, it is important to remember that Revelation 7:4–8 is describing God's people in the present, while Revelation 7:9–17 is describing God's people in the eschaton. In other words, the vision of the innumerable multitude is one that will take place at the time of the end, when all of God's people shall gather before God in a blessed state with praise. This also means that John is portraying the fulfillment of the final victory and reward of God's people who can indeed stand before God in the day of wrath (cf. 6:17) in 7:9–17.[88]

This notion of fulfillment, in fact, coincides with the evidence of John alluding to God's promise to Abraham about his seed in 7:9.[89] God has promised Abraham that he would multiply Abraham's descendants

---

87. Johnson, *Triumph of the Lamb*, 133.

88. Stewart, "The Future of Israel," 570.

89. For others who also see this connection, see Bauckham, *Climax*, 223; Beale, *Revelation*, 426–27; Mounce, *Revelation*, 171; Osborne, *Revelation*, 318; Stewart, "The Future of Israel," 570; Sweet, *Revelation*, 150.

which will not be numbered in the LXX of Genesis 13:16, 15:5, 16:10, 22:17, 26:4, and 32:13. The same promise is also captured in Hosea 2:1 (1:10) and *Jubilees* 13:20 and 14:4–5. John has taken this Abrahamic promise and has applied it to the innumerable multitude of Revelation 7. Thus, for John, the innumerable multitude is the consummate fulfillment of the Abrahamic promise.[90] This is only possible if John understands that the Abrahamic promise is not solely confined to ethnic Israel but to all God's people from every nation, tribes, peoples, and tongues (hence both Jews and Gentiles). In fact, this is the consistent witness of John throughout Revelation. He constantly shows that God's promises to ethnic Israel are being fulfilled and will be fulfilled through God's renewed community comprised of both Jews and Gentiles.[91]

This is not to say that ethnic Israel no longer has any place in God's plan of redemption. The point of the above observation is to point out that John can use and apply designations and promises made to Israel to refer to God's renewed community centered on Jesus. It is true that John's designations for the 144,000 are very specific to Israel. However, the above observation at least shows that John is fluid in his use of Jewish connotations to refer not only to Jewish Christians, but to all Christians. Since John uses references to Israel *both* to the 144,000 and to the innumerable multitude, it does not seem best to argue that the two groups are different groups, one Jewish specific and the other multiethnic, but rather that they are one and the same. The 144,000 is precisely numbered because John wants to assure the readers that God knows exactly who belongs to him and who will be secured from God's impending judgment. The innumerable multitude is not numbered because John wants to show that God will fulfill his Abrahamic promise by protecting every one of his people until they are eternally secure. In other words, it is not because

---

90. Beale, *Revelation*, 427–30.

91. Stewart, "The Future of Israel," 565. See also Beale, *Revelation*, 427. Stewart provides a selection of promises made to Israel in the OT that John applies to God's renewed community centered on Jesus. They are (1) Exodus 19:6 in Revelation 1:6 and 5:10, (2) Zechariah 4:2 in Revelation 1:12 and 1:20, (3) Isaiah 45:14, 49:23, and 60:14 in Revelation 3:9, (4) Genesis 13:16, 15:5, 32:12, and Hosea 1:10 in Revelation 7:9, (5) Ezekiel 37:26–28 in Revelation 7:15 and 21:3, and (6) Ezekiel 40–48 in Revelation 21:9–22:5. Stewart, "The Future of Israel," 566–74. To be sure, this method of interpretation and application of OT promises is not unique to John alone, but is conventional among the NT writers (i.e., Rom 9:24–26; 10:12–13; 2 Cor 5:17; 6:2, 16–18; Gal 3:7, 29; Heb 11:12; 1 Pet 2:9–10). This also does not mean that the church has replaced Israel. Rather, it is Christ who fulfilled Israel, and those who belong to him, both Jews and Gentiles, receive the blessings made to Israel in him.

they are two distinct groups that the 144,000 is numbered while the innumerable multitude is not. It is because John wants to communicate that God's people in its entirety shall be secure from now until eternity.

While there are other points that can be made for the argument that the 144,000 and the innumerable multitude are one and the same, the above points should suffice.[92] Especially the second point above is significant for the purpose of this study. As this study has shown earlier, the Lion who has conquered has turned out to be also the Lamb who was slain in Revelation 5, and this meant that in Christ, there is a redefinition of what it means to conquer. There is thus a redefinition of life, and the fact that wisdom belongs to the Lamb meant that wisdom is also redefined in Christ. However, this notion of redefined life and wisdom that are bound in Christ was implicit in Revelation 5.

Now in Revelation 7, this notion is reinforced as John uses the same technique again to refer to God's servants. As Christ is the conquering Lion of Judah, so his people are the Lion's army, 144,000 strong. As Christ is also the slain Lamb, so his people are also the Lamb's martyrs who celebrate victory.[93] This means that the followers of Christ are those who have their lives redefined in the footsteps of their master. As Christ has conquered through faithfulness even to the point of being slain, so his people must also conquer through faithfulness even to the point of being martyrs.[94]

It is these God's faithful servants who shall be protected from the divine judgments that the Lamb executes and who will stand before God

---

92. For a succinct summary of arguments for understanding the 144,000 and the innumerable multitude to be the same group, see Istrate, "Sealing the Slaves of God," 164–68.

93. Osborne notes that the white robes which the multitude wear and the palm branches in their hands serve to signify victory. Furthermore, the white robes recall the martyrs who also wore white robes in Revelation 6:11, which in turn shows that the innumerable multitude have a special connection with the martyrs of 6:11. Osborne, *Revelation*, 319–20. See also Beale, *Revelation*, 428. Beale enlists 1 Macc 13:51, 2 Macc 10:7, *Leg. Alleg.* 3.74 as example texts where palm branches signify victory.

94. Again, this must not mean that all Christians should be martyrs, for even the Apostle John was not one. Rather, it means that true believers must stay faithful to Christ despite persecution that may lead to death. Perhaps Revelation 7:14 may furnish an extra clue that this is so. In 7:14, another dimension of meaning to the white robes is given, namely that the innumerable multitude are those who have washed their robes and have made them white by the Lamb's blood. This means that they are also priests, and not simply martyrs, for it was the priests who had to sanctify their robes by means of a sacrifice before entering the tabernacle to serve in the OT (cf. Exod 29; Lev 8). See Hoskins, *Revelation*, 157–58.

and the Lamb in the end (7:9). They will celebrate in worship the victory and salvation that God and the Lamb provides (7:10).[95] As it was in Revelation 4–5, the throne room scene in Revelation 7 is once again marvelous. Following the worship of the innumerable multitude, an ever-widening crescendo of worship is captured, just as it was in 4:8–11 and 5:8–14.[96] While it was "many" angels in 5:11, it is now "all" the angels who join in the worship in 7:11. While the elders and the four living creatures "fell down" before God and the Lamb to worship (4:10; 5:8; 5:14), they now fall "on their faces" to worship (7:11). These similar, yet greater details suggest that the throne room vision of Revelation 7 is an awesome spectacle that is stronger than the one in Revelation 4–5.[97]

Rightly so, since there is one major difference between the throne room vision of Revelation 4–5 and 7: the presence of the innumerable multitude of redeemed saints. Their presence proves that the throne room vision of Revelation 7 takes place in the time of the end, whereas the throne room vision of Revelation 4–5 takes place in the present age, and attests that God's servants shall be protected from the moment they are sealed until the very end. That the innumerable multitude are believers at the time of the end is clear from the revelation given by one of the elders. In a deliberate move, one of the elders asks John at the height of the throne room vision whether he knows who these people with white robes are (7:13) and proceeds to tell John the answer (7:14). According to this elder, they are those coming out of the great tribulation, who have washed their robes in the blood of the Lamb (7:14). They are also those who shall serve God day and night in the temple and who shall experience no more suffering due to the Lamb being their shepherd (7:15–17). This certainly describes the blessedness of the eternal state reserved for the people of God. Consequently, it is fitting that the worship that those around the throne musters at the time of the end is stronger; they are celebrating the ultimate victory and the eternal redemptive work of God.

Hence, the doxology captured in 7:12 recognizes the eternal sovereignty of God.[98] The "amen" (ἀμήν) begins and ends the praise, which

---

95. As Podeszwa states, "Postawa stojąca, białe szaty oraz palmy w rękach symbolicznie wyrażają ich udział w zwycięstwie zmartwychwstania, triumfie i radości Chrystusa." Podeszwa, "Doksologie Apokalipsy," 166.

96. Fanning, *Revelation*, 268.

97. Osborne, *Revelation*, 321.

98. Beale, *Revelation*, 432.

emphatically affirms the certainty of the content of the praise.[99] The content itself has seven elements, just like the doxology of 5:12. Also, six out of the seven qualities in the doxology of 7:12 appeared in the doxology of 5:12, showing the closeness of the two.[100] One major difference, however, is that each element in 7:12 has an article, whereas in 5:12, the article only appeared with the first element and was not repeated after. This seems to be so, according to Osborne, because John wanted to cast the sevenfold praise in 5:12 as a single whole, while in 7:12 he wants to stress each element as a separate and absolute attribute of God.[101] If so, then this again must be because the worship in 7:12 is in the context of rejoicing the eschatological victory of God.[102]

It is in this context of redefining who God's servants are who shall be protected from God's judgments that the word σοφία occurs for the second time in Revelation 7:12. Furthermore, just like the first time in 5:12, σοφία occurs during the worship scene of a throne room vision, as the third element in a sevenfold praise. These similarities suggest that John wants to connect and to build upon his message expressed by the throne room visions, namely the absolute sovereignty of God and of Christ. Also, as it was the case with the throne room vision of Revelation 4–5, the throne room vision of Revelation 7 itself is also John's disclosure of wisdom. This time, John intentionally attributes wisdom to God, which suggests that true wisdom that is being disclosed also has something to do with God. In Revelation 5, true wisdom John revealed had the Lamb at the center; in Revelation 7, true wisdom John reveals has God at the center. The two revelations of wisdom are not at odds with one another but complement one another.

In Revelation 5, it was the slain Lamb who is worthy to take the scroll and to release its seals who received the sevenfold praise. This slain Lamb has wisdom, with which he shall discern the true nature of reality and execute proper judgments as a sovereign king. The Lamb thus knows what wise living entails, and even showed it by his own testimony

---

99. Beale, *Revelation*, 432. See also, Osborne, *Revelation*, 321. Many scholars note that the first amen affirms the hymn of the multitude captured in 7:10 by the angels, elders, and the four living creatures, while the second amen functions to add their own tribute on top of the praise of the multitude. Aune, *Revelation 6–16*, 471 and Lohmeyer, *Offenbarung*, 71.

100. Thanksgiving replaces wealth in the doxology of 7:12.

101. Osborne, *Revelation*, 322.

102. Osborne, *Revelation*, 322.

of slainness, which signifies his faithfulness to God. In Revelation 7, this wisdom also properly belongs to God the Father. At the time of the end, all who belong to God, including God's servants who are washed by the blood of the Lamb, shall praise God for his redemptive work and celebrate the ultimate victory. They shall acknowledge that God has wisdom, with which he has executed his redemptive work through the Lamb.[103] God also knows who are his people; they are those whose lives have been redefined in the footsteps of their sovereign king, Christ. Only these faithful servants shall be able to stand before God and enjoy the blessed state of eternity guided by the Lamb. Therefore, since Revelation 7's throne room vision takes place at the time of the end and has to do with God's order of redemptive work in history, it is very likely that the true wisdom John is disclosing particularly in Revelation 7 is that God alone has true insight into world order.[104] This would mean that any other form of insight regarding world order pale in comparison and should not be given allegiance.

SUMMARY AND CONCLUSION

In conclusion, before John shows the visions of the conflict of kingdoms and ideologies, he makes sure to let the readers know that God's kingdom is absolute; no other kingdom, whether by man or beast, can compare. He does this primarily with two throne room visions of Revelation 4–5 and 7. In these visions, God and the Lamb reign supreme; they are in control of the judgments and salvation that come upon all of creation. In this context of absolute sovereignty of God and the Lamb, John testifies that they both have wisdom. This is deliberate, for no other so-called sovereignties in the world have this wisdom in Revelation. John makes it so that only God, the Lamb, and those who belong to them have true wisdom in the book of Revelation; the rest of the world do not and are incapable of exhibiting true wisdom.

So only God and the Lamb rule with wisdom and only those who belong to them can have this wisdom. Now, two key aspects of this wisdom can be summarized based on the discussions presented in this section. First, wisdom in Revelation is the divine wisdom to know the true nature

---

103. Thus, Beale argues that wisdom in Revelation 5:12 and 7:12 is the Lamb's ability to plan and to execute redemptive history. Beale, *Revelation*, 725–26.

104. Stuckenbruck, "Disclosure of Wisdom," 351.

of reality and to execute judgments and salvation accordingly. God and the Lamb know the details and the particulars of this world, who are truly faithful to them and who are not, and judge appropriately. This means that those who belong to God also have access to this wisdom and should be able to exercise it to discern the true nature of reality, especially the deceptive nature of the kingdom of the beast.

Second, this wisdom is redefined wisdom. It is redefined by the Lamb who was slain, who conquered, and who is worthy. Thus, one can only discern what true wisdom is (what true power, wealth, and life are for that matter) through the Lamb, and it stands in sharp contrast with another reality, which is of the beast.[105] In other words, wisdom has been completely revised by the Lamb in Revelation and looks nothing like what the world might define as wisdom. This redefined wisdom furthermore is closely connected with the sacrificial work of the Lamb, which signifies faithfulness to God. In turn, those who belong to the Lamb should be able to discern and know what wise living and behavior is, which is absolute allegiance to God in the footsteps of their master, the Lamb. With this true definition of wisdom in mind, John will continue to call upon his audience to exhibit faithfulness to God and to not be deceived by the reality of the beast.

---

105. Stuckenbruck, "Disclosure of Wisdom," 350–51.

CHAPTER 3

Σοφία in Revelation as Wisdom for God's Faithful People

If the first two instances of σοφία were to claim that true wisdom belongs only to God and the Lamb, the last two instances of σοφία are especially intended to show that God's faithful people can utilize this wisdom in seeing the deceptive reality of the beast's kingdom as not to be misled by it. As this chapter will confirm, this deceptive reality of the beast has to do with its boasting that it is greater than God in power and authority, as well as its appeals to success, whether by force or by temptation, to those who will follow and worship it. Yet, wise believers are supposed to know that the beast is never greater than God, and that its time is indeed short. God's people are not to marvel and to follow the beast's ways but to stay faithful to God in understanding the true reality of the beast.

THIRD AND FOURTH INSTANCES: REVELATION 13:18 AND 17:9

As it was with the first two, the third and fourth instances of σοφία also occur at pivotal places in Revelation, this time in connection with two most puzzling figures and their identities, the first beast and Babylon the great. The last two instances moreover are found in perhaps the two most challenging passages in all of Revelation, the passages that have to do with the number of the beast and the seven heads of the beast. This chapter will seek to navigate through the discussions and debates surrounding these passages and to assess the reason why John invokes wisdom at these particular points.

Revelation 13:18

Revelation 13:18 is perhaps the most discussed verse in the book of Revelation. As such, numerous works have been published regarding it, whether academic or practical. In 13:18, John commands his readers who have wisdom and understanding to calculate the number of the beast. It is a human number, or a number of a man, which comes out to 666.

It is regarding this number that many helpful proposals, but also fanciful interpretations, have been presented. However, as Osborne laments, John's opening call for wisdom " . . . has been totally ignored in the heedless rush to link 666 with all kinds of strange and wonderful suggestions."[1] In turn, this study will keep to a minimum the recitation of the various interpretations regarding the number 666.[2] Rather, this study will focus on why John calls for wisdom at this point in the narrative, to understand the literary function of the call and its effect.

To understand more fully John's calling for wisdom in 13:18, the surrounding context must first be ascertained. Revelation 13:18 is part of a long interlude that spans from 12:1 to 14:20.[3] John made it so that this interlude divides the seventh trumpet itself into two parts. In Revelation 11:15–19, the blowing of the seventh trumpet is captured, with the theophany language ending the section.[4] However, John does not go

---

1. Osborne, *Revelation*, 519.

2. For a succinct summary of the various options, see Beale, *Revelation*, 718–28 and Osborne, *Revelation*, 519–20. For those who interpret the number to have a cryptic reference, the majority in this camp connect the number with Nero. For a representative argument for Nero, see Bauckham, *Climax*, 384–407. For symbolic interpretation, see Bodner and Strawn, "Solomon and 666," 299–312; Hoskins, *Revelation*, 252–55; Valdez, "El número 666," 191–214.

3. Most scholars agree that Revelation 12:1—14:20 form a literary unit with three major visions: the woman and the dragon (12:1-18), the two beasts (13:1-18), and the 144,000's new song and the harvest (14:1-20). See Moloney, "Tracing a Literary Structure," 651.

4. The theophany language of lightnings, rumblings, thunders, earthquake, and hail occurs in Revelation 8:5, 11:19, and 16:18–21, during the seventh seal, the seventh trumpet, and the seventh bowl. Thus, John seems to show that the seventh judgment in each of the series occurs at the same time, at the time of the end. That this theophany language has to do with the presence of God is clear from 4:5, where the same phenomenon is seen at the throne of God. If so, then the theophany language that occurs during the seventh judgment in each of the series is intended to alert the readers that at the end

σοφία IN REVELATION AS WISDOM FOR GOD'S FAITHFUL PEOPLE

straight into telling about the bowl judgments that follow the trumpets, but once again breaks the flow of the narrative, and proceeds to write about visions of a woman and the dragon, the two beasts, the 144,000 and the harvest (Rev 12–14). He shall return to the introduction of the bowl judgments that follow the seventh trumpet in 15:1.[5] In turn, the interlude of Revelation 12–14 is very important for the theological worldview of Revelation. It is here that John unpacks the reality and conflict of two kingdoms, the kingdom of God and the kingdom of the dragon or the beast, that is ongoing in this world.

In the vision of a woman and the dragon (Rev 12), John first outlines a history behind this conflict. John begins the telling of this history by introducing a woman clothed with the sun, with the moon under her feet, and who has a crown of twelve stars on her head (12:1). Some scholars readily identify this woman as the faithful Israel since Jacob, his wife, and his eleven sons are represented as the sun, the moon, and eleven stars respectively in Genesis 37:9.[6] She also gives birth to a male child whom the dragon wants to devour, but this male child is caught up to God and to his throne (Rev 12:2–5). The dragon who has seven heads and ten horns, whose tail sweeps down a third of the stars in heaven (12:3–4), is unmistakably Satan, for John tells the readers so in 12:9. The male child who shall shepherd all the nations with a rod of iron (12:5) is unmistakably Jesus the Messiah, for the words allude to the messianic text of Psalm 2:7–9.[7] This means that Revelation 12:5 is about the resurrection

---

of the seventh judgments, God or Christ is coming; it is the time of the end. For more information regarding the theophany language, see Hoskins, *Revelation*, 166.

5. John also lets the readers know that starting Revelation 12:1, a new section is beginning by stating that a great sign (σημεῖον μέγα) was seen in heaven. In 15:1, John hints once again that another section is beginning, which is actually a continuation of the storyline that he left off in 11:19, by stating that he saw another sign in heaven, great and marvelous (ἄλλο σημεῖον ἐν τῷ οὐρανῷ μέγα καὶ θαυμαστόν). Although John states that he saw another sign in heaven in 12:3, it seems clear that this does not refer to a beginning of a new section, for it is too close to 12:1 and John does not say that this one is a "great" sign.

6. Genesis 37:9 is the account of Joseph's dream where he dreams that his parents and his eleven brothers were bowing down before him. By application then, Joseph himself would be the twelfth star, which in turn matches the number of stars on the crown of the woman in Revelation 12:1. Philo, *Dreams* 2.113 in fact ranks Joseph to be the twelfth star in the dream account of Genesis 37:9.

7. *Psalms of Solomon* 17:24 also alludes to Psalm 2:7–9 in reference to the coming of the Davidic Messiah. *Psalms of Solomon* is likely to have been written between second to first century BC. In turn, *Psalms of Solomon* evidences that the Jewish people of the Second Temple period understood Psalm 2:7–9 to be messianic, which John also

and ascension of Christ, and since Jesus was born as a Jew, the argument goes that the woman of Revelation 12 must be ethnic Israel.[8]

However, it is too narrow of a view to argue that this woman represents the faithful Israelites, the remnant, who existed before the coming of Christ and onward.[9] It seems clear that not only faithful Jews are represented by the woman, but also faithful Gentiles, for Revelation 12:17 states that she has other children: those who keep the commandments of God and hold to the testimony of Jesus. These are the ones who conquer the dragon by the blood of the Lamb and by the word of their testimony (12:11), and since the church, which consists of both Jews and Gentiles, is called to conquer in Revelation (cf. 2:7, 11, 17, 26; 3:5, 12, 21; 15:2–4; 21:7), it is reasonable to understand that the woman represents the people of God in its fullness, both Jews and Gentiles. Furthermore, the description of holding to the testimony of Jesus is a mark that defines all faithful believers and not just the faithful Jews. The phrase "testimony of Jesus" (μαρτυρία Ἰησοῦ) refers to the teaching Jesus revealed to the church.[10] Jesus himself witnessed his teaching faithfully to the church (1:5), and now John (1:2, 9) and the church at large are faithful witnesses who hold to the testimony of Jesus and who proclaim it (11:3, 7).[11] Indeed, those who hold to the testimony of Jesus are all brothers and sisters (19:10) who might die because of it (20:4), and it is difficult to understand that in all these passages, John is referring solely to faithful Jews. If he did, then the conflict between the kingdom of God and the kingdom of the beast will largely have to do with Jews who are faithful believers and much of what

---

utilizes to refer to Jesus as the Davidic Messiah.

8. Walvoord is a representative of those who argue that the woman of Revelation 12 is Israel. Her children, in turn, are Jewish believers, and the persecution that the woman and her children receive is anti-Semitism. Walvoord, *Revelation*, 188–96. See also Thomas, *Revelation 8–22*, 142. Thomas takes the woman to be believing Israel and her offspring to be the believing remnant, the 144,000 of Revelation 7.

9. So also Beale, *Revelation*, 631.

10. The genitive Ἰησοῦ is a subjective genitive. So Beckwith, *Apocalypse*, 630; Hoskins, *Revelation*, 224; Mounce, *Revelation*, 242. Contra Smalley, *Revelation*, 334. That Ἰησοῦ is a subjective genitive seems clear since the genitive τοῦ θεοῦ in the phrase "commandments of God" that appears alongside the phrase "testimony of Jesus" must be a subjective genitive as well. Taking it this way, Revelation 12:17 thus defines the believers as those who keep what God commanded and who hold to what Jesus testified.

11. Hoskins, *Revelation*, 224. This writer understands the two witnesses of Revelation 11 to represent the church. This study does not have adequate space nor direct reason to present the various views and arguments surrounding the identity of the two witnesses. For an extensive treatment on this issue, see Brown, "The Two Witnesses."

John claims in Revelation would not be relevant for believers who are Gentiles, even though the book is written to the seven churches in Asia which would have been comprised largely of Gentile believers.

Thus, the present study submits that it makes far better sense to understand the woman of Revelation 12 to represent the faithful community of believers, both Jews and Gentiles. But how is it possible to make sense of the woman's history with Satan, since, as noted earlier, the earlier part of her history has to do with ethnic Israel while the latter part has to do with the church? How can she represent both at the same time and be distinct in each stage of history? It would seem that John understood the woman to have a multivalent sense or, better yet, understood the woman both historically and ontologically. As Paul Minear has put it, John discerned "an intrinsic coalescence of the heavenly and the earthly, the eschatological and the historical."[12] This allowed him to view the woman of Revelation 12 as a trans-historical reality, a comprehensive reality that is both eschatological and historical at the same time.[13]

Thus, John moves freely from seeing the woman as Israel from which Jesus the Messiah came (12:1–5) and to seeing the woman as the church in tribulation due to the oppression of the dragon (12:6–17).[14]

12. Minear, "Ontology and Ecclesiology," 100.

13. Minear, "Ontology and Ecclesiology," 96. Regarding ontology, this study thereby follows an important insight presented by Paul S. Minear. Minear proves that John clearly wrote with an ontological understanding in the book of Revelation. John introduces himself as being in Patmos and in Christ at the same time. How can he be located historically in a specific place called Patmos and yet can also claim that he is in Christ? Per Minear, John has discerned an ontological model of explaining things, and in doing so could coalesce the historical with the eschatological without forsaking one or the other. Likewise, John describes the two cities of Revelation in a trans-historical fashion. The great city embraces all the places and times that are in enmity with God; the holy city embraces all the places and times that are in comity with God. The conflict between the two cities or kingdoms is at once primordial and eschatological. Thus, for Minear, ontology cannot be separated from ecclesiology; the historical cannot be separated from the eschatological. See Minear, "Ontology and Ecclesiology," 89–105. In keeping with Minear's observation, this study understands the characters of Revelation who especially appear in John's visions of the conflict of the two kingdoms, such as the radiant woman, the beast, Babylon, and the bride, ontologically, and thereby describes them in both historical and eschatological terms.

14. There are some who understand the woman giving birth to the Messiah as a reference to Mary. For instance, see Williamson, *Revelation*, 210. While this interpretation is possible, since the woman represents the fullness of God's people of which Mary is also a part, it is unclear as to whether John and the original audience would have recognized this reference. Most Catholic scholars indeed confess that Marian interpretation is an interest that arose much later. See Ruiz, "The Apocalypse of John," 489. Thus, rather than focusing on the specific and literal side of the woman, it seems better

John also can talk about what happens in heaven due to this woman's history with the dragon (12:7–12) and what happens on earth because of the dragon's enmity with the woman (12:13–17). In all this, the story of the woman and the dragon is not disjunctive but continuous and comprehensive, for John understands the woman of Revelation 12 both historically and ontologically. So, for John and his original readers, the woman would have represented the people of God in its fullness.[15] Her history has met a radical turning point with the coming of the Messiah. Due to Christ's work on the cross, Satan has now been cast out of heaven; he can no longer approach God's throne to accuse God's people (12:7–12). Now that he cannot, Satan makes war with the rest of the woman's offspring, that is, the faithful believers in Christ (12:13–17). Yet hope is not lost, for Satan's time on earth is short (12:12) and for God's people shall be protected even through the tribulation wrought by Satan (12:6, 14–16).[16]

Through the series of visions in Revelation 12 then, John has shown the history behind the conflict between God's kingdom and Satan's kingdom that has met a decisive turning point through the work of the Messiah. For certain, Satan cannot destroy God's kingdom nor its people. He can, however, make God's people suffer and cause them harm on the earth. The question of how Satan brings tribulation upon God's people on earth is the central focus of Revelation 13. It is in fact through his two beasts that Satan brings tribulation upon God's people.

In Revelation 13:1–10, John introduces the first beast. The beast rises out of the sea and has ten horns and seven heads, with ten diadems on its horns and blasphemous names on its heads (13:1). The fact that

---

to focus on the symbolic and ontological side of the woman.

15. In a similar vein, Riley has argued that "The Woman is Daughter Zion, the idealised embodiment of God's People dear to the heart of God and central to all the workings of God's Providence." Riley, "Who is the Woman," 37. N. T. Wright moreover argued that "She represents the entire story of God's people, chosen to carry forward his plans for the nations and indeed for the whole creation." Wright, *Revelation*, 108. More will be said about the woman of Revelation 12 in chapter 4 of this study on the two-woman motif.

16. Revelation 12:6 and 12:14 state that the woman is taken away from the dragon to a place prepared and protected by God, where she will be nourished for 1,260 days or time, times, and half a time. 1,260 days and time, times, and half a time are both ways of referring to the 3½ year period of persecution the dragon and the beast will bring to God's people. The expression "time, times, and half a time" is taken from Daniel 7:25 and 12:7, where it denotes a period of oppression wrought by a pagan king upon God's people. Thus, Revelation 12 ensures that God's people, represented by the woman, shall be spiritually protected by God despite the persecution that Satan may bring. See Beale, *Revelation*, 565–68 and 646–47; Hoskins, *Revelation*, 223.

σοφία IN REVELATION AS WISDOM FOR GOD'S FAITHFUL PEOPLE   69

the beast has ten horns and seven heads shows its close relationship with the dragon who also has ten horns and seven heads (12:3).[17] The beast's seven heads have blasphemous names written on them, which indicate the first beast's nature in blaspheming God. The beast's ten horns with diadems further show that the beast exercises royal authority that goes against God's authority.

The most significant detail regarding the first beast in 13:1 relevant for this study is the fact that it rises out of the sea. In Revelation 12:18, John had mentioned that the dragon stood on the sand of the sea.[18] Now, the first beast rises out of the sea, which in turn shows that the sea is the realm of the dragon.[19] This is fitting, for the OT frequently uses the imagery of sea monsters to refer to rulers or nations that persecute God's people.[20] This also suggests that this is not the first time the dragon has done this. Throughout history, the dragon had been using sea monsters, namely rulers and nations that are opposed to God, to oppress God's people and to blaspheme God's name. The first beast of Revelation 13 then is in continuation of this scheme of the dragon. It is the great sea monster the dragon now employs to persecute the faithful believers in Christ.

Not only is the first beast a continuation of the scheme the dragon had been using all this time, it is actually the one behind all of sea monsters the dragon had employed throughout history. This is most clear in 13:2 where John's description of the beast matches the description of the four beasts that appears in the vision of Daniel 7. In Daniel 7:1–8, Daniel sees four beasts coming up out of the sea, which are interpreted to mean four kings or kingdoms (Dan 7:15–27). Interestingly, Daniel's third beast has four heads (7:6), which means that Daniel's four beasts have a total of seven heads. Daniel's fourth beast moreover has ten horns just like the first beast of Revelation. John, when describing the first beast in Revelation 13, uses the characteristics found in the four beasts of Daniel in reverse order.[21] John first states that the first beast has ten horns and seven

---

17. John will give further explanation on the beast's ten horns and seven heads in Revelation 17.

18. Some translations do not have the eighteenth verse of Revelation 12 because they have simply included it at the beginning of Revelation 13:1.

19. Smalley, *Revelation*, 335. In turn, this is one of the reasons why in the new creation, there is no more sea (Rev 21:1).

20. Hoskins, *Revelation*, 228. Hoskins lists Ezekiel 29:3 and 32:2 for Pharaoh, Jeremiah 51:34 for Nebuchadnezzar, and Psalm 74:14, 89:10 and Isaiah 51:9 for Egypt as passages that depict these rulers or nations as sea monsters.

21. Hoskins, *Revelation*, 229.

heads, which match the description of all of Daniel's beasts combined, especially the fourth beast. John then states that the first beast is like a leopard, which matches the description of Daniel's third beast. John goes on to say that the first beast's feet are like a bear's and that its mouth is like a lion's, which match the description of Daniel's second and first beasts respectively.

Thus, John intentionally goes backwards in using the description found in the four beasts of Daniel 7 as he introduces the first beast. This must be because he wants to show that the first beast was and is the power behind the four kingdoms prophesied in Daniel 7. Indeed, the first beast must have been behind all rulers and nations that oppressed God's people throughout history as the great sea monster. The first beast is all four beasts of Daniel combined into one, which suggests "extreme power" and "temporal transcendence" of the beast.[22] The beast had been the dragon's ultimate minion not just from the time of Christ and the church, but since long ago. Hence, John wants to show that, just as the enmity between the woman and the dragon of Revelation 12 has a history, the first beast of Revelation 13 also has a history. It is appropriate then to understand that John is emphasizing the ontological nature of the first beast, just as he did with the woman of Revelation 12.

John goes on to say that the dragon gave the first beast his power, throne, and great authority (13:2). This is a clear parody of the relationship between God and the Lamb who also share the throne, power, glory, and honor (4:11; 5:12-13; 7:12).[23] From 13:2 and onward, the dragon's desire for parodying the holy Trinity continues. The first beast imitates the Lamb in his work of the cross and the resurrection, namely receiving a mortal wound (ὡς ἐσφαγμένην εἰς θάνατον) and then having it healed (ἐθεραπεύθη), which in turn causes the whole earth marveling after the beast and worshipping the beast and the dragon (13:3-4).[24] But unlike the Lamb who glorified God with his mouth (cf. Jn 8:28, 38; 12:49; 13:31; 14:10; 17:1, 4), the first beast blasphemes God with his mouth (Rev 13:5-6). It also uses its authority that was given for forty-two months, which refers to the same time period of oppression wrought by

---

22. Beale, *Revelation*, 685. More detailed analysis of the use of Daniel 7 in Revelation 13 can be found in Beale, *The Use of Daniel*, 229-49.

23. Paul, *Revelation*, 231.

24. The phrase ὡς ἐσφαγμένην εἰς θάνατον unmistakably parallels the description of Christ in Revelation 5:6 as the Lamb standing as though slain (ἑστηκὸς ὡς ἐσφαγμένον).

the dragon to God's people as mentioned in 12:6 and 12:14, to persecute the saints and to rule over the people of the earth (13:7-8). It is for this reason endurance and faith on part of the saints are needed (13:9-10). John's description of the first beast thus shows that its central basis for deceiving the world into loyalty and submission to the dragon and to itself is its resuscitation from the seeming death blow.[25] Just as Christ's death and resurrection is central to the Christian faith, so also the dragon has diabolically parodied this essential aspect to bring about a deceptive faith among the earth's inhabitants.

The dragon's deception is also effectively enhanced with another minion of his, the second beast. John tells that this second beast rises from the earth, has two horns like the Lamb, but speaks like a dragon (13:11).[26] Again, the parody continues in that this beast also has horns like the Lamb, albeit the Lamb has seven horns while this one has two, but John makes it clear to his audience that the second beast does not speak like the Lamb but rather like a dragon as to not be fooled by its resemblance to the Lamb. The second beast also utilizes all the authority of the first beast on its behalf and performs great signs such as making fire fall from heaven, with which it deceives (πλανᾷ) the people of the earth into idol worship (13:12-14). John is once again intentional with the specific mention of the sign of making fire fall from heaven. This especially recalls 1 Kings 18, where Elijah defeated the prophets of Baal and proclaimed Yahweh as the true God with the same sign. This indicates that Satan, and by implication his two beasts as well, has learned something from the ordeal with Elijah.[27] The unholy trinity (Satan, the first beast, and the second beast) now uses the same signs that God's prophets used to bring glory to the one true God to deceive the people into thinking that the beast is god. In turn, this is why the second beast is also called the false prophet in Revelation (16:13; 19:20; 20:10).

25. Fanning, *Revelation*, 371.

26. The idea that the second beast rose from the earth alludes to Daniel 7:17, where the four beasts of Daniel are interpreted to be four kings that rise from the earth. Taken this way, the second beast would likely be a leading human figure or figures who deceive the people of the earth. Mounce also mentions ancient traditions speaking of two primeval monsters, one from the sea and the other from the land, that John could be drawing from (cf. *1 En.* 60:7-10; *2 Esd* 6:49-52; *2 Bar.* 29:4; Job 40:15—41:34). Mounce, *Revelation*, 255. Whatever the case may be, the clear fact that John wants to communicate is that the dragon has its own unholy trinity, which is a parody of the holy Trinity and which is unified in blaspheming God, in persecuting God's people, and in deceiving the people of the earth.

27. Hoskins, *Revelation*, 245. See also, De Waal, "The Two Witnesses," 167.

Therefore, when looking at the broad context of Revelation 12–13, it is evident that John is speaking things both historically and ontologically. The woman of Revelation 12 and her conflict with the dragon is both historical and ontological. The first beast is also both historical and ontological in that John portrays it to be the one behind the kings and kingdoms that oppressed God's people throughout history. The false prophet should be understood both historically and ontologically as well. Many attempts to identify the false prophet historically have been made by the scholars, but it is important to remember that, as the third member of the unholy trinity, the false prophet must also have an ontological aspect just like the other two members.[28]

In fact, not only does the false prophet parody the Lamb and Elijah, it also counterfeits the two witnesses of Revelation 11. Although this study analyzes only Revelation 12–14 as this is a clear section interluding in between the seventh trumpet itself, it has been shown that Revelation 12–14 also have a close connection with the interlude that occur between the sixth and the seventh trumpet, especially with Revelation 11.[29] The contextual similarities between Revelation 11 and 12–13 are particularly striking. Both describe the conflict between God's kingdom and the beast's kingdom in terms of warfare. Revelation 11:7 states that the beast will make war (ποιήσει πόλεμον) on the two witnesses and will conquer (νικήσει) them and kill (ἀποκτενεῖ) them. In 13:7, it is stated that the beast was allowed to make war (πόλεμον ποιῆσαι) on the saints and to conquer (νικῆσαι) them (cf. 12:17). Yet, Revelation 12:11 claims that the eschatological fortunes are actually reversed, for it is the saints who have conquered (ἐνίκησαν) the dragon by the blood of the Lamb and by the word of their testimony even unto death.[30] Further, both Revelation 11 and 12–13 claim that this warfare-like conflict shall go on for the same duration of time: forty-two months (11:2; 13:5), 1,260 days (11:3; 12:6), or a time, times, and half a time (12:14). No matter how one takes the period of forty-two months and identifies the two witnesses, it is very likely that Revelation 11 and 12–13 are describing the same conflict in

---

28. In a similar manner, Koch argues that apocalyptic symbols, while they can be applied to the first century context, nonetheless also have a cosmic sweep that must be recognized. This is because the present time or age and the future, eschatological time or age are not separated in the worldview of the apocalypses, but are understood to be continuous. Koch, *The Rediscovery of Apocalyptic*, 28–33.

29. For instance, Siew has argued that Revelation 11:1—14:5 is an instance of macro-chiasm and thus should be seen as a literary unit. Siew, *The War*.

30. Siew, *The War*, 71.

different languages with different focuses. Revelation 11 focuses more on the role of the two witnesses and their fate; Revelation 12–13 focus more on the unholy trinity's roles and schemes. Thus, it is safe to say that God's two witnesses are countered and foiled by the dragon's two beasts when looking at Revelation 11 together with Revelation 12–13.[31]

So in imitation of the two witnesses who receive authority from God in the presence of the Lord (11:3–4), who perform great signs such as fire coming out of their mouth (11:5–6), and who prophesy (11:3, 6, 10), the second beast also receives authority from the first beast in its presence (13:12), performs great signs such as fire coming down from heaven (13:13), and falsely prophesy and deceive (13:14; cf. 16:13; 19:20; 20:10).[32] Its deception is so effective that the people of the earth are made to worship the first beast (13:14). Those who do not worship the image of the beast are to be slain (13:15), just like the two witnesses (11:7). In all this, it is clear for John that everyone is following either God and the Lamb or the dragon. John also casts people's allegiance in terms of worship. One either worships God and gives allegiance to him, or one worships the dragon and gives allegiance to it; there is no middle ground. The critical issue on part of God's saints is whether they will exhibit endurance and faith despite the dragon's deceitful schemes and attacks (13:9–10).

It is also interesting to note how John describes the city where the dead bodies of the two witnesses are displayed in 11:8. It is the great city that is symbolically (πνευματικῶς) called Sodom and Egypt, where also their Lord was crucified (ἐσταυρώθη). In doing so, John assimilates at least five historically known cities/nations that opposed God and persecuted his people. The term "great city" refers clearly to Babylon, and by extension, also to Rome in Revelation (16:19; 17:18; 18:2, 10, 16, 18, 19, 21).[33] Sodom and Egypt are also familiar anti-God cities/nations in the OT. Finally, the city where Christ was crucified undoubtedly refers to Jerusalem. By killing God's prophets and crucifying the Messiah, even Jerusalem is numbered alongside Sodom and Egypt (cf. Matt 23:29–39; Lk 13:33–35). Regarding the reason why John does this, Minear is certainly right when he stated, "That John intentionally combined all these places

---

31. Humphrey, *The Ladies and the Cities*, 100.

32. Not only does the second beast have affinities with the two witnesses of Revelation 11, as the third member of the unholy trinity, it also has affinities with the third member of the holy Trinity, namely the Holy Spirit. See Stefanovic, *Revelation*, 371.

33. Babylon the great is the antithesis to the city of God in Revelation. More will be said in the chapter on the two-women motif.

in a single scene is indicated by his efforts to symbolize the universality of this scene."[34] The city where the corpses of the two witnesses are displayed is trans-historical or ontological, and this means that John is portraying the conflict between the beast and God's two witnesses in ontological terms, albeit while not destroying the historicity of the event.[35]

If the above treatise is valid, and if there is a close connection between Revelation 11 and 12–13, especially between the two witnesses and the second beast as shown earlier, then the above discussion furnishes another clue that the second beast of Revelation 13 should be understood not only in historical specificity, but also in ontological terms. If so, then all three members of the unholy trinity are portrayed in ontological terms by John in Revelation 12–13, as the conflict between the kingdom of God and of the beast is itself an ontological conflict. This is important to remember as the present study delves into the meaning and identity of the number 666. So, the second beast persecutes those who do not give fidelity to the first beast in worship (13:15). John continues in stating that the second beast also pressures everyone to be marked on the right hand or on the forehead so that no one can buy or sell unless one has the mark of the beast (13:16–17). Two observations must be made here. First, John is showing that worship is not only spiritual, but also has a bearing on how one lives one's life, on how one makes a living. Following the beast will give the follower the right to buy or sell, namely success and ease in making a living.[36] Second, taking the mark of the beast on the right hand or on the forehead is clearly a counterpart to taking the mark of God or of the Lamb on the forehead (3:12; 7:3; 9:4; 14:1; 22:4). This refers to one's identity and fidelity; one either belongs to God or to the beast.

So finally, in 13:18, John gives the number of the mark of the beast: 666.[37] But before giving the actual number, John calls attention on the

---

34. Minear, "Ontology and Ecclesiology," 95.

35. Minear, "Ontology and Ecclesiology," 96.

36. Keener makes the point that to withdraw oneself from an economic system so integrated with imperial worship, namely not taking the mark of the beast, was equivalent to economic suicide. Keener, *Revelation*, 353. Furthermore, Mathews states that "buying and selling," as a phrase, generally denotes activity of market trading to earn a living. He provides several examples where the phrase is used to mean this, such as Thucydides, 7.39.2.6 and Xenophon, *Anab.*, 1.5.5.8. Mathews, *Riches, Poverty, and the Faithful*, 187.

37. While there is another variant that counts the number to be 616, this study follows majority of other scholars in arguing that a stronger case can be made for the number 666 and that it is thus a preferred reading. For an argument for the number 666, see Koester, "The Number of the Beast," 2–5.

part of the readers by stating, "Here is wisdom" (Ὧδε ἡ σοφία ἐστίν).[38] By using the word σοφία, John calls to mind the first two instances of the word and the disclosure of wisdom that occurred via the two throne room visions of Revelation 5 and 7. Then he commands those who have understanding (νοῦν) to calculate (ψηφισάτω) the number of the beast, for it is a number of a man, which comes out to 666.[39] If this is a riddle John gives his readers, then he certainly expected his readers to be able to figure it out. After all, John understands that divinely guided wisdom is now available to his readers. If John's readers concur with those before God's throne room that true wisdom belongs to God and to the Lamb (5:12; 7:12), then as those who have the mark of God on their foreheads (7:3; 14:1; 22:4) and as those who have the Lamb as their shepherd who guides them (7:17), they should be able to use that wisdom to properly understand. Thus, John calls on them to exhibit and to exercise wisdom in calculating the beast's number.

This is certainly interesting and unusual, for no other works in antiquity that invoke gematria, if indeed calculating the number of the beast is one of gematria, ask the readers for wisdom.[40] In doing so, John seems to claim that no one else but his readers will be able to do the calculation and understand, since they are the ones who have had divine wisdom disclosed to them.[41] While others might be able to figure out the supposed answer, but properly understanding what the answer

---

38. Revelation 13:18's call for wisdom and understanding is similar to the call captured in Mark 13:14 and Matthew 24:15, where the call happens at an important juncture in Christ's apocalyptic discourse. This means that Revelation 13:18 is also a crucial moment in Revelation's discourse, particularly for Revelation 12–14. See Aune, *Revelation 6–16*, 769 and Osborne, *Revelation*, 519.

39. Third person imperative ψηφισάτω is a case of polite command, not of permission. Thus, the expression "let the one . . . calculate" in some English translations is misleading. See Louw and Nida, §32.15.

40. For further information on gematria and on other ancient works that utilize gematria, see Beale, *Revelation*, 718–28; Bohak, "Greek-Hebrew Gematrias," 119–21; Bovon, "Names and Numbers," 267–88; Koester, "The Number of the Beast," 1–21.

41. This study thereby is different from Koester and others who think that John was not concealing his meaning from outsiders but that just about anybody could have solved the riddle. See Koester, "The Number of the Beast," 6–7. This study instead argues that, while John surely did not need to conceal the meaning, no one but the true believers could have really solved the riddle because the outsiders would not have fully grasped nor would have accepted the meaning. Wisdom involves not just right understanding but also right behavior. Since the outsiders would have rejected what John was portraying through the riddle and would not have followed suit, even though they may have gotten the right answer, they did not really solve the riddle.

means, accepting it, and changing one's behavior in accordance to it will be available only to those who have wisdom. This is certainly in keeping with Daniel 12:10 where it is expected that only those with wisdom will understand the things of the end.[42]

However, it remains to be seen what John is specifically commanding the believers to do in Revelation 13:18. Without going through in detail what scholars have been endorsing, this study will instead succinctly discuss the major interpretive issues and options, and will promote its own understanding, especially in connection with John's use of σοφία. The first issue has to do with the method that John is asking of his readers. Those who argue for the method of mathematical calculation of some kind understand the word "to calculate" (ψηφισάτω) to denote a numerical reckoning.[43] In this camp, the majority believes the method to be gematria, which is a method of finding the numerical value of a person's name quite prevalent during John's time. On the other hand, those who view the method to be more symbolic understand the word "to calculate" to have a figurative meaning, namely, to interpret.[44] The second issue has to do with the genitive ἀνθρώπου. Those belonging to the side of a more literal, numerical calculation read ἀνθρώπου as case-specific, simply translated as a number *of a man*, thus understanding that a certain individual's number is intended to be calculated by John.[45] But those belonging to a more figurative side read ἀνθρώπου as generic, as a genitive of quality, and translate the genitive phrase as a *human* number.[46] Thus, a definite individual is not intended by John, but rather that John

---

42. See also 4 *Ezra* 12:37–38 and 2 *Bar.* 28:1. See further Beale, "The Danielic Background," 163–70.

43. Fanning is an example of this camp. He argues that the word "to calculate" refers to a mathematical calculation as attested in Luke 14:28 and that the more general sense of interpret or figure out is unattested elsewhere. Fanning, *Revelation*, 379 fn. 46.

44. Beale is a proponent of this camp. Beale argues that John always uses ἀριθμός and its cognates figuratively in Revelation (5:11; 7:4, 9; 9:16; 20:8). This means that John's command to "calculate the number" in 13:18 must be figurative as well. The beast's number thus is not to be literally calculated. Beale, *Revelation*, 721.

45. For instance, Mounce argues that the number of the beast is the number of a certain man, a definite historical person. Mounce, *Revelation*, 261. See also, Aune, *Revelation 6–16*, 769.

46. For instance, Hoskins argues that the only other instance the genitive ἀνθρώπου is used in Revelation is in 21:17, where it is clearly used as a genitive of quality. This provides an important analogy for 13:18. Hoskins, *Revelation*, 253. See also, Smalley, *Revelation*, 351.

wants show that any believer with wisdom can reckon the significance of the beast's number.

These two issues combined thereby have a bearing on the interpretation of the beast's actual number: 666. Those holding to a more literal side of mathematical calculation understand the number to refer to a definite person, the vast majority today advocating that the number points to Nero or a Nero-like figure.[47] Nero, who was a persecutor of Christians and who was rumored to come back in the future (Nero *redivivus* myth), would be a fitting type for the future antichrist. On the other hand, those holding to a more figurative side understand the number to simply signify that the beast, no matter how mighty it may seem as it imitates God, still falls short of God.[48] After all, God's number is 7, which signifies

---

47. Scholars in this camp usually claim that, when Nero Caesar in Greek is written in Hebrew letters (קסר נרון), it yields a numerical total of 666. Further, if Nero Caesar in Latin is written in Hebrew, it yields 616, because in Latin, the name is written as Nero rather than Neron in Greek. It is argued that the lack of final n, which has a numerical value of 50, will drop the total numerical value from 666 to 616, and this means that the name of Nero even works for the variant reading that states the beast's number to be 616. While it is objected that the normal spelling of "Caesar" in Hebrew is קיסר, which should yield a numerical total of 676 due to the added yodh, but an Aramaic document has been found from the Judean desert that spells "Caesar" as קסר. Scholars also readily note the Nero *redivivus* myth that was supposedly well-known during John's time, a belief that Nero the great persecutor will return as the embodiment of Satan (cf. *Sib. Or.* 3:63–74; *Mart. Asc. Isa.* 4:2–8), and that this was what John had in mind in Revelation 13:18. For those who argue for the beast's number to be referring to Nero or a Nero-like figure, see Aune, *Revelation 6–16*, 722, 770–71, 780; Yarbro Collins, *Cosmology and Eschatology*, 117–18; Fanning, *Revelation*, 380; Giesen, *Offenbarung*, 315–18; Gumerlock, "Nero Antichrist," 347–60; Klauck, "Do They Never Come Back?," 683–98; Koester, *Revelation*, 597–99; Koester, "The Number of the Beast," 9–11; Kraybill, *Imperial Cult*, 161–64; Osborne, *Revelation*, 520–21. Osborne sees Nero to be the best option for the beast's number but confesses that it is still only a tantalizing possibility.

In a similar vein, there are scholars who argue that 666 is a triangular number with the root of 36. The argument goes that 36 is also triangular, itself with the root of 8. The number 8 then is connected with Revelation 17:11 where the beast is said to be the eighth king. Thus, these scholars note that the mention of 666 in 13:18 prepares the readers for the eighth king of 17:11, whose identity is closely associated with Nero. For those who observe 666 as a triangular number, see Bauckham, *Climax*, 390–96; Farrer, *Revelation*, 158–59; Keener, *Revelation*, 354; Lohmeyer, *Offenbarung*, 118–19.

48. For those who take the beast's number to have a symbolic significance, see Beale, *Revelation*, 721–22; Hoskins, *Revelation*, 254–55; Morris, *Revelation*, 168–69; Smalley, *Revelation*, 352; Valdez, "El número 666," 191–214; Walvoord, *Revelation*, 210. Minear has also succinctly raised objections as to why the identification of the beast with Nero does not work as many suppose. Minear, "The Wounded Beast," 93–101; Minear, *I Saw a New Earth*, 118–19. For a more detailed argument against the Nero theory, see Tonstad, "Appraising the Myth," 175–99.

perfection or completeness, but the beast's number is only a threefold 6, which signifies imperfection.[49]

Perhaps a better answer lies in understanding that this is not an either/or question, but a both/and one. As the current section of this study strived to show, John clearly understood and portrayed the conflict between God's kingdom and the beast's kingdom in ontological terms since Revelation 12. The woman of Revelation 12 is ontological, a transhistorical portrayal of God's faithful people. The dragon, the first beast, and the second beast all have features that are ontological. They have been imitating God, deceiving the people of the world, and persecuting God's people throughout history. This is most clear in John's depiction of the first beast in 13:2 where the beast is described in beastly terms that resemble Daniel's four beasts. This shows that the beast is an ontological or a trans-historical reality; it had been behind the kingdoms of the earth that oppose God and his people throughout history.

Therefore, when John spoke about the number of the beast, he likely had this ontological reality in mind. The essence of the argument regarding the number of the beast between the scholars is about which aspect is in the foreground of John's thinking when he called his readers to calculate the beast's number, whether historical or symbolic. If one believes that John had the historical aspect in the foreground of his mind, then one will argue that the number refers to a definite, historical person. If one believes that John had the symbolic aspect in the foreground, then one will argue that the number has a symbolic significance. This study is instead arguing that John had the ontological aspect in the foreground of his mind when he spoke about the beast's number. Thus, the issue is not really whether the number is historical or symbolic. The number is ontological, because the beast itself is an ontological reality in a trans-historical conflict with God's kingdom and his people, and if ontological, then the number has a comprehensive aspect, both historical and eschatological.

Surely Nero, as a persecutor of God's people, would be an embodiment of the evil that the beast represents in a specific time in history.[50] Yet, Nero is not all that the beast represents. The beast is multivalent, and

---

49. God, when viewed as a Trinity, would yield a number of 777. In contrast, as the unholy trinity, Satan and his henchmen yield a number of 666. See Schreiner, *The Joy of Hearing*, 37; Smalley, *Revelation*, 352; Torrance, *The Apocalypse Today*, 86.

50. Beale and McDonough, "Revelation," 1131.

σοφία IN REVELATION AS WISDOM FOR GOD'S FAITHFUL PEOPLE 79

Nero would be part of that multivalency.[51] John, by way of design, has made the beast's number in Revelation 13:18 quite mysterious, and one specific answer to the riddle cannot give an adequate solution to all that John communicates of the beast in Revelation 13.[52] Again, this is likely because John wants to portray the beast and his number to be multivalent, or better yet, ontological. No matter how the beast manifests itself in specific time and history, what Revelation's readers must understand is that it is only a part of the bigger picture. This is why John began his long interlude on the conflict between God's kingdom and the beast's kingdom with the woman clothed with the sun, her male child, and the dragon in Revelation 12.

What Revelation 12 has shown was that this conflict began long ago. Also now, due to the work of Christ on the cross, the condition of the conflict has met a drastic turning point. The dragon has been defeated and has been thrown down to the earth (12:7–9). The kingdom of God has won a decisive battle (12:10). The devil knows this, and he also knows that his time is short (12:12). With little time he has, he now makes war with the rest of the woman's children, namely the faithful believers in Christ (12:17).

With great urgency and wrath, the devil schemes with his two beasts in deceiving the world into idolatrous worship and in persecuting God's people (Rev 13). To be clear, the devil has been working with the first beast throughout history even before the time of Christ's first coming (cf. 13:2). But now, because the devil knows his time is short, his two henchmen work even more in deceiving the people of the earth. The new tactic, as John emphasizes it time and time again, that they use in their deception is imitating the Lamb (13:3, 11, 12, 14). By imitating the Lamb and by showing off their imitation, they make the people marvel at and give worship to the first beast (13:3–4, 8, 12–14).

In all this, the cosmic conflict between the two kingdoms remains in the foreground of John's mind. He wants his readers to understand this ontological history of conflict, that it is not only ongoing, but is also quite rigorously being manifested in the world as the wrathful dragon makes war with the believers of Christ. The urgency for endurance and loyalty that the believers must exhibit toward God is now greater than

---

51. Witherington expresses something similar when he states that " . . . the veiled nature of such gematric games allows John's text to have a certain multivalency." Witherington III, *Revelation*, 179.

52. So also, Bodner and Strawn, "Solomon and 666," 312.

ever. John's triple "if anyone" (εἴ τις) clauses (13:9–10) and double "here is" (ὧδέ ἐστιν) exhortations (13:10, 18) especially convey great urgency and seriousness of what is at stake.[53] There is also an increasing pressure to defect, as the dragon's two beasts work hard in deceiving the world into following them and into persecuting those who do not.[54] But in the end, John states that the beast's number 666 is only a human number or a number of a mere man. Either way, the number is intended to show that, the beast, no matter how much it claims to be greater than God, will in truth never be greater.[55]

Those with wisdom should be able to see this ontological reality and should not be deceived by the beast. In fact, they must call to mind the disclosure of wisdom of the throne room visions and realize once again that the Lamb has supreme authority to judge the world and its people, and that God likewise has true insight into world order. The Satanic trio may seem as if it is controlling the world, but its authority pales in comparison to the Lamb and to God. Therefore, no matter what happens in this physical world, the believers who have divine wisdom and understanding must recognize past the deception and must show loyalty to God and the Lamb by holding fast to Christ's commands and testimony, knowing that the beast's kingdom is no match for God's kingdom.

Hence, the call for wisdom functions in fact not to read the beast's number one-dimensionally on the part of the readers. To understand John's calling as simply using gematria or other mathematical formulas in figuring out the beast's name does not do justice to all the significance that the number may entail. What John wants is for the readers to use divine wisdom to understand the bigger picture, namely the cosmic conflict between the two kingdoms that are being manifested historically and tangibly, to realize without mistake that the beast's kingdom cannot match God's kingdom, although it may seem in time as if the beast's kingdom is mighty, and not to be deceived but to stay loyal to God's kingdom no

---

53. Tonstad, "Appraising the Myth," 197.

54. Minear, *I Saw a New Earth*, 119. Minear states that discernment is thereby required to see the beast's circuitous lines of attack (Rev 13:18) as to not give in to the pressure to defect.

55. Whereas the beast's number is human and can be calculated, the Lamb's name is altogether different and cannot be calculated in Revelation. This moreover shows that the beast cannot match the Lamb no matter how much it tries to imitate him. In Bovon's words, "In the book of Revelation we find a similar consciousness of the inadequacy of any human name for Jesus Christ: 'He has a name inscribed that no one knows but himself' (Rev 19.12)." Bovon, "Names and Numbers," 279.

matter what. Thus, to summarize, the call for σοφία in Revelation 13:18 is not simply calculating what the beast's number signifies, though that is part of it, but on a larger scale necessitates two aspects: to understand the ontological reality of the two kingdoms and to exhibit proper behavior with urgency, namely staying faithful to God and to the Lamb and not defecting to the beast's side.[56] Indeed, those with σοφία do not take the beast's mark (13:16–17); they instead have the Lamb's name and God's name written on their foreheads (14:1).

In turn, John goes on to make sure to let the readers know in Revelation 14 that the fate of those who stay loyal to God is eternally secure.[57] They will stand on Mount Zion with the Lamb and sing a new song that only they know (14:1–5). The phrase "new song" especially recalls Revelation 5:8–10, where the heavenly hosts sang a new song of praise about the Lamb redeeming his people and his conquest of evil (cf. 15:2–4).[58] The Lamb with wisdom (5:12) will ensure final victory, and his redeemed people with wisdom (13:18) shall also join in the new song of praise in victory in the end. The hour of judgment is surely coming (14:6–7), and Babylon (14:8), as well as those who follow the beast, will surely fall (14:9–11).[59] Therefore, John encourages his readers once again and calls on them to exercise endurance in staying loyal to God (14:12–13; cf. 13:10). The day of reaping is coming, and those who stay faithful to God shall be properly reaped (14:14–16), whereas those who do not shall be gathered into the great winepress of the wrath of God and be judged (14:17–20). Those with divine wisdom are to understand and to recognize this ultimate reality and to act accordingly.

---

56. Again, wisdom thus entails both right understanding and right behavior. Stuckenbruck, "Disclosure of Wisdom," 359.

57. Osborne is certainly correct when he states, "This is an incredibly rich chapter, especially since it contrasts the future of the saints with that of the sinners." Osborne, *Revelation*, 523.

58. Smalley, *Revelation*, 356.

59. Revelation 14:8 provides the first instance where Babylon is mentioned in the book and serves as a nice foreshadow into Revelation 17–18, the main section on Babylon. This is not surprising and is probably intended, for Babylon serves as another dimension into how the beast deceives the people of the earth and how it uses them to persecute God's people. In other words, Revelation 12–14 and 17–18 are sections both dealing with the conflict of the two kingdoms, especially showing how the beast is operating in the current world. It is thus quite significant that both sections include John's specific call to σοφία for the readers (13:18; 17:9). John wants his readers to think about the reality of the beast's kingdom and its fate, and not to align themselves to this kingdom.

Revelation 17:9

The mention of Babylon in Revelation 14:8 brings this study suitably to Revelation 17, where Babylon is properly introduced and where another instance of the word σοφία occurs. To look at things in a larger context first, Revelation 17:1—19:10 can be considered as one major section that deals with the reality and fate of Babylon the great. In order to properly understand the purpose and function of this major section however, it is necessary to begin with the ending of Revelation 16. In Revelation 16:17–21, John narrates the very final judgment of the twenty-one judgments, namely the seventh bowl judgment. With it, God announces that "It is done" (γέγονεν), that God's judgment is finally completed (16:17). The familiar theophany language of lightnings, rumblings, thunders, and earthquake, a great one in fact, that follows God's announcement indicates that it is now the end (16:18). Christ is coming back. John's eschatological language of every island fleeing away, mountains being gone, and great hailstones falling upon people further envisages that the end is now here (16:20–21).

But in the midst of John's theophany and eschatological language of the end, he adds a peculiar detail of cities falling (16:19). On one hand, since Christ's coming means the final victory of God's kingdom, it is fitting that the cities of the nations fall at the coming of Jesus. Although the kings of the world all gather for war against God on the great day of God (16:14–16), instead of winning, their cities fall.[60] This suggests complete demolition of the worldly system and structure by God at the coming of Jesus.[61] God's kingdom and his people will win in the end.

On the other hand, it is not just the cities of the world falling, but also the great city (ἡ πόλις ἡ μεγάλη). This recalls Revelation 11:8 where John stated that the corpses of God's two witnesses will be in the street of the great city that is symbolically or spiritually called Sodom and Egypt, where their Lord was also crucified. As noted in the previous section of this study, the great city must be viewed ontologically as the epitome of all cities in history that opposed God and his people. It is also called Babylon in Revelation (16:19; 17:18; 18:2, 10, 16, 18, 19, 21). Babylon the great is the capital city of the beast and is thus the main target of God's wrath.[62] John is noting that what the angels have warned in 14:8–10 shall

---

60. Thomas and Macchia, *Revelation*, 289.
61. Smalley, *Revelation*, 415.
62. Hoskins, *Revelation*, 301.

have come to pass when the last judgment occurs. Babylon and her allies who take the mark of the beast will drink the wine of God's anger that is unmixed in the cup of his wrath. God has not forgotten about Babylon (16:19); Babylon and her allied cities/nations shall surely all fall when the end comes and God's wrath is poured out.

Now, how God will give Babylon the cup of the wine, that is, his fierce anger (16:19; τὸ ποτήριον τοῦ οἴνου τοῦ θυμοῦ τῆς ὀργῆς αὐτοῦ)[63] is the subject matter of Revelation 17:1–19:10, the main section on Babylon. John thereby does not go on to tell about what happens when Jesus comes back after his narration of the seventh bowl judgment at the end of Revelation 16, but digresses to give a rather lengthy treatment regarding Babylon the great in 17:1—19:10. John will pick up and continue telling about the second coming of Jesus and thereafter in 19:11. Nevertheless, this lengthy digression on Babylon evidences that it is important to John and to his readers. John wants his readers to fully know the reality and fate of Babylon, and he even puts off his narration about the very end times to do so.

Thus, in 17:1, John actually goes back in time a bit and states that one of the seven angels having the seven bowls came to him to show the judgment of the great harlot. By the end of Revelation 16, all seven bowls have been poured out. The fact that the angel in 17:1 still has the bowl suggests that this vision is taking place *before* the pouring of all seven bowls, not after.[64] This is also comparable to 21:9 where John states that one of the seven angels having the seven bowls full of seven last plagues came to him to show the bride of the Lamb. The detail of the same angel showing John both the great harlot and the bride indicates that there is a connection between the two women figures. Indeed, John will claim that the connection is actually one of great antithesis, for the great harlot belongs with the beast whereas the bride belongs with the Lamb. Hence, whereas the angel will take John to the wilderness to show him the great harlot (17:3), the same angel will take John to a great and high mountain to show him the bride (21:10).

In any case, before John will mention how and why the great harlot will be judged, he first makes an unusual effort in giving a detailed

---

63. This writer has taken the last genitive construction τῆς ὀργῆς αὐτοῦ adjectivally, while taking the last two genitives appositionally. See also Beale, *Revelation*, 843.

64. Osborne understands Revelation 17:1—19:4 to be a further explanation on the sixth and seventh bowl judgments. Osborne, *Revelation*, 607. So also, Beale, *Revelation*, 847.

description of the great harlot (17:1-6).⁶⁵ John wants his readers to know the full reality of the great harlot so as to not be enticed by her and partake in her sins. First, the harlot is described as sitting on many waters (17:1). According to the angel, "many waters" signify "peoples, multitudes, nations, and tongues" (17:15), and this fourfold way of speaking about the entire world shows that the harlot exhibits much influence upon the whole world.⁶⁶ The nature of her influence is captured in 17:2. John states that the kings of the earth have committed harlotry (ἐπόρνευσαν) with her and that the earth dwellers have become drunk with her wine, that is, her harlotry (τῆς πορνείας αὐτῆς).⁶⁷ Thus, deed befitting of her title, the great harlot, Babylon has influenced many people of the world, both high and low, through harlotry. The nations and their people have become intoxicated (ἐμεθύσθησαν) with her, which suggests that they have repeatedly engaged in immoral behavior with this woman.⁶⁸

65. This is unusual, for John does not make such detailed effort in providing descriptions for other women figures in Revelation. In fact, the bride of Revelation 21 is quickly transformed into a city and is described in terms of a city, the New Jerusalem, but the great harlot of Revelation 17 has a prolonged description as a woman, albeit supernatural, before being described as a city. This shows that learning about the great harlot on the part of the readers is important to John. The reason must be because John's audience currently lives alongside the great harlot (cf. 18:4). Her enticing nature is dangerous, enough to make John himself marvel at her (17:6), and the readers must know her true identity and fate in order not to be deceived by her.

66. In the OT, Babylon is noted as a city located on many waters (Jer 51:13), which in turn provides an important connection to Babylon the great in Revelation. Further, Tyre and Nineveh were also cities associated with many waters (Isa 23:3; Nah 2:8) and both were called harlot cities in the OT (Isa 23:15-17; Nah 3:4). Tyre was also known for wealth and Nineveh for sorcery, and both defied God and enticed people to worship idols (see Ezek 26-28 for Tyre and Nah 3 for Nineveh). While the historical Babylon is never called a harlot in the OT, Ezekiel 23:17 does speak about the harlotry of the Babylonians. There are also other harlot cities in the OT, such as Jerusalem (Ezek 16:15), that serve as the backdrop for Revelation's Babylon. As such, Babylon the great in Revelation is an amalgamation of all harlot cities in history, representing enticement of people via wealth and sorcery, to persecute God's people and to defy God in worshiping the beast (Rev 17-18). She is thus fittingly called "the mother of harlots and of earth's abominations" (Rev 17:5). For more information on harlotry in Revelation, see Hoskins, *Revelation*, 308-14 and Robinson, "Sexual Immorality Language."

67. This writer takes the genitive string τῆς πορνείας αὐτῆς appositionally, describing what is meant by the harlot's wine.

68. The metaphor of intoxication is an allusion to Jeremiah 51:7 (Jer 28:7 in LXX), where it is stated that the historical Babylon makes the nations drink from her wine. Although not stated in Revelation 17:2, Jeremiah 51:7 includes the disastrous consequence of this intoxication, namely that the nations went mad or wavered. The same allusion to Jeremiah 51:7 is also found in Revelation 14:8. See, Aune, *Revelation 17-22*, 932. Thus, while Revelation 17:2 states that the people of the earth have become drunk,

The language of harlotry and of intoxication here is clearly metaphorical. In the Old Testament, to commit harlotry or to be a harlot (זָנָה) is often used metaphorically to refer to actions of unfaithfulness to God by committing idolatry (cf. Exod 34:16; Lev 17:7, 20:5; Deut 31:16; Ps 106:36–39).[69] The same sense is being used in Revelation 17:2 as well to indicate that the kings of the earth, as well as the earth dwellers, have committed harlotry by unfaithfully compromising with the great harlot, especially in lucrative trading with her for wealth, and in doing so, have committed idolatry by following the beast.[70] Harlotry requires payment, and in Revelation, to commit harlotry with the great harlot requires a payment of giving allegiance to the beast.[71] John is painting in very graphic and ghastly terms to make sure his readers recognize that compromising with the beast's city is in fact, committing idolatry. The great harlot uses worldly wealth and power to entice people very effectively. People of the world are following the beast when they seek to associate with the great harlot in order to satisfy the desires of the flesh whether they realize it or not.[72]

Also important to note regarding harlotry and intoxication in Revelation 17:2 is Hosea 4:11–12. In Hosea 4, God accuses Israel of harlotry and prophesies about her judgment. In the midst of the accusation, God combines harlotry and wine and claims that the people of Israel have cherished these things which take away understanding (לֵב) in Hosea 4:11.[73] God goes on to say that the people ask wood and staff to declare oracles to them, because a spirit of harlotry makes the people to err or to

---

it also means that the nations have become drunk.

69. Beale, *Revelation*, 250, 519–20, 848–49; Hoskins, *Revelation*, 310. See *HALOT*, s.v. "זנה." See also, BDAG, s.v. "πορνεύω" and Thayer, s.v. "πορνεύω."

70. This is most explicit in Revelation 18, where those who have compromised with the great harlot all weep and mourn because of the lost wealth and ceased opportunity in trading with her.

71. Hoskins, *Revelation*, 310; Robinson, "Sexual Immorality Language," 147–49. Robinson is correct in seeing that the mark of the beast in Revelation 13 that people must receive in order to trade shows that the required payment for trading with the beast's city, the great harlot, is allegiance to the beast.

72. Hoskins, *Revelation*, 313.

73. The term לֵב literally means "heart." In Hosea, the word "heart" refers to the seat of understanding and volition (2:14; 7:6, 11, 14; 10:2). Further, in Hosea 4:14, the word בִין is used to refer to discernment or understanding, and God states that people without understanding shall come to ruin. According to Dearman, this statement from God is a proverb, and the verb בִין is a vocabulary of the wise. Dearman, *Hosea*, 166. Thus, the language of intoxication and harlotry are within the realm of sapiential language, and this is also true of Revelation.

go astray (4:12). Thus, harlotry and wine are connected to idolatry and to lack of understanding, and both lead to ruin. In the same way, John uses the language of harlotry and of intoxication in Revelation 17:2 to show the idolatrous and erring ways of people as they associate with the great harlot. Although John does not explicitly claim it, he would also concur with Hosea that the people of the world who are drunk with the harlot's wine and who commit harlotry with her lack understanding, and this will lead to their demise. On the other hand, John will call upon the people of God to exhibit wisdom and understanding (Rev 17:9), which will lead them to eternal victory.

In 17:3, the great harlot's connection with the beast becomes clear as John says that the woman is sitting on a scarlet beast that is full of blasphemous names and that has seven heads and ten horns. This is unmistakably none other than the first beast, for the description matches what is true of the first beast in 13:1. The woman is also sitting on the beast, which must mean that she is enthroned on the beast (cf. 17:1).[74] Everything that the beast has this woman exercises, and she is thus properly called the beast's city. As John will later show, however, she does not really reign over the beast, but the beast is simply using her to deceive the world into following it, for the beast will turn against the woman and destroy her (17:16). This shows that the beast is not faithful and following the beast will only end in one's downfall.

Starting with 17:4, John begins to paint a close-up picture of the great harlot.[75] He first notes her attire. The harlot is clothed in purple and scarlet and is adorned with gold, jewels, and pearls. There is a debate as to where John took the details of her clothing and adornment from.[76] As

---

74. Aune, *Revelation 17–22*, 934.

75. Scholars often note that Revelation 17:1–6 is a case of visual ekphrasis. See Aune, "Intertextuality," 158; Rossing, *Two Cities*, 77; Royalty, *The Streets of Heaven*, 129, 177, 215. Visual ekphrasis can be defined as vivid, visual description that stirs imagination and emotion. As such, it increases the motivational force of the author's argumentation. See Stewart, "Ekphrasis," 227–40.

76. Some argue that Ezekiel serves as the antecedent for the great harlot's attire. See Vanhoye, "L'utilisation," 440–42 and Ruiz, *Ezekiel*, 324. Others argue for alternative prophetic sources such as Jeremiah or Isaiah. For the former, see Court, *Myth and History*, 141. For the latter, Fekkes, *Isaiah*, 102. Rossing argues that these proposals are not fully convincing. Whereas these prophetic oracles condemn the whoring cities such as Jerusalem, Tyre, or Babylon and vindicate God's judgement upon them, Revelation's goal is more hortatory: to persuade the readers to sever ties with Babylon. This hortatory function resembles more Proverb's warning against the evil woman than the prophetic oracles against the whoring cities. See Rossing, *Two Cities*, 76–77. Still, Glancy and Moore argue that, although recourse to the OT in understanding the great harlot is

this study has shown above, it is likely that John is drawing a composite picture of the great harlot, and this means that John is likely pulling from multiple sources. In any case, the harlot's attire suggests very clearly that she is wealthy. She is not an ordinary πόρνη of a low-class ladder but an exalted one. After all, even the kings of the earth want to associate with her for her wealth (cf. Rev 18:9).

John also notes a golden cup in the harlot's hand. This continues the imagery of wealth and exaltation, but John makes sure of the discrepancy. It is a cup full of abominations and impurities of her harlotry (17:4). Thus, although the woman may look grandiose, she is in fact vulgar and degrading. She is like a lowly harlot proclaiming her availability to service all for a price, drunk with wine, during a rowdy dinner party.[77] She welcomes and entices all people to sin, and those who drink with her will also commit abominations and become unclean or defiled.[78]

Then John reports on her forehead. On her forehead is written a name of mystery: Babylon the great, the mother of harlots and of earth's abominations (17:5). In Revelation, one's character and one's ultimate allegiance is closely tied to one's forehead. God's people have the mark or the name of God and of the Lamb on their foreheads (3:12; 7:3; 14:1; 22:4). On the other hand, the beast's people have the mark or the name of the beast on their foreheads (13:17; 14:9, 11; 16:2; 19:20). The great harlot also has a mysterious name on her forehead that tells something about her nature. She is the *great* Babylon, the culmination of all anti-God cities in history.[79] She is also the *mother* of harlots and of earth's abominations,

---

relevant, so is work on ancient Greek and Roman prostitution. They thus look at Greek and Roman sources to show that the great harlot of Revelation resembles, albeit not perfectly, a Roman prostitute in the streets. Glancy and Moore, "How Typical," 551–69. Perhaps it is better to understand John to be portraying the great harlot with multiple antecedents instead of arguing for a single source, because as this study will show, the great harlot is a multivalent symbol.

77. Glancy and Moore, "How Typical," 561.

78. Hoskins notes a double significance for the harlot's cup or wine. "It represents both enticement to sin and the sins that those who partake commit." Hoskins, *Revelation*, 319.

79. Babylon is a suitable name, for it is a prominent city in the OT known for its harlotry (Jer 51:44–52; Isa 21:9), merchantry (Ezek 16:29; 17:3), and oppression of God's people (Jer 51:11, 24, 34–35, 49). That the harlot of Revelation 17 is called the great Babylon suggests that she is the culmination of all harlot cities. Gregory argues that John intentionally chose the name Babylon, and not any other name such as Tyre, to describe the great harlot of Revelation because the name guarantees her destruction and the Lord's triumph as prophesied by the OT prophets such as Isaiah, Jeremiah, Ezekiel, and Daniel. This in turn brings assurance and encouragement to those who

the origin and influencer of idolatry and all that God detests.[80] She clearly does not belong to God, for her titles stand in great antithesis to God.

Babylon's opposition to God is especially brought to light in 17:6 as John tells that the woman is drunk with the blood of the saints and with the blood of the witnesses or martyrs of Jesus. For the second time, John claims that he saw (εἶδον; cf. 17:3) the woman, which signals that John is sure of what he saw, and she is unmistakably a persecutor of God's people. Apparently, Babylon's wine of harlotry that the earth dwellers came to be drunk on (17:2) is the blood of God's people. This means that harlotry or idolatry in Revelation has a direct connection with persecution of God's saints; those who commit harlotry by worshipping and following the beast will also persecute followers of Christ. The picture of the woman (and also those who commit harlotry with her) drunk with the blood of God's people makes John's visual ekphrasis of Babylon all the more ghastly. While she may look magnificent and desirable, she in reality is meretricious and despicable. She is not to be marveled at for any reason.[81]

Now that this study has looked at how John introduced and portrayed the great harlot, it is fitting at this point to consider her identity before moving to John's interpretation of the harlot beginning with Revelation 17:7. Scholars who emphasize the notion that John's visions largely have to do with the situation contemporaneous to the author's own time argue that the great harlot is Rome.[82] This historical approach claims that

hear and read Revelation. Gregory, "Its End Is Destruction," 137–53.

80. Rossing rightly argues that Babylon's motherhood is the same expression suggested by the phrase "Jezebel's children" in Revelation 2 and by the relationship between the radiant woman and her children in Revelation 12. The expression signifies Babylon's power to extend its authority and influence on its followers. Rossing also notes other biblical and classical texts where the expression is used for major cities that have given birth to daughter cities (Ezek 26:6; Isa 47:8; 2 Sam 20:19; Bar 4:10; Gal 4:26). Rossing, *Two Cities*, 83.

81. John states that he marveled greatly (lit. marveled with a great marvel) when he saw the great harlot (17:6). John does not state his reason for this great marvel. Whatever the reason may be, he is quickly rebuked by the angel in 17:7. Marveling is a response that those who do not belong to God give to the beast (13:3; 17:8), and conversely the believers must not marvel at anything that is of the beast.

82. deSilva argues this clearly when he states, "John creates one of the most memorable—and negative—pictures of Rome in extant literature." deSilva, "Strategic Arousal of Emotion," 17. According to deSilva, John deliberately portrays Rome grotesquely in Revelation 17–18 in order to evoke feelings of enmity and indignation toward Roman imperialism on part of his audience. deSilva, "Strategic Arousal of Emotion," 17–25, 31. Yarbro Collins has argued similarly, namely that John presents serious charges against Rome in order to mitigate against the arousal of pity on part of the audience as they hear and read about Babylon's judgment. Yarbro Collins, "Revelation 18," 185–204.

the seven heads of the beast are identified to be seven mountains or hills on which the harlot sits in 17:9 and that this refers to the topography of Rome as the city on seven hills.[83] In turn, when John states that the seven heads of the beast are also seven kings in 17:10, this must mean seven Roman emperors.[84] Connection is also made with the beast being the eighth king in 17:11 to emperor Nero, since this approach understands the mark of the beast in 13:18 to be referring to Nero. But this approach is not without difficulties. There is no indisputable standard of counting the Roman emperors, and scholars disagree on whom they should start with, whether Julius Caesar or Augustus, and on how to deal with the short-reign emperors such as Galba, Otho, and Vitellius.[85] More significantly, if the great harlot is Rome and the eighth king is the Roman emperor Nero, then this means that Revelation 17–18 has long been fulfilled and is no longer directly relevant, but as this study has shown in the discussion of Revelation 12–14, the beast is not simply historical but ontological, and the great harlot also has an ontological side that must be recognized.

Consequently, other scholars who are not satisfied with the historic approach espouse the symbolic approach.[86] This approach notices that the number seven has a highly symbolic meaning in Revelation, representing completeness or totality.[87] Similarly, the number seven can also symbolize the divine arrangement of history and of the world, which was the sense widely used in the ancient world.[88] Thus, the beast's seven heads

83. So Boring, *Revelation*, 179–80; Caird, *Revelation*, 216–17; Court, *Myth and History*, 125–28; Prigent, *L'Apocalypse*, 261; Swete, *Apocalypse*, 220–21.

84. See, for example, Wilson's daring statement that "Virtually all scholars agree that this is a reference to the Roman emperors." Wilson, "The Problem," 599.

85. Baines, "Identity and Fate," 77. Aune has a succinct summary of the alternative ways of counting the Roman Emperors in Aune, *Revelation 17–22*, 946–48.

86. So Aune, *Revelation 17–22*, 948; Beale, *Revelation*, 869; Beasley-Murray, *Revelation*, 256–57; Beckwith, *Apocalypse*, 704–8; Hoskins, *Revelation*, 328–31; Lohmeyer, *Offenbarung*, 143; Mounce, *Revelation*, 317; Sweet, *Revelation*, 257.

87. Baines, "Identity and Fate," 77; Bauckham, *Climax*, 30, 405; Mounce, *Revelation*, 317.

88. Aune, *Revelation 17–22*, 948; Smalley, *Revelation*, 436; Yarbro Collins, *Cosmology and Eschatology*, 126–27. Smalley does give examples from Revelation (cf. 1:11, 16; 2:1; 5:1; 6:1; 10:3–4; 15:1; 16:1; 21:9) where the number seven is used figuratively in this manner, but it is not at all clear whether the number seven does take on this sense in the examples Smalley provides. Also, both Aune and Smalley do not provide any examples from ancient works that do take the number seven figuratively in this manner. Yarbro Collins, however, does give examples from ancient works where the number seven is used as an organizing principle and as having a major cosmic role (cf. Philo, *On the Creation*, 102–3). For these examples, see Yarbro Collins, *Cosmology and Eschatology*,

signify either the epoch of Roman Empire in its totality or the entire history of the world kingdoms in its totality. As the previous section of this study has shown, the first beast's seven heads and ten horns reflect the combination of all four beasts of Daniel 7, and this would certainly mean that Revelation's first beast was what was behind the earthly kingdoms in history.[89] If the first beast's seven heads refer to either kings or kingdoms of the world throughout history, then it follows that the great harlot who rides this beast should also be understood symbolically as the beast's city, as the beast's economic and religious system throughout history that stands in sharp contrast to God's city, the New Jerusalem.[90] However, there is disagreement among scholars who take the symbolic approach as to whether the great harlot will manifest physically as one specific city or empire in the future or not.

As it was for the mark of the beast, this study takes a both/and approach and understands the great harlot to be ontological as well as historical.[91] The great harlot is the opposite reality and female figure to the bride of the Lamb in the book of Revelation. As Revelation's *great city*, Babylon is also the antithesis to the *holy city* (cf. Rev 11:2), the New Jerusalem. Babylon is both the *great* harlot and the *great* city, because she is the symbol of all harlotry, whether persons or cities/nations, in leading people astray into idolatry and in persecuting God's people. But she is, first and foremost, a comprehensive reality, a trans-historical model that encompasses all harlot persons, cities, and empires that have existed throughout history. This is why, as it was noted earlier, that John adjoins famous harlot cities/nations of history into this one city, namely the great city in Revelation 11:8. In Paul Minear's words,

---

55–127.

89. See Bauckham, *Climax*, 404 and Beale, *Revelation*, 869 for further information on the use of Daniel 7 in the portrayal of the first beast.

90. Beale, *Revelation*, 853–54; Fanning, *Revelation*, 440–41; Hoskins, *Revelation*, 308–9.

91. Beale in fact comes closest to this view. He understands the beast to be transtemporal since John applies features of Daniel's four beasts to this one beast. This one beast with seven heads thus signifies wicked kingdoms that likely span all of history. During John's time, this beast's embodiment, of course, was Rome. Beale, *Revelation*, 869. Hoskins views the great harlot in typological terms. She is the great antitype of the people and cities that were harlots in the OT. This study differs from Hoskins in that the great harlot is not simply the antitype, but in fact an ontological reality, a metanarrative that runs behind all people and harlot cities that defy God and persecute God's people throughout history. Hoskins, *Revelation*, 309, 361.

> There operated within his mind a 'symbolism of the centre', a perspective which accented simultaneously both the particularity of five cities and their common origin and destiny. For John, space functioned in such a way as to unite Sodom and Rome, not to separate them. Time did not separate the Pharaohs from the Roman emperors but brought them together. He perceived each separate place-time in terms of its content, i.e. that corporate historical action which 'filled it'. He discerned behind this action a 'trans-historical model' which linked each story to the others.[92]

Therefore, Babylon the great in Revelation is not just Rome. She is also not just a city or a certain system that is economic or religious that will arise in the future time of the end. She is all of these things. She is an ontological reality that has existed throughout history wherever and whenever the beast's influence in eliciting idolatry and persecution of God's people, namely harlotry, is manifested. During John's time, she was Rome. At the same time, she was also locally manifested as Jezebel in the Thyatira church (2:20–29). In the history of the past, she was manifested as the historical Babylon, Tyre, Sodom, Egypt, and even that part of Jerusalem which defied God and committed harlotry (11:8). John was able to bring all these historical persons and places together because he understood a common trans-historical and trans-temporal reality behind them. Just as he perceived an ontological identity and history of God's people and city (cf. Rev 11, 12, 21), he also perceived an ontological identity and history of the beast's harlot that is also a city (cf. Rev 11, 13, 17–18). This is Babylon the great that stands in great antithesis to the bride of the Lamb and to the New Jerusalem in Revelation. This study in turn will continue to proceed in discussing the fourth occurrence of the word σοφία in 17:9 with this ontological context of Babylon the great in mind.

After giving a detailed portrayal of the great harlot in Revelation 17:1–6, John then proceeds to give an extended interpretation of the woman in 17:7–18.[93] At the end of 17:6, John has come to marvel at the woman. This is apparently a wrong response, for the angel rebukes John for his marvel and moves on to tell him about the mystery (μυστήριον) of the woman and of the beast that carries her (17:7). It seems that John's marvel

---

92. Minear, "Ontology and Ecclesiology," 96.

93. Aune notes that the vision of Babylon the great is the only vision in Revelation with an extended interpretation. Aune, *Revelation 17–22*, 915.

had to do, at least in part, with Babylon's name of mystery (μυστήριον) that tells something about her nature (17:5). The angel knows that there is nothing marvelous about her and wants John to clearly know her nature and fate. In turn, John wants his readers to understand clearly as well in order not to elicit the same mistaken response of marvel that he once made.

And the great harlot's nature is closely associated with the first beast. Although she rides the beast and looks grandiose, she does not control the beast; the beast controls her. In fact, she is nothing but a pawn in the beast's scheme in deceiving the world into following it, and everything she is has to do with all that the beast aspires.[94] Thus, the angel begins with the mystery of the beast first and not with the mystery of the woman, for the beast is ultimately what is behind her.

The essence of the mystery of the beast, as the angel tells John in 17:8, is that the beast "was, and is not, and is about to come up from the abyss, and goes to destruction" (ἦν καὶ οὐκ ἔστιν καὶ μέλλει ἀναβαίνειν ἐκ τῆς ἀβύσσου καὶ εἰς ἀπώλειαν ὑπάγει). This is basically an imitation of God, for God is the one "who was, and who is, and who is coming" (ὁ ἦν καὶ ὁ ὢν καὶ ὁ ἐρχόμενος; 4:8). This designation for God is an interpretation of the divine name Yahweh and has to do with the eternal nature of God.[95] But the beast, no matter how close of an imitation of God it may be, will never be like him, for while God is the one "who is and who is coming," the beast is the one "who is not and who goes to destruction." The beast is not eternal and is in fact overwhelmingly inferior to God.[96]

The designation of the beast also parodies Christ. The phrase "was, and is not" imitates Jesus's death and resurrection.[97] This especially recalls Revelation 13:3 where the beast is said to have received a mortal wound but yet was healed. Revelation 13:3 goes on to say that the whole earth

---

94. The beast uses Babylon to make people of the earth to commit harlotry, namely getting them to worship the beast (17:2). The beast also uses Babylon to persecute God's people (11:7–8; 17:6), and apparently the beast even used her in crucifying Christ and in trying to display his seeming defeat (11:8). Thus, the two main aspirations of the beast (cf. Rev 13), namely getting people to commit idolatry and to persecute God's people, are also what Babylon is all about.

95. Bauckham, *Theology*, 28–30. Bauckham also helpfully notes that the third part of the formula is not the future form of the verb "to be" but the present participle of the verb "to come," and this shows that God's eternity is not something separated from his creation. God, in fact, chooses to relate to his creation with his eternity, and his future coming will bring all things to a proper fulfillment in his eternal nature.

96. Hoskins, *Revelation*, 326.

97. Osborne, *Revelation*, 615.

marveled after the beast, and the same response by the people is captured in 17:8. Revelation 17:8 further states that it is those whose names are not written in the book of life before the foundation of the world will marvel when they see the beast, which Revelation 13:8 portrays as worshipping the beast. This means that marveling has to do with following and worshipping the beast, and it is apt that the angel rebukes John for his marvel at the great harlot. No believer should marvel at anything or anyone that has to do with the beast. Again, the beast tries hard in imitating God and the Lamb, but it does not even come close to be one worthy of true worship. The beast's end is assured; it will go to destruction.

The mystery (μυστήριον) of the beast and of the woman is thus found to be ironically unremarkable. The beast and the woman are not at all marvelous; they are less than mundane. The reason for the earth dwellers' marvel at the beast is clear according to the angel. It is because the beast that they see is one that "was, and is not, and is to come" (ἦν καὶ οὐκ ἔστιν καὶ παρέσται; 17:8).[98] As the people see the beast's seeming death and resurrection, its godlike power and authority, and its ostensible perpetuity, they follow the beast in worship. But the irony of it all is that the beast "is to come" only to go to destruction. The people of the world whose names have not been written in the Lamb's book of life think that the beast "is to come" in glory, but the believers should make no mistake. It "is to come" only to be destroyed.

At this point, it is pertinent to define and describe the term "mystery" (μυστήριον) as it is used in Revelation in general and Revelation 17:7 in particular. The word μυστήριον occurs in four places in Revelation: 1:20, 10:7, 17:5, and 17:7. In all four, μυστήριον refers to something that was largely hidden but is being revealed.[99] The content of which is being revealed is eschatological in nature. This characteristic of mystery in Revelation, namely eschatological content that was hidden but is being revealed, matches the use of mystery in the book of Daniel 2 and 4.[100] While this study cannot delve into a detailed analysis of the use of

98. The participle of seeing (βλεπόντων) in 17:8 can be adverbial, modifying the verb "to marvel," or substantival, modifying "those who dwell on the earth." Either way, the participle ultimately has a causal sense in this context. The earth dwellers marvel because they see the beast. Beale, *Revelation*, 867.

99. Hence, μυστήριον involves content and its interpretation. Beale and Gladd, *Hidden but Now Revealed*, 43.

100. While there is a debate as to where the term μυστήριον in the NT should find its precedence from, many scholars, especially since Raymond Brown, have come to accept that the background lies in OT or Jewish apocalypticism, not in Greek or other

μυστήριον in Daniel and in Revelation, two observations must be made here. First, Gladd has argued convincingly that there is a close connection between mystery and wisdom in Daniel 2:17–23.[101] Daniel calls Nebuchadnezzar's dream and its interpretation a μυστήριον (רז in Hebrew; Dan 2:18), and later blesses God when God revealed the mystery to him, saying that God is the one who gives wisdom to the wise and reveals deep and hidden things to people (2:20–23). Hence, μυστήριον can be defined as revelation of God's wisdom,[102] and this is especially true of Revelation 17:7–18 where the term μυστήριον occurs in conjunction with σοφία. Second, Beale has noted persuasively that mystery involves not only a revelation of hidden eschatological content, but also the unexpected manner in which the eschatological content will be fulfilled.[103] Again, this is true of Revelation 17:7–18, for the mystery of the beast and of the woman also includes the fact that their demise is unexpected and ironic.

In short, in line with the usage in Daniel, Revelation uses the term mystery to show the eschatological reality of the beast and of the great harlot. First, the two will come to exert royal authority on this earth (17:9–12, 15, 18). Yet, the irony will be that the beast will only reign a short while (17:10, 12) and will then go to destruction (17:8, 11). The great harlot's demise is especially unexpected, for she will in fact be destroyed by her most trusted ally, the beast (17:16–17). What John wants to communicate to his readers is that those who have divine wisdom can understand this eschatological reality.

With this notion of mystery in mind, the current study shall proceed to analyze the rest of the angel's interpretation of the beast and of the harlot. As it was seen, the above analysis of Revelation 17:8 shows that the verse runs parallel to Revelation 13, especially verses 3 and 8.[104] This means that Revelation 17 shares affinities with Revelation 13, both dealing with the existence of the beast and its collaborators. If so, then it is likely that John has in mind the same ontological reality of the beast

---

pagan settings. For a history of research on the term μυστήριον, see Gladd, *Revealing the Mysterion*, 8–16. Within the Jewish background, the book of Revelation most likely utilizes the book of Daniel for the significance of the term μυστήριον. See Beale, *Use of Daniel*, 12–22. This is especially supported in light of the fact that Revelation alludes to Daniel quite frequently especially regards to the beast. Even the harlot's mysterious title, Babylon the great, finds partial allusion to Daniel 4. See also, Beale, *Revelation*, 858.

101. Gladd, *Revealing the Mysterion*, 26–31.
102. Gladd, *Revealing the Mysterion*, 31.
103. Beale, *Revelation*, 858. So also, Tabb, *All Things New*, 169.
104. So Aune, *Revelation 17–22*, 940.

σοφία IN REVELATION AS WISDOM FOR GOD'S FAITHFUL PEOPLE   95

in Revelation 17, and by extension also of the harlot, as he did in Revelation 13. Thus, the mystery of the beast and of the harlot in fact is not simply eschatological but ontological. Furthermore, since the same call of exhibiting wisdom is made in 17:9, as it was with 13:18, it is possible to expect John's call of wisdom to have the same function: to encourage the readers to perceive the true reality of the beast and of the harlot as to not be deceived by them.[105]

So, in 17:9, John calls his readers to exercise wisdom by saying, "Here is the mind that has wisdom" (ὧδε ὁ νοῦς ὁ ἔχων σοφίαν).[106] He goes on to state the interpretation of the angel, namely that the seven heads of the beast are seven mountains on which the harlot sits (17:9), and that the seven heads/mountains are seven kings, five of whom have fallen, one is, and the other has not yet come (17:10). But when the seventh king does come, whenever that may be, it is decreed (δεῖ) that he reigns for only a little while.[107] The very fact that the seven heads of the beast can represent both mountains and kings demonstrates that John is being multivalent in his portrayal of the mystery of the beast.[108] The reference to the seven mountains may allude to the idea that Rome was the beast's empire during John's day, since Rome was known as a city with seven hills.[109] But

---

105. Aune, *Revelation 17–22*, 941; Beale, *Revelation*, 725, 867; Osborne, *Revelation*, 617; Smalley, *Revelation*, 435.

106. Scholars differ on whether the call for wisdom in 17:9 refers to what John has said in preceding (especially 17:8) or what he says in following (especially 17:10–14), with the seeming majority opting for the former option. See Aune, *Revelation 17–22*, 941; Fanning, *Revelation*, 443; Osborne, *Revelation*, 617; Smalley, *Revelation*, 435. Beale, however, argues for both before and after. Beale, *Revelation*, 867. This writer agrees with Beale in that the call for wisdom refers to perceiving the whole content of Revelation 17. Revelation 17 has to do with the judgment of the great harlot. In telling of her judgment, John also tells of the mystery of the beast and of the harlot, which require revelation of God's wisdom to understand the mystery. The overall context suggests that Revelation 17, at the very least, should be taken as one unit, with the portrayal of the harlot and the subsequent interpretation of her mystery, which also involves the beast who holds close partnership with her, making up that unit. If so, then it is more likely that the call for wisdom in 17:9 has to do with understanding all of reality portrayed in Revelation 17, and not just a few verses.

107. The verb δεῖ implies divine sovereignty in setting out times and events according to the sovereign plan of God. Fanning, *Revelation*, 75, 445; Pokes, "δεῖ," *EDNT* 1:280.

108. So also, Keener, *Revelation*, 409.

109. Cf. Cicero, *Att.* 6.5; Pliny, *Nat.* 3.66–67. For further information on Rome as the city with seven hills, see Aune, *Revelation 17–22*, 944–45; Osborne, *Revelation*, 617; Swete, *Apocalypse*, 220.

the word "mountain" (ὄρος) can also connote strength in Revelation,[110] and coupled with the number seven which can mean completeness or perfection as being God's number, the reference to the seven mountains can also allude to the idea that the beast tries to equal his power to that of God by exhibiting his influence over the kings and kingdoms of the world. In turn, since the harlot sits on the seven mountains, this would mean that she is enthroned in Rome, or whichever kingdom the beast exerts his authority.

Either way, taken ontologically, the beast, through the harlot cities in history, has been wielding a wide net of influence over the people of the earth. Using Babylon's alluring appeal, the beast ultimately has been deceiving people into harlotry with her. The beast's deception is now enhanced by imitating the death and resurrection of Christ. Now more than ever, the people of the earth marvels at the beast's godlike power and authority, being exploited especially with the promise of financial success (cf. Rev 13:16–17; 18) offered by the great harlot. John envisions that this narrative will continue until the time of the end. However, those with divine wisdom should know that, not only will the final fate of the beast and of Babylon is destruction, but also that their time is short. So, John further states that the seven heads/mountains are also seven kings, five of whom have fallen, one is, and the other to come shall only remain for a short time (17:10). Whether the seven kings refer to Roman emperors or to world empires, John's point is clear.[111] Since five kings are already in

---

110. So Beale, *Revelation*, 868; Minear, *I Saw a New Earth*, 235–36.

111. For those who wish to understand historical antecedents to the seven kings as Roman emperors, see, for example, Charles, *Revelation*, vol. 2, 69–70; Fiorenza, *Revelation*, 97; Ford, *Revelation*, 289–90; Klauck, "Do They Never Come Back?," 690–98; Prigent, *L'Apocalypse*, 261; Rissi, *Time and History*, 80–82; Swete, *Apocalypse*, 220; Wilson, "The Problem," 598–99. As noted earlier, there are varying debates on how to count the seven Roman emperors. For a succinct summary of the varying proposals, see Aune, *Revelation 17-22*, 946–48 and Osborne, *Revelation*, 618–19. David May has recently proposed a new method in counting the seven Roman emperors using Roman imperial coins, arguing that the fallen five refers to Augustus, Tiberius, Claudius, Galba, and Vespasian, and that the current sixth refers to Titus and the future seventh as Domitian. May, "Counting Kings," 239–46. Nevertheless, May believes that the best way to account for the seven kings is not only figuring out the historical antecedents, but actually combining the historical and the symbolic together. For examples of those who argue for a symbolic understanding of the seven kings, see Beale, *Revelation*, 869–72; Beasley-Murray, *Revelation*, 257; Hoskins, *Revelation*, 327–31; Lohmeyer, *Offenbarung*, 143; Mounce, *Revelation*, 317; Smalley, *Revelation*, 435–36. Since this study argues that the beast is an ontological reality, the seven kings are understood to be both historical and eschatological. While the beast currently exerts its authority through the historical kings or kingdoms, whether they are Roman emperors or other empires, the point is

the past, with the sixth one currently exercising authority in the present, and since even the seventh king to come will only reign for a short time, the reign of the beast and of the harlot in fact has only a little time left.[112]

If the understanding of the beast's seven heads as discussed above is hard enough, scholars' quest for grasping the mystery of the beast is further complicated by what John says in 17:11. According to John, the beast that shall go to destruction is itself an eighth king, and yet belongs to the seven. Scholars are probably right in that they again see the beast's parody of the resurrection in this verse.[113] Just as Christ was raised on the first day of the week, which can be considered as the eighth day, so the beast will be raised and come as the eighth king in order to deceive and to reign on the earth.[114] But unlike Christ who reigns eternally, John makes it clear that the beast shall only reign a short while and go to destruction. However, the parody of Christ alone cannot account for John's expression that the beast is an eighth and yet belongs to the seven.

Those who understand the myth of Nero *redivivus* to be at work in this verse argue that the eighth emperor is the resurrected Nero, although they disagree over which emperor is in view. For instance, Klauck argues that the emperor Domitian is the Revelation's beast, the eighth king, in whose person Nero came back, but still reserves himself by stating, "Of course, more than a well-directed guess is not possible."[115] Klauck none-

---

that the beast's reign is close to coming to an end. After that, the beast shall simply be no more.

112. Yarbro Collins, *Cosmology and Eschatology*, 67.

113. For instance, Beale, *Revelation*, 875–76; Osborne, *Revelation*, 620–21.

114. Bauckham helpfully notes that while the beast's parody of Christ is found in both Revelation 13 and 17, there is one major difference: time. Revelation 13's parody is focused on the beast's scheme in the present age, whereas Revelation 17's parody is focused on the beast's scheme in the future, near the time of the end. In other words, the beast in Revelation 13 parodies Jesus's first coming, but the same beast in Revelation 17 parodies Jesus's second coming. In turn, those who focus on the Nero *redivivus* myth understand Revelation 13 and 17 as one and the same event, for they recognize only one event of Nero's return. But this does not seem to correspond well with the context of both chapters, for Revelation 13 seems to portray the work of the beast in the present, whereas Revelation 17 seems to portray its work in the future. Bauckham, *Climax*, 431–41, esp. 438–39. This study concurs with the sentiment of Bauckham in that the Nero myth was not at the foreground of John's mind as he penned Revelation 13 and 17 and that Revelation 13 does focus on the beast's scheme in the present age, while Revelation 17:7–14 especially focuses on the beast's scheme at the time of the end.

115. Klauck, "Do They Never Come Back?," 696. Far more confident than Klauck is Josef Schmidt. Schmidt has argued that the combination of words "mind" and "wisdom" in 17:9 has the same function and meaning as it did in 13:18, namely to figure out the historical referent (wisdom) by means of gematria (mind). Thus, to have a "mind,"

theless believes that the Nero myth faces a healthy future, and can account for Revelation's idea of the beast destroying the great harlot, namely the city of Rome, for according to the Nero myth, Nero does come back with his Parthian allies to destroy the city of Rome and to rule once again.[116] However, upon close examination, the data from the myth really does not match Revelation 17 closely as Klauck argues. Domitian did not take the throne by allying with Parthia, nor did he ever destroy the city of Rome. Hence, while Nero *redivivus* myth might have been on John's mind as he wrote Revelation, it is hard pressing to argue that it was the controlling factor in John's depiction of the beast. The Nero myth might be able to explain partially why the beast can be the eighth king and yet belong to the seven, since according to the myth, the original Nero can be counted among the five kings who have fallen and since Nero, or someone like him, will come back in the future as the eighth king, but it does not provide the entire picture.

Those who reject the view that Revelation 17:10–12 has to do with succession of Roman emperors argue instead that the passage refers to succession of kingdoms or empires throughout history.[117] This view, however, also cannot give adequate explanation as to why the beast can be the eighth king (or kingdom) and yet belong to the seven. For one, there is no agreement as to what definite qualifications are required to be an "empire." More importantly, it is unsure in what manner a certain empire in the past can be resurrected and rise to dominance in a current world already saturated with plentiful nations. Although one can argue

---

is to utilize gematria, and this will beget "wisdom," the historical referent. Schmidt then goes into a series of gematric calculations to arrive at *divus* as the name for the beast, which is in fact a blasphemous part of the human name, *divus Claudius*. For Schmidt, *divus Claudius* refers to Nero, the last Claudian, and while John did not really fear the return of a Claudian, he did fear the resurrection of the religious policy of the last Claudian, hence the warning in Revelation 17. Schmidt also argues that John was writing during the time of Vespasian, the sixth king, clearly evidenced from 17:10, and that John did not believe Titus would succeed the throne as the seventh king, hence the description of political turmoil when the seventh king comes in 17:11–12. But since Titus did succeed the throne without any political complications, this means that John was wrong. For Schmidt, the very fact that John was wrong about the future seventh king shows that he lived during the time of the sixth king, Vespasian. Schmidt, "Νους und Σοφια," 164–89. Schmidt's calculations are fanciful at best and his declarations do not do adequate justice to the internal evidence and context of Revelation. Schmidt's arguments thus should not be received wholeheartedly.

116. Klauck, "Do They Never Come Back?," 698.

117. See, for example, Auberlen, *The Prophecies of Daniel*, 264 and Maier, *Offenbarung*, 272.

that the seven kings refer to the fullness of worldly kingdoms throughout history, for the number seven can symbolize perfection, but this alone still cannot explain why the beast is the eighth king.[118] If the number seven means completeness, then the addition of the number eight seems redundant.

In turn, the two views presented above, namely the successive emperors view and the successive kingdoms view, largely argue that after the seventh king or kingdom comes an eighth. Instead, this study shall argue that the beast is *both* the seventh king and the eighth king.[119] The beast will be the final seventh king who will come at the time of the end to rule for a short while. At the same time, the beast can be considered the eighth king, since it was the authority behind its seven heads, namely the anti-God kings and kingdoms throughout history. This seems like the most natural way of understanding Revelation 17:11 in light of what this study has been advocating regarding ontology.

First of all, it is very logical to think that the beast would be the final seventh king who is to come. In 17:10, John states that only one king lies in the future, the seventh king. This is in keeping with the significance of the number seven in Revelation. As this study has shown, the number seven in Revelation is God's number that signifies perfection or completeness. The very reason why the beast has seven heads is to parody God and to rival his power. In other words, the beast's rule is summed up in its seven heads. If so, then it is natural to understand that the seventh head of the beast would be the final, climactic seventh king, with whom the rule of the beast throughout the ages would be complete.[120] This would be none other than the beast itself.

If the above reasoning is valid, then it makes good sense why John states that the beast is "of the seven" (ἐκ τῶν ἑπτά) in Revelation 17:11.[121]

118. For examples of scholars who argue for the idea of the fullness of secular kingdoms, see Ladd, *Revelation*, 229; Thomas, *Revelation 8–22*, 297; Walvoord, *Revelation*, 251–54.

119. The same argument is essentially captured in the article by Paul Hoskins. Hoskins, "Another Possible Interpretation," 86–102.

120. Hoskins, "Another Possible Interpretation," 97. Although Bauckham claims that the seven heads/kings represent the complete series of evil, he still entertains the possibility that the beast might be the eighth, "a kind of final excess of evil." But this seems inconsistent, for if seven kings represent *complete* series of evil, why is there a need for an *excess*? See, Bauckham, *Climax*, 405.

121. This writer takes the preposition ἐκ to be partitive. Thus, the beast is "one of the seven," precisely because it will manifest itself as the seventh head/king. Some others seem to take the preposition as source, thereby understanding that the beast somehow

Since the beast itself will come as the final, climactic seventh king, it is perfectly suitable to claim that the beast is "one of the seven." But John also states that the beast is an eighth (αὐτὸς ὄγδοός ἐστιν). To understand how the beast can be both the seventh and the eighth king, it is important first to note that the title of the beast in 17:11 has affinities with its title in 17:8. In 17:8, the beast's title is mentioned twice as one "who was, and is not, and is about to rise from the abyss, and departs to destruction" as well as one "who was, and is not, and is to come." The beast's title in 17:11 retains "who was, and is not" as well as "who departs to destruction," but the title about its future coming or arising has been changed into an elaboration that the beast is an eighth and is of the seven. In light of 17:10 where John claims that only the seventh king is left in the future as noted above, it makes all the more sense to understand that the beast shall be the seventh king itself. However, the very fact that John elaborates the beast's future coming as not only the seventh but also eighth suggests that he wants to express something about the full reality of the beast to his audience.

As this study has advocated repeatedly, John's statement that the beast is an eighth and is one of the seven is yet another evidence that John is understanding the beast as an ontological reality. While the beast itself will come as the final seventh king, it is more than simply the seventh. The beast is also the eighth king because it is the ultimate reality behind its seven heads. The story of the beast does not only lie in the future when it finally comes only to go to destruction. The beast's story has a past and a present, because it has been working behind its heads, five of which have fallen and one currently rules (17:10). Hoskins summarizes it well:

> The beast is more than just the seventh king, he is also an eighth king, because he is and has always been the power behind the seven kings, his seven heads (17:11). As the second member of the dragon's unholy trinity, he is greater than merely the sum of his heads.[122]

---

is "from the seven," meaning that it is either descending from the seven or is made up of the seven. See Beale, *Revelation*, 876; Hughes, *Revelation*, 186; Miguéns, "Los 'Reyes,'" 18. However, when thinking of the overall context of Revelation regarding the identity of the beast, it seems more likely that the seven kings receive their authority from the beast, rather than vice versa. In other words, the source of the beast's authority and power does not come from the seven kings; the seven kings instead derive their authority and power from the beast.

122. Hoskins, "Another Possible Interpretation," 102.

σοφία IN REVELATION AS WISDOM FOR GOD'S FAITHFUL PEOPLE 101

Thus, the beast is both the seventh and the eighth king. The beast has been ruling through its heads throughout history. As it was shown in Revelation 13, John describes the beast's appearance as an amalgamation of Daniel's four beasts, meaning that the beast was the one behind the kings and kingdoms in history that defied God and persecuted God's people. John wants to show that the story of the beast and its kingdom is ancient and has always rivaled the story of God's kingdom in history.[123] Hence, the beast can be considered an eighth king, for it was the power behind all anti-God kings and kingdoms throughout history. However, at the time of the end, the beast itself shall come as the final, climactic king to rule with its ten horns/kings for "one hour" (17:12–13).[124] Together they shall wage war against the Lamb, but the Lamb will conquer them (17:14). This implies that those who stand with the Lamb will also emerge victorious in the end, and John specifically describes them as "called, chosen, and faithful" (κλητοὶ καὶ ἐκλεκτοὶ καὶ πιστοί) in 17:14.

Thus, as John speaks about the mystery of the beast, he invokes wisdom on the part of the readers in order that they may not be deceived. Yes, the beast has been ruling throughout history through its heads. But its end is near; only the seventh king, the beast itself, is left to come in history. Even when it finally comes, its rule will be very short. It will try to wage war against the Lamb and his people, but it will ultimately be conquered and destroyed. The beast's end will be ironically futile and unimpressive. Believers who have divine wisdom should be able to see this truth and should not align themselves with the beast, no matter how successful and influential its authority may seem in the present. Instead, they must stand with the Lamb who will emerge victorious, knowing that they are called and chosen by God. They are also faithful, meaning that they must stay loyal to the Lamb. Loyalty to God is what is required to be the followers of the Lamb.

Those with divine wisdom should also see the truth about Babylon. After the mystery of the beast, John further tells of the mystery of the great harlot in 17:15–18. Her end is incredibly ironic and inexplicable.

---

123. Scholars frequently note that Revelation 12–14 contains the story of the conflict of the two kingdoms. See Bauckham, *Theology*, 88–94; Mounce, *Revelation*, 229; Osborne, *Revelation*, 454–55. Yarbro Collins has even termed Revelation 12 especially as "combat myth." Yarbro Collins, *The Combat Myth*, 116–45.

124. The "one hour" parallels John's statement in 17:10 that the beast shall remain only a little while whenever it comes. Thus, the expression suggests that the beast's rule as the final seventh king will be very short, which gives encouragement and comfort for the believers who are reading/hearing Revelation.

Although the harlot has great influence over the people of the world (17:15), the beast, together with the ten horns/kings, shall hate the harlot and shall destroy her when the time comes (17:16).[125] This ironic conclusion of the harlot proves two things. First, unlike the Lamb (cf. 1:5; 19:11), the beast is not faithful; it will consume its own allies whenever and however it sees fit.[126] Second, although the beast's hatred will be what destroys her, it will ultimately be God's judgement.[127] The beast will simply be fulfilling God's purpose (17:17). It is this woman, the great city that has dominion (βασιλείαν) over the kings of the earth (17:18), who shall meet a tragic end as the ten kings hand over their dominion (βασιλείαν) to the beast (17:17; cf. 17:13). This is betrayal at its finest; it is also a somber reminder that no earthly dominion is absolute. True dominion lies with the Lamb, for he is "Lord of lords and King of kings" (17:14).

Wise believers who understand the soon-to-be-finished reality of the beast and of the harlot should take comfort in knowing that their end is near and should not partake in their demise by associating with them. They may look grandiose and invincible with their influence over

---

125. Literally translated, the beast and the ten horns are said to make the harlot desolate and naked, to devour her flesh, and to burn her up in fire. Some feminist scholars argue that Revelation 17:16 portrays a rape of a woman's body. For these feminist critiques, see Pippin, *Death and Desire*, 57–58; Selvidge, "Powerful and Powerless Women," 164. However, Barbara Rossing has argued convincingly that the vocabulary used to describe the harlot's destruction in 17:16 actually has to do with a city being besieged rather than a rape of a woman. The word "desolate" (ἐρημόω) is a specific term of destruction for cities, not of a woman's body. This is especially clear in Revelation 18:17 where the same word is used by the merchants to bemoan the devastation of Babylon's wealth, not of her physical body. While the word "naked" (γυμνός) is not specific like the word "desolate" and is more indeterminate, the context of Revelation makes clear that John is not using the word in sexual terms. In Revelation 3:17–18, the same word is used to bring accusation to the Laodicean church for being proud of their wealth. There, the word does not have sexual connotations, nor is it gender specific. In the same way, the word "naked" in 17:16 also does not seem to have sexual connotations, for the context of Revelation 18 makes clear that the focus is the city of Babylon being stripped of its economic and political status. Thus, it would be unwise to dwell upon the idea of mistreatment of woman in Revelation 17, for then, one will miss out on what John is trying to communicate in the overall context of the fall of Babylon in Revelation 17–18 and of the entire book of Revelation. For Rossing's arguments, see Rossing, *Two Cities*, 88–97.

126. Hoskins, *Revelation*, 335. Hoskins helpfully notes that the same pattern of harlot cities' triumph and demise is captured in the OT. This shows how the beast has not been faithful throughout history, and it will be the same for the great harlot in the time of the end. Hoskins, *Revelation*, 333–34.

127. The idea of the harlot burning up in fire is closely connected with God's judgment (cf. 8:7; 18:8).

the kings and peoples of the earth, but their true reality is deceitful. They are not faithful either. In fact, the story of the beast is marked by betrayal. The beast has used harlot cities throughout history to spread its net of influence over the people of the earth, but the relationship never lasts forever. The beast has betrayed time and time again its harlot cities and has left a trail of destruction. John envisions that this story of betrayal and destruction will continue up until the time of the end. The beast promises great things to those who worship it, but John's vision of the judgment of the great harlot shows that the beast is not trustworthy. The beast, even though it itself will come, will only reign for a short while and shall go to destruction by the Lamb. The beast's and the harlot's grandeur shall turn out to be utterly ghastly when the short time that they have runs out.

This is the mystery of the beast and of the harlot that John wants his readers to realize by exercising wisdom. Like 13:18, the readers must call to mind the ultimate reality already disclosed to them through the throne room visions of Revelation 5 and 7, that the Lamb has already inscribed victory and that the sovereign rule and worship of the Lamb and of God shall ensue forever, unlike the beast and Babylon.[128] John also wants his readers to act rightly upon their realization. This is clearly captured in Revelation 18:4–8. A call is made from heaven, "Come out of her, my people so that you may not take part in her sins and so that you may not receive her plagues" (18:4). Whatever the specifics John had in mind with the call to come out, one thing is clear: God's people must not associate with Babylon as do the kings and people of the earth.[129] God's people must not partake in the sinful ways of Babylon and commit harlotry with her, all to grow rich from her power,[130] for if they do so they will be participating in her sins, which will ultimately lead to partaking in the judgment of God when it finally comes to her (18:1–3, 5, 7–8). Thus, this is an issue of boundaries between two cities, either the beast's city, Babylon or God's

128. Cf. Stuckenbruck, "Disclosure of Wisdom," 356, 358.

129. This study has no space for getting to the specifics of what this call to come out in 18:4 entail. Obviously, the call does not simply mean packing everything and leaving Babylon to go into the mountains to live physically separated. God commands the believers to be the light of the world and to be witnesses in the world (cf. Rev 11). The call, rather, means that the believers must not participate in the sinful ways of Babylon and must not commit harlotry with her. Hoskins, *Revelation*, 342; Smalley, *Revelation*, 447. This refusal to go along with the sinful ways of Babylon is comprehensive, and includes economic, social, political, and spiritual resistance. Richard, *Apocalypse*, 135.

130. Mathews is correct in seeing that Babylon's reasons for demise especially emphasize her sin of deception by the promise of wealth and economic success she can provide. Mathews, *Riches, Poverty, and the Faithful*, 204.

city, the New Jerusalem, and how one responds to the commands of God or the Lamb such as recorded in 18:4 decides which boundary one falls in.[131] In other words, showing loyalty to God by obeying his commands evidences that one belongs in the New Jerusalem; showing loyalty to the beast by committing harlotry with the great harlot evidences that one belongs in Babylon. It is either-or; there is no in-between.

But there is more. Not only do God's people must come out of Babylon, they must also "pay her back" and "repay her double," as well as to "mix a double portion" and to "give her a like measure of torment and mourning" (18:6–7).[132] These four imperatives, along with the imperative to "come out" in 18:4, present a challenge to interpreters. Initial reading of these commands seems to suggest that John is envisioning here not of passive resistance, but of active rebellion. Yet, the overall context of Revelation seems to suggest more of a passive form of resisting.[133] Hence, scholars who want to avoid the idea of God's people being involved actively in the punishment of Babylon argue that the four imperatives found in Revelation 18:6–7 are not directed toward God's people as it was in 18:4, but to other addresses such as heavenly beings.[134] However, the immediate context of Revelation 18:4–8 does not show any evidence of

---

131. Minear, "Ontology and Ecclesiology," 102. Minear goes on to say that "This is why the exhortations of the prophet are so strategic for understanding his visions."

132. It is noted that the doubling language in 18:6 could also be translated as "duplicate." In this way, the meaning is to render a fitting equivalent of punishment to Babylon. See Kline, "Double Trouble," 171–79.

133. Revelation 11 especially seems quite clear on this. The two witnesses, while their prophesying is a torment to those who dwell on the earth, nonetheless are killed by the beast. There does not seem to be any hint about the witnesses performing a violent retaliation which gets them killed in the process. After all, even John was on the island of Patmos in tribulation because of his witness of the gospel (cf. 1:2; 1:9), and the context does not suggest any other reason, such as active rebellion, other than John's faithful proclamation of the word. Even the letters to the seven churches (Rev 2–3) emphasize faithfully holding onto the promise of Jesus despite suffering, to endure and to repent, and do not call the churches to be involved in any type of violence or rebellion. See also, Yarbro Collins, "The Political Perspective," 241–56. Middleton, however, argues instead that martyrdom is an act of violent resistance, for the martyr is directly participating in the divine act of violent judgment. Middleton, *The Violence of the Lamb*. Still, Revelation does not seem to envision Christians actively performing and inciting direct violence against others.

134. For instance, Swete claims that "The Command is addressed of course not to the 'people of God,' but to the ministers of Divine justice, the yet untrained and unknown forces which the Seer saw gathering for the work of destruction." Swete, *Apocalypse*, 229. For others who entertain the possibility of heavenly beings as the addresses of Rev 18:6–7, see Bauckham, "The Economic Critique," 50 and Yarbro Collins, "Revelation 18," 193.

any shift in the addressee, and the natural reading of the passage suggests that it is God's people who are to "pay Babylon back."[135]

However, the challenge to understand how God's people can participate in the judgment of Babylon without engaging in active vengeance can be explained quite simply. It is that the believers are to participate by remaining faithful to God. As this study has indicated, God's people are to conquer Satan by the blood of the Lamb and by the word of their testimony (cf. Rev 12:11). This is not a conquering by military vengeance, but a conquering by faithfulness to God and to the Lamb even to the point of death.[136] Yarbro Collins is basically correct when she argued that Revelation uses holy war traditions to promote a model of passive resistance where God's people participate in the judgment synergistically in martyrdom.[137] Bauckham also argues alongside Yarbro Collins that the people of God wins Revelation's holy war through their suffering witness and martyrdom, although he understands a more active role of martyrdom in the holy war than Yarbro Collins.[138]

This participation in God's judgment is clearly captured in Revelation 18:20, where God's people are called to rejoice over Babylon's destruction because "God has judged *your* judgment (τὸ κρίμα ὑμῶν) against her."[139] Apparently, God's people have been crying to God for judgment on those who shed their blood (6:10), and the demise of Babylon who shed the blood of the saints (17:6) is God's answer to their cry. Not only will it be God's judgment, but 18:20 envisages that it will also be the judgment of God's people against Babylon. This is economically possible since God's people participate in the judgment, hence it is God's judgment (18:8) as well as their judgment (18:20), and it will be because of the persecutions Babylon has enacted upon God's people for their faithfulness to God. Understood in this manner, the commands such as to "pay Babylon back" or to "mix a double portion" in 18:6–7 suggest

---

135. Elliott, "Who Is Addressed," 101.

136. So also Klassen, "Vengeance," 305–9.

137. Yarbro Collins, "Political Perspective," 241–56.

138. Bauckham understands that Revelation substitutes armed revolt with faithful witness to the point of martyrdom in its depiction of the holy war. As believers follow the Lamb in the path of suffering witness, they participate in his victory over evil. Bauckham, "Christian War Scroll," 17–40.

139. This writer considers the genitive ὑμῶν to be subjective genitive rather than objective genitive. See Hoskins, *Revelation*, 352 and Fanning, *Revelation*, 467 for the subjective genitive view. See Osborne, *Revelation*, 655 for the objective genitive understanding.

that God's people are to participate in the judgment of Babylon by being faithful witnesses to the point of martyrdom. It is as if each persecution of God's people is heaping God's anger for judgment upon Babylon, and the saints' faithfulness to God which leads to suffering and persecution will be what ultimately "pays her back."[140] At the time of the eschaton, when Babylon, the beast's city that lured people into harlotry with her and into persecuting God's saints with her, is finally judged, God's faithful people shall further perform a prophetic role of serving that judgment to her.[141]

In the end, the proleptic dirges of Revelation 18 serve two purposes: (1) to announce God's judgment upon Babylon's evil and (2) to call the audience to separate from Babylon.[142] First, Babylon is judged because of her pride and wealth (18:7), as well as because of her sorcery and persecution (18:23–24).[143] The three main dirges, namely the laments of the kings of the earth (18:9–10), of the merchants (18:11–17a) and of the sailors (18:17b–19) especially emphasize mourning over Babylon's wealth, showing that wealth is one of the main tools that the beast, via Babylon, uses to deceive people of the earth into following it.[144] Importantly, one

---

140. Elliott, "Who Is Addressed," 112.

141. Rossing understands the imperatives of 18:4–7 to be influenced by the tradition of Jeremiah, especially Jeremiah 25:17. This is surely correct, for the idea and language of the cup of judgment that Babylon drinks, which is quite unique to Jeremiah, is prevalent in Revelation 17–18. If so, then John is also understanding a prophetic role of God's people where they will serve that judgment to her, namely "mixing a double portion in the cup she mixed" and "giving her a like measure" (18:6–7), just like Jeremiah who was commanded by God to make all the nations to whom God sent him to drink from the cup of wrath (Jer 25:15–17). Rossing, *Two Cities*, 124–25.

142. Rossing, *Two Cities*, 113. Rossing is again correct in understanding that the laments in Revelation 18 is proleptic since they are foretelling the destruction of Rome *before* its destruction. This is in contrary to Royalty who understands the laments as epideictic, as speeches upon the event of the destruction of the city. Royalty, *Streets of Heaven*, 197–98. While this writer also understands the dirges of Revelation 18 to be proleptic, this writer however understands them to be foretelling not simply the destruction of Rome, but the destruction of the eschatological city of the beast that will occur at the time of the end. In any case, the proleptic nature of the laments shows that this is deliberative rhetoric, to foretell Babylon's judgment and to assure the readers that it is coming. If so, it is all the more urgent for the audience to take the call to "come out" seriously.

143. Among these, sorcery as the reason for Babylon's judgment is interesting. Sorcery, by nature, involves deception. It also draws power from a source other than God. With sorcery, Babylon fools people into thinking that she is more powerful than she really is and gets them to commit harlotry with her. In this way of deception, Babylon is clearly connected with Satan, the beast, and the false prophet (12:9; 13:14). Hoskins, *Revelation*, 356.

144. Mathews notes that while the kings of the earth have already been introduced

σοφία IN REVELATION AS WISDOM FOR GOD'S FAITHFUL PEOPLE 107

should not fail to notice that in these laments, there is no remorse or repentance over participating in Babylon's sins by the people of the earth. They simply mourn over the loss of the opportunity of wealth and luxury that Babylon once offered. Thus, there is only the announcement of God's judgment on Babylon; no opportunity for repentance is offered.

Second, from the laments, the believers on the other hand should realize the vainness of chasing after the affluence the kingdom of the beast offers. The people of the earth are so blinded, they cannot look beyond Babylon and toward God even after her destruction.[145] They know that God had judged her, or at least the kings of the earth do (18:10), but their lament is mostly about their current loss of wealth. It appears they do not care whether the beast or Babylon had deceived them or whether it was wrong to have followed the ways of the beast. This shocking response by the people of the earth is intended to produce resentment over pursuing after the affluence that the beast offers and alleviating the tension between choosing God's way or the beast's way on the part of God's people.[146] Indeed, the believers better "come out" of Babylon, or they will be looking like the people of the earth lamenting.

---

in Revelation, the merchants have gone unnoticed until Revelation 18. The fact that the merchants get an extended discourse in Revelation 18 as they are introduced is very significant, and this evidences that the issue of earthly wealth is important for John. Moreover, John portrays the merchants as desiring affluence, which blind them to God's coming judgment. For Mathews, the portrayal of the lament of the merchants is one evidence among others he presents that his understanding of the theology of wealth in Revelation is basically correct, namely that the faithfulness to God is incompatible with affluence in the present age. Mathews, *Riches, Poverty, and the Faithful*, 204–18.

145. One should not miss the connection here with the Laodicea letter (3:14–22). Christ rebukes the Laodicean church for not realizing that they are blind, and this blindness has to do with the believers thinking that they are rich and do not need anything (3:17). It is those who turn to Christ who shall be truly rich and who shall be able to "buy" (ἀγοράζω) from him an eye salve in order to truly see (3:18). In other words, those who belong to Christ are not going to be blind, but they will be able to see the reality properly.

146. Cf. Yarbro Collins, *Crisis and Catharsis*. Yarbro Collins argues that by portraying the demise of Babylon and the lament of the people, John produced catharsis for the audience, thus relieving the tension caused by the perceived crisis under Roman rule that the audience faced. This encouraged the audience to "come out" of Babylon all the more, which Yarbro Collins understands to be a radical withdrawal from the social, political, and economic sphere. While this writer agrees with Yarbro Collins' understanding that Revelation 18 has the effect of encouraging the believers to disassociate from Babylon, this writer does not believe that John is advocating the kind of radical separatism that Yarbro Collins understands. Even Yarbro Collins is unclear as to what this radical separatism looks like, although she admits that it does not mean total disconnection, the kind espoused by the Qumran community. Whereas the believers

Instead of lamenting, the believers must rejoice over God's judgment against Babylon (18:20). Babylon shall soon be "no more" (18:21–23).[147] When God's judgment finally comes to her, there shall be crescendos of hallelujahs in heaven (19:1–10). Whereas Babylon, the beast's city is judged and destroyed, the bride, God's city will stand ready (19:7–8). The saints who stay faithful to God to the end will be the ones who will be invited to the marriage supper of the Lamb (19:9).

In the meantime, God's people should heed God's call to disassociate from the sinful ways of Babylon. They must remain faithful to God despite persecutions wrought about by Babylon, despite her alluring appeals of success in exchange for committing harlotry with her. John's call for wisdom in 17:9 is specifically intended to exhort God's people to "see" the entirety and the sureness of this truth, to "see" through the deception of the beast and Babylon. Those with wisdom will indeed stay loyal to God with endurance to the very end as urged in the book of Revelation. As Yarbro Collins states, "There is a divine plan, all is in God's control, and the outcome will be advantageous to those loyal to God's will as revealed in the book."[148]

SUMMARY AND CONCLUSION

This chapter has sought to understand how John's call for wisdom functions within the two most challenging passages in Revelation: 13:18 and 17:9. In both passages, the function is the same: to call the readers to see the true reality of the beast and of his kingdom, to not be deceived by the beast, and to remain absolutely faithful to God despite the temptations to defect and despite the persecutions the beast may exert. The call for wisdom also reminds the readers of the ultimate reality of the throne room, that it is God and the Lamb who are forever victorious and whose kingdom will last forever. Wisdom is thus more than simply figuring out the number of the beast or the identity of Babylon. It is about knowing reality as a whole that has been disclosed in Revelation and discerning the pattern and allegiance of one's life accordingly.

---

must separate from the sinful ways of Babylon, but this does not necessarily entail that the believers sever all ties in the social and economic sphere. If then God's people would not be witnesses of Christ in this world.

147. The repeated phrase of "no more" (οὐ μὴ ... ἔτι) in these verses especially show the utter and complete destruction of Babylon.

148. Yarbro Collins, *Cosmology and Eschatology*, 137.

The beast, through the second beast and through Babylon, has been deceiving the people of the world throughout history into worshipping it via the appeals to its power and to success. Yet, those who belong to God and to the Lamb have access to the divine wisdom. With this divine wisdom, they must look past the deception and see the true reality of the beast's kingdom, that it can never compare with the grandeur of God's kingdom, that it only has a little time left, and that the beast's kingdom, along with the promise of successful living it gives, shall all be destroyed in the end when God judges it. Those with divine wisdom do not only understand this reality but also exhibit right behavior accordingly. They must "come out" of Babylon and stay completely loyal to God no matter what. John wants his audience to truly understand this ontological reality and to live faithfully to God, and has thus invoked σοφία in strategic places to garner their understanding and to elicit their loyalty. In the end, the uses of the word σοφία in Revelation function to exhort the readers toward a certain ethical behavior, a life of unwavering fidelity to Christ.

CHAPTER 4

Two-Women Motif outside of Revelation

As it was noted briefly in chapter 3 of this study, one major wisdom motif John utilizes in the book of Revelation is the two-women motif. John's use of the two-women motif has been especially brought to light by Barbara Rossing's seminal work, *The Choice between Two Cities*. In this work, Rossing mainly argues that John's characterization of the great harlot on one hand and of the bride on the other is largely influenced by a wisdom tradition known as the two-women topos. She is especially helpful in understanding the contrast between the great harlot and the bride through her careful analysis of Revelation 17–20.

This study's purpose in turn is not to prove that the two-women motif exists in Revelation. Rossing has already done that. Rather, this chapter and the next seek to build upon Rossing's work and to analyze more comprehensively how John evokes this sapiential motif throughout the book of Revelation. While Rossing discussed in detail the great harlot (Rev 17–18) and the bride (Rev 19–20) in terms of the two-women motif, she spent little amount of attention regarding other women figures in Revelation, namely Jezebel of Revelation 2 and the radiant woman of Revelation 12.[1] This study argues that Revelation utilizes the two-women

1. The main reason for this seems to be because Rossing does not believe the radiant woman of Rev 12 and the bride of Rev 19–20 to be identical. Similarly, while Rossing sees some connection between Jezebel of Rev 2 and the great harlot of Rev 17–18, she does not discuss in detail their relationship since she believes anti-polemic against Rome is the main emphasis in Revelation, of which Jezebel does not belong. For Rossing, the great harlot is the anti-Rome polemic, whereas Jezebel is a mere anti-false-prophet polemic. Within the anti-imperial polemic of Revelation, only the great

topos not so narrowly as Rossing understands, as anti-imperial polemic (hence only the great harlot and the bride are to be included), but much more comprehensively as anti-Satan or anti-beast polemic. This is because John's worldview in Revelation is deeply spiritual, with the beast's kingdom being constantly on the move to persecute, to deceive, and to tempt people into following the beast rather than God. In this understanding, the two-women topos can be expanded to include Jezebel and the radiant woman.

Furthermore, while others have noted the connections and contrasts between these women, such as between Jezebel and the great harlot and between the radiant woman and the great harlot, they have not really done so in terms of the two-women motif.[2] This chapter will look at how the extrabiblical and biblical literatures use the two-women topos, apart from Revelation, and the next chapter will analyze all of the women figures in Revelation through the lens of the two-women motif. This examination will produce a more robust picture of how this motif functions in the book. In the end, this study will argue that John utilizes the two-women motif in characterizing the women figures in Revelation in order to encourage his readers to shun the evil woman (i.e., Jezebel, the great harlot) and to embrace the virtuous woman (i.e., the radiant woman, the bride). Only by doing so, will John's audience stay loyal to God resolutely until the end. It will also be recognized that John moreover gives an added twist to the two-women motif. Not only are his readers encouraged to embrace the virtuous woman, but they should in fact be the embodiment of the virtuous woman herself.

---

harlot and the bride operate as the two-women topos, and Rossing thus focuses only on these two women figures. Rossing, *Two Cities*, 11–12. This study however disagrees with Rossing in that it argues that the four women figures are indeed connected closely. The anti-imperial polemic in Revelation is not only political, social, economical, and religious as Rossing understands, but is itself deeply spiritual. In other words, the anti-imperial polemic is not the main emphasis John wants to tackle in Revelation; rather, the primary focus of Revelation is to encourage the believers to stay faithful to God in all areas of life against the schemes of the enemy, namely Satan and the beast. Thus, Revelation's main emphasis is anti-Satan or anti-beast, not simply anti-Rome. Viewed within this spiritual worldview that John paints in Revelation, the four women figures are indeed connected. The two-women topos in Revelation does not simply operate as anti-Rome polemic, but as anti-Satan or anti-beast polemic.

2. For an example of the former, see Robinson, "Sexual Immorality Language." For an example of the latter, Bruns, "Contrasted Women," 459–63.

EXTRABIBLICAL BACKGROUND

Before delving into how the two-women motif functions in Revelation, it is necessary first to look at how other literature in the ANE and around John's time uses the same motif.[3] This will aid in comparing John's usage to other usages, in recognizing what features of the motif are the same and what features are different. This section will analyze the extrabiblical literature in which the two-women motif is employed in terms of elements set forth by Rossing, namely (1) the personification of an either/or choice as two women figures, (2) the visual description of two women, (3) the moral contrast between the two women figures, and (4) the ethical appeal to embrace the one and renounce the other.[4]

Graeco-Roman Literature

The oldest known material that furnishes the two-women topos is the Heracles story. Philosopher Prodicus in the sixth century BC is thought to have produced the original version, of which Xenophon procured an extended quotation in his *Memorabilia* (4th cen BC). In this story, Heracles is seen to have come to a mature age, a stage in life where he must choose which path to take, whether of virtue or of vice (Xenophon, *Mem.* 2.1.21). He is met with two women, one who is fair and the other attractive (Xenophon, *Mem.* 2.1.22). The fair woman is described as having a body adorned with purity (καθαρειότητι), having eyes with modesty (αἰδοῖ), prudent (σωφροσύνῃ) in appearance, and being clothed in white (λευκῇ). The attractive woman is described as being plump and soft, having her skin adorned so that she can appear as white and pink, exaggerated in appearance, having eyes with openness, and having dressed so as to display her charms.

When the two women see Heracles, the attractive woman outruns the fair woman to get to Heracles first, to woo him into following her. She promises an easy-going life of enjoyment and pleasantries, and when asked by Heracles what her name is, she gives up her name as "Vice" (Κακία; Xenophon, *Mem.* 2.1.23–26). Meanwhile the fair woman also reaches Heracles and attempts to persuade him into following her instead.

---

3. According to Rossing, "The story of two women, one good and one evil, each seeking to woo a young man, is a favorite cliché in ancient literature." Rossing, *Two Cities*, 17.

4. Rossing, *Two Cities*, 18.

The fair lady, whose name turns out to be "Virtue" (Ἀρετή), promises not a life of pleasure, but a life of truth where right deeds and hard effort bring honor (Xenophon, *Mem.* 2.1.27–28). The two women then proceed to give further reasons as to why Heracles should not follow the other, with Virtue's argument being the lengthy and thorough one (Xenophon, *Mem.* 2.1.29–33). Virtue's charge against Vice is significant: "You force lust when there is no need, by all kinds of tricks and by using men as women" (Xenophon, *Mem.* 2.1.30).[5] The moral of the story as cited in *Memorabilia* is obvious: one must also think about one's life and choose one's path wisely (Xenophon, *Mem.* 2.1.34).

This story of two women who signify two paths, one of virtue and the other of vice, became a stock moral fable in the ancient world, as evident from the numerous citations by other authors in antiquity.[6] According to Rossing, by combining rhetorical techniques of personification, comparison, and visual description, the ethical charge that the two-women topos brings is especially effective.[7] As such, the two-women topos has been modified by the ancients to treat a variety of topics. The basic framework remained intact, namely two personified women, their visual contrast, and the exhortation to follow one and reject the other, but the two women's identities were changed to serve other purposes.[8]

Cicero, *De Officiis*

In *De Officiis*, Cicero explicitly mentions the Heracles story found in the words of Prodicus in Xenophon, as he discusses the choice of careers people make in life (*Off.* 1.32.118).[9] In his discussion regarding careers, Cicero claims that most people do not have such an experience that Heracles had in life, in which he had two women or two paths to

---

5. The English translation of *Memorabilia* is from Xenophon, *Memorabilia. Oeconomicus. Symposium. Apology.*, trans. E. C. Marchant and O. J. Todd, LCL 168 (Cambridge, MA: Harvard University Press, 2013).

6. Rossing, *Two Cities*, 19. Rossing gives many examples of writers who cited the Heracles story such as Dio Chrysostom, *Or.* 1.66–84; Lucian, *Bis acc.* 21; Julian, *Or.* 2.57; Philo, *Sacr.* 20–35; Justin Martyr, *2 Apol.* 11; Clement of Alexandria, *Paed.* 2.10.110; Cicero, *Off.* 1.32.118; Quintillian, *Inst. orat.* 9.2.36.

7. Rossing, *Two Cities*, 21–25.

8. Rossing, *Two Cities*, 25.

9. Cicero's *De Officiis* is usually dated to be from 44 BC, written in the last year before his death. The version of the work used in this study is Cicero, *De Officiis*, trans. Walter Miller, LCL 30 (New York: Macmillan, 1913).

contemplate about and to choose from since young age. Rather, people make immature choices early in their lives concerning their careers before clearly understanding what may be best for them (*Off.* 1.32.117), and they are usually influenced by the teachings of their parents and by the popular opinions of the day (*Off.* 1.32.118). Cicero thus changes the two women's identities from choices of morality to choices of careers to suit his discussion. In doing so, Cicero does not elaborate upon the two-women topos, but makes use of it in a short and concise manner.

Tabula of Cebes

A pseudonymous text from the first century AD called *Tabula of Cebes* also makes use of the Heracles story to a significant extent.[10] Alleged to be written by Cebes of Thebes, this work seems to have been well known in antiquity as several writers such as Tertullian (*Praescr.* 39) and Lucian of Samosata (*Merc. cond.* 42) do mention it in their works. The *Tabula of Cebes* captures a dialogue between a young narrator and an old man regarding the meaning of a painting found on a certain votive tablet at the entrance of the shrine of Cronus. The painting pictures a mountain with a series of gateways that one must pass through in order to get to the top. There are various female figures who are poised along the way. According to Fitzgerald and White, the underlying structure of the contents of the dialogue " . . . is really nothing more than an expanded form of the Prodicus myth."[11]

The dialogue begins as the young narrator asks the old man for an explanation of the fable captured on the painting. The old man in turn proceeds with a caution before giving the young narrator his explanation (*Ceb. Tab.* 3.1). The caution is simple but instructive; one must pay attention and understand the fable to be wise (φρόνιμοι) and happy (εὐδαίμονες), but if one does not, one will become foolish, unhappy, sullen, and stupid (ἄφρονες, κακοδαίμονες, πικροὶ, ἀμαθεῖς). With this the explanation commences. The mountainous scenery, as it turns out, is "Life" (Βίος), and the large crowd standing at the gate are those who are about to enter Life (*Ceb. Tab.* 4.2). There is also a throne alongside the gate on which a woman sits who has a cup in her hand and who has

---

10. Fitzgerald and White argue that first century AD is a likely date for the *Tabula of Cebes*. Fitzgerald and White, *The Tabula of Cebes*, 3–4.

11. Fitzgerald and White, *The Tabula of Cebes*, 14.

a persuasive appearance (*Ceb. Tab.* 5.1). She is called "Deceit" (Ἀπάτη) who leads all man astray, and everyone drinks from her cup of ignorance and error as they enter Life without exception (*Ceb. Tab.* 5.2—6.1).

Once in, the people are greeted by various female figures who promise them good life, and they are led by these women as they wander aimlessly in Life. One significant female figure that everyone wants to associate with is Fortune (Τύχη) who gives and takes away possessions such as wealth and glory from men (*Ceb. Tab.* 7.1—8.4). In the next enclosure after the second gate, there are adorned women who are called Incontinence, Profligacy, Covetousness, and Flattery who seek to persuade men to accept them so that they may trick the men and take whatever they have received from Fortune (*Ceb. Tab.* 9). The result of spending time with these women is disgraceful slavery in which people end up committing all kinds of injurious acts (*Ceb. Tab.* 9.3–4). Once the men are in this stage, they are delivered to Retribution (Τιμωρία) and are punished to spend the rest of their lives in total unhappiness unless Repentance (Μετάνοια) happens to encounter them (*Ceb. Tab.* 10).

It is interesting that Repentance is described to be making her own choice (ἐκ προαιρέσεως) as to whom she wants to encounter (*Ceb. Tab.* 9.4). Nonetheless, to the one she makes herself known, a chance at true life is given. Repentance introduces the man to Opinion, who in turn leads the man to true Education. If the man welcomes Opinion, he is saved and can reach happy life; if the man does not, then he is led astray once again by False Education (*Ceb. Tab.* 11.2). The road to true Education may be difficult, but once a man reaches there, he is purified of all the evils he received throughout his journey in Life and is led to the Virtues (*Ceb. Tab.* 19). Contrary to the evil women who were adorned, the Virtues are simple and are not artificially adorned, yet attractive (*Ceb. Tab.* 20.2). When the Virtues have received the man, these women lead the man to the ultimate end, the highest citadel in Life where their mother Happiness (Εὐδαιμονία) dwells (*Ceb. Tab.* 21). By reaching Happiness, the man finally receives power to become truly happy and blessed; he is victorious (*Ceb. Tab.* 23.4—24.1).

In turn, the fable of the *Tabula of Cebes* is intended to teach a lesson in life: one must not be deceived by the evils in life, as represented by the malicious women, but must attain a virtuous life of true happiness, as represented by the noble women. The lesson is thus the same as that of the Heracles myth. Yet, the original myth is made much more elaborate and complex. The choice between virtue and vice is not so simple as if it occurs so clearly in life and once for all time. It occurs throughout one's life and one must continuously navigate past the deception and strive to reach the end goal. To communicate this truth, the *Tabula of Cebes* uses multiple women figures and not just two women to represent virtue or vice. Still, all the women figures do belong to either camp, and each woman represents one aspect from either the virtues or vices.

Lucian of Samosata, *The Dream or Lucian's Career*

Written in the second century AD, Lucian recounts how he came to choose his literary career in his autobiographical work, *The Dream*. His family wanted Lucian to be apprenticed as a sculptor, but his apparent dislike of the trade made him run away from home. Sometime later after his success as a literary composer, he was returning home, and he probably wrote this work in order to provide a fanciful account of the reason why he chose a literary career over sculpting to his family.[12] To do this, Lucian uses the two-women topos from the Prodicus myth. He claims that in his dream, he saw "Two women (Δύο γυναῖκες), taking me by the hands, were each trying to drag me toward herself with might and main" (*Somn.* 6). One was like a workman with unkept hair; the other was fair and dignified with nice dress. Each persuaded Lucian to choose her over the other and he ended up choosing Education (the fair lady) over Sculptor (*Somn.* 7–14), thus his reason for leaving home to pursue a literary career. In doing so, Lucian changes the two women's identities from choices of morality to choices of careers just like Cicero. But Lucian's Sculptor, representing the bad choice, is not attractive as the bad woman in other works. His purpose in telling this dream was also that "... those who are young may take the better direction and cleave to education" (*Somn.* 18).

Silius Italicus, *Punica*

An orator named Silius Italicus makes use of the Prodicus myth to encourage a military campaign in his Latin epic poem about the second War with Carthage, *Punica*.[13] He tells a story of a young soldier named Scipio, troubled in heart whether to take the position of a general to lead the already decimated army to war in Spain (*Punica.* 15.1–19). As Scipio

12. Harmon, *Lucian*, 3:213.
13. Punica was written at the end of the first century, during the reign of Domitian.

contemplates, he is met by two women, Virtue and Pleasure, who fly down from the sky (*Punica*. 15.20–22). Silius also details the two women's appearance, with Pleasure being attractively adorned with purple and gold while Virtue being modest in snow-white robe (*Punica*. 15.23–31). Pleasure speaks first and tries to persuade Scipio to not go to war: "Take my advice, and cease to fight against danger and expose your life to the storm of clashing weapons. Unless you abandon the worship of her, stern Virtue will bid you dash right through battle and flame" (*Punica*. 15.38–41).[14] Virtue reacts and is able to finally persuade Scipio to go to war (*Punica*. 15.68–123). For Silius, the two-women topos works as two choices, to war (Virtue) or not to war (Pleasure), with the former winning in the end.

Aelius Aristides, *Orations*

Aelius Aristides is another orator who makes use of the Prodicus myth, but in the opposite manner to that of Silius Italicus. Written between 147–149 AD, Aelius' *Oration* 24, named *To the Rhodians, on Concord*, purports to urge the Rhodians to choose Concord (ὁμόνοια), not Strife (στάσις). In doing so, Aristides personifies and casts Concord as the stereotypical good woman and Strife as the stereotypical evil woman. Aristides' description of Concord is as expected: charming and harmonious in every detail (Aristides, *Or*. 24.44). On the opposite end, however, the description of Strife is not as expected. Instead of being attractively adorned, she looks like her true self: bitter, gloomy, and atrocious (Aristides, *Or*. 24.44). Aristides' argument from his portrayal of the two women is simple: "Indeed, it is worth all things for all men to pursue earnestly for concord (καὶ μὴν ἅπασι μὲν ἀνθρώποις τοῦ παντὸς ἄξιον σπουδάζειν ὑπὲρ τῆς ὁμονοίας)."[15] Aristides' use of the two-women topos thus comes out to be quite the opposite of Silius as he changes and flips the two women's identities. The good woman now represents concord, not strife as it was for Silius, and in doing so, choosing the good woman reaps the opposite choice and outcome to that of Silius.

---

14. The English translation is from Silius Italicus, *Punica*, vol. 2, trans. J. D. Duff, LCL 278 (Cambridge, MA: Harvard University Press, 1934).

15. *Or*. 24.45. The English translation is the author's own. For the work in Greek, see Keil, *Aelii Aristidis Smyrnaei*.

Dio Chrysostom, *Discourses*

Dio Chrysostom is another figure who uses the Heracles story for political means, but in a much more elaborate way than Silius or Aristides. In his *First Discourse on Kingship*, written for emperor Trajan at the end of the first century, Dio tells his version of the Heracles story which he claims to have received from an old lady (*Or.* 1.53–56). One day, when Zeus saw that young Heracles was fit to be a noble ruler, he sent Hermes to instruct him (*Or.* 1.65). Hermes in turn took Heracles to a mountain path that divided into two roads to two peaks, one called Peak Royal and the other called Peak Tyrannous (*Or.* 1.66–67). Heracles then was able to tour both peaks, starting with Peak Royal. On Peak Royal was a woman enthroned, beautiful, radiant, and clothed in white (*Or.* 1.70), whose name turned out to be Lady Royalty (Βασιλεία; *Or.* 1.73). She was also surrounded by other virtuous women such as Justice, Civic Order, and Peace. On Peak Tyrannous, another woman was enthroned, Lady Tyranny (Τυραννίδα), with whom men were infatuated, who counterfeited Royalty and was adorned with gold, ivory, and every color, but in reality whose throne was flimsy and whose scowl was ugly and forbidding (*Or.* 1.78–80). She likewise was surrounded by other women such as Cruelty, Insolence, and Lawlessness, but they were obviously not like those who surrounded Royalty. After the tour of both peaks, Hermes asks Heracles to make a choice and his choice is apparent: Royalty "whom I admire and love (θαυμάζω καὶ ἀγαπῶ)" (Or. 1.83).[16] Dio's elaboration of the Heracles story is very detailed in the description of the two women, and he seeks to persuade Trajan to be Heracles in choosing the path of benevolent ruler (Lady Royalty).

While not a two-women topos per se, Dio further captures the danger of evil women in his two other discourses, namely the *Fourth Discourse on Kingship* and the *Fifth Discourse on Kingship* (also known as the *Libyan Myth*). In his *Fourth Discourse*, Dio casts himself in the role of Diogenes and speaks boldly to Alexander the Great (Trajan): "Therefore, O perverse man, do not attempt to be king before you have attained to wisdom" (*Or.* 4.70). With this, Dio mentions the Libyan myth and advises Trajan that a good king must especially prevail over women who are "extremely dangerous and savage," meaning that Trajan must not

---

16. The English translation used for Dio Chrysostom's *Discourses* is from Dio Chrysostom, *Discourses 1–11*, trans. J. W. Cohoon, LCL 257 (Cambridge, MA: Harvard University Press, 1932).

succumb to the sweetness of evil desires to be a wise and noble king (*Or.* 4.73). This Libyan myth is told in detail in Dio's *Fifth Discourse*. He makes it clear that the myth has to do with human passion (ἐπιθυμία) as he tells the story (*Or.* 5.4). In Libya, there lived a "dangerous and savage" species of animal, with the face and the upper body of a beautiful woman and with the lower body of a snake, which lured men with a passionate desire for sexuality (*Or.* 5.5–14). When men become infatuated with them and come near, these beasts (θηρία) grab them, kill them, and eat them (*Or.* 5.15). Likewise, Dio argues, men must resist their beast-like passions that lure them with guile (*Or.* 5.16–17).

Justin Martyr, *Second Apology*

Justin Martyr is one among the early Christian writers who utilized the two-women topos. Written to defend Christians from unjust persecutions under prefect Urbicus, Justin's *Second Apology* is addressed to the Roman senate and even to the emperor, although there are numerous instructions for Christians on how to live one's life faithfully. In this work, Justin invokes the Prodicus myth mentioned by Xenophon to praise the virtue of the Christians and their courage in the face of death. He links those who are persecuting Christians with the woman figure Vice to form his argument. Justin states:

> For Vice, veiling her actions in the beauties which properly belong to Virtue and are genuine [though only by imitation of incorruptible things, for she possesses and can produce nothing which is incorruptible], enslaves groveling people, clothing Virtue in the ugliness which properly belongs to herself.[17]

The implication thus is that the persecutors of Christians do so because they have been deceived with false virtues. However, the true virtues, although they may look ragged as the woman figure Virtue, are possessed by the Christians, and they endure the persecutions without fear because they know God who is just sees everything (*2 Apol.* 11–12). Justin's presentation of the two-women topos is close to that of the book of Revelation in that Vice deceives and enslaves the people of the world while Virtue belongs with the Christians. Yet the two women are neither

---

17. Justin Martyr, *2 Apol.* 11. The English translation is from Barnard, *St. Justin Martyr*, 82.

elaborated nor developed in a detailed, complex manner as that of Revelation.

Clement of Alexandria, *Paedagogus*

Clement of Alexandria is another early Christian writer who made use of the Prodicus myth. As he teaches on the subject of modest dressing in his *Paedagogus*, Clement enlists Prodicus' delineation of Virtue and Vice, along with other scriptural supports, to admonish Christian women to dress with decency (*Paed.* 2.10.110). Wanton women dress like Vice, in superfluous attires that are brightened up with color. On the contrary, Virtue is pictured as " . . . standing simply, clothed in white, pure: this is virtue, adorned only with her modesty (that is the way fidelity ought to be, virtuous and modest)."[18] Thus, Clement takes the Prodicus myth and specifically emphasizes the two women's clothing in order to teach women to dress themselves modestly. Nothing other than the images of Virtue and Vice from the myth are used in doing so.

Maximus of Tyre, *Philosophical Orations*

Second century orator Maximus of Tyre uses the Prodicus myth to build his own myth by changing the identities of the two women in his *Oration 14* on friendship and flattery.[19] To do so, Maximus first summarizes the original Prodicus myth, noting the two women's appearance and clothing (*Or.* 14.1). Then he states, "Come then, let us too fashion a myth of our own, with a pair of roads and a good man and, in place of Virtue and Pleasure as guides, the Friend and the Flatterer" (*Or.* 14.1). In his own modification of the original myth, Maximus retains the idea of contrasting appearance and clothing worn by the two figures, as well as their alluring call, especially by the Flatterer, to the passerby. Maximus claims that "But if our man is a man like Heracles, he will choose the true guide, the Friend, just as Heracles chose Virtue" (*Or.* 14.2). Maximus evidences

---

18. The English translation is from Clement of Alexandria, *Christ the Educator*, trans. Simon P. Wood, The Fathers of the Church 23 (New York: Fathers of the Church, Inc., 1954).

19. The actual manuscript title of this oration is τίσιν χωριστέον τὸν κόλακα τοῦ φίλου (By What Criteria Should One Distinguish Flatterer from Friend?). Maximus of Tyre, *The Philosophical Orations*, 124. The English translation used in this study is also from this work.

well how one can take the two-women topos and modify it to suit one's ethical needs. It is also important to note that Maximus has retained the description of contrasting appearance of the two figures, their alluring call, and the representation of two women as two paths. These are the essential features of the two-women topos that make it especially effective.

The *Shepherd* of Hermas, *Ninth Similitude*

Arguably the most popular Christian book in the second and third centuries, the *Shepherd*, basically a collection of revelations by a prophet named Hermas, utilizes the two-women topos in critiquing and exhorting Christians to remain holy in the *Ninth Similitude*.[20] In this ninth parable, Hermas is guided by an angel and sees an enormous white rock with a gate and twelve glorious virgins who stand around the gate, "clothed in linen tunics and beautifully belted" (Herm. *Sim.* 9.2.1–4). These virgins help the men to build a tower upon the rock by carrying the stones for them (Herm. *Sim.* 9.3—9.5). However, when the lord of the tower comes and examines the tower, he does not deem it fit, and the men continue to build the tower with the help of the virgins (Herm. *Sim.* 9.6—9.9.4). Perplexingly, another group of twelve women are introduced, "extremely beautiful in appearance, dressed in black, belted, with uncovered shoulders and loose hair," who are ordered to take the stones away from the tower (Herm. *Sim.* 9.9.5–6).

The angel later explains the vision to Hermas. The white rock is the Son of God (Herm. *Sim.* 9.12), the tower is the church, and the virgins are holy spirits (Herm. *Sim.* 9.13.1–2). The other group of women represent evil desires who seduce men from working on the tower, and those who follow these women are to be cast out from the house of God (Herm. *Sim.* 9.13.8–9), for the church of God must be clean (Herm. *Sim.* 9.18.3–4). Hermas' warning to these unfaithful Christians is telling: "But if they do not repent, they are already handed over to the women who take away their lives" (Herm. *Sim.* 9.21.4; cf. 9.20.4; 9.22.4; 9.26.6–8). On the other hand, the exhortation is clear: Christians must repent and remain faithful to God, holy and pure, so that they may truly live. The *Ninth Similitude* is quite similar to the book of Revelation in terms of its ethical appeal via

---

20. Ehrman, *The Apostolic Fathers*, vol. 2, 162. The English translation used in this study is from this work as well.

the use of the two-women topos. Perhaps it was influenced by Revelation, which is likely an earlier work than the *Shepherd*.

Philostratus, *Vita Apollonii*

Philostratus also makes use of the Heracles story as he recounts the life of Apollonius of Tyana in his work, *Vita Apollonii*.[21] At a certain point in Apollonius' life, he goes to Egypt to interview the naked sages there to inquire of their wisdom (*Vit. Apoll.* 6.10). As Apollonius discourses with Thespesion, the eldest of the naked sages, the latter uses the Heracles story to defend the superiority of the wisdom of the naked sages from that of the wisdom of the Indians. Philostratus observes as he narrates this event that Thespesion did this because Apollonius had a high view of the wisdom of the Indians, which Thespesion wanted to discredit. So Thespesion mentions the Heracles story by Prodicus and likens the wisdom of the Indians with Vice and the wisdom of the naked sages with Virtue, thereby changing the identity of the two women to be distinct philosophical systems or wisdoms. In the process, the two women's attires are specifically emphasized, to promote the idea that while the wisdom of the Indians may look fancy like Vice, in truth it is lacking, and while the wisdom of the naked sages may look ragged like Virtue, in truth it is a superior wisdom. In a way, this presentation of the women's clothing and its implication is similar to that of Justin Martyr.

Conclusion

The above examples of works show the familiarity and popularity of the two-women topos in antiquity. By changing the identities of two women, and by further elaborating upon the topos, writers and orators were able to bring about their intended argument or exhortation. Important to note is that, in all the above examples, the motive for utilizing the two-women topos is ethical; people have used it to show which is the proper way to live and to exhort others to follow suit. In doing so, they have made four features of the two-women topos to stand out.

---

21. *Vita Apollonii* was written in the third century AD and recounts the life of a charismatic teacher from the first century. The version of the work used in this study is Philostratus, *The Life of Apollonius of Tyana: Books 5–8*, vol. 2, trans. Christopher P. Jones, LCL 17 (Cambridge, MA: Harvard University Press, 2005).

First, the contrasting identities/realities are personified as two women. Characteristics (happiness, education, concord, strife, etc.) and even philosophical systems (e.g., Philostratus) are personified, and although the writers use multiple women figures as they deem necessary (e.g., *Tabula of Cebes*), these figures still belong in either camp, either good or evil woman. Second, the two women's appearance and clothing are emphasized and contrasted, with the good woman usually described as simple, pure, and in white and the evil woman described as adorned, excessive, and in multiple colors, to show their true or deceptive nature.[22] Third, the two women usually try to persuade men, and this is true especially of the evil woman. Fourth, there is an exhortation to choose between the two women, whether implicitly or explicitly.[23] In turn, these four features do appear in the book of Revelation.

Before turning to the Jewish literature, one final caveat must be made. This study does not intend to argue that John has borrowed the two-women topos from the Heracles story popular during his time. Since the Heracles story was a stock topos, John would have made use of the topos without directly and consciously borrowing from the Heracles story. Better yet, as this study will argue along the way, John has likely borrowed the two-women topos from Proverbs 1–9 and has combined another feature from the Old Testament, namely the personification of cities as women, to bring about his own unique rendition of two women who represent two paths as well as two cities/kingdoms. This uniqueness of John makes his presentation of the two women topos all the more pivotal and complex. In any case, John's rendition of the two-women topos does exhibit all the familiar traits of the stock two-women topos popular during his time.

Second Temple Jewish Literature

This section examines the Jewish literatures around John's time that utilize the two-women topos. Since Revelation is steeped in Jewish materials, understanding how Revelation is similar and different in using the

---

22. It is true that Lucian's bad woman in his work, *The Dream*, is not attractive, but this may be because Lucian did not need to cast her as being deceptive. She simply represents a bad choice.

23. Rossing argues that, among the four features, the first and the fourth elements are essential to the two-women topos. Rossing, *Two Cities*, 37–38.

two-women topos from the Jewish literature will further aid in recognizing how the topos is operating and is functioning in Revelation.

Sirach

Sirach is a summary of the wisdom teachings of its proposed author, "Jesus son of Eleazar son of Sirach of Jerusalem" (Sir 50:27).[24] This would make the book's date to be around 180 BC.[25] Ben Sira begins by giving a high place to wisdom, that God has created her before all things from eternity (1:1–10), that those who love God shall receive wisdom (1:10), and that to fear God is the beginning of wisdom (1:14–20), a statement reminiscent of Proverbs. Wisdom's divine qualities are also praised, that she teaches her children, that life, joy, and glory are available to those who come to her, and that those who serve her are actually ministering to the Holy One himself (4:11–14). For these reasons, Ben Sira calls his students to come to her with all their soul and might (6:26; cf. 14:20–27).

Wisdom is in fact a mother and a bride who will not fail whoever comes to her (15:1–6). Wisdom's extraordinary status is especially communicated in Sirach 24 as wisdom praises and glorifies herself with the highest honor. In the closing section of Sirach, Ben Sira confesses that he pursued after wisdom like a lover since he was young and, more importantly, before he decided his path in life (51:13–21, esp. v. 13). In turn, he concludes by exhorting his students that they also must decide their path in following wisdom.

On the other hand, one woman figure who represents the opposite reality to wisdom is conspicuously missing in Sirach. No woman other than wisdom is personified and is given a voice and a role in Sirach. Rather, Ben Sira simply warns his students not to associate with wily women, lest they be seduced and be plunged into destruction (9:1–9). He further states, "I would rather live with a lion and a dragon that live with an evil woman" (25:16).

Ben Sira thus portrays wisdom as a perfect companion people should strive after. Yet, it is important to note that Ben Sira also equates wisdom with the Torah (24:23–24; cf. 33:2–3; 39:1–11). This is why wisdom is said to have found a dwelling place in Israel via the command of

---

24. The English translation used in this study is from Michael D. Coogan, ed., *The New Oxford Annotated Apocrypha*, 4th ed. (New York: Oxford University Press, 2010).

25. Ben Sira's grandson translated the original Hebrew work into Greek in Egypt around 117 BC.

God (24:7–8). In effect, it follows that to have wisdom, one must obey and keep the law of God. Sirach does not have a feature where two women are rivaled in wooing people to follow one and forsake the other. While wisdom and other wily women may be contrasted, the contrast is meager at best. In Sirach, wisdom simply reigns supreme and there is no life that is worth living outside the confines of wisdom.

Wisdom of Solomon

Wisdom of Solomon is similar to Sirach in that it also elevates wisdom to a high status that no evil women figures can match.[26] Written between late first century BC and early first century AD, the author, who claims to be king Solomon, praises the quality of wisdom in this work of encomium and exhortatory discourse.[27] From the beginning, the author seems to personify wisdom as if she has a mind of its own, namely that she will not dwell with deceitful and sinful people (1:4) and that she is a kindly spirit who will not free blasphemers (1:6). Her personification is made explicit in 6:12–16 as wisdom is portrayed as a lover who one must seek and desire. In fact, in line with the good woman from the two-women topos, wisdom is described as going around and seeking those who are worthy of her, and once found, "she graciously appears to them in their paths" (6:16). Loving her will lead to immortality and a kingdom (6:17–21), and the author expresses his desire to make known what wisdom is and how she came to be to his readers (6:22).

Thus, in a major section on wisdom (6:22—10:21), the author, in the implied role of king Solomon, describes his life of quest for wisdom and the benefits wisdom can bestow upon the one who finds her. Here, wisdom receives divine qualities similar to those of Sirach. Wisdom is the fashioner of all things (7:22); she is holy, all-powerful, overseeing all things (7:22–24). She is indeed the breath of the power of God (7:25) and the reflection of eternal light (7:26). Against wisdom, "evil does not prevail" (7:30). For Solomon, she is a bride whom Solomon sought and desired earnestly since youth (8:2—9:18). Wisdom protects (10:1), rescues (10:6), and prospers the righteous man (11:1). Therefore, Wisdom of Solomon is akin to Sirach in that wisdom is described as a supreme bride one must pursue after. Only wisdom as the good woman figure is

---

26. Rossing, *Two Cities*, 46.
27. Coogan, *Apocrypha*, 69. The English translation is also from this work.

emphasized in the work, and it is as if no other woman figure deserves a mention.

Philo of Alexandria

Philo (c. 20 BC–50 AD) was a Jewish philosopher who was steeped in Greek philosophy. He is known for using allegory in his attempt in integrating Greek philosophy with Scripture. In several places of his works, Philo utilizes the two-women topos in discussing biblical themes and characters. In *De cherubim*, Philo argues that virtuous and wise men from Scripture such as Abraham, Isaac, Jacob, and Moses are not described in the Bible as knowing women, and this means that their spouses were not actually women, but "are in reality virtues" (*Cher.* 41).[28] In *De congressu eruditionis gratia*, he likewise allegorizes the biblical characters, Sarah and Hagar, as virtue and education which wise Abraham had for his wife and concubine respectively (*Congr.* 23). The pair of Leah and Rachel, as well as Bilhah and Zilpah, are also allegorized as virtues which men must take in order to be virtuous until the end (*Congr.* 25–33).[29] In *De fuga et inventione*, Philo explains that the calling of Jacob to flee from Esau to the house of Bethuel, his mother (Rebecca)'s father, is a calling to go and find a safe haven in the house of wisdom from life's troubles (*Fug.* 42–50). Thus, Philo interprets Bethuel, Rebecca's father, as Wisdom (*Fug.* 51–52), and this effectively makes Rebecca to be Wisdom's daughter and the command to Jacob to find a wife from the house of Bethuel to be a command to find virtues connected to Wisdom.[30]

The most extensive use of the two-women topos by Philo is found in *De sacrificiis Abelis et Caini* (*The Sacrifices of Abel and Cain*). Here, Philo contrasts Cain and Abel as two contrasting realities, vice and virtue respectively (*Sacr.* 1–10). He states, "Thus vice will carry off the honour of precedence in time, virtue the precedence in repute and honour and good name" (*Sacr.* 16).[31] To explain further the contrasting realities of virtue and vice, Philo summons a familiar two-women topos:

> For each of us is mated with two wives, who hate and loathe each other, and they fill the house of the soul with their jealous

---

28. Philo, *Philo in Ten Volumes*, vol. 2.
29. Philo, *Philo in Ten Volumes*, vol. 4.
30. Philo, *Philo in Ten Volumes*, vol. 5.
31. The English translation is from Philo, *Philo in Ten Volumes*, vol. 2.

contentions. And one of these we love, because we find her winning and gentle, and we think her our nearest and dearest. Her name is pleasure. The other we hate; we think her rough, ungentle, crabbed and our bitter enemy. Her name is virtue (*Sacr.* 20).

Philo also describes the appearance of the two women in line with the two-women topos. Pleasure is like a harlot (πόρνης), her posture is prideful, her face and hair are decorated, and her clothing is extravagant with flowers, ornaments, and jewels (*Sacr.* 21). She also has her closest friends with her, all eleven of them who represent other vices (*Sacr.* 22). Pleasure promises blessings and happiness to people, provided that "if you will dwell with me" (*Sacr.* 22–25).

After Pleasure's presentation comes Virtue's warning call, fearing that people may be seduced by Pleasure. Virtue is like a free-born citizen, her person is serene and modest, her clothing is plain, and her adornment is of good sense and virtue (*Sacr.* 26). She is also accompanied by a large company of other women figures who represent other virtues (*Sacr.* 27). She advises that Pleasure's promises are deceptive, and if one chooses her gifts, then one will basically become a fulfillment of immorality (*Sacr.* 28–32). Quite interesting is the fact that Virtue lists a long list of vice that will befall on the person who chooses Pleasure in doing so. On the other hand, while there may be toil and hardship in choosing Virtue (*Sacr.* 35), one will truly be blessed.

Although Philo does not specify the source of his two-women topos, whether it be from Proverbs 1–9 or the Heracles story, he is nonetheless an important example of a writer who integrated the two-women motif with Scripture. Personification of the two women, the contrasting description of their appearance and clothing, their alluring appeal, and the exhortation to choose virtue over vice are all present. Also interesting is the fact that the two-women motif is not described in terms of one's life journey or path. Rather, it is described in terms of living or dwelling with the women, and this is much more in line with Proverbs than it is with the original Prodicus myth.

Qumran Dead Sea Scrolls

Among Second Temple Jewish literature, Qumran's Dead Sea Scrolls provide a significant piece of evidence regarding the use of the two-women topos. This is because the Scrolls offer "a crucial link for understanding how a two-women *topos* that originated in wisdom setting could flourish also in an apocalyptic setting."[32] This is important, since the book of Revelation also utilizes the two-women topos and it is an apocalypse. Comparing Revelation with the Dead Sea Scrolls then would prove fruitful.

The main texts for the two women figures at Qumran are 4Q184 (The Wiles of the Wicked Woman) and 4Q185 (A Sapiential Work). Both texts can be dated to the first century BC and both draw heavily on Proverbs 1–9.[33] In 4Q184, the main subject is the evil woman. The text begins by introducing her as utterly corrupt in every way:

> She [. . .] utters futility and in [. . .]. She is always looking for depravities, [and] whets the word[s of her mouth, . . .] and implies insult, and is [bu]sy leading the community astray with non[sense.] Her heart weaves traps, her kidneys n[ets. Her eyes] have been defiled with evil, her hands grasp the pit, her feet descend to act wickedly and to walk in crimes. [. . .] (are) foundations of darkness, and there are plenty of sins in her wings. Her [. . .] (are) night gloom and her clothes [(are) . . .] Her veils are shadows of the twilight and her adornments diseases of the pit. Her beds {her couches} are couches of the pit, [. . .] (are) deep ditches. Her lodgings are couches of darkness and in the heart of the nigh[t] are her tents. In the foundations of gloom she sets up her dwelling, and camps in the tents of silence, in the midst of eternal fire.[34]

The evil woman's clothing and adornments are also mentioned, but instead of describing what she wears, the text simply claims that her clothes are twilight and her adornments diseases of the pit. Her dwelling place is especially brought to light, namely that it is of darkness, death, and the underworld. The wisdom psalm moreover highlights the evil woman's seductive nature:

> In the city squares she veils herself, and in the gates of the village she stations herself, and there is no-one who can ke[ep her] from (her) incessant [fornicat]ng. Her eyes scan hither and thither, and she raises her eyebrows impudently, to spot a just

---

32. Rossing, *Two Cities*, 41. Emphasis original. See Collins, "Dead Sea Sect," 25–51 for the argument that the Qumran community's setting was apocalyptic.

33. Crawford, "Lady Wisdom and Dame Folly," 360.

34. 4Q184, lines 1–7. The English translations of the Dead Sea Scrolls are taken from Florentino García Martínez and Eibert J.C. Tigchelaar, eds., *The Dead Sea Scrolls: Study Edition*, 2 vols (Leiden: Brill, 1997).

ma[n] and overtake him, and a [no]ble man, to trip him up; the upright to turn (from) the path. (lines 12–14)

Thus, the evil woman of 4Q184 is a harlot who must be avoided, and the psalm warns its readers not to "possess" or "hold" her (cf. lines 8–11). The description of the evil woman's snare of men to lead them astray at the city gates especially reminds of Proverbs 7:10–12 and 9:13–18. Yet she seems to be more than the simple "strange woman" from Proverbs 1–9; 4Q184's evil woman is more than human, more cosmic in scope, and seems to represent evil in embodied form.[35] As such, she is closely connected with the underworld in 4Q184. Although this psalm does not present a woman figure who is the counterpart to the evil woman, the stark warning not to associate with the evil woman suggests that there is still an implicit exhortation to choose the right woman over the other in line with the two-women topos.[36]

In 4Q185, a clear counterpart to the evil woman of 4Q184 is presented, namely Wisdom. In 2:8–15, Wisdom is praised with macarisms:

> Blessed is the man to whom she has been given, the son of ma[n ...] ... The wicked persons should not brag, saying: She has not been given to me and not [... God has given her] to Israel, and like a [g]ood gift, gives her. He has saved all his people, but has destroyed those who hate [his wi]sdo[m ...] Whoever glories in her should say: one should take her as po[ssess]ion and find her and ho[ld] fast to her and get her as an inheritance; with her [there are long d]ays, and greasy bones, and a happy heart, rich[es and honour.] His mercies are her youth, and [his] salvation [...] ... Blessed is the man who does her, does not deceive her, does not slander against [her,] does not [with a] fraudulent [spir]it seek her, nor holds fast to her with flatteries. (lines 8–14)

Here, Wisdom is described as a personified female figure whom the people of Israel must possess in order to live a blessed life ordained by God. The blessed nature of finding Wisdom especially recalls Proverbs 3:13–18. However, there are two crucial differences. Whereas Wisdom of Proverbs is very much active in seeking out people to follow her, Wisdom of 4Q185 seems to be very passive. "She is given by God, sought by humans, and possession of her brings rewards, but, at least in the material

---

35. Crawford, "Lady Wisdom and Dame Folly," 360–62; Quick, "The Hidden Body," 235.

36. So also, Harrington, *Wisdom Texts from Qumran*, 34–35.

we have, she does not act."[37] Furthermore, Wisdom of 4Q185 is closely associated with the Torah, hence the emphasis that she was given by God to Israel. This connection of Wisdom to the Torah was also stressed by Ben Sira.

Still, it is important to note that Wisdom is personified as a woman figure in 4Q185 despite her passiveness. Whereas Wisdom's human-like features such as her body parts, posture, and clothing are missing, unlike the description of the evil woman in 4Q184, the readers are nonetheless exhorted to "possess her" to be blessed. This is the opposite of the evil woman in 4Q184 where it states that those who "possess her" will descend to the netherworld (line 11). Thus, when 4Q184 and 4Q185 are taken together, a clearer picture emerges. In line with the stock two-women topos, readers are exhorted to choose Wisdom and forsake the evil woman.

In addition to 4Q184 and 4Q185, there are few other works among the Dead Sea Scrolls that mention personified female figures. 4Q525 (4QBeatitudes), dated to be from the second half of the first century BC, is a wisdom literature that also contains eschatological language.[38] First, frag. 2 ii 1–7 states thus:

> Blessed are those who adhere to her laws, and do not adhere to perverted paths. Bles[sed] are those who rejoice in her, and do not burst out in paths of folly. Blesse are those who search for her with pure hands, and do not pursue her with a treacherous [heart.] Blessed is the man who attains Wisdom, and walks in the law of the Most High, and directs his heart to her ways, and is constrained by her discipline and alwa[ys] takes pleasure in her punishments; and does not forsake her in the hardship of [his] wrong[s,] and in the time of anguish does not abandon her, and does not forget her [in the days of] terror, and in the distress of his soul does not loathe [her.] For he always thinks of her, [and places her] in front of his eyes in order not to walk on paths [. . .]

Wisdom is also mentioned in frag. 5:

---

37. Crawford, "Lady Wisdom and Dame Folly," 363.

38. 4Q525's editor, Émile Puech notes that 4Q525's vocabulary is close to that of the canonical book of Proverbs. Puech, "4Q525," 82. Elisa Uusimäki further claims that 4Q525's Proverbs-like wisdom is combined with eschatological language. Uusimäki, *Turning Proverbs towards Torah*, 180–81. The alternate name of 4QBeatitudes comes from the repeated use of macarisms and recalls Psalm 1 and Matthew 5.

Those who fear God keep her paths and walk in [...] her laws, and do not reject her reproaches. Those who understand will acquire [...] Those who walk in perfection keep away from evil and do not reject her admonishments [...] they bear. The skilful dig her paths, and in her depths they [...] they watch. Those who love God humble themselves in her and in [...]

In these passages, Wisdom is clearly personified as a female figure, and there is also a repeated pronouncement that those who possess her are blessed. This parallels 4Q185's portrayal of Wisdom and the macarisms that are associated with her. Also, like 4Q185, Wisdom in 4Q525 seems very passive and is clearly connected with the Torah (2 ii 4).[39] Furthermore, 4Q525 frag. 15 (par. 5Q16 1–2 + 5) contains mentions of the evil woman's house. While the evil woman herself does not seem to be directly mentioned in the discovered fragments of 4Q525 currently in possession, scholars such as Tigchelaar have noticed that fragment 15 parallels the description of the house of the evil woman in 4Q184.[40] This means that 4Q525 frag. 15 also emphasizes the nature of the house of the evil woman, who can also be called Folly, just like 4Q184, namely that her house reeks of death of the underworld. If so, then 4Q525 likewise has the implicit exhortation to the readers to choose Wisdom and to shun Folly. To choose Folly would be eschatologically catastrophic.

Two of the noncanonical psalms in the Great Psalms Scroll from Cave 11 (11Q5 or 11QPsa) also mention Wisdom as a personified figure. A sapiential hymn of Psalm 154 states thus:

> For, wisdom has been granted in order to make YHWH's glory known, and in order to recount his many deeds she has been taught to man: to make his power known to ordinary people, to instruct his greatness to those lacking judgment, those who are far from her gates, those who are withdrawn from her entrances . . . . Her voice is heard from the gates of just ones, and from the assembly of devout ones her song; when they eat to bursting they speak about it, and when they drink in unison with one another; their meditation is on the Law of the Most High, their words (are meant) to make his power known. How distant from wicked people is her word, from all arrogant people her knowledge! (lines 3–6, 12–15)

---

39. For a detailed analysis between 4Q185 and 4Q525 and the relationship between Wisdom and the Torah in these texts, see Uusimäki, "'Happy Is the Person,'" 345–59.

40. Tigchelaar, "Lady Folly and Her House," 371–81. See also, Uusimäki, *Turning Proverbs towards Torah*, 173.

Like 4Q185 and 4Q525, Wisdom here is closely associated with the Law or Torah. The acrostic poem of Sirach 51:13–30 found in Cave 11 is quite different. Wisdom as a personified female is a clear theme, but the author writes of an erotic desire and pursuit for Wisdom, something not found in the other texts of Qumran mentioned above. Verses 13–14 begin with these words: "When I was young and innocent, I sought wisdom. She came to me in her beauty, and until the end I will cultivate her."[41] The erotic desire for Wisdom seems to climax in verse 19: "I burned with desire for her, never turning back. I became preoccupied with her, never weary of extolling her. My hand opened her gate and I came to know her secrets." So wonderful it is when one acquires Wisdom that the author exhorts his readers to find her as well (verses 23–30).

Thus, in Qumran literature, the evil woman figure underwent a major change. She is not a mere human, but a "chthonic night demon" who must be avoided at all costs.[42] The good woman figure of Wisdom on the other hand is especially connected with the Torah. This connection with the Torah may explain why Wisdom is not hypostasized fully with human-like features. Yet, she is nonetheless personified, and the two female figures do function as two choices. Since Qumran's setting was apocalyptic, it would have been apt for the community to emphasize Folly's evil nature so that the people may continue to stay faithful to God in view of the eschaton. This emphasis on Folly is akin to Revelation's emphasis on the harlot.

Conclusion

Second Temple Jewish literature affirms the Jewish people were familiar with the two-women topos. Philo, as a philosopher, utilized the motif in ways very similar to the Graeco-Roman world. The motive in doing so was ethical as well: to exhort the readers to choose the good woman and to dwell with her while forsaking the evil woman. Nonetheless, a special feature in the Jewish literature was in elevating the good woman figure to a high status where she does not compare with any other, especially the evil woman (Sirach and Wisdom of Solomon). The good woman is specifically called Wisdom and is identified with the

---

41. The English translation of the acrostic poem is taken from Skehan, "The Acrostic Poem," 387–400.

42. Crawford, "Lady Wisdom and Dame Folly," 365–66.

Torah. Qumran, on the other hand, also emphasized the nature of the evil woman and connected her with the underworld. This emphasis of the evil woman seems to have stemmed from Qumran's apocalyptic setting, so that the people would stay faithful to God in view of the eschaton. In turn, this is quite similar to Revelation's emphasis on its evil woman figure, the Harlot.

BIBLICAL BACKGROUND: PROVERBS 1–9

Within the biblical corpus, the only place other than Revelation where the two-women topos is present is Proverbs 1–9. Proverbs 1–9's literary structure and setting revolve around two main aspects: a father's or a teacher's lessons to his son or student and Wisdom's speeches.[43] While there have been voluminous materials written on the historical and theological identities of Wisdom and the Strange Woman of Proverbs 1–9, what matters here is looking at how these two women figures conform to the stock two-women topos and what their rhetorical functions are.[44] This study also is not concerned with the dating of Proverbs 1–9 and thus with the possibility of influence, whether the author of Proverbs 1–9 borrowed the two-women topos from existing literature in the ANE and used it or whether the topos was already in the author's mind to begin with since the topos was a stock motif well-known by the people of the day. More important for this study is the relationship between Proverbs 1–9 and Revelation, and whether the latter's author has used Proverbs 1–9 in shaping his own two-women topos for his purposes. This is quite likely since Revelation is steeped in OT allusions in general and since the author undoubtedly used other materials from the OT such as the personification of cities as women in portraying the two women of Revelation in particular.

Proverbs 1:20–33 introduce Wisdom the good woman as calling out in the noisy streets, marketplaces, and at the entrance of the city. Thus, Wisdom is pictured as intentionally going to where the people are and speaking to the passersby. She warns them that if they do not listen to her, they will come to ruin because they hated knowledge (Heb: דַּעַת; Grk: σοφία) and did not choose the fear of the Lord (1:29). On the other

43. Whybray, *Proverbs*, 63.
44. For the history of research on Wisdom and the Strange Woman, see Ahn, "Personified Woman Wisdom," 134–40; Forti, "The *Isha Zara*," 90–96; Fox, "Ideas of Wisdom," 613–33; Fox, *Proverbs 1–9*, 134–41 and 333–45.

hand, those who listen to her will dwell secure (1:33). Here, Wisdom is not just any ordinary woman, although she is very near to those who seek her, but seems to take on divine authority. As such, she calls people to repent (שׁוּב) and proclaims, "I will pour out my spirit (רוּחַ) to you" (1:23).[45] Her stark warnings of judgment (1:26–27) further evidence that she has divine authority as that of God. To reject Wisdom (1:24–25) thus is to reject Yahweh (1:29).[46] Yet, she is also given by Yahweh (2:6), which suggests that she is not equal to Yahweh.

Wisdom is next mentioned in 3:13–18. A macarism (אַשְׁרֵי) begins and ends this section, to emphasize the enormous blessing that comes to the person who finds and holds Wisdom. She is more precious than jewels and her ways are pleasant and peaceful (3:14–17). Most interesting is the connection between Wisdom and the tree of life. The tree of life in ANE and in Israel represent healing and eternal life, as it is in Proverbs (cf. Prov 3:7–8, 21–26; 4:13, 22; 8:35) and in Revelation (cf. Rev 2:7; 22:2).[47] The author of Proverbs claims that those who hold Wisdom shall reap the benefits of the tree of life, and this is also true of the book of Revelation.

Proverbs 4:1–9 again claim similar benefits for those who cherish Wisdom. Yet, the father's plea to his sons to get wisdom is especially direct and strong.[48] They must not forget nor reject their father's instruction, and they must get wisdom and understanding no matter what (4:5).[49] Then, as if Wisdom is a bride or a powerful patroness, the father commands his sons not to forsake her but to love her, which will turn out for their security (4:6).[50] They must prize her highly, and if they do, Wisdom

---

45. This study uses the ESV for scriptural references unless otherwise noted.
46. Trible, "Wisdom Builds a Poem," 515.
47. Waltke, *Proverbs*, 259.
48. Fox, *Proverbs 1–9*, 176.
49. The LXX differs and instead of having the double command to get wisdom and to get understanding as it is in the MT, it simply reads, "keep the commandments" (φύλασσε ἐντολάς). It is likely that the translator of the LXX freely translated from the Hebrew to fit Proverbs into his or her own Hellenistic context. See Tan, "Where Is Foreign Wisdom," 699–708. As it was shown in this study, later Jewish writers did equate Wisdom with the Torah, and the LXX's rendering may reflect that tendency as well. In any case, the concept of Wisdom is certainly present in Proverbs 4:1–9 in particular and in Proverbs 1–9 in general, whether Hebrew or Greek.
50. Scholars debate whether Wisdom is personified as a lover or not in this passage. Fox does not think Wisdom is portrayed as a lover in 4:1–9 but is a powerful patroness who rewards her faithful protégés. Fox, *Proverbs 1–9*, 174 and 178. Waltke thinks Wisdom is portrayed both as a bride and a patroness. Waltke, *Proverbs*, 280. Either way,

shall bring exaltation and honor to them (4:8–9). She is a noble figure who returns the sons' loyalty and love with gracious benefits.

The counterpart to Wisdom, namely the Strange Woman, is first introduced in 2:16–19. She is described as a "foreign" (נָכְרִי) woman (2:16; 5:20; 6:24; 7:5), but Proverbs 23:27 does connect her with being a harlot (זנה) as well. This promiscuous woman is a danger to men for she lures them with smooth words (2:16). As such, her lust for men causes her to willfully violate her covenant with her husband and thus with God (2:17).[51] Her house is further connected with death, so that those who choose to fornicate with her will not come back to the path of life (2:18–19).

Proverbs 5:1–14 continue this line of thought regarding the Strange Woman. Opposite to 4:1–9, the father's plea is strong in 5:1–14 as he warns his sons to avoid the Strange Woman at all costs. The lips of this woman drip honey and her words are smoother than oil, but in truth she is bitter as wormwood and sharp as a two-edged sword (5:3–4; cf. Eccl 7:26). Her ways end in death and Sheol, the exact opposite of the ways of Wisdom which are the path of life (5:5–6; cf. 3:17–18; 4:11–13). So, the father implores his sons not even to go near her and her house lest their lives are ruined (5:7–13). This evil woman must not be desired, and one must not let her capture one's heart even with her eyelashes (6:24–25).

Not only does Proverbs present the two women and their benefits or lack thereof separately, but also compares the two side by side. In 5:18–19, the father calls on his sons to rejoice in the "wife of your youth." With sexual language, the wife is likened to a lovely female deer whose breasts fill her husband with delight, and the father admonishes his sons to be intoxicated (literally, to be led astray) always in her love. In contrast, the father does not wish his sons to be intoxicated with the Strange Woman and to embrace the bosom of this foreign woman or a harlot (5:20). Here, the "wife of your youth" is being compared with the Strange Woman, and the exhortation is clear: choose the former woman and reject the latter. Since the Strange Woman is the counterpart to Wisdom in Proverbs, one could understand that Wisdom is being portrayed as a bride (the "wife of your youth") here in 5:18–20. At the very least, the "wife of your youth" is closely associated with Wisdom and could be understood as belonging to the company of Wisdom, if not the same.[52]

---

the sons are exhorted to love this female figure.

51. Waltke, *Proverbs*, 231.

52. This study has seen that the two-women topos can be used in a way that there could be multitude of female figures who belong to either camp, whether to the

Proverbs 7–9, in many ways, can be considered the height of the two-women topos. Both Wisdom's and the Strange Woman's alluring calls to men are captured in extended form in this long section. The Strange Woman first makes an appearance in 7:6–20. She is pictured as looking out the window of her house to see which man she could seduce (7:6–9). She then meets the man of her choice, dressed as a harlot (7:10). Once her victim is chosen, she becomes even more brazen by waiting for him in the corners of the streets and of the market and by seizing him and kissing him without hesitation (7:11–13).[53] Her sweet words to her victim are captured in 7:14–20. Not only is she a harlot, but also an adulterer, for she says to her victim that her husband has gone a long journey and is not home, so she has prepared her house as a house of love until morning.[54] Thus, the father warns his sons not to become her prey and go down the way of death and of Sheol (7:21–27).

The stark contrast to the evils of the Strange Woman is in Proverbs 8:1–36. Unlike the dark and shady tone of the evil woman's invitation, Wisdom's call is bold and open.[55] She stands where people are and where everyone can see, and raises her voice (8:1–3). She speaks boldly to men to hear her, for what she says is righteous and true (8:4–11). She claims virtues such as counsel, wisdom, strength, riches, honor, and righteousness for herself, and argues that those who seek her shall find her and by her they shall reign (8:12–21). Then, from 8:22–31, Wisdom seems to proclaim her godlike status.[56] She states that God has brought her forth before creation and that she was actually beside God when he created the

---

company of Virtue or of Vice.

53. Yee helpfully notes that the descriptions of the Strange Woman being loud, not staying at home but lying in wait in the street and in the market in 7:11–12 are some of the very words that describe Wisdom in 1:20–21. There, Wisdom is described as being in the street and in the market, crying out loudly. Yet, unlike the Strange Woman who does not "stay" (שׁכב) home, Wisdom "dwells" (שׁכן) in prudence (8:12). Yee, "The Foreign Woman," 62.

54. Yee further brings out the contrast between Wisdom (the "wife of your youth") and the Strange Woman. In 5:18–19, the father exhorted his son to let the good wife fill (הור) him with her love. In 7:18, the harlot pleads the man, "let us take our fill (הור) of love till morning." Apparently both women can give the man his fill of love, but there is a major difference. "The love of the true wife will fill her beloved at all times. The love of the *'iššâ zārâ* is transitory. It lasts until morning, until the return of her cuckolded husband." Yee, "The Foreign Woman," 63.

55. Fox, *Proverbs 1–9*, 265.

56. Ahn even argues that Proverbs 8:22–31 express Wisdom's divine preexistence. Ahn, "Personified Woman Wisdom," 144, 147–48.

heavens and the earth.⁵⁷ With that level of authority, Wisdom declares blessings (macarisms) upon those who listen to her and who keep her ways (8:32–34). The reason is obvious: to Wisdom belongs life and favor from Yahweh and to reject her means death (8:35–36).

If Wisdom's transcendence was the theme of Proverbs 8, Wisdom's ordinary reality is the theme of Proverbs 9:1–6.⁵⁸ Proverbs 9 is also the climax of the two-women motif, for the Strange Woman's call (Prov 7) and Wisdom's call (Prov 8) come head-to-head in a conflict of banquets. First, Wisdom is pictured as a woman who has built a large house with seven pillars so that she can become a noble hostess who throws a noble banquet (9:1).⁵⁹ Hence she prepares a feast and sends out her young women to call from the highest places in town so everyone can hear, to invite men to the feast (9:2–5). The nature of Wisdom's banquet is explained as life and understanding (9:6). Quite important for this study is the idea of Wisdom having a company of young women. On the one hand, if one believes that the "wife of your youth" (cf. 5:18–19) mentioned in Proverbs is not the same woman figure as Wisdom, then one will at least now have to include her in the company of Wisdom. On the other hand, Wisdom having a company of other women on her side means that even Scripture uses the two-women topos in a complex way that involves multiple women figures and not just two. This raises the possibility that John's use of the two-women topos in Revelation may also involve multiple women figures, if indeed John uses the two-women topos with Proverbs in mind.

Proverbs 9:13–18 portray the other banquet, namely the Strange Woman's banquet. She is now called "Folly" (תּוּלִיסָב). She also has a house and calls people to her banquet from the highest places in town just like Wisdom (9:14). Her words of invitation mirrors that of Wisdom's as well (9:15–16). However, there is a major difference. Whereas Wisdom's invitation to the banquet was to eat and drink what she has prepared so that

---

57. There is a debate as to what it means by God has "brought her forth" (הנק). It could either mean possession/acquisition or creation/procreation. The former would allow the interpretation that Wisdom was preexistent just like God. The latter would mean that Wisdom was created or begotten by God, and thus derives its existence from God. For a summary of the debate, see Fox, *Proverbs 1–9*, 279–80; Waltke, *Proverbs*, 408–9. Both Fox and Waltke opt for the creation/procreation option as with many others. No matter the case, Wisdom is being portrayed as supernatural in Proverbs 8:22–31 and closely connected with Yahweh.

58. Ahn, "Personified Woman Wisdom," 144.

59. Waltke notes that the mention of "seven" pillars points to an exceptionally large building that can entertain large guests, as well as perfection (cf. 6:16; 24:16; 26:16, 25). Waltke, *Proverbs*, 433. If so, then this has affinities with Revelation.

the invitees can live and walk in the way of understanding (9:2, 5–6), Folly's invitation to her banquet is to eat and drink stolen goods, and the invitees are actually in the presence of death and Sheol (9:17–18).

Conclusion

Thus, Proverbs uses the glaring contrast between Wisdom and Folly, and invites the readers to obviously choose Wisdom and her ways and to shun Folly. Choosing Wisdom will lead to life and understanding; choosing Folly will lead to death and Sheol. Cast in terms of a father's instruction to his sons, Proverbs 1–9 contain repeated plea of the father to his sons to choose Wisdom and to choose the "wife of your youth." While the two women's attires are not emphasized, their nature and reality are clearly stressed.

A significant detail to note is Proverb's portrayal of Wisdom. Wisdom, the good woman, is portrayed in both supernatural and natural terms. She is a supernatural being who is closely connected to Yahweh but at the same time she is an ordinary woman in the streets. She is also the "wife of your youth." Wisdom seems to be both ontological and historical. She has a company of other good women as well. These features in turn, as this study will argue, do appear for the good woman figure of Revelation, the bride.

On the other hand, Folly does not seem to have such a divine quality and status as that of Wisdom but is emphasized only as an ordinary harlot in Proverbs. She is also called Strange Woman and foreign woman but is not really portrayed as a reality on par with Wisdom. She does have an abnormal power though in seducing men, but her seduction leads to death and Sheol. Even this is similar to the portrayal of the great harlot in Revelation. Revelation's Babylon that gets destroyed completely cannot match the New Jerusalem that comes down from heaven. This does not mean that John has borrowed strictly and solely from Proverbs in depicting the two women of Revelation. Rather, the above observation shows that Proverb's two-women motif did have an influence upon John, and this study shall proceed in examining the two-women topos of Revelation in light of Proverbs, as well as other sources presented above.

SUMMARY AND CONCLUSION

But first, it is necessary to define what two-women topos is based on the analysis presented in this chapter before moving on to examine the two-women topos of Revelation. This will help highlight which parts of the motif are the same or similar and which parts are novel in the book of Revelation. The two-women topos is a sapiential motif in which two ethical choices are represented by two women or two camps of women—one good and the other evil—contrasted to bring about the author's intended exhortation to embrace the correct one and to forsake the other. To make the ethical appeal more recognizable and effective, the author might accentuate one woman over the other, personify the two types of women, and/or provide visual descriptions of the women. In the case of Revelation, all of the aforementioned elements are present, and the provided definition of the topos is well-suited to its context, as the following chapter will demonstrate. Moreover, as noted in the introduction of this chapter, the most novel feature of the topos in Revelation is that, not only are the readers exhorted to choose the good woman, but also to actually embody the good woman themselves. This will also be examined in greater detail in the following chapter.

CHAPTER 5

Two-Women Motif in Revelation

When viewed through the lens of the two-women topos, the main chapters for the evil woman figure in Revelation, namely the great harlot or Babylon, are chapters 17–18. The main chapters for the good woman figure, namely the bride or New Jerusalem, are chapters 21–22. Thus, it is fitting to start with these chapters and their surrounding contexts first before turning to other chapters that concern the other two female figures in Revelation. In the end, this chapter will show that all four female figures in Revelation—Babylon, the bride, Jezebel, and the radiant woman—are connected and are cast in terms of the two-women topos as belonging either to the camp of the virtuous woman or of the evil woman. John's basic exhortation via his use of the topos is for his audience to embrace the virtuous woman and to shun the evil woman. The ethical choice represented by the two camps of women in turn has to do with the purpose of Revelation, namely, to encourage the readers to remain faithful to God despite the temptations to defect. This chapter will also bring out what features of the topos are the same and what features are novel in Revelation. It is in fact the unique features that make John's use of the topos all the more significant and effective.

THE EVIL WOMAN BABYLON

Revelation 17–18 deal with the evil woman figure and her demise. She is called the great harlot or Babylon the great (also known as the great city). John first makes a mention of Babylon in Revelation 11:8. There, Babylon is revealed as the great city that shall parade the corpses of the two witnesses. Whether the two witnesses symbolize generally the church or more specifically certain faithful individuals, the fact of the matter is that the great city takes part in persecuting God's people. Babylon is thus evil, and as was noted in chapter 3 of this study, the city stands as the epitome of all anti-God cities/empires in history. John thus states that the great city is symbolically called Sodom, Egypt, and Jerusalem where Christ was crucified (11:8). As such, the great city Babylon is unmistakably the beast's city that performs a major role in persecuting God's people.

Consistent with the portrayal of the evil woman figure of the two-women topos, Babylon is fittingly associated with death and destruction in Revelation. However, a major difference of Revelation with other works that utilize the two-women topos is that the emphasis is not on the demise of those who associate with her, although this notion is clearly present, but on the demise of the evil woman herself. Babylon's demise is thus called for in Revelation 14:8 and 16:19. In 14:8, an angel announces the fall of Babylon in this manner: "Fallen, fallen (ἔπεσεν ἔπεσεν) is Babylon the great." This announcement alludes to other prophetic calls of demise in the OT (i.e., Jer 51:7-8 [28:7-8 in LXX], Isa 21:9) and should thereby be understood also as a prophetic call of certainty.[1] The announcement of 14:8 further parallels the prophetic call made during the portrayal of Babylon's actual demise in 18:2. This means that the call of Babylon's demise in 14:8 is proleptic and anticipates Revelation 17–18. The reason for Babylon's demise is stated in 14:8 as well, and it is because she made all nations drink the wine that produces the passion for her harlotry.[2] John will explain further what her wine entails in Revelation 17. In any case, the fact that she can get all the nations to drink with her suggests her powerful seducing ability as a harlot, and this is in accordance with the two-women topos, especially with the evil woman figure in Proverbs. Moreover, Revelation 14:9–10 shows clearly that committing harlotry with Babylon is closely connected with worshipping the beast (idolatry) and will lead to "the wine of God's wrath." Committing harlotry with

---

1. Aune, *Revelation 6–16*, 829. Aune notes that the two aorist verbs ἔπεσεν ἔπεσεν are proleptic or prophetic perfect, which emphasizes the certainty of the fall as if it had already occurred.

2. The string of genitives concerning Babylon's wine can be understood in various ways. For a summary of different options, see Osborne, *Revelation*, 538–39. This writer concurs with Osborne and understands the genitives to mean that Babylon's wine is one that produces or results in passion for her harlotry.

"HERE IS WISDOM"

Babylon is undoubtedly a spiritual issue, and passion (θυμός) for her harlotry (14:8) will lead to God's wrath (θυμός; 14:10).[3]

Revelation 16:19 captures Babylon's destruction in a pithy manner. In 16:17, the last of the twenty-one judgments, namely the seventh bowl judgment, has been poured out. With this God's judgment is complete, as God himself from the throne speaks, "It is done (γέγονεν)!" Moreover, Jesus's second coming is portrayed in 16:18 with a familiar theophany language, signaling that it is now the time of the end. Then John states that "God remembered Babylon the great."[4] God did not forget about her and her judgment, and it shall come to pass as announced in 14:8–10. Babylon shall surely drink the cup of God's wrath (16:19). Hence John states that the great city was split into three parts, suggesting a complete destruction.[5]

Babylon's Portrayal as the Evil Woman

Revelation 17–18, the main section on the evil woman figure of Revelation, Babylon, catalogue her destruction in a vivid and detailed manner. Also, unlike the above passages that mention Babylon, Revelation 17 especially personifies Babylon as a woman and not simply as a city.[6] John

---

3. Other than Revelation 14:8, the word θυμός is used eight other times in Revelation to mean "wrath" (12:12; 14:10, 19; 15:1, 7; 16:1, 19; 19:15). Thus, Hoskins argues that the harlot's wine of wrath in 14:8 is God's wine of wrath in 14:10, and that Babylon causes the nations to drink from the cup of God's wrath by inciting people to commit harlotry with her. Hoskins, *Revelation*, 274. This means that Hoskins understands the word θυμός to have a single meaning, namely "wrath." However, this writer agrees with Osborne that the word θυμός may have a double meaning of both passion and wrath, with the former meaning being in the foreground in 14:8 and the latter meaning in the foreground in 14:10. Osborne, *Revelation*, 539. Osborne does not mention the reason for this, but this writer argues that, in light of the two-women topos, the notion of the evil woman Babylon enticing people to be passionate about committing harlotry with her makes perfect sense. In any case, whether one understands Babylon's wine as the cup of God's wrath or as a passion for harlotry, Revelation is clear that falling into the seductress Babylon's hands will end in God's fierce judgment.

4. The same notion of God remembering Babylon is also found in Revelation 18:5. There, the reason for Babylon's destruction is because God has remembered her sins.

5. Smalley, *Revelation*, 415.

6. Rossing notes that the very mention of harlotry in 14:8 suggests that two distinct traditions are being used by John regarding Babylon: the siege oracles against foreign nations with a prophetic context for the cup of wrath on one hand and the evil woman traditions on the other hand in which the cup of wrath does not occur. Rossing, *Two Cities*, 65–66. While this writer agrees with Rossing that the two-women topos is in the background of 14:8 along with the prophetic calls against sinful cities/nations from

begins by calling her "the great harlot" (17:1), a clear signal that he wants to portray Babylon as an evil woman figure like that of Proverbs. She is also described as sitting on many waters, which the angel later interprets to John as peoples, multitudes, nations, and languages (17:15). Thus, she is fittingly called the *great* harlot, for she has enticed the whole world to associate with her. Even the kings of the earth have committed harlotry (ἐπόρνευσαν) with her, and the earth dwellers have become drunk with her wine, that is, her harlotry (17:2). If Revelation 14:8 simply stated that all the nations have become drunk with her wine, 17:2 adds a further detail: it is not just the people in high positions but also the ordinary people who have become enticed by Babylon's intoxicating wine of harlotry. As noted in chapter 3 of this study, the people's engagement in harlotry with Babylon is not a one-time occurrence; the intoxication language suggests instead that this is a repeated crime. The great harlot has a successful campaign of seduction upon the people of the world.

John also makes clear the harlot's connection with the beast in 17:3. John sees her riding the beast, which would mean that she exercises the authority of the beast. The beast is behind her, and the beast is the one supporting her. Nevertheless, Revelation 17:8 (cf. 17:11) claims with certainty that the beast rises from the abyss and goes to destruction. Since the great harlot is closely associated with the beast who itself is connected with the abyss and destruction, it would be correct to recognize that the great harlot is also connected with the abyss and destruction. This is in conformity with Proverbs and with the Qumran literature that portray the evil woman and her house to be of death and Sheol. But unlike Proverbs and the Qumran literature, Revelation will go further in actually portraying the evil woman's own death and destruction.

The harlot's appearance is noted in 17:4–6. John sees the woman, dressed in purple and scarlet, adorned with gold and precious stones, and holding a golden cup that is full of abominations and impurities of her harlotry (17:4). As also noted in chapter 3 of this study, scholars understand the description of the harlot's attire to be derived from either the OT or the Greek and Roman sources. Those who lean to the OT turn to the prophetic oracles that condemn harlot cities such as Jerusalem or Babylon and that pronounce judgment on them; those who lean to the Greek and Roman sources see similarities in description between the

---

the OT, the two-women topos is not emphasized there. It is with Revelation 17 that the two-women topos really comes to the fore as John clearly personifies Babylon as an evil woman in a detailed manner.

harlot of Revelation and the actual harlots of the Roman empire. While these are helpful backgrounds to the great harlot of Revelation, they still do not fully explain Revelation's purpose in introducing the destruction of Babylon. The OT's prophetic oracles' main purpose in condemning the harlot cities is vindication, to show that God's judgments on them are just, and those who compare Revelation's harlot with the harlots of the Roman empire simply do so for the sake of appraisal.

On the other hand, John's purpose in portraying the destruction of Babylon is more hortatory, to urge his readers to disassociate from Babylon (cf. 18:4), and this more closely resembles the function of the two-women topos as found in the book of Proverbs than any other.[7] In fact, Babylon's appearance is a stock description of the evil woman figure of the two-women topos. The excessive adornment of color is a prominent feature of the evil woman from the topos and can be found even in the original Prodicus myth (Xenophon, *Mem.* 2.1.22). The company of evil women from the *Tabula of Cebes* are all excessively adorned, unlike their counterpart, the noble women who are simple (*Ceb. Tab.* 20.2). The evil women in *Punica* (*Punica.* 15.23–31) and in Dio Chrysostom's *Discourses* (*Or.* 1.78–80) are also attractively adorned with purple and gold. While Proverbs does not detail the Strange Woman's attire, she is nonetheless called a harlot, which would implicitly mean that she is attractively adorned, like that of the great harlot of Revelation. Hence, there is a good reason to understand that the two-women topos akin to that of Proverbs is at work in John's portrayal of Babylon, along with other OT backgrounds.

Next, John describes that Babylon has a golden cup in her hand (Rev 17:4). While Revelation 14:8 and 17:2 mentioned that Babylon made all the nations drink from her wine and 14:10 and 16:19 stated that those who worship the beast as well as Babylon herself shall be judged by drinking from the cup of the wine of God's wrath, 17:4 is the first instance in Revelation that Babylon actually has a golden cup which she uses to make the nations become intoxicated. This identifying item of Babylon must be special as to make John to take notice. The metaphor of intoxication from the harlot's wine is also extended in 17:4 by clarifying that her wine actually has to do with abominations and impurities of her harlotry. Thus, those who are enticed by Babylon's wine become abominations and

---

7. So also, Rossing, *Two Cities*, 76–77.

unclean in the sight of God, and they shall not enter New Jerusalem, the counterpart to Babylon (21:27).[8]

Scholars readily identify Babylon's golden cup to be from Jeremiah 51:7. After all, Jeremiah 51:7 clearly states that Babylon was a golden cup in Yahweh's hand, making the nations drink of her wine. Jeremiah 51:8–10 go on to pronounce Babylon's demise, the ensuing wailing by the people upon her destruction, and the call to forsake her as God has brought judgment upon her. One can obviously see the close connection between Revelation 17–18 and Jeremiah 51:7–10. However, there is one major difference. Whereas Jeremiah explicitly makes Babylon to be Yahweh's golden cup, namely His instrument of judgment, Revelation portrays Babylon's golden cup to be her own.[9] In Revelation, Babylon's golden cup has more to do with being Babylon's effective instrument in seducing the people of the world than symbolizing God's instrument of judgment. Thus, the golden cup in Babylon's hand in Revelation 17:4 is filled with abominations and impurities of Babylon's harlotry, not with God's wrath or anger.[10] Apparently, something else is at work in Revelation 17:4 than simply Jeremiah 51:7.

In fact, Babylon's strategy in seducing and deceiving people with wine and intoxication has more to do with the evil woman figure from

---

8. Hoskins notes the close relationship between harlotry/idolatry and uncleanness in the OT and the fact that nearly all of the sins in Revelation's vice lists are labeled as abominations in the OT. Thus, it is fitting that Babylon's cup is full of abominations and impurities, for abominations and uncleanness belong together. Those who commit harlotry with Babylon actually have committed abominations before God, and they are unclean. As such, they shall not enter New Jerusalem (Rev 21:27). Hoskins, *Revelation*, 318–20.

9. Scholars like Fanning, Osborne, and Smalley also note this difference, but they do not elaborate as to why this is so. Fanning, *Revelation*, 438; Osborne, *Revelation*, 611; Smalley, *Revelation*, 430. Beale explains the difference quite simply, namely that, although the wine comes from the hand of Babylon, it is ultimately from the hand of God. Beale, *Revelation*, 855. While this is helpful, Beale's clarification still does not adequately explain why Revelation 17:4 explicitly equates Babylon's wine with her own harlotry and not in any way with God.

10. Aune has noted that the Targum of Jeremiah 51:7 does turn Babylon's cup into a metaphor for her sin. Aune, *Revelation 17–22*, 935. However, the Targum of Jeremiah is likely from the fourth century AD, and it is thus improbable that Revelation's author would have borrowed the metaphor from it. For the date of the Targum of Jeremiah, see Hayward, *The Targum of Jeremiah*, 34–38. Although one can still argue that the Jewish writers were interested in Jeremiah long before the emergence of the Targum, but it is virtually impossible to prove that John would have known about this pre-targumic material, especially the information about Babylon's cup.

the two-women topos than Jeremiah or any other OT prophetic works.[11] This is clear from Proverbs' portrayal of the evil woman figure, the Strange Woman. Proverbs 2:16 states that this woman is a danger to men because she has the ability to seduce men with smooth words. Indeed, her lips drip honey and her words are smoother than oil (5:3–4). Proverbs 5:20 further warns the readers not to be intoxicated with the Strange Woman. This woman is a harlot and an adulterer and has an abnormal ability of seducing men (7:6–20). Her alluring call may be sweet, but Proverbs repeatedly warns the readers not to be deceived, for her way is actually the way of death and of Sheol (2:18–19; 5:5–13; 7:21–27). Hence, the seducing and deceiving language that are absent in Jeremiah or in any other prophetic works of the OT regarding Babylon likely have come from Proverbs' portrayal of the evil woman as John painted a composite picture of the great harlot in Revelation.

Some scholars have also noted a remarkable parallel between Revelation's portrayal of Babylon and the woman called "Deceit" in the *Tabula of Cebes*.[12] In the *Tabula*, Deceit sits on a throne by the gate and has a cup in her hand, with which she makes everyone to drink from in order to lead them astray in life (*Ceb. Tab.* 5.1—6.1). The concepts of sitting on a throne (cf. Rev 17:1, 3), of a cup in the woman's hand (cf. Rev 17:4), of making people to drink from the cup (cf. Rev 14:8; 17:2, 6), and of deceiving and leading people astray (cf. Rev 18:23) are notions all found in Revelation's portrayal of Babylon. It is important to reiterate that the *Tabula of Cebes* was written during the first century AD, around the same time as Revelation. This strongly suggests that the stereotypical evil woman from the two-women topos was a familiar theme that the people of the first century would recognize.[13]

What all of this means is that the golden cup in Babylon's hand does not simply connote Babylon's sins or God's wrath. If the possibility of the presence of the two-women topos is allowed, and this study is advocating that it is present, then Babylon's cup also represents the evil woman's seducing and deceiving nature. As a harlot, Babylon deceives people by

---

11. So, Rossing, *Two Cities*, 80. Callahan thus suggests that Babylon of Revelation 18 should be studied in comparison with the female topoi from both prophetic and sapiential works. Callahan, "Apocalypse as Critique," 55.

12. Aune, *Revelation 17–22*, 936; Charles, *Revelation*, vol. 2, 65; Prigent, *L'Apocalypse*, 258; Swete, *Apocalypse*, 216; Wettstein, *Novum Testamentum Graecum*, vol. 2, 820.

13. Rossing, *Two Cities*, 80.

making them intoxicated with her wine from her cup, and John is claiming that the content of her cup, namely her wine, is her harlotry. The concept of an evil woman who is a harlot and who wants to seduce men through intoxication is the stock pattern of the two-women topos and, once again, John is likely drawing this concept from Proverbs as he portrays Babylon as the evil woman figure of the book of Revelation. Since John uses other passages from the OT in formulating his portrayal of Babylon, it is fitting that he would also use Proverbs in his formulation, although other Jewish wisdom literature, as well as the Qumran literature, that invoke the two-women topos are not far off. In turn, this is one strong evidence that should caution those who read and study apocalypses to stop solely looking for connections with prophecy. Revelation, at the very least, should be studied with minds open not only for connections with the Hebrew prophets, but also for sapiential themes and works, especially Proverbs.

In any case, John turns his attention next to Babylon's name written on her forehead in Revelation 17:5. The forehead signifies one's identity and allegiance, and once again John identifies her as a harlot who is an abomination.[14] This is the second time in Revelation 17 so far that the personified Babylon is categorized as a harlot. The word "abomination" (βδέλυγμα) occurs three times in Revelation, with the first two instances occurring in 17:4–5 in connection with Babylon. The third instance of the word occurs in Revelation 21:27, where John states that the one who does what is abominable (βδέλυγμα) will not enter the New Jerusalem except for those who are written in the Lamb's book of life. Obviously the one who decides what is abominable or not is God, and since abomination is being contrasted with being written in the book of life and with having access to God's New Jerusalem in 21:27, the word has a spiritual connotation.[15] Since the word "harlot" or "harlotry" also has a spiritual connotation in Revelation as it pertains to idolatry, Babylon's name as a harlot and as an abomination signifies that, not only does she stand in antithesis to God, but also that her evil nature and identity likewise has a spiritual connotation. Moreover, she is actually named as the *mother* (μήτηρ) of prostitutes and of earth's abominations, suggesting that she

---

14. Huber states, "For John, however, the great whore is not just an elite woman who has traded status for enslavement; she is aligned with evil itself." Huber, "The City-Women," 315.

15. BDAG notes that the word βδέλυγμα is often used in the OT for things pertaining to idolatry (polytheistic cult) and for things that defile a sacred place. BDAG, s.v. "βδέλυγμα." This is also true of Revelation. So also, Thayer, s.v. "βδέλυγμα."

is the climax and amalgamation of all anti-God cities and evil women throughout history. Rossing is certainly correct in understanding that the motherhood language here is the same expression as "Jezebel's children" (2:20–23) and "the [radiant] woman's children" (12:17).[16] This means that John is portraying the conflict of God's kingdom and the beast's kingdom also in connection with the stories of two women and their children, and it will be important to analyze all references to female figures and their children in Revelation.

Babylon's antithetical standing against God becomes crystal clear as John testifies that he saw the evil woman drunk with the blood of the saints and martyrs of Jesus in 17:6. As the dragon, who is Satan, tries to exterminate the radiant woman's children, namely the church, in 12:17, so does Babylon. The intoxication language is made grotesque by suggesting that Babylon is drunk with the blood of God's people; she has shed the blood of so many as to be drunk by it. This once again evidences that Babylon's spiritual or religious side is very prominent in John's introduction of her in Revelation 17.[17] While her economic significance is noticeable especially in Revelation 18, one cannot dismiss her spiritual significance. The root of her evil is clearly spiritual, and to stress her political or economic aspects while ignoring her spiritual aspect does not do full justice to John's portrayal of her in Revelation.

In conclusion, Babylon is clearly depicted as a personified woman figure in Revelation, especially in Revelation 17. The visual description of her attire matches the description of the evil woman figure of the two-women topos. She is also clearly marked as a harlot, a great one at that, and as an abomination. John makes no mistake in presenting who she is: an evil woman the believers must watch out for. As an evil woman, she has the authority of the beast and performs the work of Satan in shedding the blood of the saints. The root of her evil is spiritually motivated. She moreover has an amazing ability in seducing and deceiving the world into committing harlotry with her, a stock motif of an evil woman of the two-women topos. She is also a mother of prostitutes and of the earth's abominations, suggesting that she has children who are like her. The above analysis evidences that John has utilized the two-women topos in his depiction of Babylon along with other OT allusions. In the end, the

---

16. Rossing, *Two Cities*, 83.
17. So also, Beale, *Revelation*, 859.

description of Babylon in Revelation 17 is intended to create a sense of antipathy toward the adorned woman.[18]

Babylon's Demise as the Evil Woman

After the angel's interpretation of the mystery of the beast (Rev 17:7–14), the mystery of the harlot is described from 17:15 onward. Her mystery, as it turns out, actually has to do with her unexpected and ironic destruction. Babylon shall be destroyed by its most trusted ally, the beast and its ten horns. John states that the beast and its ten horns will hate (μισήσουσιν) the harlot, they will make her desolate (ἠρημωμένην) and naked (γυμνὴν), they will eat (φάγονται) her flesh, and burn (κατακαύσουσιν) her with fire (17:16). This shows that the beast is not faithful; it will turn on those who are on its side. Yet, John claims that the beast's betrayal and attack on Babylon ultimately stems from God, that God is the one who has put into the beast's heart to carry out his purpose (17:17). God can even use the beast's character in bringing about his will in destroying the harlot. Thus, the evil woman's complete demise is succinctly captured in Revelation. This is something that is lacking in other works that utilize the two-women topos. Revelation, by telling of Babylon's own destruction, and not just the destruction of those who associate with her, seems to take the warning not to choose the evil woman from the two-women topos further.

Regarding this destruction of Babylon, some scholars have argued that John is depicting a literal maltreatment of a woman's body in 17:16. Marla Selvidge understands Revelation 17:16 to be detailing the harlot's painful death by rape (ἠρημωμένην), fire (ἐν πυρί), and cannibalism (κατακαύσουσιν).[19] Selvidge believes that there is even a hint of joy and jealousy on part of the author as he details the harlot's death, for if he cannot enjoy her, then no one should be able to.[20] Tina Pippin likewise argues that 17:16 describes a rape of a woman's body and claims that this passage is the "most vividly misogynist passage in the New Testament."[21] Recently, Pillay has argued that to dismiss the feminist reading of Revelation's Babylon and her demise for the sake of patriarchal

18. Huber, "The City-Women," 315.
19. Selvidge, "Powerful and Powerless Women," 164.
20. Selvidge, "Powerful and Powerless Women," 165.
21. Pippin, *Death and Desire*, 58.

ethos of Revelation is irresponsible and immoral.[22] If the feminist reading of Revelation 17–18, or any other readings of gender for that matter, is understood to be the sole trope that John is utilizing for his portrayal of Babylon, then the protests of the feminist scholars do seem to have value.

In response, Fiorenza's insight against this type of feminist interpretation is worth mentioning. Fiorenza states, "One must avoid absolutizing and universalizing gender as a basic category of analysis."[23] In other words, some feminist interpreters of Revelation take gender to be the exclusive lens with which to construe Revelation, but it is important to recognize that gender is not and cannot be the sole trope. Revelation is much more complex, and one must account for "the vacillation and ambiguity of a text" that can move freely between different images and symbols.[24] The poetic and symbolic language world of Revelation requires one to seek to understand it with multiple venues.[25] This means that the context of Revelation 17–18 does not permit an interpretation that is solely in sexual terms.

Thus, although John portrays Babylon as the evil woman figure of the two-women topos, and although this is a significant imagery that must be recognized, one should not expect this to be the sole trope that is at work regarding Babylon as do some of the feminist interpreters. John has woven a complex image of Babylon that is also spiritual as well as political, and all of these must be taken into account. In fact, vital to John's portrayal of Babylon is not only the two-women topos, but also city imagery from the Old Testament. As mentioned earlier in this study, scholars see Ezekiel to be at work in John's portrayal of Babylon. With regard to the demise of Babylon in Revelation 17:16–18, Ezekiel 16 and 23 are readily enlisted to be the background materials.[26] Ezekiel 16 and 23 both deal with the metaphor of God punishing his adulterous wife as the jealous husband.

However, it is very important to recognize that John does not follow the exact wording of either Ezekiel 16 or 23. The word used in the

22. Pillay, "Reading Revelation 18," 421–36.
23. Fiorenza, *Revelation*, 215–16.
24. Fiorenza, *Revelation*, 217.
25. Recently, Tōniste has argued similarly that to ignore the multiple layers of meaning Revelation produces, especially its intertextuality, is to dismiss its literary and canonical nature. To do so is to fail in making good biblical interpretation. Tōniste, "John and Women," 104–5.
26. For instance, Ruiz, *Ezekiel*, 359–78, esp. 364 and Vanhoye, "L'utilisation," 440–42.

expression, "they will make her desolate," is ἐρημόω, and this is not found in the Ezekiel text. While the idea of leaving the harlot naked can be found in Ezekiel 16:39 and 23:29 (cf. Hos 2:5), Ezekiel actually uses the word ἐκδύω for the stripping of her clothes (Ezek 23:26; cf. Hos 2:5).[27] John has conspicuously exchanged ἐρημόω for ἐκδύω, and this is likely because ἐρημόω is a specific term for destruction of cities without any sexual connotations.[28] Ezekiel 29:12, in fact, employs ἐρημόω to refer to the destruction of cities and nations, and Revelation 18:17 and 18:19 employ the word also to refer to the destruction of the great city and to the loss of wealth as a result. Rossing's claim from this observation has strong merit: "Revelation's choice of 'lay waste' (ἠρημωμένην) as the first of the list of punishments against Babylon in Rev 17:16 makes clear the intent to weight the imagery of Babylon's destruction toward the devastation of a city or landscape rather than a woman's body."[29]

Likewise, the exact expression of eating her flesh is also not found in either Ezekiel 16 or 23. Ezekiel 23:25 has the expression of cutting off of the harlot's nose and ears, followed by the expression of being eaten by fire which has some affinities with Revelation 17:16, but it may be a stretch to argue that this alludes to the eating of flesh language in Revelation 17:16.[30] Scholars in turn have listed other possible candidates for the eating of flesh expression from other parts of the Old Testament, such as Psalm 27:2, Micah 3:3, and Isaiah 49:26, but the contexts are too different to merit viable connection. In the end, it is inconclusive exactly where John may have gotten the eating of flesh language from. However, important

27. The word for "naked" (γυμνός) can be used for the shame of a woman's body, as it is in Ezekiel, but also for the shame of cities. In fact, the word is used in Revelation 3:17–18 to refer to the shaming of the Laodicean church for their boasting in wealth. Obviously the Laodicean church is not a literal woman but a community of believers, and the warning to the church of its nakedness is not sexual but economic. This shows that one should not automatically understand a sexual connotation just because the word γυμνός is used, and this is true for Revelation 17:16. See Rossing, *Two Cities*, 92–97.

28. Rossing, *Two Cities*, 90–91. Few recent scholars nonetheless argue that the adjective ἔρημος is used in Isaiah 54:1 to refer to childless women, a text which Paul also cites in Galatians 4:27. For these scholars, this proves that the word ἔρημος and its cognates can be used for female abuse, and it necessarily follows that the employment of the word ἐρημόω in Revelation 17:16 can also take on a negative sexual connotation. See Fletcher, "Flesh for Franken-Whore," 159–60 and König, "The 'Great Whore,'" 6. However, this argument basically ignores John's careful usage of OT allusions, in this case Ezekiel, and should thus be approached with caution.

29. Rossing, *Two Cities*, 92.

30. So Ruiz, *Ezekiel*, 367.

to note here is that the eating of flesh language is clearly an expression used for destruction of cities or persons irrespective of sexual connotation in the Old Testament. Psalm 27:2's eating of flesh language refers to the psalmist himself, probably David (hence, not a woman), namely that the enemies are trying to eat the psalmist's flesh, and this does not refer to any kind of sexual exploit but simply the psalmist's destruction. Micah 3:3 refers to the rulers of Israel eating the flesh of the people of Israel, namely mistreating and destroying God's people, and Isaiah 49:26 refers to God making the oppressors eat their own flesh, meaning that God will judge and destroy those who oppress God's people. In these passages, there is no hint of any kind of sexual exploitation. This shows that John, as he described the demise of Babylon in Revelation 17:16, deliberately deviated from using Ezekiel's language of the harlot's demise and changed the expression once again in order to diminish the sexual connotation that comes from the female imagery of the great harlot.

So John states in Revelation 17:18 that the woman is the great city (ἡ πόλις ἡ μεγάλη) as if to concretize his notion that, when he is talking about the harlot's demise, he is describing it in terms of the destruction of a city and not so much of a woman. König has argued that " . . . from a literary-theoretical point of view, it is important to state that the city does not 'end' and the woman does not 'start' at a specific, identifiable point within the text . . . In the case of the female cities, the woman never exists completely without the city and the city is never purely wood and stone."[31] While the latter notion may be true, the former must be qualified. When John's careful usage of the Old Testament, in this case Ezekiel, is taken into account, one can see that he intentionally and masterfully avoided language that describes judgment on a woman but instead used language that is neutral and that has to do with destruction of a city in 17:16. This shows John's intention; he wants the city metaphor to come to the fore and wants to avoid accentuating female abuse when it comes to the harlot's demise. In other words, 17:16 is a specific, identifiable point where the woman does "end" and the city does "start."[32] Nonetheless, while Babylon's demise is cast in terms of a city's destruction, the ethics of the two-women topos is still lurking in the background. So, John will call upon God's people to not to choose her (18:4).

31. König, "The 'Great Whore,'" 7.

32. Ruiz claims similarly, "Finally, it is quite clear that Rev 17,16–18 prepares us for the shift that takes place in Rev 18 from an emphasis on the metaphor of the Prostitute to the metaphor of Babylon." Ruiz, *Ezekiel*, 377.

The Ethical Choice: "Come Out"

After John's succinct statement on Babylon's demise in Revelation 17:16–18, he proceeds to narrate a series of pronouncements of judgment and proleptic dirges on Babylon's destruction in Revelation 18. Revelation 18 has been noted by many to be carefully composed structurally, but not everyone agrees on how to precisely subdivide the chapter. Yet, there are clues in the text that aid in understanding how Revelation 18 is generally structured, and for the purpose of this study they are sufficient in meaningfully situating the ethical choice found in 18:4–8 within the overall context of the chapter. First, there are three explicit voices from heaven that give organization to the chapter in verses 1, 4, and 21.[33] Interestingly, 18:1–3 and 18:21–24 both contain the angels' pronouncement of judgment on Babylon, with the former spoken by an angel with a mighty (ἰσχυρᾷ) voice (v. 1) and the latter vocalized by a mighty (ἰσχυρὸς) angel (v. 21). Second, 18:4 clearly begins a new division, for another voice from heaven (ἄλλην φωνὴν ἐκ τοῦ οὐρανοῦ) speaks, followed by three identifiable laments (v. 4–20).[34] Furthermore, Rossing is certainly correct in seeing another parallel between 18:4–8 and 18:20 with both containing imperatives followed by ὅτι clauses.[35] When the above clues are taken into account, one can understand the structure of Revelation 18 in this manner:

A. 18:1–3 – Proclamation of judgment by an angel with a mighty voice.
  B. 18:4–8 – Imperatives followed by ὅτι clause.
    C. 18:9–19 – Three laments by the kings, the merchants, and the sailors.
  B' 18:20 – Imperative followed by ὅτι clause.
A' 18:21–24 – Proclamation of judgment by a mighty angel.

Viewed in this chiastic manner, the three laments in 18:9–19 seem central to the whole structure, especially the lament by the merchants which take up the most space (vv. 11–17a). This in turn evidences that Babylon's wealth and the vain of going after it is emphasized especially in Revelation 18.[36] While this may be so, also important are the impera-

---

33. Fanning, *Revelation*, 455.

34. Fiorenza thus claims that Revelation 18 is a strong unitary composition called a triptych. Fiorenza, *Revelation*, 98–99.

35. Rossing, *Two Cities*, 100–1.

36. Callahan thereby argues that Revelation 18 functions as a critique of political economy of Rome, and it teaches that a Christian must not compromise one's faith for the sake of the material benefits. Callahan, "Apocalypse as Critique," 46–65. Mathews

tives found in 18:4–8 and 18:20, for John directly exhorts his readers to behave in a certain way in relation to Babylon. In fact, all of 18:4–20 are especially important, for John brings in another speaker from heaven to address God's people in these verses.[37] This speaker is none other than God, for he calls the believers, "my people" (ὁ λαός μου).[38] God himself rarely speaks in Revelation, especially with such urgency, and this shows in turn how important the imperatives in 18:4–8 and 18:20 must be.[39] God exhorts his people to "come out" of Babylon (18:4) and calls them to "rejoice" over her (18:20), and these responses are in direct contrast with the responses of lament by the people of the world (18:9–19).

The nature and entailment of the ethical exhortations in Revelation 18 was discussed in chapter 3 of this study. This chapter concerns how the exhortations function in terms of the two-women topos. As the evil woman figure of the two-women topos, Babylon has apparently been promising a life of affluence to those who choose her (13:16–17; 17:2, 4; 18:3, 7, 9, 11–19). So sweet is her alluring that people who choose her are described as being drunk (17:2), as Babylon herself is drunk (17:6), and John tells that they still miss her even after she is destroyed by God (18:9–19). Yet, Revelation warns in a stark manner that her path is death and Sheol (cf. Prov 2:18–19; 5:5–6; 7:21–27; 4Q184; 4Q525 frag. 15). She seeks to mislead others so that they may follow her way of folly, yet nothing but lament awaits those who choose her and her path. Revelation, by going further than other works that use the two-women topos, actually describes the evil woman's complete destruction, while her demise as a woman is indeed mitigated by highlighting her destruction in terms of a city, an ingenuity on John's part, and in doing so makes the ethical warning not to follow her all the more powerful.

This must be because John understands his visions to be an apocalyptic drama of the end. He thereby emphasizes the evil woman figure

---

claims that Revelation 18 is the book's climax of economic critique, developing a worldview that demonizes worldly economic system and that postpones true material blessing for the faithful to the future age. Mathews, *Riches, Poverty, and the Faithful*, 197.

37. This study agrees with Bauckham that the whole section of 18:4–20 is the words of the voice from heaven. Thus, the three laments are also the words of prediction by the heavenly voice on how the people of the world will respond to the fall of Babylon. Bauckham, *Climax*, 340–41.

38. So Beckwith, *Apocalypse*, 714. Even if one argues that the speaker is not God himself but another angel, the message is still from God. Cf. Stefanovic, *Revelation*, 528.

39. For information on the urgency of God's command in 18:4, see Hoskins, *Revelation*, 342.

even more so than the Qumran literature because following her reaps eternal consequences. Revelation is clear: to follow the harlot is to participate in her sins, which is especially tied to the accumulation of wealth.[40] To choose her is to commit harlotry, which is akin to worshipping the beast and rejecting the worship of God.

So God himself commands his people to come out of her lest they take part (συγκοινωνέω) in her sins (18:4). Mathews notes that the word συγκοινωνέω occurs elsewhere only one other time in Revelation 1:9 where John claims that he is a partner (συγκοινωνὸς) in the tribulation, God's kingdom, and steadfast endurance in Jesus.[41] This suggests that in Revelation, one either participates in the affluent lifestyle afforded by Babylon or in the life of faithfulness despite suffering for God. John clearly has chosen the latter and wants God's people to join with him in the life of loyalty to God. To do so, one must "come out" of her, which is to reject the evil woman Babylon whose path is the path of death, and choose God's side; there is no middle ground.[42] God's people must stand with him when he judges her and must "pay her back" and "repay her" alongside God.[43] Instead of lamenting, they must "rejoice" over God's judgment on her (18:20). Indeed, choosing God's side means choosing the good woman New Jerusalem, whom John will continue to introduce starting Revelation 19.

THE VIRTUOUS WOMAN NEW JERUSALEM

Revelation 19:1–8 is a portrait of what rejoicing looks like for those on God's side. Strings of hallelujahs are shouted for God's righteous judgment upon the great harlot who corrupted the earth with her harlotry (see esp. verse 2). Then, during the last hallelujah praise, the bride of the Lamb is introduced for the first time in Revelation (19:6–8). Not only are God's people called to praise God for his judgment upon the great harlot (19:2–3), they are to praise God, for the bride of the Lamb has made herself ready for the marriage (19:7). This suggests that the bride is the counterpart to the great harlot in Revelation. If the great harlot is the

---

40. Mathews, *Riches, Poverty, and the Faithful*, 200.

41. Mathews, *Riches, Poverty, and the Faithful*, 200.

42. Again, to "come out" of Babylon is to reject her sinful ways. It would not mean radical separation. See footnote 146 on page 140 of this study.

43. What these commands mean was discussed in chapter 3 of this study.

evil woman God's people must avoid, the bride is the good or virtuous woman God's people must welcome. The Lamb's bride, as John will show, is also called the New Jerusalem.

New Jerusalem's Portrayal as the Virtuous Woman

It is true that the bride is mainly portrayed as a city in Revelation, but her personification as a woman is nonetheless present. On the other hand, as seen above, Babylon is emphasized in her personification as a woman. This emphasis of the personified evil woman and the lack thereof for the virtuous woman is quite akin to the tendency of the Qumran literature that invoke the two-women topos. It would seem that in apocalyptic settings, the evil woman figure is emphasized more so than the good woman figure in order to warn people of the imminent danger of the evil and to encourage them to stay loyal to the good. Still, New Jerusalem takes an important place in Revelation not only as a city but also as a woman.

In fact, the very title of the *bride* itself in Revelation's introduction of the New Jerusalem in 19:7 suggests a woman figure. Rossing's observation is insightful: "Whereas the Babylon preview of Rev 14:8–10 names only a city without any hint of a woman, the preview of Rev 19:7–9 introduces only a woman and her marriage to the lamb, with no mention of her city traits or city name."[44] This not only suggests that the bride is the very opposite reality of Babylon, but also that John wants to make sure the readers recognize the bride as a woman figure. The fact that John seemingly introduces the bride as a woman right after his telling of the destruction of Babylon without delay suggests that he has the two-women topos in mind.[45] By introducing the bride as the Lamb's good woman on the heel of the demise of the evil woman Babylon, John is showing his readers that, after they "come out" of Babylon, they must choose and align themselves with the right woman, the bride.

Of course, John does not disclose the bride's identity in 19:7–8 nor say much about her appearance. Yet what little detail John gives is hugely significant. First, John states that the Lamb's bride has made herself ready (ἡ γυνὴ αὐτοῦ ἡτοίμασεν ἑαυτὴν), and that it is for the marriage of the Lamb (ὁ γάμος τοῦ ἀρνίου). This notion of divine marriage is an important one. Since long ago, the Old Testament prophets utilized the

---

44. Rossing, *Two Cities*, 136.
45. Rossing, *Two Cities*, 141.

theme of divine marriage to express God's everlasting relationship with his people (i.e., Isa 49:18; 54:5–10; 61:10; 62:4–5; Jer 2:2; 31:31–32; Ezek 16:8, 32, 60–63; Hos 2:14–20).[46] Jesus himself also used the imagery of a wedding feast to refer to the kind of eschatological salvation he brings about and to make sure his people participate in the banquet as faithful invitees (Matt 22:1–14; Lk 14:16–24).[47] Paul, moreover, called the church, the bride of Christ (Rom 7:2–4; 2 Cor 11:2; cf. Eph 5:25).[48]

Important to notice here is that the notion of divine marriage and feast can be used in two ways, whether God's people become the bride herself or they are a third party, invitees to the marriage feast. Jesus seems to have used it in the latter manner, and Paul the former. However, the boundary between these two ways is not always clear cut. As mentioned above, the OT prophets described God as the bridegroom and either Israel or Jerusalem as the bride to express God's relationship with his *people*. This is because Israel and Jerusalem (or Zion) are more than simply a nation or a city. They represent the people of God.[49] This is especially clear in Isaiah 62 where in verses 2–4, Jerusalem or Zion is closely connected to the land of Israel and in verses 10–12, the city is closely connected with God's people (hence the phrase, "daughter of Zion" in verse 11).[50] Furthermore, the sexual immorality language so prevalent in the book of Revelation also appears in the Old Testament to refer to idolatry and unfaithfulness of not only Jerusalem as a harlot city (i.e., Jer 3:6–10; Lam 1:8–9; Ezek 23:11–35), but also God's people (i.e., Exod 25:16; Lev 17:7; 20:5; Num 25:1–5; Deut 31:16; Ps 106:36–39; Jer 5:7; Hos 4:12). This goes

---

46. Fekkes, *Isaiah*, 235.

47. Fiorenza, *Revelation*, 102.

48. Thomas argues that the bride in Rev 19:7–8 is the church alone and chronologically cannot include Israel. Per Thomas, OT saints rise during the time of the millennium (20:5–6) and are thereby not present during the time of the rapture and of Christ's return. Thomas, *Revelation 8–22*, 367–69. This writer, however, understands the bride to include all the redeemed, both Jews and Gentiles. The church as the bride of Christ is transnational. Anyone, irrespective of race or nationality, can be God's people through faith in Christ. This is because Christ has fulfilled the OT promises regarding God's people, and anyone can be part of God's people in Christ. This fulfillment of God's people now displays in the form of the church, the body of Christ. This does not mean that the church has somehow replaced Israel. Rather, the church, as a transnational reality, includes those redeemed from Israel as God's people. Patterson seems to understand similarly as he believes the bride of Rev 19 likely includes all the redeemed. Patterson, *Revelation*, 343–45.

49. Hoskins, *Revelation*, 367.

50. This helpful insight is from Paul Hoskins. See, Hoskins, *Revelation*, 367.

to show that the biblical writers regarded the city of Jerusalem and its people to be virtually indistinguishable as to use the nuptial imagery as well as the imagery of harlotry to both the city and the people to infer the same kinds of relationship between God and his people.

Hence, when it comes to the nuptial imagery of Revelation 19, one should not solely impose that the bride is the city of New Jerusalem and not the people of God.[51] Although the emphasis is on God's people being invitees to the marriage feast between the Lamb and the bride, one must understand that there is a close relationship of identity between God's people and the bride as well.[52] This emphasis of calling the readers to the marriage feast of the Lamb and the bride is probably from John's desire to compare and contrast the bride as the right woman to pursue from the Harlot, the evil woman.[53] In doing so, he strategically urges his readers that, after they shun the evil woman, they must choose the right woman, because it is this right woman who gets married to the Lamb. In other words, this is a choice between unfaithfulness/harlotry with the beast by siding with Babylon and faithfulness/loyalty to Christ by siding with New Jerusalem. This is akin to the author of Proverbs who tells his sons to choose the right bride and to stay far away from the strange harlot.

However, Proverbs, as well as any other works that utilize the two-women topos, encourages the readers to choose the virtuous woman for themselves, and in the case of Proverbs, to marry the good bride themselves.[54] In contrast, Revelation's bride belongs to the Lamb alone, and

---

51. Rossing actually argues that the bride represents the city of New Jerusalem and not the people of God in Rev 19:7–9 since the church or audience of Revelation is not scripted in the role of bride here. Rossing wants the good woman tradition from the two-women topos to stand out, but in doing so depreciates biblical allusions and in turn, does not see the close connection between the nuptial model of God's people as invitees to the wedding and the nuptial model of God's people as the bride. Rossing, *Two Cities*, 137–38.

52. Against Rossing's position, Miller argues that the bride is the church, namely the people of God. Miller, "The Nuptial Eschatology," 301–18. Hoskins even observes that the "first love" that the Ephesian church/believers abandoned in Revelation 2:4 has to do with their love for Christ as Christ's bride. Hoskins, *Revelation*, 75. Bauckham rightly understands that the New Jerusalem is both a place and people. Bauckham, *Theology*, 132–40. Likewise, Tabb, *All Things New*, 180. Huber moreover connects the bride with the idea of a virgin, and since God's people are called virgins in 14:4, the effect is that God's people who are virgins and who follow the Lamb wherever he goes must follow to the point of becoming his bride and wife. Huber, "The City-Women," 317–18.

53. So Rossing, *Two Cities*, 137.

54. For other works that describe wisdom as the bride the audience must espouse, see especially Sir 15:2–6 and Wis 8:2–16. See also Sirach 51, 4Q185, and 11Q52.

the readers are invited to their marriage. This proves that John is not following the standard two-women topos strictly. If he did, then he would want his readers to take and to marry the Lamb's bride themselves, and this would constitute adultery/harlotry which Revelation so adamantly opposes. No, John wants God's people not to defile themselves with women, for they are virgins (Rev 14:4).

John apparently has gone further with the two-women topos. Yes, the believers must choose the right woman, the bride, just as the author of Proverbs urges his sons to choose the right bride. Yet, at the same time, the bride is the Lamb's woman. John has ingeniously combined the good woman imagery from the stock two-women topos with the biblical nuptial model of God's people as God's wife to argue that the bride is whom the believers must strive for and that they must, in fact, be the bride at the same time. John has cleverly removed the conflict that arises from solely using the two-women topos as described above in doing so. Pursuing the Lamb's bride is no longer harlotry but a holy marriage union with the Lamb.

Rossing is thus only half right when she rejects the model of "audience-as-groom" in order to avoid the understanding that John somehow is encouraging his readers to take the Lamb's bride for themselves and marry her instead.[55] This is well-intended, for scholars such as Tina Pippin have been known to express distress, thinking that John is allowing the audience's desire for violence and sex to roam free for the bride in Revelation 19:7–9.[56] But clearly the audience is not the groom, the Lamb is. Notwithstanding, the audience is still encouraged to choose the bride according to the two-women topos, and Rossing, in order to make sense of the text, argues instead that the audience is not called to desire the bride herself, but rather her gifts and inheritance.[57] While this may soften the issue, it still does not adequately explain what desiring the bride's gifts may entail. After all, what really is the difference between desiring the bride herself and desiring what she can give?

Better is to understand that the audience is called to desire the bride to the point of becoming her themselves. This makes perfect sense in light of the biblical allusions John is utilizing in 19:7–9 and avoids Rossing's dilemma above altogether. John's ability to combine different imageries and biblical metaphors and to emphasize one over the others

55. Rossing, *Two Cities*, 139.
56. Pippin, *Death and Desire*, 82–86.
57. Rossing, *Two Cities*, 139.

in different points in the same narrative is not new. This study has shown one such instance regarding the harlot's demise in 17:16–18. While John does emphasize the good woman imagery in 19:7 to encourage his readers to choose the right woman, he also has the biblical metaphor of God's people as God's bride in mind as well. Hence, the real effect becomes thus: choosing the good woman really means one becomes the Lamb's bride.

This is made clear in Revelation 19:8 as John states that the bride is wearing fine linen (βύσσινον), bright and pure (λαμπρὸν καθαρόν), and that her clothing is actually the righteous deeds of the saints. First of all, the description of the bride's clothing and appearance cannot be explained with the biblical model of nuptial imagery alone and is in fact a stereotypical description of the good woman from the two-women topos. Wisdom texts that make use of the two-women topos employ the words "bright" and "pure" to describe the virtuous woman's appearance (Cf. Xenophon, *Mem.* 2.1.22; Clem. Alex. *Paed.* 2.10.110; Dio Chrysostom *Or.* 1.70; *Tabula of Cebes* 12.2; 14.4; 19.1; 20.2; 21.3), and Proverbs 31:22 describes the good bride's clothing as that of fine linen. Biblical scholars argue correctly that Isaiah 61:10 is being alluded in Revelation 19:7–8, but the said Isaian passage does not contain the words "bright," "pure," or "linen" in the description of God's bride.[58] Again, John must have intentionally added these words to successfully invoke recognition of the good woman of the topos to urge the audience that the bride is the right woman they must espouse as the counterpart to evil Babylon.[59] As the counterpart, the bride's clothing parallels or contrasts with certain aspects of Babylon, such as her purity over against Babylon's impurities (Rev 17:4) and her bright fine linen over against the brightness and the fine linen taken away from Babylon (18:12, 14, 16).[60] "The clear sense is

---

58. Fekkes argues that, among the OT passages that employ the nuptial imagery, Isaiah 40–66 stand behind Revelation's nuptial imagery in general and Isaiah 61:10 stands behind Revelation 19:7–8 in particular. This is because only Isaiah utilizes the bridal imagery in a spiritual sense and in a consistently positive manner akin to Revelation. While some understand that Ezekiel 16 may lie behind Revelation 19:7–8, Fekkes objects in claiming that Ezekiel 16 portrays Jerusalem in a negative manner as the unfaithful bride, which does not conform to the positive portrayal of the bride in Revelation. Only Isaiah 61:10 has various parallel concepts and themes with Revelation 19:7–8 to constitute viable allusion. Yet even Fekkes concedes that " . . . the dictional connections between Rev 19:7–8 and Isa 61:10 are in individual cases doubtful or inexact." Fekkes, "His Bride," 272–74.

59. Rossing, *Two Cities*, 141.

60. Rossing, *Two Cities*, 143.

that Babylon's clothes and splendor have been 'taken from her' (ἀπώλετο ἀπὸ σοῦ, Rev 18:14) and given (ἐδόθη αὐτῇ, Rev 19:8) instead to the bride."[61]

Furthermore, John specifies that the bride's clothing is actually the righteous deeds of the saints (19:8). Rossing simply argues that this does not mean that the bride is identical to the saints but rather that the bride is acknowledging the saints' righteous deeds by wearing them.[62] But the most natural reading of this passage makes it out that the audience is in fact the bride.[63] This is all the more certain when one understands that Isaiah 61:10 is in the background of Revelation 19:8. Just as Isaiah's bride (Israel) expresses that God has covered her with a robe of righteousness (Isa 61:10), so Revelation's bride (church) was given a clothing of righteous deeds of the saints.[64] Thus, John combines the good woman imagery from the two-women topos with the biblical nuptial imagery of God's people as the bride to masterfully claim that the Lamb's bride is the one the audience must pursue and that they should indeed become this bride by righteous deeds. In other words, choosing the right woman is through the saints' obedient service to God in faith and perseverance (cf. Rev 3:5; 6:11; 7:14; 13:10; 14:12–13).[65] Again, this is not simply about moralistic choosing of which woman one wants to take. The issue is more spiritual; choosing the good woman really means fidelity to God in faith and obedience.

Then, in Revelation 19:9, "The metaphor changes from vv. 7b–8 (the bride represents God's people) to v. 9 (the guests represent God's people)."[66] John has changed the metaphor once again to the theme of messianic banquet or, to the nuptial imagery of God's people as invitees, to further inspire his readers to absolutely long for the Lamb's marriage with the bride. In 19:9, the angel commands John to write (γράψον), which adds authority to what is written. And what is written is actually a blessing (μακάριος): "blessed are the ones who are invited to the marriage

---

61. Rossing, *Two Cities*, 143–44.

62. Rossing, *Two Cities*, 139–40.

63. So Beale, *Revelation*, 940, 945; Charles, *Revelation*, vol. 2, 128; Fanning, *Revelation*, 480–82.

64. Fekkes, "His Bride," 273.

65. In Revelation, righteous deeds are only possible because the saints have been cleansed via the Lamb's act of sacrifice (7:14). Christian works then flow from what Christ has done, as believers obediently live in actual conduct. See Hoskins, *Revelation*, 367–68.

66. Fanning, *Revelation*, 482.

feast of the Lamb." With this, John has succinctly and successfully introduced the counterpart to Babylon, namely the bride, in 19:7–9. The bride is the right woman God's people must long after, for she is the one who gets blissfully married to the Lamb. God's people must strive also to become that bride. Although John's introduction of the bride may be succinct, his invitation to choose the bride is effective, as he has skillfully combined various metaphors including the good woman imagery of the two-women topos to bringing about his intended encouragement and persuasion.

New Jerusalem's Rise as the Virtuous Woman

Interestingly, John never really describes the anticipated marriage between the Lamb and the bride. Instead, John transforms the good woman figure into a magnificent city called New Jerusalem in Revelation 21–22. Just as Babylon was both a woman and a city, so the bride is both a woman and a city. John will continue to compare the bride with Babylon in terms of a city in Revelation 21–22, the main section on the New Jerusalem of Revelation. However, although John makes comparison between the bride and Babylon for the bride is the antithesis of Babylon, the comparison is really one of exceptionality. John wants to show that in truth, New Jerusalem is unmatched in its beauty and magnificence, and not even Babylon at its height can compete against her.

John's visionary section on New Jerusalem begins with him seeing a new heaven and a new earth (21:1–8).[67] He also sees the holy city New Jerusalem coming down from heaven, prepared as a bride adorned for her husband (21:2). By describing New Jerusalem as a prepared bride (νύμφη), John communicates that the holy city is in fact the Lamb's bride (γυνή) he introduced in 19:7.[68] This holy city is also "from God" (ἀπὸ τοῦ θεοῦ), signaling that she has a divine origin (cf. 21:10).[69] Unlike the

---

67. Dempsey argues that Rev 21:1–8 is by far the most stunning vision that communicates of a radical transformation, an intimate relationship, and an everlasting hope. Dempsey, "Revelation 21:1–8," 400.

68. Although vocabularies differ, it is clear that the New Jerusalem of Rev 21–22 is the Lamb's bride of 19:7. In Rev 21:9, John uses both words, νύμφη and γυνή, to call the holy city, "the bride, the wife of the Lamb." See, Thomas, *Revelation 8–22*, 442. It seems that he used the word γυνή in 19:7 in reference to the Lamb's bride in order to recall for the readers Proverb's virtuous wife and the importance of choosing her instead of the evil woman.

69. Beckwith, *Apocalypse*, 751.

harlot Babylon whose authority stems from the beast (17:3, 7), the bride, New Jerusalem's authority is from God.

The reason stated in 21:3 why New Jerusalem comes down from heaven and from God to the new heaven and new earth is very important. It is because God wills to dwell with his people. God will no longer stay in heaven separated from his creation, especially from his people; he will personally come to dwell with them, and they will be his people when the time comes.[70] New Jerusalem is thus an ultimate place of perfect communion where God and his people meet without anything blocking or hindering the way.[71] This relational and spiritual aspect of New Jerusalem is so emphasized by John that the audience cannot help but understand New Jerusalem as more than simply a city. As this study has shown, the nuptial imagery in Revelation 19:7-9 uses both the imagery of God's people as invitees and of God's people as the bride. In other words, John uses the marriage metaphor to invite his readers to New Jerusalem as well as to become part of the bride herself. The same is true of Revelation 21-22. By calling New Jerusalem, "bride" (21:2, 9), John invokes the same metaphor to invite his audience to embrace New Jerusalem. Just as Babylon represented both its people, namely the people of the earth, and a place, the New Jerusalem also represents both God's people and their dwelling place.[72] After all, Jesus himself promised those who conquer that he would put the name of New Jerusalem on them in

---

70. Rev 21:3 contains deliberate covenantal language (cf. Lev 26:11-12; Ezek 37:27; Zech 2). John is signaling that with the coming of New Jerusalem, there will be absolute and everlasting relationship between God and his people. See Aune, *Revelation 17-22*, 1122-23; Bauckham, *Climax*, 311-12; Beale, *Revelation*, 1046.

71. Osborne notes that there is never again any other descent from heaven to earth after the New Jerusalem in Revelation. The New Jerusalem is the final descent from heaven, and the heaven and the earth finally become one with the coming of the holy city. Osborne, *Revelation*, 732.

72. Osborne, *Revelation*, 733. For further support on understanding New Jerusalem as both God's people and place, see Pattemore, *The People of God*, 200. While Gundry argues for New Jerusalem being God's people, he nonetheless admits that a city can represent both its inhabitants and their dwelling place. Gundry, "The New Jerusalem," 256. Thomas also understands the figure of a bridal-city to capture two characteristics of the New Jerusalem, namely God's relationship with his people (i.e., the bride) and the life of the people in communion with God (i.e., the city), and claims, "The bride is both the people of God and the seat of their abode, the new Jerusalem." Thomas, *Revelation 8-22*, 442. Thus, while the New Jerusalem can be an actual place, it can also represent God's people, since there is a close identity between the city and its inhabitants. See also, Schreiner, *The Joy of Hearing*, 158.

Revelation 3:12, which indicates a close identity between New Jerusalem and the believers.

Since God himself will dwell among his people, there shall be reversal of fortunes in the new creation. This is indicated by a series of "no more" (οὐκ ἔτι) in 21:1–4. First, the sea is no more in the new heaven and new earth (21:1). Aune is correct in understanding that the sea must be functioning here as a negative symbol as to be singled out as missing in the new creation.[73] The sea is the place of evil in the book of Revelation (cf. 12:18; 13:1), and its absence in the new creation means that evil wrought by Satan does not exist.[74] Furthermore, the sea was a place of idolatrous trade activity with Babylon (18:10–19; cf. 8:9). In terms of the two-women topos then, the seductive and idolatrous economic commerce with Babylon is no more; perfect enjoyment of New Jerusalem is what is left in the new creation. Just as the Israelites came to enjoy God's inheritance in the new land after the parting of the Red Sea, God's people will come to fully enjoy their inheritance in the new creation without any old-world barriers after the eschatological Red Sea departs.[75] The threats of evil and of judgment that defined the old world for the believers will be replaced with complete salvation and vindication in the new world, the highlight of which is the New Jerusalem.[76]

Second, death, mourning, crying, and pain are no more (21:4). This parallels the sea being no more in 21:1 and explains it in further detail. The dissolution of the sea also means the dissolution of all sufferings that identified the old creation.[77] So, John alluded to Isaiah 51:10 in Revelation

---

73. Aune, *Revelation 17–22*, 1119. Beale lists five ways the word "sea" (θάλασσα) is used in Revelation: the origin of cosmic evil (4:6; 12:18; 13:1; 15:2), the unbelieving nations (17:2, 6), the place of the dead (20:13), the primary location of the world's idolatrous trade activity (18:10–19), and the literal body of water (5:13; 10:2; 14:7). He understands all five uses to be at work in Rev 21:1. Beale, *Revelation*, 1042. Osborne, however, argues that the first two uses are primary in 21:1, thus understanding that the word "sea" is being used symbolically in that passage. Osborne, *Revelation*, 731. This writer agrees with Beal with the first four symbolic uses but is hesitant with his fifth literal usage. In any case, all would agree that the absence of sea in the new creation means removal of bad things the sea represented in the old creation.

74. So Bauckham, *Theology*, 49–50; Lee, *New Jerusalem*, 269; Osborne, *Revelation*, 731; Roloff, *Offenbarung*, 198; Smalley, *Revelation*, 524.

75. This new Exodus motif has been recognized by several scholars. For an effective argument of the function of the new Exodus motif in Rev 21:1, see Mathewson, "New Exodus," 243–58.

76. For a more thorough treatment of the difference between the old and the new creation alluded by the sea imagery, see Moo, "The Sea That Is No More," 148–67.

77. Smalley, *Revelation*, 539; Swete, *Apocalypse*, 278.

21:1 to invoke the new Exodus motif and alludes to Isaiah 51:11 in Revelation 21:4 to claim that the going away of the sea further denotes the going away of the sufferings.[78] What is more, both 21:1 and 21:4 also utilize Isaiah 65:17–20 in reference to the passing away of the old.[79] The peculiar difference between Isaiah 65 and Revelation 21:4 seems significant. Whereas Isaiah 65:17–20 list three items, namely weeping, crying, and death, that will be no more when the new heaven and new earth come, Revelation 21:4 lists four items (death, mourning, crying, and pain). This may be deliberate on John's part to make the list fourfold.[80] The number four signifies the entire world in Revelation,[81] and John seems to have intentionally made his list fourfold to signal that all the old world's sufferings will be done away with the coming of the new creation.

The new creation clearly is the pinnacle of God's blessings as he himself shall dwell with his people in the New Jerusalem, and as such, no old adverse fortunes that befall the believers shall exist in the new. It shall only be an eternal state of joy and peace. God is trustworthy and true, and what he declares shall come to pass exactly as he promised (21:5). Indeed, God himself speaks with authority in 21:6: "To the thirsty, I will give from the spring of the water of life without payment." Just as Christ offered living water to the thirsty (Jn 4:10; 7:37–38), so God offers the water of life to those who long for the new heaven and new earth. Mathewson is correct in seeing several allusions regarding this life-giving water to Isaiah 55:1, Ezekiel 47:1–12, and Zechariah 14:8.[82] Also important to note that these OT prophetic books equate the water with the Holy Spirit (cf. Isa 44:3; Ezek 36:25–27), just as John 7:39 does.[83] Thus, it is very possible that Revelation 21:6 is referring to the Holy Spirit as the sustaining source of eternal life. If so, then all three members of the Trinity are found to be at work in the new creation: God brings about the new creation, the Lamb marries the bride, and the Spirit sustains the eternal life.

---

78. Mathewson, "Isaiah in Revelation," 202.

79. Fekkes, *Isaiah*, 254.

80. Isaiah 65's weeping, crying, and death parallel Revelation 21's mourning, crying, and death. If so, the only item missing from Isa 65 but added to the list of Rev 21 is pain.

81. Bauckham, *Climax*, 31.

82. Mathewson, *New Heaven and New Earth*, 80–83.

83. In addition to Rev 21:6, 22:1 and 22:17 also make mention of the water of life. For scholars who understand the reference to the Holy Spirit in these verses, see Hoskins, *Revelation*, 433, 457; Paul, *Revelation*, 344–45; Rainbow, *Johannine Theology*, 369, 409; Swete, *Apocalypse*, 294–95.

Yet, it may also be that wisdom traditions stand behind Revelation 21 and not just the prophetic traditions. While the aforementioned prophetic passages such as Ezekiel 37:27 and Zechariah 2:10–11 (cf. Lev 26:11–12) do make strong sense of God dwelling with his people in terms of covenantal language, they do not feature the explicit language of God "descending" to do so as in Revelation 21:2–3.[84] This notion of the divine descending to dwell on earth has more affinities with the wisdom traditions of Proverbs and Sirach 24. In Proverbs, wisdom proclaims her own godlike status in heaven (Prov 8), but then claims that she has built her house among men to invite them to her banquet (Prov 9:1–6). Similarly in Sirach, wisdom claims that she was first in the presence of God and that God then commanded her to dwell in Israel (Sir 24:1–12). In both these sapiential texts, the invitation toward God's people to choose to dwell with wisdom who was in heaven but now has come down for their benefit is strong, just like Revelation 21.

Furthermore, God himself speaking to offer water of life to the thirsty without payment in Revelation 21:6 has correspondences with Sirach 24:19–34 to merit viable allusion.[85] The same is true for Revelation 22:17 where the same invitation for the water of life is made, albeit this time it is offered by John.[86] In Sirach 24:19–21, the wisdom figure calls people to come to her to eat and to drink, and claims that "those who drink of me will thirst for more (cf. 15:3)." This is akin to the bride calling people to come to take the water of life in Revelation 22:17. In fact, the motif of the spring or fountain of living water is frequent in sapiential literature.[87] Revelation 21:6 has God offering the water of life to the thirsty, and this water is from *the spring*. None of the prophetic works that stand in the background of Revelation 21:6 as noted above specify that the living water comes from a spring. Yet, Proverbs 16:22 (cf. 5:18) states that wisdom is a fountain of life, and Sirach 24:25–34 compare wisdom as an overflowing water from a water channel to a river and then to a sea.

The phrase, "without payment" may recall the ending of Sirach 51:25 where the author urges the readers to acquire wisdom without

---

84. Rossing, *Two Cities*, 149.

85. Rossing, *Two Cities*, 150.

86. While the invitation to the thirsty to come take the water of life in 22:17 directly comes from John, one could argue that the Spirit, the bride, and even Jesus himself are together with John in calling people to come. See Fanning, *Revelation*, 563.

87. Fishbane, "Well of Living Water," 3–16.

money.[88] The same invitation is happening in Revelation like bookends, one at the beginning of the New Jerusalem vision (21:6) and one at the end (22:17), both urging the readers to choose to take the water of life. All these correspondences suggest the likelihood of John using the wisdom traditions along with the prophetic traditions, and it is with the wisdom traditions that John's invitational nature to desire and to participate in the New Jerusalem really comes out to the fore and becomes effective. It is true that the phrase, "without payment" is found in Isaiah 55:1 and that the said passage is invitational in nature. However, it has been noted that Isaiah 55:1 itself is based on a wisdom form of invitation to a feast, notably found in Proverbs 9:5–6 and Sirach 24:19–21.[89] In any case, John's intended effect to his readers is clear with the thirsting for the water of life language; they must strive for the perfect satisfaction of the life-giving water in the new creation. Only those who conquer will inherit this promise (Rev 21:7), a clear charge to the readers to endure and to stay loyal to Christ. The invitation for this inheritance is "without payment," which is completely the opposite of Babylon's offer of riches at a price of busy commerce. What the bride can offer freely stands far above Babylon's most luxurious trades. Which invitation to choose, whether Babylon's appeal or the bride's, should be very easy to decide.

John's account of the blessed state of the new creation comes to its apex with the description of the holy city, New Jerusalem (21:9—22:5). Even here, John writes in a way that further invites his readers to choose the bride. It is well known that John's portrayal of New Jerusalem is modeled after Ezekiel's depiction of the new city and temple (Ezek 40–48).[90] Yet significant differences emerge. First, John emphasizes the city's great and high wall and its twelves gates with detail, which Ezekiel does not do. Ezekiel 40:5 does mention a wall surrounding the future temple, but it seems like a normal wall, not "great and high" like Revelation 21:12. Furthermore, Revelation 21:14 states that the wall of New Jerusalem has twelve foundations with twelve names of the Lamb's apostles written on them, and no foundations are mentioned in connection with the wall in

---

88. Rossing, *Two Cities*, 152.

89. This was first suggested by Begrich, *Studien zu Deuterojesaja*, 59–60. Clifford took it a step further by arguing that this is a divine invitation to the feast of life. Clifford, "Isaiah 55," 27. See Oswalt, *Isaiah*, 435.

90. This study does not deny that other prophetic works such as Isaiah are behind John's depiction of New Jerusalem. This study is simply affirming that Ezekiel 40–48 have the major influence on Revelation's New Jerusalem and that comparing the differences between the two books is fruitful.

Ezekiel. Regarding the twelve gates, Ezekiel 48:31–34 do also mention them as having the names of the twelve tribes of Israel inscribed just like Revelation 21:12–13, but John adds a new detail of twelve angels being situated at the gates.

These differences suggest that John wants to emphasize the grandiose nature of New Jerusalem, incomparable to Babylon that is destroyed. He also wants to show that New Jerusalem is not simply a city grandeur, but represents a people perfected. The angels being at the gates recall Revelation 2–3 where the angels were closely associated with the seven churches.[91] With the mention of twelve names on the gates and twelve names on the foundations, John has altogether twenty-four names being inscribed at the wall of New Jerusalem. This further recalls the twenty-four elders who were around the throne (cf. 4:4), who represent the people of God in its fulness.[92] Even if one does not see a connection with the twenty-four elders, the message is the same. The twenty-four names signify that New Jerusalem represents the perfected people of God.

The wall with twenty-four names of God's people is moreover comparable to the bride's clothing and adornment, since both characterize how one looks on the outside. The holy city as a virtuous woman was clothed with fine linen, bright and pure, and John stated that her clothing is the righteous deeds of the saints (19:7–8). Now, as John portrays the holy city as a virtuous city, he claims that the city's clothing, namely its wall and the gates, has the names of the saints written on them. John also claims that when he saw the Lamb's bride descending from heaven as a city (21:9–10), she had the glory of God, whose radiance (φωστήρ) was like precious stones (21:11). In Scripture, radiance (φωστήρ) is another way of referring to God's glory as it is reflected in his people (cf. Dan 12:3; Matt 5:14; Phil 2:15).[93] As the bride was adorned bright and pure with the righteous deeds of the saints (19:7–8), so New Jerusalem is adorned with

---

91. Beale, *Revelation*, 1068.

92. The series of twelves also have been connected with the twelve signs of the zodiac, to the point that New Jerusalem is an astral city, akin to the celestial cities deities had in the sky, albeit Revelation is portraying that New Jerusalem is a celestial city par excellence. See Malina, *New Jerusalem*, 45–65, esp. 55. However, it is likely that what John directly had in mind with the mention of the series of twelve names has to do with the people of God, since he clearly specifies that these are the names of twelve tribes of Israel and of the Lamb's apostles, not names of some constellations. For those who see a reference to the fulness of the people of God in the series of twelve names, see Beale, *Revelation*, 1068–69; Lee, *New Jerusalem*, 279; Mounce, *Revelation*, 390–91; Osborne, *Revelation*, 751–52; Smalley, *Revelation*, 548–49.

93. Beale, *Revelation*, 1066.

brilliant radiance of God's glory as it is reflected by the saints. Thus, as the bride was so identified with the people of God in 19:7–8, so is the New Jerusalem so identified with the people of God in 21:9–14. The holy city is more than just a city; it represents God's people.[94]

Furthermore, John meticulously details the kinds of precious stones used to build the wall and the gates of the holy city as he now moves in closer to look at the city (21:15–21). This obviously adds to the impressive stature of the city, as well as its invitational quality. The wall is made of jasper (21:18), and since John already told that the city's wall was radiating like jasper, clear as crystal (hence, transparent), when he first saw the city from afar (21:11), it must be that as John moved in closer to examine the city, he could see through the transparent jasper wall the inside of the city, which was pure and clear gold (21:18, 21). John's ingenious, yet subtle, telling of this visionary experience thus invites the readers to long to see the city as well.[95] Also of significance is John's deliberate description of the twelve stones used to adorn the foundation of the wall. This incredible adornment reminds the readers of Babylon's adornment with precious jewels, but only so much better.[96] The enumeration of twelve stones according to the Lamb's twelve apostles' names clearly emphasizes the importance of being part of God's people through the Lamb's work, which he began with calling his special group of disciples.[97] These features combined further encourages the church to persevere to attain the blessings of New Jerusalem.

Second, unlike Ezekiel, Revelation's New Jerusalem has no temple (21:22). Vogelgesang is correct when he stated that this great divergence from Ezekiel 40–48 where seven of nine long chapters describe the future temple must be deliberate and radical.[98] Even the sectarian community at Qumran, although they saw themselves as a temple (1QS 8:1–7; 9:3–6), similar to the New Testament's idea of the church community as a temple, still understood that the eschatological temple would be rebuilt

---

94. See also the conclusion by du Rand, "The New Jerusalem," 275–302.

95. Rissi, *The Future*, 71.

96. Royalty states that Rev 21:15–21 contain the most concentrated and detailed amplification of any wealth imagery in Revelation. In doing so, John creates a vision of Jerusalem that is more extravagant than any other city. Royalty, *Streets of Heaven*, 227–34.

97. Hoskins, *Revelation*, 448.

98. Vogelgesang, "The Interpretation of Ezekiel," 77.

(4QFlor; *DNJ*).⁹⁹ The reason that John gives for the negation of the temple building in New Jerusalem is astonishing. It is because the Lord God and the Lamb are the city's temple (Rev 21:22). The temple represents God's presence among his people. The fact that there is no temple building in the New Jerusalem and that God and the Lamb are its temple means that the whole city is the temple, for God's immediate presence is there.¹⁰⁰ John means to show that there is such a perfect presence of God and a perfect relationship with God in New Jerusalem. This is something radically new: a welcoming sight indeed.

Third, unlike the gates in Ezekiel's temple, the twelve gates of New Jerusalem are always open, and people are invited to enter them (21:24–26). In Ezekiel, the temple's east gate is conspicuously shut and may never be opened so that no one may enter by it (Ezek 44:1–2). Furthermore, Ezekiel emphasizes the limited nature of the twelve gates as he states that the gates are *exits* of the city, through which people go out to cultivate the land (48:30). In Revelation, precisely the opposite is emphasized. The gates provide *entrance* into New Jerusalem. This is clear when looking at John's repeated use of the preposition εἰς (Rev 21:24–26).¹⁰¹ Those who are written in the Lamb's book of life can enter the gates into New Jerusalem freely (21:27). This invites the audience to enter the city as well, and to choose this city over Babylon all the more.

Fourth, the new paradisiacal condition inside New Jerusalem far exceeds Ezekiel's vision of the sanctuary (Ezek 47:1–12). Ezekiel's vision also references water flowing out from the threshold of the temple, becoming a river which runs into the Dead Sea. This water turns the sea into fresh water and brings life wherever it goes. However, in Revelation, the river of life flows from the throne of God and of the Lamb and through the middle of the street of the city (Rev 22:1–2). The first difference is expected given the fact that God and the Lamb stand in place of the temple (21:22). The second difference is more significant. Whereas Ezekiel focuses on the river of life going out of the city to bring life wherever it goes, John focuses on the fact that the river of life runs through the heart of the city, with no mention of it running outside the city. Since New Jerusalem signifies the people of God as well, John must be communicating that " . . . the life of the perfected kingdom of God fills all God's people."¹⁰²

99. Lee, *New Jerusalem*, 281–82.
100. Bauckham, *Theology*, 136.
101. Rossing, *Two Cities*, 154.
102. Lee, *New Jerusalem*, 290.

Moreover, whereas Ezekiel mentions trees bearing fruit every month whose leaves are for healing growing from the banks of the river (Ezek 47:12), John explicitly mentions the tree of life growing on the side of the river inside New Jerusalem (Rev 22:2). This reminds the readers the Garden of Eden with the tree of life and river (Gen 2:9; 3:22), but unlike the condition of the Garden of Eden where Adam and Eve were prohibited from eating from the tree of life after they sinned, God's people can now eat freely from the tree of life with no restrictions. Proverbs 3:18 states that wisdom, the virtuous woman, is a tree of life to those who choose her, and Revelation shows that the tree of life is indeed available to those who choose the bride. New Jerusalem, in essence, is a perfect paradise unlike anything the old creation has ever envisioned. There will be neither curse nor night; only blessing and perfect relationship with God and his people will eternally exist (Rev 22:3–5).

This portion of the study has analyzed the invitational nature of God's city, the New Jerusalem. While New Jerusalem is mainly described in terms of a city in Revelation 21–22, the fact that she is called the bride in 21:2 and 21:9 connects her with the bride of 19:7-8, which in turn means that the good woman imagery of the two-women topos is continuing, albeit very implicitly, in Revelation 21–22. In fact, New Jerusalem is described as more than a city as it also represents God's people, and this is in line with the description of the bride in 19:7-8 where she also represented God's people. By using the OT city imagery where the city and its people are intimately linked, John in effect argues that God's people must not only long for the coming of God's city, but also strive to become a part of that city. This is also in line with the exhortation in 19:7-8, namely for God's people to not only desire the bride, the good woman, but also to become that bride themselves. Moreover, the invitational nature of the description of New Jerusalem cannot be explained by prophetic traditions alone, but it is likely that John has weaved sapiential traditions alongside the prophetic traditions to make God's city truly welcoming. If so, this matches with the purpose of the two-women topos, which is to make the good woman figure desirable as to spur people to make the right choice in wanting her.

The Ethical Choice: "Come"

After the portrayal of the bride as God's perfect city, New Jerusalem, John continues to urge his readers to choose the bride in the closing section of Revelation. First, John confirms the veracity of his prophecy contained in the book of Revelation via the angel's endorsement and more importantly, via Christ's very own words (Rev 22:6–16). In doing so, John adds to the gravity of situation. The prophecy has been given and the visions have been cast, the last of which was the portrayal of New Jerusalem. The readers now must seriously decide whether they will stay faithful to Christ and align themselves with the bride by keeping the words contained in Revelation (22:7, 9, 11, 12, 14), or whether they will succumb to the ways of the beast and fornicate with Babylon into destruction (22:11, 12, 15).

Then, John proceeds to let the virtuous woman speak for herself. In Revelation 22:17, the bride is once again personified and truly speaks, "Come."[103] "Her invitation to 'Come' (Rev 22:17) recalls the invitation to the banquet in Rev 19:9 and the invitations of other feminine wisdom figures from Proverbs, Sirach, and the moralists, who also call out to passerby to come to them."[104] Her command to come is buttressed by making sure that she is not speaking alone, but together with the Spirit. In doing so, John essentially validates the bridal New Jerusalem's invitation as divinely sanctioned.

Rossing argues that this bride cannot be the church, although she is the same bridal figure of Revelation 19:7–9.[105] However, as this study has shown, the bride signifies the church, and is not simply a feminine wisdom figure or a city that stands opposite to Babylon.[106] The bride's adornment and the bridal New Jerusalem's foundations and gates are identified closely with the saints (19:8; 21:12–14). New Jerusalem itself is a symbol of perfect and immediate relationship between God and his people. If God is the city's temple, then his people are the city. The bridal New Jerusalem is a place and people at the same time. This is nothing new; cities and their inhabitants have been used interchangeably to refer to the same entity. Thus, when the bride beckons the audience to come,

---

103. This would be the only instance in Revelation where the bride speaks for herself.

104. Rossing, *Two Cities*, 161.

105. Rossing, *Two Cities*, 160–61.

106. Aune states thus: "Here the bride must be the personification of the Church." Aune, *Revelation 17–22*, 1228.

it is as if the church as an organic and ontological whole is calling the present believers to make a choice to be part of herself.

It has also been noted that the call to "come" is for the Lamb to come back soon.[107] This fits the context, since Christ himself stated twice that he will come soon (22:7, 12). Hence, 22:17 has the Spirit and the bride responding with a petition of maranatha (cf. 1 Cor 16:22; Rev 22:20) to the Lamb. The Spirit would prophetically beckon Christ to come, and the bride would also want him to come, for she longs for her husband. The people who are hearing John's prophecy and who desire the water of life will also want Christ to come back soon (22:17).

However, it is also possible to understand the call to be referring to the audience as this study has done.[108] The latter half of Revelation 22:17 more likely addresses the readers to come, and the same can be true for the former half.[109] Moreover, there is an allusion to Isaiah 55:1 in Revelation 22:17, and the Isaian text clearly calls everyone who thirsts to come to the waters and to buy without price. If so, then Revelation 22:17 is also calling people who are thirsty to come take the water of life without price. More importantly, John has compared and contrasted Babylon with New Jerusalem using the two-women topos. One of the essential elements of the topos is the two women's alluring calls to people to choose one over the other, with the right choice obviously being the virtuous woman. Since New Jerusalem of Revelation is the virtuous woman, it is fitting that she would call people to "come" to her. Whereas the audience must "come out of" Babylon, they must "come" and "enter" the gates of New Jerusalem.

Thus, the call to come in Revelation 22:17 is likely a call to people to come choose New Jerusalem. The eschatological church as the bride is longing for present believers to stay faithful and persevere, so that they will partake in the blessings of new creation. To give this solemn, divine charge one last time, John, in the closing section of his letter, lets the bride and the Spirit speak to call the readers to faithfulness. To twist or

---

107. For scholars who argue for the position that this is a call for Jesus to come, see Fanning, *Revelation*, 563; Hoskins, *Revelation*, 478–79; Smalley, *Revelation*, 577.

108. See also, Bauckham, "Revelation," 1305; Beale, *Revelation*, 1148–49; Ladd, *Revelation*, 294–95; Mounce, *Revelation*, 409; Osborne, *Revelation*, 793.

109. Beasley-Murray takes the first two imperatives as a call to Jesus and the last two as addressed to people. Beasley-Murray, *Revelation*, 343–44. While this may be possible, the tight proximity of the imperatives would weigh more towards seeing the imperatives as a unit, addressing the same individual or individuals.

to miss John's prophecy, and thereby his charge, would be detrimental to one's outcome (22:18–19).

John's goal in giving his prophetic revelation to the church is thus hortatory. The book of Revelation is not simply John's apocalyptic take on the situation surrounding his time nor is it just aimed at giving information about the future. It is paraenetic; John is advising his audience to stay committed to God and to the Lamb in light of the future. Rossing argues that Revelation's exhortations have political and economic dimensions, not just moral, since New Jerusalem is God's alternate city with an entire political economy.[110] While this may be true, she does not recognize that New Jerusalem is overarchingly spiritual. In order to participate in the political and economic blessings of New Jerusalem, one does not simply follow morals acceptable to God and to the Lamb. Just as following Babylon means worshipping the beast (13:3–4, 8; 17:8), following New Jerusalem means worshipping God (19:9–10). Those who can enter New Jerusalem are those who wash their robes (22:14), and John made clear that it is the believers who wash their robes in the blood of the Lamb (7:14) and who can worship God day and night (7:9–12, 15). The believers are also those who keep the commandments of God and hold to the testimony of Jesus (12:17), and holding to the testimony of Jesus is the same as keeping faith in Jesus (14:12). Faith is a spiritual matter, and staying faithful to God and thereby entering New Jerusalem would necessitate faith in Christ.

CONCLUSION: BABYLON AND NEW JERUSALEM

Therefore, while both New Jerusalem and Babylon are political and economic realities, the foundational reality is spiritual. Both are representative cities for the kingdoms of God and of the beast. The conflict of the two kingdoms, which John portrays as ongoing (Rev 12–14), has at its core a conflict of worship.[111] This is why John distinguishes between those who worship the beast and those who worship God throughout Revelation.[112] Those who have the mark of the beast on their foreheads

---

110. Rossing, *Two Cities*, 157–58.
111. Bauckham, *Theology*, 34–35.
112. Morales recently has argued that there is a third group of people in Revelation, namely the nations. If the saints belong to God and if the earth dwellers belong to the beast, the nations act in Revelation as a middle-man, whom both God and the Lamb on one hand and Satan and the beast on the other contend for. Thus, Morales understands

will worship the beast (Rev 13) and those who have the name of God on their foreheads will worship God (Rev 14:1–5), each with radically different endings for eternity.

Because John knows this, and because John recognizes that Satan works hard in persecuting the saints and seducing people to follow him, he uses the two-women topos along with other biblical motifs to portray two cities/kingdoms as two women to further describe this spiritual reality in the closing section of Revelation. Just as Satan tempts people to follow him through his two beasts, so Babylon the evil woman allures people to choose her. Yet believers must recognize that God wants them to persevere and stay faithful despite Babylon's charms, and so John portrays the bridal New Jerusalem as a virtuous woman who beckons them to their true home. In doing so, John's paraenetic goal in exhorting his audience to stay loyal to God is cleverly enhanced. John's portrayal of two contrasting women cities is thus a sapiential polemic that is anti-Satan.

Yet John's use of the two-women topos in making his paraenetic appeal is not merely conventional. Personification of Babylon and of New Jerusalem, their visual descriptions and contrasts, and the exhortation to shun Babylon and to embrace New Jerusalem, to be sure, are stock elements found in the topos. However, John has also combined other OT motifs such as the nuptial imagery and city imagery in his portrayal of Babylon and of New Jerusalem to further his cause. This allowed John to describe Babylon's own destruction and not just those who associate with her, an element missing from the stock two-women topos. More importantly, in the case of New Jerusalem, the OT nuptial and city imageries allowed John to closely identify his readers with the bride, also an element missing from the topos. By doing so, John persuades his readers not only to desire the good woman, but also to actually be the good woman themselves. This ingenuity makes the ethical appeal of the two-women topos even more effective as John can exhort people not only to follow the right woman and to shun the wrong woman, but also to argue that they in fact must be the right woman themselves and that real and complete destruction awaits those who choose to associate with the wrong woman.

---

a more nuanced view of the characters that appear in Revelation (saints, nations, and earth dwellers), rather than a dualistic view (those who belong to God and those who belong to Satan). Morales, *Shepherd of the Nations*. While this may be true, it still does not change the fact that John portrays two destinies in Revelation. Everyone will either worship the beast and go to destruction or will worship God and go to new creation. There is no middle destiny.

TWO OTHER WOMEN FIGURES IN REVELATION

Since John's use of the two-women topos is not just anti-imperial or political but is spiritual at its basis, it becomes important to look at other female figures in Revelation to see how they may contribute to John's overall two-women motif. The other female figures in question are Jezebel of Revelation 2 and the radiant woman of Revelation 12. Rossing excludes these two figures from the two-women topos since they are not related to the anti-imperial polemic of Revelation. This study differs from Rossing in arguing that John's use of the two-women topos is not anti-imperial but anti-Satan, and if so, the two other female figures in Revelation find their lot in the topos as well due to their relationship with Satan. This section will show that Jezebel and the radiant woman are indeed connected with Babylon and New Jerusalem, and that when these connections are viewed in light of the two-women topos, John's exhortation to choose New Jerusalem and to shun Babylon becomes not a distant calling but one that is uncomfortably close to home. The call to choose between the two is local and ongoing, and people must decide and persevere in their decision every day of their lives.

The Woman Jezebel

The person named Jezebel appears in the letter to the church in Thyatira (Rev 2:18–29). The letter to Thyatira is considered by many to be the center piece of the seven letters. It is the longest of the seven and is climactic in two important aspects, namely the judgment of Christ and compromise with idolatry.[113] Regarding the first aspect, this is the only letter where Christ claims that the time for repentance has passed and only judgment remains.[114] Regarding the second, it seems that spiritual compromise was most severe in Thyatira. Ephesus had rejected false teachers (2:2) and Pergamum had some, not all, who followed the false teachings of Balaam and of the Nicolaitans (2:14–15), but Thyatira had been tolerating the false teacher Jezebel for some time (2:20).[115] Thus, it

---

113. Hoskins, *Revelation*, 92.

114. While there are also no calls for repentance in the letters to Smyrna and Philadelphia, this is because Christ has only good things to say about these two churches.

115. Hoskins, *Revelation*, 92. Osborne also notes that a stronger verb ἀφίημι (to tolerate) is used in the Thyatira letter to denote a more serious nature of spiritual compromise than what was used in the Pergamum letter, which was ἔχω (to have). Osborne, *Revelation*, 155.

seems fitting that Jezebel would be singled out by Christ in this climactic letter, for she serves as a serious example for John's readers of what Christ will do to someone who does not repent but continues the life of idolatry.

The name Jezebel recalls a significant figure from the Old Testament. Queen Jezebel, who was a foreign wife of king Ahab, is known in 1 Kings to have led Israel to worship other gods such as Baal (1 Kgs 16:31; 18:4, 13; 21:25–26). She is also famous for trying to kill God's prophet Elijah (1 Kgs 19:1–3). Jehu in later years describes her as one whose harlotries and sorceries seduced many (2 Kgs 9:22; cf. 2 Chr 21:13).[116] Her influence was woefully enormous; she is one of the most famous women in Israelite history who led God's people astray to commit harlotry/idolatry. This queen has many affinities with the false teacher at Thyatira as to have her name summoned by Christ in the letter. The connection suggests that the church in Thyatira was also facing a serious threat from her.

It is thus possible that the name Jezebel as it is used in Revelation could be a code name, and not the person's real name. It is also possible that the name stands for a group of false teachers who were inciting idolatry, and not just for a specific individual.[117] While these are worthwhile conjectures, it is more important to notice that Christ in the letter to Thyatira specifically calls this person or group "woman" (γυνή) in Revelation 2:20. By labeling her deliberately as a woman, John seems to want to portray her as an evil woman figure.[118] This becomes clearer considering John's extensive use of the two-women topos in Revelation 17–22. It is well-known that John has a tendency to introduce a theme in the earlier chapters, which he elaborates further as the chapters

---

116. The root word used for Jezebel's harlotry is זנה for both OT passages. Since both passages are referring to Jezebel's influence on people in leading them to commit idolatry, the word זנה takes on a symbolic meaning of committing idolatry in these passages, and not the literal meaning of physical adultery. The case is the same in Revelation. John uses the words πορνεία and πορνεύω to refer to Jezebel's harlotry in Rev 2:20–21, but it has a symbolic meaning of enticing people to commit idolatry like her. For those who argue for a symbolic meaning of harlotry in reference to Jezebel of Thyatira, see Beale, *Revelation*, 261; Caird, *Revelation*, 44; Keener, *Revelation*, 134; Mounce, *Revelation*, 86–87.

117. For a succinct summary of various identities of Jezebel that have been proposed, see Weima, *The Sermons*, 135–37.

118. There is a variant reading where some manuscripts add the genitive σου to have it say "your wife Jezebel" in Rev 2:20. If so, then she would not be a regular harlot but someone's wife, most likely a wife of a leader of the church. Either way, she would still be an evil woman figure. Proverb's evil woman figure is also someone's wife who seduces other men to commit harlotry with her (Prov 7:10–20).

progress.[119] This means that the information from later chapters is helpful in understanding what John has said prior and vice versa, and the same is true for the *woman* Jezebel.

Jezebel, whoever this person may represent, is clearly vile, since Christ states that he is against the Thyatiran church for tolerating this woman. Most interesting is Christ's description of the woman which foreshadows Babylon the great. First, Christ claims that she calls herself a prophetess (2:20). Irrespective of how one understands the existence of female prophets in the early church, she must be a false prophetess like queen Jezebel of the Old Testament and like the second beast, the false prophet.[120] Queen Jezebel, who serves as a model for the Thyatiran Jezebel, was charged with sorcery (2 Kgs 9:22), and the only figure who is specifically charged with sorcery in Revelation is Babylon the great (Rev 18:23). It is also noteworthy that Babylon of Revelation sheds the blood of prophets and saints (17:6; 18:24), just like queen Jezebel of the Old Testament. This suggests that being a sorcerer is very much the same as being a false prophet, since their authority does not stem from God; God is not the source of their power.[121] This also means that the evil woman Jezebel of Thyatira has a connection with the evil woman Babylon the great via the evil queen Jezebel of the Old Testament.

Second, like the second beast, Jezebel of Thyatira teaches and seduces (πλανάω) people to commit harlotry (πορνεύω) and to eat food sacrificed to idols (2:20). In fact, the verb to seduce (πλανάω) occurs elsewhere in Revelation to describe not only the actions of the second beast (13:14; 19:20), but also Babylon the great (18:23) and Satan (12:9; 20:3, 8, 10).[122] This deceptive nature of Jezebel thus links her with the unholy trinity and with the harlot Babylon. The verb to commit harlotry (πορνεύω) likewise connects her with Babylon who also made people to commit harlotry with her (17:2; 18:3, 9). Since Jezebel's action of harlotry is closely linked with eating food sacrificed to idols in 2:20 (cf. 2:14), it is likely that harlotry here takes on a symbolic meaning of idolatry as

---

119. This study has analyzed one such instance of this tendency, the theme of conquering, in chapter 2.

120. Although queen Jezebel is not directly called a prophetess in the OT, she did seem to have led a group of prophets (1 Kgs 18:19; 19:1-2) and was charged with sorcery (2 Kgs 9:22).

121. Rodney Thomas argues that Revelation understands any power that does not stem from God as wrong and disloyal. Only power that has God as its source is accepted by John. Thomas, *Magical Motifs*.

122. Weima, *The Sermons*, 137.

it is the case with Babylon. Hence, just as the harlot Babylon seduces people of the world to commit idolatry, so Jezebel seduces God's servants to commit idolatry as well. These connections show that Jezebel's source of power and teaching is in fact Satan, just as Babylon's source of power comes from the first beast and ultimately from Satan (17:3).[123] Accordingly, Christ claims that Jezebel's teaching has to do with the deep things of Satan in Revelation 2:24. The issue with the harlot Jezebel is thereby spiritual at its core, and Christ will judge her for it.

Since Jezebel refuses to repent even though enough time was given (2:21), Christ announces that he will throw her onto a bed (ἰδοὺ βάλλω αὐτὴν εἰς κλίνην; 2:22). This reference to her punishment by Christ is hotly debated.[124] On the one hand, there are those who understand this to be a non-sexual reference for sickness (hence, a sickbed), whether the word κλίνη has a sexual connotation or not. Aune and Beale argue similarly that the reference is a Hebraism, meaning to cast upon a bed of sickness for punishment.[125] Fee and Weima see a sexual connotation in the word κλίνη, but nonetheless argue that the expression of throwing Jezebel onto a bed is an intended irony: the bed of harlotry has now become the bed of illness and suffering.[126] On the other hand, there are those who understand Christ's punishment to be sexually violent. Pippin and Streete suggest that the reference is pornographic and sexually violates and humiliates a female entity.[127] Whether Jezebel stands for an actual woman or not, the fact of the matter is that John is exerting a male dominance and violence in his letter to Thyatira.

The key issue here is how one will understand the word κλίνη. However, it is important to reiterate that the Thyatiran Jezebel is not just any woman. If her connection with Babylon the great is allowed, then she is surely being described as an evil woman figure of the two-women topos. The stock ending for the evil woman figure of the topos and her followers is death, and this is especially emphasized in the Qumran literature (4Q184; 4Q525) and Proverbs. Thus, the expression of casting Jezebel

123. Hoskins, *Revelation*, 96.

124. See Heister, "Jezebel's Punishment," 186–99 for a great summary of varying positions and their advocates on Rev 2:22.

125. Aune, *Revelation 1–5*, 205 and Beale, *Revelation*, 263. Support given for understanding the phrase as Hebraism for illness is Exodus 21:18, 1 Maccabees 1:5, and Judith 8:3.

126. Fee, *Revelation*, 40 and Weima, *The Sermons*, 143–44.

127. Pippin, *Apocalyptic Bodies*, 60 and Streete, *The Strange Woman*, 154–55.

onto a bed most likely refers to death as punishment, which is expected of an evil woman figure. This is confirmed in Revelation 2:23 where Christ states that he will strike Jezebel's children dead. The notion of a woman having children also appears in Revelation 12 with the radiant woman and her offspring (12:17) and in Revelation 17 with the harlot Babylon being a mother of prostitutes (17:5).[128] In all these cases, the maternal relationship is symbolic, and children refer to full-pledged followers.[129] If Christ announces that he will bring death to Jezebel's children, namely Jezebel's fully devoted followers, then it is to be expected that Jezebel herself will face death as well.[130]

Therefore, κλίνη likely refers to a deathbed, a funeral bier.[131] While most scholars understand the word as a sickbed, this would be suitable as long as they understand that it refers to illness that leads to death. The charge that κλίνη has a sexual connotation may be true, but it must be a play on words; Christ is trying to bring out the ironic ending to this spiritual harlot by claiming that her bed of harlotry has now been replaced with a deathbed. A woman is not really attacked sexually here by Christ; Christ is simply throwing Jezebel upon a deathbed for her evil. Yes, the woman Jezebel is described in sexual terms, but this is because John is following the Old Testament precedence where idolatry is described in terms of harlotry. Better yet, John is employing the two-women topos and is describing Jezebel in terms of an evil woman figure. Thus, she is described as a harlot, following the topos, and her feet go down to death, as expected of an evil woman from the topos (cf. Prov 2:18–19; 5:5–6; 7:21–27; 9:18). John does this, not because he wants to exert male dominance, but because he wants his audience to recognize that Jezebel is the evil woman whom they must choose not to follow.

Jezebel was thereby an evil woman figure incarnate who was causing havoc in the Thyatiran church.[132] Whoever this person may have been,

---

128. Rossing also notes this connection, although she rejects the idea that Jezebel of Rev 2 should be associated with Babylon of Rev 17–18. Rossing, *Two Cities*, 83.

129. So likewise, Osborne, *Revelation*, 159.

130. This study understands Jezebel's children in Rev 2:23 and people who commit harlotry with her in Rev 2:22 to be different groups. People who commit harlotry with Jezebel are people who are drawn to her but have not become full members of her circle. As such, they still have an opportunity to repent, unlike Jezebel and her children.

131. So Hort, *Apocalypse*, 30. See also, Baughan, "Anatolian Funerary *Klinai*." Baughan notes of beds for the placement of the dead (κλίνη) that are found regularly in the tombs of Asia Minor.

132. This study thus argues that Jezebel was a historical person in the church at

this figure posed a serious threat to God's servants, and Christ brought swift judgment after an opportunity for repentance was exhausted. As such, Jezebel herself can be considered a child of the great harlot Babylon, whom Jezebel has as a mother (cf. Rev 17:5). Like her evil mother, Jezebel the evil daughter seduced people, led people to a life of idolatry, and made them disloyal to God as a result. She must not be tolerated and those who have entertained an association with her must repent from her works (ἐκ τῶν ἔργων αὐτῆς; 2:22), meaning they must sever their ties with her. Rather than choosing Jezebel and her works, God's saints must conquer and keep the Lamb's works until the end (ὁ τηρῶν ἄχρι τέλους τὰ ἔργα μου; 2:26). The Lamb is the one who knows everyone's hearts, and he will give according to everyone's works (ἑκάστῳ κατὰ τὰ ἔργα ὑμῶν; 2:23).

Therefore, people have two choices: choose Jezebel and keep her works or choose the Lamb and keep his works, with the latter choice obviously being the right one (2:26–28). This is a foreshadow of the conflict of the two kingdoms which John elaborates in the later chapters of Revelation. Just as people must come out of Babylon (18:4), they must disassociate with Jezebel. Just as people must not choose the beast and what its kingdom can offer (Rev 13, 17–18), they must not choose Jezebel and what she can offer. Rather, they must choose the Lamb and what his kingdom can offer, which is supreme authority to rule the nations (2:26–28). This means that the Lamb's kingdom is far superior to the one Jezebel belongs to, which is satanic at its basis (2:24). This is politics that has spirituality at its core. Which side one follows and worships determines which kingdom one is loyal to. Jezebel belongs obviously to the kingdom of the beast and should thus relate to Babylon, who also belongs to that kingdom. Both evil figures, in turn, fittingly end in destruction.

The Radiant Woman

Curiously, the Lamb states that he does not lay any other burden to the rest (τοῖς λοιποῖς) in Thyatira who does not associate with Jezebel (2:24). They simply need to hold fast to what they have and keep the Lamb's works until the end (2:25–26). Pollard is basically right when he understands

---

Thyatira. This is the view held by most scholars. It is difficult to understand Jezebel to be a symbol for a reality bigger than the church, for instance, Rome, considering the local flavor embedded in John's letters. Rather, it is more likely that each of the local churches in Asia Minor had their own localized problems with which Christ deals in the letters.

a connection between the λοιπός of Thyatiran church (2:24) and the λοιπός of the radiant woman (12:17).[133] Per Pollard, "The localized conflict between the 'Jezebel' figure and the λοιπός in Thyatira anticipates the author's globalization of the war against the remnant of Rev 12:17 by Queen Babylon and the enemy powers presented in the latter half of the book."[134] Another way to put it would be that the threat of Jezebel against the Thyatiran believers is but one of local manifestations of the cosmic threat by the satanic powers and by Babylon against God's people, represented by the radiant woman. The connection becomes stronger as both remnants are described with the actions of keeping (τηρέω) and holding (ἔχω) in 2:24–26 and 12:17. Throughout Revelation, these are terms that describe the faithful believers (cf. 1:9; 2:13; 3:11; 14:12; 19:10; 20:4; 22:9), and one can safely understand that λοιπός refers to those true believers who are loyal to God and to the Lamb. In any case, the above observation shows that Jezebel of Thyatira is not only connected with the great harlot Babylon, but also with the radiant woman of Revelation 12. However, unlike with Babylon, Jezebel's relationship with the radiant woman can be described not in terms of affinity, but in terms of enmity.[135]

In Revelation 12, John describes the enmity between the radiant woman and the dragon. This enmity is portrayed in ontological terms as the cosmic Satan pursues to devour the woman and God protects the woman from harm (12:13–16). Unable to touch her, Satan becomes furious and goes after her children instead (12:17), which John describes as being materialized in this world through Satan's two beasts (Rev 13) and Babylon (Rev 17). Their combined effort and scheme to hurt the radiant woman's children are simple yet effective; they deceive the people of the world to follow and worship the dragon (13:3–4, 13–14; 14:8; 17:2), and together they persecute her children, namely God's saints (11:7–10; 13:7–10, 15–17; 17:6). Yet, if God's true saints persevere and endure despite the persecution until the end (1:9; 2:2, 13, 19, 25; 3:10–11; 13:10; 14:12), the Lamb will invite them to the marriage supper, and they will be his bride (19:6–9; 21:1—22:17). In this great and cosmic conflict, all four female figures are connected.

---

133. Pollard, "The Function of Λοιπος," 45–63.

134. Pollard, "The Function of Λοιπος," 45.

135. So Duff argues that the radiant woman stands in opposition to Babylon and that Jezebel stands in a relationship of equivalence to Babylon. In fact, the positive female figures, namely the radiant woman and the bride, stand in opposition to Jezebel and Babylon. Duff, *Who Rides the Beast?*, 85.

The radiant woman's identity was examined in chapter 3 of this study. Here, the focus is on her connection with the other female figures in Revelation in terms of the two-women topos. In Revelation 12:1, John states that this woman (γυνὴ) was clothed (περιβεβλημένη) with the sun, with the moon under her feet, and with a crown of stars upon her head. Scholars readily identify this portrayal to be coming from Genesis 37:9–10,[136] and rightly so, since the woman represents God's people, but there is conspicuously no mention of the sun, the moon, and the stars being someone's clothing and appearance in the said text. It is thereby likely that John is deliberately describing the radiant woman in terms of the two-women topos. This woman is basically clothed with the heavenly luminaries, and thus her appearance is one of pure brightness. As mentioned earlier, one of the stock imageries of the virtuous woman of the two-women topos is bright and pure clothing. John seems to have added the detail of the radiant woman's attire as he introduced her for the first time in Revelation 12 to communicate that this woman is a virtuous woman figure.

Furthermore, the description of the radiant woman's clothing has close affinities with another virtuous woman figure in Revelation, namely the bride. In 19:8, John states that the bride was clothed (περιβάληται) with pure and bright linen. In 21:23, John reports that the bridal New Jerusalem has no need for sun or moon to shine on the city, since the glory of God and the Lamb gives it light.[137] Elsewhere in Revelation, the Lamb is described as having a face that is like the sun (1:16; 10:1),[138] and this would mean that New Jerusalem the bride is certainly bright due to the Lamb whose glory far eclipses heavenly luminaries. One might argue then that the radiant woman and the bride are separate entities, for the

---

136. For instance, Beale, *Revelation*, 625; Fanning, *Revelation*, 349; Smalley, *Revelation*, 315.

137. It is also possible to understand this verse to be stating that the Lamb himself is the glory of God. For instance, see Paul, *Revelation*, 355.

138. This writer understands the angelic figure of Rev 10 to be the Lamb himself, due to the many references of divinity in 10:1. This figure also seems to almost argue with God and win (10:4–11), which is only possible if the figure is the Lamb and not an angel. For those who also understand the angelic figure of Rev 10 to be the Lamb, see Beale, *Revelation*, 522–25; Kraft, *Offenbarung*, 147. Osborne argues instead that this figure is not the Lamb himself, but rather an angelic representative of the Lamb who possesses his traits. Osborne, *Revelation*, 406. So also, Smalley, *Revelation*, 258. Whether the figure of Rev 10 is the Lamb himself or an angelic representative, it is nonetheless true that having a face like the sun is a divine quality in Revelation.

former is clothed with heavenly luminaries while the latter has no need and is not.

Nevertheless, when the two-women topos is considered, both the radiant woman and the bride are clearly portrayed as virtuous woman figures, since both are described as having bright clothes. The difference in the *quality* of their clothing must be since the bridal New Jerusalem finds its status in the new creation, while the radiant woman is described in terms of what is happening here and now. In other words, the radiant woman represents God's people before the Parousia, while the bride represents God's people in the eschaton.[139] Thus, this study advocates that they are in fact the same woman, depicted differently based on the time periods portrayed. Räpple is basically correct when she states, "The virtues of an honorable woman are engraved into the female image of the bride (Rev 21:2, 9; 22:17), the woman (Rev 19:7), and the mother (Rev 12:1–6)."[140]

Therefore, unlike the relationship between the two evil women figures, namely Jezebel and Babylon, where Jezebel is not equal to Babylon but can be construed as Babylon's offshoot, the relationship between the two virtuous woman figures is one of equal standing. Understood in this way, it becomes possible to see that, with regard to Jezebel and Babylon, Revelation portrays the threat of the evil woman not as distant and vague, but as quite real, one that can even be manifested in the local church. With regard to the radiant woman and the bride, Revelation depicts the story of God's people throughout history leading up to the consummation using the two women. The bride as God's people in the eschaton lies in the future and is someone John's readers must look forward to. The radiant woman as God's people before the Parousia is someone John's readers must identify with in the present. Yes, she and her children are under attack by Satan, but John's readers know that God has secured her safety (12:14–16). They must persevere and stay faithful to the Lord despite the

---

139. One could also understand the radiant woman in a derivative sense, meaning that the bride is the primary virtuous woman figure and the radiant woman belongs to the bride's group or company. There are ample examples where the virtuous woman has a company of other good women in literature that utilizes the two-women topos. However, it is more likely that the radiant woman and the bride are same woman, just described in terms of different time periods, since both represent God's people as this study has shown. Bauckham argues similar to this study. He understands that the New Jerusalem of the future has a forerunner in the present, namely the radiant woman of Rev 12 and the holy city of Rev 11. New Jerusalem of the future also has an opposite in the present, namely Babylon the great harlot. Bauckham, *Theology*, 128.

140. Räpple, *Metaphor of the City*, 196.

threat as her children (12:17), which is another way of saying that they must continually align themselves with the radiant woman in the present.

Since the radiant woman is the virtuous woman figure of Revelation, she has comparable and opposite characteristics to Babylon the great, and by extension, to Jezebel. First, whereas the radiant woman is a sign from heaven and is clothed with heavenly luminaries (12:1), Babylon sits upon many waters (17:1) and is clothed with splendid but pretentious fabrications of man (17:4).[141] This shows the qualitative difference between the radiant woman and Babylon: the former heavenly and the latter earthly. Second, both are mothers, but the radiant woman is described in the act of giving birth, "the maternal act par excellence" (12:2), while Babylon is negatively called the mother of harlots and of earth's abominations (17:5; cf. 2:23).[142] Moreover, whereas Satan endangers the radiant woman's children (12:4, 17), the Son of God threatens Jezebel's children (2:23), and in both contexts, reference to Psalm 2:8–9 is used regarding ruling with a rod of iron (2:27; 12:5).[143] Third, the radiant woman is nourished by God in the wilderness despite threats of death by the dragon (12:6, 14), whereas Babylon is drunk with the blood of the saints in the wilderness (17:6) and is eventually destroyed by the beast (17:16).[144]

These points of contact between all four women figures in Revelation show that John is deliberately comparing and contrasting the radiant woman and the bride on the one hand and the great harlot and Jezebel on the other. Scholars have noted these connections in various ways. Bruns and Duff, for instance, focus primarily on the contrast between the radiant woman of Revelation 12 and the great harlot of Revelation 17.[145] Few others have opted for the opposite, arguing that these two women are actually the same woman.[146] In any case, for these scholars, the radiant woman and the great harlot are primary female characters in Revelation.

---

141. Bruns, "Contrasted Women," 459–60.
142. Duff, *Who Rides the Beast?*, 86.
143. Duff, *Who Rides the Beast?*, 92–93.
144. Duff, *Who Rides the Beast?*, 86.
145. Bruns, "Contrasted Women," 459–63; Duff, *Who Rides the Beast?*, 83–96. It is true that Duff analyzes all four female figures and compares them all. However, Duff understands the relationship between the woman of Rev 12 and the harlot of Rev 17 to be primary, while comparisons between other women are secondary.
146. The proponents of this view are succinctly summarized in Razafiarivony, "Woman of Revelation 17," 134–49. In his article, Razafiarivony debunks this view and argues that the two women are not the same. Needless to say, the view that argues for the radiant woman to be the same woman as Babylon is in the minority.

Rossing focuses on the contrast between the great harlot of Revelation 17–18 and the bride of Revelation 19–22, understanding that these two figures are primary.[147] Yet, when the two-women topos is expanded to include all four women figures in Revelation, a more balanced picture emerges.

SUMMARY AND CONCLUSION

First, Jezebel of Revelation 2 is a local manifestation of Babylon of Revelation 17–18. They are both described in terms of the evil woman figure of the two-women topos. Second, the radiant woman of Revelation 12 is the bride of Revelation 19–22.[148] They are both described in terms of the virtuous woman figure of the two-women topos. Thus, John has two pairs of women, two virtuous and two evil, appearing in Revelation in juxtaposition.[149]

John employs these women figures in strategic places in Revelation, one in Christ's central letter to the church, one in describing the beginning of the spiritual and political conflict between God's kingdom and the beast's kingdom, and two at the end of Revelation, to effectively exhort

---

147. Rossing, *Two Cities*.

148. Again, this study goes against Rossing in identifying the radiant woman to be the same as the bride. Rossing does not believe the two women are the same and enlists Yarbro Collins as another scholar who concurs with her. Yarbro Collins, in her work *Combat Myth*, indeed does not see the two women as identical since she understands distinct sources to be at work for each woman. For her, the radiant woman of Rev 12 is a queen of heaven according to the combat myth, while the bride of Rev 19–22 is the New Jerusalem, symbolic of the Christian community, according to the holy city tradition. Yarbro Collins, *Combat Myth*, 66, 71, 132, 230. However, Yarbro Collins' focus on John's utilization of combat myth believed to be scattered throughout Revelation in fragmented nature eludes her from seeing other intricate connections within the text, especially the connection between the radiant woman and the bride. Yarbro Collins, in another work, nonetheless admits that on one level, the woman of Rev 12 is the heavenly Israel whose destiny foreshadows that of the followers of Jesus, her "seed." Yarbro Collins, *Cosmology and Eschatology*, 115, 130.

149. So Duff, *Who Rides the Beast?*, 95–96. Selvidge understands the juxtaposition of these pairs as well but comes to a different conclusion. She thinks the independent and powerful women (Jezebel and Babylon) are portrayed as evil, while the helpless and passive women (the radiant woman and the bride) are portrayed as good. According to Selvidge, John does this to attack a powerful religio-political establishment that he does not agree with. Selvidge, "Powerful and Powerless Women," 157–67. However, these general characteristics of the good and the bad women are in line with the two-women topos, which Selvidge does not see. Further, the bride directly speaks in Revelation 22:17 whereas Babylon and Jezebel do not, and this is hardly passive.

his readers using the two-women topos. The kingdom of the beast's influence is powerful, as Babylon deceives and allures the people of the world to commit harlotry with her. This is a real threat that is felt even within the confines of the church, Jezebel being the example. At the core of this threat lies Satan who seeks to oppose the kingdom of God and to destroy God's people, the radiant woman. This conflict is not merely religious or political but is one that is deeply spiritual. It is also a real conflict that is currently ongoing in this world in the present.

God's people thus have a choice to make. They can either follow Jezebel and Babylon and commit idolatry or they can follow the radiant woman and the bride and stay loyal to God. The former promises life abundant in this world that is coming to an end; the latter promises life perfect in the new creation that is eternal. This is a classic moral choice presented by the two-women topos, and the right choice is obvious. God's people must continually choose to align themselves with the radiant woman in the present, looking toward that day when the bride will be made ready.

If God's people can endure and stay faithful through the persecutions, they will be invited to the marriage supper of the Lamb. In fact, they will not only be invitees, but will also be the Lamb's bride. They will enjoy all the blessings that come at no cost forever. Hence, Revelation calls people to come out of Babylon and to come to the bride instead. Which woman one chooses to associate with determines to whom one shall remain loyal, and for John, the choice is none other than the virtuous woman. And to make his ethical appeal to choose the right woman even more effective, John apparently has gone further with the two-women topos. He actually tells of the evil woman's complete destruction and gets his readers to so identify with the virtuous woman. This makes John's purpose in exhorting his readers to stay faithful to God by following and being the virtuous woman all the more powerful.

CHAPTER 6

Blessings and Vice Lists in Revelation

ONE OF THE COMMON wisdom forms used in apocalyptic literature is blessings and vice lists (macarisms and woes).[1] These ethical catalogues can be defined as lists of characteristics or behaviors that should be welcomed or avoided by the people to whom they were written.[2] As such, these lists complement one of the functions of apocalypses, which is to modify the recipients' views and behaviors to conform to transcendent perspectives.[3] The book of Revelation also employs macarisms and vice lists to exhort the readers to a certain behavior. Although issues have been raised by scholars regarding the provenance of these catalogues in Jewish and Christian literature, since the Old Testament lacks these lists, this study will not address the problem of origin and influence but will focus on how the macarisms and vice lists function in Revelation.[4]

---

1. John Collins signals this at Collins, "Wisdom, Apocalypticism," 174–79. Collins also argues from 1 *Enoch*, Sir 2:12–14, 41:8–9, and 2 *Enoch* that virtue and vice lists likely have a wisdom origin, rather than prophecy. Collins, *Seers, Sibyls and Sages*, 395–96.
2. Aune, "Lists, Ethical," 670–72.
3. Aune, *Literary Environment*, 195, 231.
4. For discussion regarding origin and influence, see Conzelmann, *1 Corinthians*, 100–1; Du Toit, "Ethical Lists," 59–62; Easton, "Ethical Lists," 1–12; López, "Vice Lists," 178–95; Wibbing, *Die Tugend*. An issue related to the problem of origin is whether the virtue and vice lists of the New Testament are conventional, meaning they merely follow the lists of the day, or contextual, meaning they are specifically adopted to fit the goal of the author's discourse. Easton, for instance, argues more for the side of the NT's virtue and vice lists being conventional. Easton, "Ethical Lists," 8. For arguments for the lists being contextual, see Aune, *Literary Environment*, 195 and Du Toit, "Ethical Lists," 61–62, 91. As this study will show along the way, the lists in Revelation are fitted specifically for what John wishes to communicate and emphasize.

Another significant factor regarding ethical catalogues is determining what constitutes a list. To count as a list, some argue that the list must contain at least three related items or descriptions.[5] According to this criterion, there are three vice lists in Revelation (9:20–21; 21:8; 22:15).[6] Yet, Revelation 21:27 has two vices and one virtue, thus totaling three items. While the catalogue in 21:27 may not be a vice list proper according to modern standards, it is an ethical list nonetheless, and this study shall take the opportunity to examine it along with the other well-known three. Moreover, it must also be recognized that Revelation does not have a virtue list. Revelation nonetheless employs several macarisms throughout, and instead of simply cataloguing items, the macarisms detail the kinds of actions or goals the readers are to strive to attain. As such, their function is also paraenesis, namely, to demand the audience to seriously take up the way of life revealed.[7] This means that the macarisms in Revelation complement the vice lists in terms of function; the former exhorts by revealing the proper way of living, while the latter exhorts by revealing wrong behaviors. Therefore, this study shall analyze the macarisms alongside the vice lists. The end goal will be to understand how these macarisms and vice lists function in relation to the overall purpose of Revelation.

MACARISMS IN REVELATION

There are seven macarisms (μακάριος, μακάριοι) in the book of Revelation (1:3; 14:13; 16:15; 19:9; 20:6; 22:7, 14). Nwachukwu, in his study of macarisms in Revelation, suggests that John seems to have deliberately limited them to be sevenfold, to symbolize the fullness of blessing that comes by heeding them, to strengthen the force of his approach to the various situations and concerns addressed in Revelation, and to give unity to the whole book.[8] Macarisms can be further defined as formulaic expressions of blessedness common in wisdom and apocalyptic literature

---

5. Robinson, "Sexual Immorality Language," 156. This issue is also raised in McEleney, "Vice Lists," 203.

6. These three are readily acknowledged by several scholars. See Aune, "Lists, Ethical," 670; Easton, "Ethical Lists," 4; Hatfield, "Rhetorical Function," 15.

7. Betz, *Sermon on the Mount*, 96–97. Although Betz is commenting on Matthew's macarisms, the same must be true of other macarisms in the NT in terms of function. See also, Trax, "Happy Reading," 305–6.

8. Nwachukwu, *Beyond Vengeance*, 63–64.

with the function of implicitly motivating the audience to make an active and proper decision.[9] For Revelation, in which John seeks to exhort his readers to persevere and to stay faithful to God in the midst of ongoing persecutions and temptations from the beast's kingdom, the macarisms must function then to strengthen John's exhortation for faithfulness.[10] In this section, each of the seven macarisms in Revelation will be investigated to understand how each are functioning in their own contexts. Exceptions to this are the macarisms of Revelation 1:3 and 22:7, which will be examined together due to their similarities. In fact, these two macarisms serve almost as bookends to the book. Then, the macarisms will be viewed as a whole in the overall context of Revelation to draw a conclusion with regard to their purpose.

Macarism 1 and 6: Revelation 1:3 and 22:7

The first macarism occurs at the end of the superscription or preface of Revelation (1:3). The superscription itself (1:1–3) provides information regarding the provenance of John's words and authenticates them. According to John, the words contained in the book of Revelation have a divine origin. They are none other than the revelation of Jesus Christ, which God gave him, and have subsequently been passed on by his angel to John (1:1).[11] John also introduces himself as Christ's servant who testifies to the word of God and to the testimony of Jesus Christ, of all that he saw (1:2). Not only does John's characterization of himself authenticate him as a faithful believer and a true prophet (cf. 1:9; 11:7; 12:11, 17; 19:10; 20:4), but it also authenticates his message contained in the book of Revelation. The transmission of this revelation is clearly truthful and is from God and Christ, and John's readers can trust it and heed it.

Indeed, to give a clear indication that John's words contained in Revelation are truthful and to set the tone of urgency and of sternness

---

9. Stewart, "Soteriology," 134. See also, Bieder, "Die sieben Seligpreisungen," 29–30, Fiorenza, *Revelation*, 189, and Rossing, *Two Cities*, 136.

10. Cruz, "The Beatitudes," 272.

11. Revelation 1:1 seems to state that Christ has received the revelation from the Father, and then Christ has sent his angel bearing that revelation to John. This is comparable to 22:6 where John states that it was God the Father who sent his angel to John with the revelation. This suggests not only that Christ and the Father are one, but also that the origin of the revelation is ultimately from both the Father and the Son. Thus, not only are John's words the revelation of Jesus Christ, but also the revelation of God the Father.

that compels the readers to observe the prophecy with careful minds and with immediate actions, John concludes his superscription with a macarism.[12] John states that blessed is the one who reads aloud (ἀναγινώσκω), the ones who hear (ἀκούω) the words of this prophecy, and the ones who keep (τηρέω) the things written in it, for the time is near (1:3).[13] To be "blessed" (μακάριος) means to be fortunate to receive and to enjoy the privilege of God's favor on one's life.[14] This is in fact the only macarism in the entire Bible where blessing is applied to reading something. This suggests that John's words are very important, and reading them is absolutely crucial to one's life, if one wants to receive God's blessings. John is envisioning here that, as the churches get together to read aloud the prophecy contained in the book of Revelation, and as the people take heed, God will absolutely bless them, for this is a prophecy from God himself.[15]

But just reading aloud and listening attentively are not enough. To be blessed further requires one to hear and to keep the words. The words "to hear" and "to keep" work as a synthetic parallelism to make a call for obedience.[16] Therefore, before the actual giving of the contents of the prophecy, John makes sure to let his readers know that the authentic prophecy he is about to present is something that must be obeyed. This shows that Revelation is not just about prediction, but an ethical exhortation.[17] John's macarism in Revelation 1:3 is essentially the same as Jesus's macarism in John 13:17: "If you know these things, blessed are you if you do them."

Obedience to John's prophecy is all the more urgent "for the time is near" (ὁ γὰρ καιρὸς ἐγγύς). As he is about to show, living as faithful people of God will be very difficult due to the seductions and persecutions from Satan and its alliances. Temptations to defect will be very strong. Yet John knows that the devil's time is short (cf. Rev 12:12; 17:10–12; 18:10,

---

12. Nwachukwu, *Beyond Vengeance*, 75.

13. Fanning argues that the awkwardness of the macarism's grammar, namely the switching from the singular to the plural, comes from a common practice in the ancient world of a speaker reading a text out loud to an audience. Fanning, *Revelation*, 78.

14. BDAG, s.v. "μακάριος" and Louw and Nida, §25.119.

15. Nwachukwu argues that the action of reading aloud provokes reflection and confession, creating a confessional response akin to that of OT public readings, such as one captured in Neh 8:18. He also understands John may be repeating Christ who stated that if one abides in his word, that one will be a true disciple in Jn 8:31. Nwachukwu, *Beyond Vengeance*, 78.

16. Cruz, "The Beatitudes," 273.

17. Cruz, "The Beatitudes," 273.

17, 19). The time (καιρὸς), meaning the critical and decisive moment for the fulfillment of all John has seen and heard, is close at hand, and John wants his readers to take seriously what he is about to write to them and obey them carefully.[18] Thus, the first macarism functions to give a solemn ethical injunction and motivation to persevere in faithful obedience for the readers. The fact that this macarism to obey John's prophecy is given before the actual presentation of that prophecy suggests that the purpose of the book of Revelation has a strong paraenetic side.

The sixth macarism, which mirrors the first macarism, occurs in 22:7 during the epilogue of the book. The epilogue (22:6–21), in fact, contains two macarisms. The seventh and final macarism occurs in 22:14. What is interesting is that the final macarism is buttressed with the final vice list of Revelation (22:15), and Revelation 22:14–15 is the only place in Revelation where a macarism and a vice list occur together. One could assume easily that this must be the case because John wants to give an exhortation to his readers on which identity they must take on and which they must shun one last time before he finishes his prophecy. Taking the seventh macarism aside then, the sixth macarism, together with the first, work as bookends to the book of Revelation.

The context in which the sixth macarism occurs also mirrors the context in which the first macarism occurs. As noted above, the first macarism's immediate context has to do with the provenance and authenticity of John's prophecy. In Revelation 1:1, John states the precise identity and nature of his prophecy, namely that it is the revelation of Jesus Christ, and how the prophecy came to him via an angelic mediator. With this statement of authenticity, John is able to argue in 1:3 that the one who reads aloud, hear, and keep his prophecy is blessed. The same context occurs once again in 22:6 as the angel claims the authenticity of the prophecy and states how this prophecy came to John and to other believers via an angelic mediator.[19] It is with this same statement of authenticity John states in 22:7, using Jesus's own voice, that blessed is the one who keeps (τηρέω) the words of the prophecy of this book. Hence, John escalates

---

18. Mounce, *Revelation*, 43–44.

19. There is a debate whether the speaker of Rev 22:6 is an angel or Christ himself. It is likely an angel, for the tone with which this speaker speaks is different from 22:7 where Christ himself speaks. If an angel, it would be the same angel as in 21:9. So Osborne, *Revelation*, 780. Furthermore, the prophecy (literally, the faithful and true words) mentioned in 22:6 does not refer only to the New Jerusalem vision (21:9–22:5), but to the entire content of the book itself. So, Thomas and Macchia, *Revelation*, 391.

the importance of heeding the words in Revelation by having the sixth macarism pronounced by Christ himself who is coming soon (22:7a).

However, the sixth macarism does not mirror the first macarism exactly in content. There is a major difference. The blessing in Revelation 22:7 does not include the first two items from the first macarism, namely the blessing on those who read and who hear, but only retains the third item, namely the blessing on the one who keeps the words of the prophecy. This difference is quite natural, for by this point of the book of Revelation, John's readers have now read and heard the prophecy contained in it. What is left is to actually keep John's words. In fact, John's words must be kept precisely as it is written; tampering with its contents will mean God's judgment and the loss of one's share in the new creation (22:18–19).

On the one hand, this warning communicates the high importance of John's prophecy due to its divine authenticity and reliability, and of keeping it. On the other hand, this exhortation to keep John's words must include not only obeying the specific commands given throughout Revelation, but even more so in receiving the teaching of the book and living in accordance to it.[20] It has to do with shaping one's life in a manner consistent with Christ (2:26; 3:3), in obedience to God's commands (12:17; 14:12), and in worship to God (22:9).[21] Simply put, to keep John's words is to stay loyal to God and Christ. Therefore, the sixth macarism also functions to give an exhortation to the readers to stay faithfully obedient to God. By providing another blessing to keep the words of prophecy contained in Revelation towards the end of the book, and even having Christ himself voicing out this blessing, John effectively and solemnly brings an ethical charge that cannot be shoved aside.

Macarism 2: Revelation 14:13

The second macarism occurs near the end of the interlude regarding the conflict between God's kingdom and the beast's kingdom (12:1—14:20) in 14:13. John begins this interlude by showing the history of enmity between God's people (the radiant woman) and the dragon (Satan) in Revelation 12. This enmity is described in further detail in Revelation 13 as the dragon, together with his two beasts, seduces the people of the

---

20. Hoskins, *Revelation*, 469–70.
21. Koester, *The End*, 46–47. So also, Stewart, "Soteriology," 134.

world to follow and worship him and persecute God's people. Yet, hope is not lost as John shows in Revelation 14 the ultimate blessing reserved for those who follow Christ and the ultimate doom awaiting those who follow the beast. It is also starting with Revelation 14 that John focuses on God's judgment upon the beast's kingdom and its people (Rev 14–19), and it is fitting that John would first compare the radically different fates awaiting those who belong to God's kingdom and those who belong to the beast's kingdom in Revelation 14.

It is in this context of the conflict between the two kingdoms and their final ends the second macarism is announced. Revelation 14:13 begins with a heavenly command to write (γράψον), which suggests that an important message will follow.[22] The following message is a blessing: "Blessed are the dead who die (ἀποθνῄσκοντες) in the Lord from now on." Considering the context in which this macarism occurs, it seems to express martyrdom as a blessing. As the beast's kingdom persecutes God's people, there are bound to be believers who are killed, as Revelation 2:13 testifies. However, despite the sufferings and dangers that believers might face, they must endure and keep the commandments of God and their faith in Jesus (14:12). In other words, God's people must exhibit faithfulness and obedience no matter the threat. Indeed, this is obedience even to the point of death, and John states, by means of the authoritative heavenly voice, that blessed are those who die in the Lord.

However, the very language of the macarism seems to indicate more than simply death by martyrdom. In fact, the blessing specifies that blessed are the dead who die (ἀποθνῄσκω), not who are killed (ἀποκτείνω; cf. 2:13), and it is those who die "in the Lord from now on" who are blessed. On the one hand, the language seems to include every believer who dies in the Lord, whether the cause of death was martyrdom or natural. On the other hand, the phrase "from now on" (ἀπ' ἄρτι) suggests that this blessing is not reserved for life in the new creation only, but can be experienced and declared in the present.[23] In any case, what is clearly important here is whether or not they died "in the Lord," which refers to the believers' regenerated existence lived in union with Christ.[24]

22. Cruz, "The Beatitudes," 274.
23. Osborne, *Revelation*, 544; Stewart, "Soteriology," 135.
24. Fanning, *Revelation*, 396 fn. 40. See also, Beale, *Revelation*, 767. Beale argues that the phrase ἐν κυρίῳ is a dative of sphere, although it could also include a causal aspect. In any case, Beale notes that the phrase refers to the believers' identification with the Lord.

This also means that this blessing is not for everyone who dies, irrespective of one's faith, but is squarely contingent upon the life and death of Christ.[25]

Just as Christ lived his life in obedience to God, suffered because of it, and died, believers likewise can suffer and die due to their obedience to God and the Lamb. But death was not the end for Christ. He rose again and conquered (cf. 5:5, 9), and the slaughtered Lamb is a sign of victory for those who suffer on behalf of him.[26] In short, the believers find their identity in Christ who conquered by suffering and death, and if so, they are blessed when they suffer and die, for this means that they are also conquering and have sealed their victory. The result of their conquering is the blessedness and reward of rest.[27] Again, this is only available to those who are "in Christ" or who are "in the Lord," not anybody else.

So the Spirit concurs by saying, "yes" (ναί). God's people are indeed blessed, for they may rest from their toils because their works follow them (14:13). This is obviously not referring to a work-based salvation of any kind. Bieder argues rightly that this release from toil means the end of the believers' trials, tribulations, and their life of faith on this earth.[28] The idea is essentially similar to Wisdom of Solomon 3:1: "But the souls of the righteous are in the hand of God, and no torment will ever touch them." Furthermore, the claim that the believers' works follow them serves as a confirmation that they are indeed in Christ.[29]

Thus, the saints' works that are done on this earth in obedience to God and in faithfulness even to the point of death confirm that they do belong to Christ. As people who are in the Lord, they are joined together with Christ who suffered, died, and thereby conquered. This life of victory is also available to those who suffer even to the point of death for the sake of God's name. Hence, the saints are blessed even now when they suffer, because their suffering means that they are conquering. Their blessedness will find its fulfillment when they enter the new creation. The

---

25. Nwachukwu, *Beyond Vengeance*, 109. Revelation uses the title "Lord" to refer to both God (cf. 1:8; 4:8; 6:10; 11:15; 22:6) and Christ (cf. 11:8; 17:14; 22:20–21). Rev 14:13 likely refers to Christ, not God the Father, when looking at its immediate context (the Lamb and his followers vs. the beast and its followers) and when considering that the phrase "in the Lord" (ἐν κυρίῳ) is an often-appearing phrase in the NT in reference to Christ.

26. Kowalski, "Martyrdom and Resurrection," 55–56.

27. Stewart, "Soteriology," 135.

28. Bieder, "Die sieben Seligpreisungen," 22–23.

29. Cruz, "The Beatitudes," 275.

second macarism functions then to assure and to encourage God's people to stay loyal to God no matter the earthly cost, no matter what conflict the beast's kingdom may bring.

Macarism 3: Revelation 16:15

John interjects the third macarism in his vision of the sixth bowl, which is about the battle of Armageddon (16:12–16).[30] When the sixth bowl is poured out, the river Euphrates is dried up, to prepare the way for the kings from the east (16:12). Irrespective of whether this river is the literal Euphrates or symbolic, and who these kings from the east may represent, what is clear is the fact that these kings stand with the unholy trinity, thereby opposing God and his people, and that it is God who is in control and who allows them to gather for battle. After all, it is the angel of God who dries up the great river with the sixth bowl. John also tells that at this time of the sixth bowl, the unholy trinity will call and assemble the kings of the world for battle on the great day of God the Almighty (16:13–14). John states that the place they will assemble is called Armageddon (16:16).[31]

That this battle will take place on the great day of God indicates John is describing the time of the end. At this time, all three members of the unholy trinity will work together to call and to gather the kings of the whole world for battle. This is a gruesome picture, especially if one is reading or hearing Revelation for the first time and does not know the

---

30. Some scholars have noted the abruptness of the third macarism in 16:15, arguing that it must not have been at the present location originally. Cf. Aune, *Revelation 6–16*, 896; Charles, *Revelation*, vol. 2, 49. However, this study agrees with many others who argue for the appropriateness of 16:15 in its present location. Cf. Beckwith, *Apocalypse*, 684; Bieder, "Die sieben Seligpreisungen," 20; Caird, *Revelation*, 208; Morris, *Revelation*, 193; Mounce, *Revelation*, 300; Smalley, *Revelation*, 411. Nwachukwu also argues for the appropriateness of the macarism's current location and observes that John has a tendency to break the flow of his narrative. Nwachukwu sees examples of this tendency in Rev 3:11; 12:6, 13–17; 14:8; 21:1–2; 22:5, 7, 12, 20. Nwachukwu, *Beyond Vengeance*, 140.

31. The exact meaning and location of Armageddon is debated. See Osborne, *Revelation*, 594–96 for a survey of different opinions. For a survey of how people have understood Armageddon throughout history, see Burnet and Detal, "Armageddon," 193–219. Perhaps the best option would be to understand the word Armageddon to be comprised of two Hebrew words, *Har* and *Magedōn*, which means mountain or hill of Megiddo. Megiddo is a well-known place in the OT associated with biblical battles, which in turn would be a suitable name of the place for the final battle on the great day. Cf. Hoskins, *Revelation*, 297–98; Mounce, *Revelation*, 301; Paul, *Revelation*, 272.

information contained in subsequent chapters. John is claiming that the whole world will side with the dragon, the beast, and the false prophet and will wage war against God and his people. If a person sides with God, then this means that a vast army of the whole world will come against God's camp that the person belongs to, and he or she will have to face a fierce threat of an unavoidable battle. This is a clear and sure danger that is coming one's way if one decides to stick to God's side.

Thankfully, John does not leave his readers alone in hopeless anxiety of an impending doom. He interjects in 16:15 with an exhortation from Christ himself. Christ proclaims, "Behold," thus grasping attention, "I am coming like a thief; blessed is the one who stays awake and who keeps his garments on, that he may not go about naked and that they may see his exposure." The pithy sapiential saying about coming like a thief by Jesus recalls Revelation 3:3 as well as the Synoptic Gospels (Matt 24:42-44; Lk 12:35-40; cf. Mk 13:33-37).[32] This thief motif, like other instances in the New Testament, refers to the second coming of Christ.[33] Since John had been portraying the battle of the great day of God, Christ's second coming must be his return as the warrior king. In essence, John is telling his readers that this battle of Armageddon is not a hopeless battle of an impending doom if one faithfully sticks to God's side. Not at all, for Christ the warrior king will come and win the day, and God's people will join in the victory.

The thief motif also has another function. It emphasizes the suddenness of Jesus's coming and exhorts watchfulness. This call for watchfulness is further enhanced by a macarism. The macarism itself points to two characteristics God's people must take on, namely staying awake and keeping one's garments on. If not, they will have to go about naked and expose their shame when Christ returns suddenly. Thus, watchfulness includes not losing sight of Jesus's coming (viz., staying awake).[34] It also involves faithful perseverance (viz., keeping one's garments on).[35] The

---

32. Vos, *The Synoptic Traditions*, 77.

33. Nagy, "Come Like a Thief," 16–17. Nagy argues that, although there is a change of genre in the thief motif, since the Synoptic Gospels use the motif in parables whereas Revelation does not, the message and function are very similar. Bauckham calls this change of genre, "deparabolization." In the process of deparabolization, the parable form is dissolved and is turned into a metaphor or simile, and in doing so the thief motif and the interpretation are not separated as in parables but are joined together as in Revelation. Bauckham, "Synoptic Parousia Parables Again," 129–34.

34. Nwachukwu, *Beyond Vengeance*, 143.

35. Cruz, "The Beatitudes," 276.

message is very similar to Jesus's words to the church in Sardis (3:2–5), albeit it was more of a warning in the Sardis letter while it is more of an encouragement here in Revelation 16.

All in all, the message of 16:15 is aptly stated by Cruz: "Without such persistence, ethical integrity, and those good works that wrap one like a garment, a person is naked before God, and to one's shame it becomes evident that one is not 'in Christ.'"[36] John's interjection in Revelation 16:15 with its macarism so cleverly shifts attention from a great battle the unholy trinity will bring about to the importance of Christ's second coming and the preparedness God's people must exhibit for the return. "Revelation 16:15 is an encouragement that while the satanic powers are gaining strength, Christ is assuring his people of his coming."[37] The third macarism also then functions to exhort the readers to faithful obedience and perseverance despite what the unholy trinity may bring against God's people and in light of Christ's second coming.

Macarism 4: Revelation 19:9

The fourth macarism occurs at the end of a large section concerning Babylon the great (Rev 17:1–19:10). In Revelation 17–18, John has introduced Babylon the harlot and has described her mystery and her destruction. Starting 19:1, a series of hallelujah praises ensues in heaven at the result of Babylon's destruction (19:1–8). 19:6–8 especially introduce the promise of the messianic banquet or marriage feast, as well as the bride, the contrasting woman figure to Babylon. It is after this that the angel gives a macarism of the invitation to the messianic banquet (19:9).

The fourth macarism is comparable to the second macarism. In both cases, there is a preview of a major woman figure, Babylon in the case of second macarism (14:8–10) and the bride in the case of fourth macarism (19:7–8). Interestingly, the Babylon preview only names the city without any hint of a woman, whereas the bride preview only introduces the woman without any hint of her city traits.[38] It is following both previews macarisms (14:13; 19:9) are given, apparently to exhort the audience on

---

36. Cruz, "The Beatitudes," 276. Nwachukwu argues that nakedness refers to spiritual emptiness. Nwachukwu, *Beyond Vengeance*, 147. In any case, nakedness is a symbol of judgment as sins are exposed by God (cf. Isa 20:1–4; Ezek 16:36, 23:10, 29). So, Osborne, *Revelation*, 594.

37. Nagy, "Come Like a Thief," 23.

38. Rossing, *Two Cities*, 136.

how they should relate to these two women figures.³⁹ With the second macarism, the implicit exhortation was that the audience must not associate with Babylon, the city of the beast's kingdom, even if this may result in death. With the fourth macarism, the explicit exhortation is that the audience must associate with the bride, the Lamb's woman, by participating in the messianic feast. Furthermore, both the second and the fourth macarisms begin with the command to write (γράψον), showing that the following promises are important. These similarities and contrasts between the second and the fourth macarism suggest that John has intentionally made the two to be related and compared in connection with the two major women of Revelation, namely Babylon and the bride.

The actual message of the fourth macarism is as follows: "Blessed are the ones who are invited to the marriage supper (δεῖπνον) of the Lamb" (19:9). As the following verses reveal, the Lamb will come at the time of the end to destroy the army of the unholy trinity (19:11–21), thereby completing the missing picture of the battle of Armageddon introduced in 16:12–16 where the third macarism occurs.⁴⁰ For the enemies, the Lamb will come as a conquering king and will carry out the decisive battle of victory by destroying them. For the followers of the Lamb, a reverse fortune awaits them: a celebration of victory instead of judgment and punishment.⁴¹ In fact, John stresses this reversal of fortunes by using the same word δεῖπνον to refer to two different kinds of supper or banquet God prepares in Revelation 19. On the one hand, the faithful are invited to the marriage supper or the messianic banquet where there will be celebration for the fulfillment of God's redemption (19:9).⁴² On the other hand, the birds are invited to the great supper of God where the wicked will be the banquet these birds will feed upon (19:17).⁴³ Clearly, one does not want to join the latter supper or banquet.

Therefore, the Lamb's people are indeed blessed, for they are given the privilege to dine with him in a messianic banquet of celebration. As this study has noted in the previous chapter, there is a metaphor change here: the bride is God's people in 19:7–8 but the guests are God's people

---

39. Rossing, *Two Cities*, 136.

40. Osborne states regarding the battle scene of Rev 19:19–21 thus: "This is a direct continuance of 16:14, 16." Osborne, *Revelation*, 688. So also, Aune, *Revelation 17–22*, 1064 and Fanning, *Revelation*, 490.

41. Nwachukwu, *Beyond Vengeance*, 160–61.

42. Fanning, *Revelation*, 482.

43. Keener, *Revelation*, 455.

in 19:9.[44] By changing the metaphor and by addressing the macarism to God's people who are now guests of the marriage feast in 19:9, John is able to strongly encourage his readers to make sure they gain the honor of being invited to the Lamb's banquet (cf. 3:20–21). The notion of marriage promises the perfect communion between the Lamb and his people, and if God's people remain faithful, they will be participants to this marriage. In the end, the kingdom of the beast will fall, and God's people will celebrate together with the Lamb. The fourth macarism is intended to instill hope and to strengthen the faith of God's people in the midst of temptations and persecutions.[45]

Macarism 5: Revelation 20:6

The fifth macarism is given at the end of the vision of the millennium (20:1–6). The fifth macarism is also the only macarism in Revelation where the blessing is combined with a second designation, "holy" (ἅγιος). It thereby goes like this: "Blessed and holy is the one who has a part in the first resurrection." The two designations, blessed and holy, are virtually synonymous, but the designation "holy" could refer to the believers' priesthood.[46] In any case, the two designations combined especially denote the privileged position of the believers in the millennium.

The exact nature and timing of the millennium has been hotly debated with no resolution in sight. This study does not intend to add another voice in this debate, but rather will proceed in analyzing how the fifth macarism functions in its context. At the same time, it will be impossible to fully avoid discussing how different views understand the text of Revelation 20:1–6. This study will however keep the discussion to a minimum with the hope of focusing on the intended effect of the fifth macarism for the readers of Revelation.

The immediate context of 20:1–6 must first be looked at. Following their defeat, two members of the unholy trinity, namely the beast and the false prophet, are captured and are thrown into the lake of fire, while the rest are slain by the conquering Lamb (19:20–21). Conspicuously, one member of the unholy trinity, namely the dragon, is not thrown into

---

44. Beale, *Revelation*, 945; Fanning, *Revelation*, 482.

45. Cruz, "The Beatitudes," 277.

46. Beale, *Revelation*, 1002; Smalley, *Revelation*, 510. Both refer to Pierre Prigent as one who seems to have first argued that the designation "holy" refers to the saints' priesthood. Prigent, *L'Apocalypse*, 312.

the lake of fire like the other two. Rather, the dragon is bound by an angel and is thrown into the bottomless pit for a thousand years (20:1–3). The reason for this is given in 20:3: so that the dragon might not deceive the nations until the thousand years are completed. However, after the completion of the thousand years, John says that Satan will be released for a short time, will once again deceive the nations, will gather them for battle against God's camp, will once again be defeated, and will finally be thrown into the lake of fire where the other two members of the unholy trinity are (20:7–10).

Thus, lodged in-between the two battle stories (19:11–21; 20:7–10) is the vision of the millennium (20:1–6). The actual information regarding the millennium is found in the short verses of 20:4–6. John sees thrones and those who sat upon them, to whom judgment was given in their favor (20:4). Revelation 20:4 alludes to Daniel 7:22 where God declares judgment on the oppressor of God's people, the little horn, and states, "Judgment was given for the saints of the Most High (Dan 7:22a)." As a result, the time comes when the saints take possession of the kingdom (Dan 7:22b). John, by alluding to Daniel 7 in Revelation 20, is noting the fulfillment of Daniel 7's prophecy in the second coming of Christ and in the establishment of the millennium. Since Daniel 7:22 is at work in Revelation 20:4, it is more likely that Revelation 20:4 is claiming that God is the one who has judged the unholy trinity in favor of the saints, rather than stating that God has given the authority to judge to the saints.[47] In any case, the fact that the saints get to sit on the thrones is significant. Whereas Satan is "dethroned" during the millennium, the saints are "enthroned." This denotes a change of status; the saints will be esteemed highly to a privileged position of kingship.

John also sees the souls of the beheaded believers, as well as those who did not worship the beast and who did not receive its mark, coming to life (ζάω) and reigning with Christ for a thousand years (20:4).[48] He

47. Hoskins, *Revelation*, 397–98. Contra, Osborne, *Revelation*, 705.

48. This study does not understand Rev 20:4 to be talking about a single group, namely the martyrs. While the focus of the immediate context is on the martyrs, the overall context of Revelation suggests that all saints are in view here. This study thus argues that the phrase οἵτινες οὐ προσεκύνησαν τὸ θηρίον οὐδὲ τὴν εἰκόνα αὐτοῦ καὶ οὐκ ἔλαβον τὸ χάραγμα ἐπὶ τὸ μέτωπον in 20:4 does not modify τὰς ψυχὰς τῶν πεπελεκισμένων διὰ τὴν μαρτυρίαν Ἰησοῦ καὶ διὰ τὸν λόγον τοῦ θεοῦ, but is referring to a more inclusive group, namely all the saints, in addition to the martyrs. After all, Christ promised all those who conquer that he would give them the right to sit with him on the throne (3:21; cf. 2:26–27; 5:10). For scholars who posit the all-saints view, see Beale, *Revelation*, 1000; Hoskins, *Revelation*, 399; Swete, *Apocalypse*, 262. For those

notes further that the rest of the dead did not come back to life until the thousand years were completed, and that the believers' coming to life is the first resurrection (ἀνάστασις) in 20:5.[49] The meaning of the phrase "first resurrection" has been subject to much debate. On the one hand, those who argue that this refers to the future bodily resurrection of the saints claim that in Revelation, the notion of "coming to life" is used elsewhere to indicate Jesus's resurrection (2:8; cf. 13:14; Jn 5:28–29).[50] Hence, John intends to argue that the saints will also come back to life bodily the same way as Jesus and this sets them apart from the rest of the dead who still have to face the second death, the lake of fire (cf. 20:6, 14). On the other hand, those who argue that the first resurrection refers to the spiritual coming to life, not physical, understand it either as a spiritual regeneration that occurs the moment a person comes to faith in Christ or as an entrance into the intermediate state.[51] They note that the language of "coming to life" and of "resurrection" does not always have to mean a literal, physical resurrection, but can also mean something spiritual (cf. 3:1). Furthermore, Kline has argued that the second death in 20:6 is the spiritual death of the unbelievers and that the death of the believers in 20:4 is literal and physical. This means that there is a "criss-crossing pattern" of connections between the two deaths, and if so, there are also two corresponding resurrections, the first one being spiritual (20:5) and the second one being physical (20:12–15).[52]

---

who posit the only-martyrs view, see Beasley-Murray, *Revelation*, 293–94; Beckwith, *Apocalypse*, 740; Mounce, *Revelation*, 365. In any case, Osborne's words are certainly of value: "I believe it is indeed the martyrs who are the focus throughout 20:4 but that all the saints are also intended in the larger context." Osborne, *Revelation*, 705.

49. Beale makes a valid case. If only the martyrs are in view in 20:4 and not all the saints, then "the rest of the dead" in 20:5 will naturally include the other saints who died without martyrdom. If so, it is strange to number the non-martyred saints along with the unbelievers. Furthermore, these non-martyred saints would not be part of the first resurrection and will not enjoy the blessings that come with it, such as becoming God's priests and reigning with Christ for a thousand years (20:6). This does not seem likely when looking at the overall context of Revelation. However, if all the saints are in view in 20:4, then this awkwardness goes away. Beale, *Revelation*, 999–1000.

50. For instance, Fanning, *Revelation*, 505–6; Hoskins, *Revelation*, 400.

51. For the former, see Wright, *Resurrection*, vol. 3, 474–75. Wright however reserves himself by saying that the spiritual regeneration view is a suggestion and that "This metaphorical use of 'resurrection' language to denote the believer's present status seems to me a partial parallel at least to use in Revelation 20.4 of 'the first resurrection.'" For the latter, see Beale, *Revelation*, 1004–17. Smalley seems to entertain both possibilities. Smalley, *Revelation*, 510.

52. Kline, "The First Resurrection," 370–72. Kline's arguments have been countered

No matter which view of the "first resurrection" one may embrace, it is clear that this first resurrection is a special privilege.[53] So John claims, "Blessed and holy is the one who has a part in the first resurrection" (20:6). If the first resurrection involves only the martyred saints, the reader is encouraged nonetheless, especially if one is facing suffering on account of faith, for dying a martyr's death will reward one with the blessings of the first resurrection. Whether the first resurrection refers to a future, bodily resurrection of the saints or a spiritual resurrection of some kind, the reader is encouraged no matter what, for this resurrection gives one a privilege of being a priest of God and of reigning with Christ for a thousand years (20:6). In fact, whichever view one may have regarding the millennium, John's macarism in 20:6 stands true, and the emphasis remains the same.

John's emphasis is especially brought out by his juxtaposition of the first resurrection and the second death. To the saints belongs the first resurrection; to the unbelievers belongs the second death. Christ has assured the church at Smyrna that the one who stays faithful unto death will receive the crown of life and that the one who conquers will not be hurt by the second death (2:10–11). This blessed assurance is being fulfilled in Revelation 20 as John sees the saints coming to life during the millennium and as the unbelievers are judged during the great white throne judgment to the lake of fire (20:11–15). John can thus exclaim that blessed and holy is the one who can receive the first resurrection, for the second death has no power over them (20:6). Quite the contrary, John claims twice to make sure the audience knows that the saints will reign with Christ (20:4, 6).

Therefore, as Revelation nears the end, John brings out the stark contrast of destiny between the people of God and the people of the beast. The people of the beast will take part in the second death, the lake of fire. All members of the unholy trinity, no matter how much of a fight they think they can bring against God and his people, will be dealt with

---

by many, including Michaels, "The First Resurrection," 100–9 and Hughes, "The First Resurrection," 315–18. Fanning captures the major weakness of the spiritual view well: "One of the problems for views that read these as primarily spiritual 'resurrections' of one kind or another is that it requires amazingly complicated explanations of why the wording does not mean what a straightforward reading of it appears to yield." Fanning, *Revelation*, 506.

53. One can find a great summary of both premillennial and amillennial positions regarding the first resurrection in Waymeyer, "The First Resurrection," 3–32. Waymeyer himself however opts for the premillennial position.

swiftly and fittingly and be sent to the lake of fire. On the other hand, God's people will take part in the first resurrection and will reign with Christ. Their lot is with God and with the Lamb in the new creation (cf. Rev 21–22). John, with his fifth macarism, stresses the truth that those who are in Christ participate in only one death.[54] After that, there is no more death for them but only resurrection. If one faithfully stays on the Lamb's side, one will receive the benefit of fellowship with Christ and the victory that comes with it. The fifth macarism aptly functions to motivate the audience to see past this world and to stay faithful, for resurrection awaits them.

Macarism 7: Revelation 22:14

The seventh and final macarism of Revelation occurs in the epilogue (22:6–21). The epilogue contains two macarisms (22:7, 14), but the seventh macarism is the only macarism in Revelation that is followed by a vice list (22:14–15). Considering the significance of the number seven in Revelation, it is fitting that this seventh one closes the series, for it describes the blessing of the final destiny of God's saints and encourages the audience to reach it. The blessing is complete with the seventh macarism, because there cannot be any further blessing than being able to enter New Jerusalem and being able to enjoy the ultimate benefits of God's city.

John has just finished his major and final vision of the new creation and of New Jerusalem (21:1—22:5). Then, at the beginning of the epilogue, he has reiterated the divine origin, hence the importance, of his prophecy (22:6–13). In doing so, he has emphasized for the readers the critical nature of faithfully obeying the words of the prophecy using a macarism (22:7). Now, to motivate his audience one last time to persevere until they obtain the everlasting inheritance of God's holy city, John gives them a final blessing. The macarism states, "Blessed are the ones who wash their robes, that they may have the right to the tree of life and that they may enter the city by the gates" (22:14).

The notion of washing one's robes evokes the audience several prior places in Revelation where the same or similar idea were expressed. In Revelation 3:4, Christ mentions the faithful few in Sardis who have not soiled their garments and who shall walk with him in white. In its context, these are the few who have believed in Jesus and continue to faithfully

---

54. Nwachukwu, *Beyond Vengeance*, 189–90.

follow him by keeping what they received and heard (3:3). As such, these are also the ones who conquer and who will be clothed in white clothes (3:5; cf. 3:18; 6:11). The notion of conquering was looked at chapter 2 of this study. True conquering involves two aspects in Revelation: the need to be covered by the Lamb's blood and the Christlike manner of faithful obedience (12:11; cf. 2:10, 13; 6:11; 11:7; 13:10; 14:12). Additionally, in Revelation 7:9–14, John sees those who are clothed in white clothes worshiping God before the throne and is told that these have washed their robes and have made them white in the blood of the Lamb.

Thus, it must be that the washing of robes also involves two aspects just like the idea of conquering. First, one must be washed clean by the blood of the Lamb (1:5; 3:18; 5:9; 7:14). Just as John's other writings, Revelation portrays Christ's active involvement in the saints' cleansing.[55] Second, while the cleansing of believers and the receiving of perfectly white garments are the work and the gift of the Lamb (3:4–5, 18; 6:11; 7:14), the believers also must persevere in faithful obedience in order to attain the Lamb's final, perfect gift of white garments (3:3–5; 7:14; 12:11; 13:10; 14:12; 19:8). In other words, the saints participate in the washing of robes as they persevere in faith and in obedience.[56] This second aspect is also attested in John's other writings such as 1 John 1:6–10.

John so states that the blessed are those who wash their robes in Revelation 22:14 to encourage his audience to persevere in faithful obedience. Then he provides the picture of the ultimate end reward one final time. Those who wash their robes are blessed precisely because they get to have the right to the tree of life and because they can enter New Jerusalem by the gates. In the vision of the New Jerusalem (21:1—22:5), the central images were the gates, the city, and the tree of life.[57] John, by recalling all three images, claims that all the blessings of New Jerusalem

---

55. Hoskins, *Revelation*, 474. Hoskins refers to Jn 1:29; 3:5, 8; 6:51–58, 63; 13:5–10; 19:34 and 1 Jn 1:7, 9; 2:2 as places where the idea of Christ's or the Spirit's active part in the cleansing of people are captured.

56. Hoskins, *Revelation*, 475. This could be why some manuscripts have the words, "Blessed are the ones who do his commands" (ποιουντες τας εντολας αυτου) instead of "Blessed are the ones who wash their robes" (πλυνοντες τας στολας αυτων) in Rev 22:14. In any case, the saints' participation in the washing of robes does not mean they somehow earn salvation. Revelation is clear that Christ is the one who provides the white garments. This is more of a case of "already, but not yet." The saints are cleansed and are wearing clean clothes already due to the Lamb's work on the cross. However, their final cleansing and the receiving of clean clothes await the consummation. Until then, they must persevere and run the race faithfully, so to speak.

57. Beale, *Revelation*, 1139.

will be available to those who stay loyal to God and to the Lamb. Furthermore, John seems to have deliberately placed the mention of the tree of life before the mention of entering the city. In the vision of the New Jerusalem, John naturally saw the city first, entered it, and saw the tree of life with all its benefits. Now, he reverses the order to possibly emphasize the source of the blessing than the location.[58] In doing so, he is specifying the target for his readers. They must persevere faithfully until they reach their final prize at the finish line, the tree of life.

John's final macarism hence works to give the readers their ultimate goal they must strive to attain. They must enter God's holy city and succeed in reaching the full benefits of the tree of life. The tree of life, which had been inaccessible since the time of Adam and Eve (cf. Gen 3:22–24), has now been made accessible by the cleansing power of the Lamb's blood. If God's saints persevere faithfully despite the temptations and persecutions of the beast's kingdom, they will have the right to the tree in the eschaton.[59] Indeed, if they wash their robes and not soil them until the end, they will be blessed. John's last macarism thus functions to motivate the readers to be determined in their obedient loyalty to God with their eyes fixated on the final prize.

Conclusion: Macarisms as a Whole

The seven macarisms are clearly placed strategically by John throughout Revelation. The first and the sixth macarisms work like bookends to Revelation, sealing John's words as authentic prophecy revealed to him by God and the Lamb. To think otherwise would turn John into a liar, and John had been adamant to claim that liars have no place in the New Jerusalem (Rev 21:8, 27; 22:15).[60] If he is not a liar, then it is pressing all the more to listen and obey the words contained in Revelation, for the ones who do so will be blessed (1:3; 22:7).

The second to fifth macarisms occur in the context of the conflict between God's kingdom and the beast's kingdom. The second macarism claims that the blessed are those who die in the Lord, encouraging the believers to stay faithful no matter the cost (14:13). The third macarism

---

58. Cruz, "The Beatitudes," 280.

59. *1 Enoch* 25 also mentions the tree of life and the notion that its fruit will be given to the righteous and holy when all things are over.

60. Nwachukwu, *Beyond Vengeance*, 239.

occurs in John's telling of the last battle of Armageddon, and functions to motivate the readers to fix their eyes on Jesus's second coming and to be prepared for it despite what the unholy trinity may bring against God's camp and people (16:15). The fourth macarism occurs on the heels of the destruction of Babylon, encouraging the readers not to choose Babylon but to stay loyal to the Lamb, in order to be invited to his marriage supper (19:9). The fifth macarism claims that the first resurrection belongs to the people of God, of whom the second death has no authority (20:6). This is a sure assurance that emboldens the readers to look forward to.

Finally, the seventh macarism gives one final encouragement to the readers by announcing who the rightful heirs to all the blessings of the eschaton are (22:14). Those who wash their robes are the rightful heirs, meaning those who persevere in faithful obedience. Amid prophesying about the unholy trinity's persecution of God's people, God's coming judgment, and Jesus's victory at his second coming, John has embedded macarisms throughout to exhort God's people to faithful obedience to God. Those who stay loyal to God and who keep his commands are truly blessed, for they will share in the future reward in God's new creation.[61] Cruz has rightly noted that certain themes are repeated in John's macarisms: emphasis on obeying the words of prophecy, rewards awaiting faithful believers, importance of possessing proper garments, and emphasis on the imminence of fulfilment of these promises.[62] Clearly, the macarisms show John's dual concern for eschatology and ethics.[63] John's ethics, in turn, has to do with remaining faithful to God with the behavior of the blessed life of overcoming in order to participate in eternal life.[64]

VICE LISTS IN REVELATION

Provided that Revelation 21:27 is counted, there are four vice lists in Revelation (9:20–21; 21:8, 27; 22:15). Along with virtue lists, vice lists were one of the common, stereotyped paraenetic forms that provided a list of unacceptable behaviors, thus provoking conformity to the values acknowledged by a given community.[65] In Revelation, the vice lists elicit

---

61. Schreiner, *The Joy of Hearing*, 50.
62. Cruz, "The Beatitudes," 280–1.
63. Cruz, "The Beatitudes," 281.
64. Osborne, *Revelation*, 789; Stewart, "Soteriology," 136.
65. Aune, *Literary Environment*, 194–95.

the readers to modify their behaviors so that they may continue in a way of life that is deemed acceptable by John. This section will examine each of the four lists in its context to understand more clearly what John had intended.

Vice List 1: Revelation 9:20–21

The first vice list occurs during the vision of the sixth trumpet (9:13–21). The sixth trumpet is also called by John as the second woe (Ἡ οὐαὶ ἡ δευτέρα; cf. 9:12; 11:14), and it is fitting to find a vice list here. The sixth trumpet vision is strange. The readers are told that when the sixth trumpet is blown by the sixth angel, the angel is commanded to release the four angels who are bound at the great river Euphrates (9:13–14). John also explains that these four angels have been prepared especially for the occasion, timed down to the precise hour, and that the purpose of releasing these four is to kill a third of mankind (9:15).

As if the fifth trumpet (the first woe) was not bizarre enough, the sixth trumpet goes further in its harshness. The peculiar and frightening locust army from the abyss in the fifth trumpet vision at least did not have the authority to kill mankind (9:1–11), but these four angels of the sixth trumpet will actually have the right of killing a third of mankind.[66] The name of the river, Euphrates (cf. 16:12), brings further ominous note to John's readers. The river marked the boundaries for Israel (cf. Gen 15:18; Josh 1:4) and for Rome.[67] Something being done to this river or at this river would mean danger, especially invoking a threat of an invading army.[68]

---

66. Some argue that the four angels of the sixth trumpet are the same as the four angels mentioned in Rev 7:1. For instance, see Kiddle, *Revelation*, 161–63. The precise identity of these four angels is not given by John, however. Many nonetheless understand them to be evil in character. See for instance, Smalley, *Revelation*, 236. Aune observes that, although angels of punishment are known in Jewish apocalyptic literature (cf. 1 En. 53:3; 56:1; 62:11; 63:1; 66:1; 3 En 31:2; 32:1; 33:1), the specific mention of their grouping as four angels is not known. Aune, *Revelation 6–16*, 537–38. This must be a novel feature of John. Knowing the significance of the number four in Revelation, the four angels of punishment in Rev 9:13–15 must mean that their authority to kill a third of mankind is not limited regionally but affects the whole world.

67. Paul, *Revelation*, 181; Thomas and Macchia, *Revelation*, 187.

68. For Israel, it would recall historical conquests by foreign nations such as Assyria and Babylon, and the complete destruction that followed. Cf. Isa 7:17—8:8; Jer 46. For Rome, it would mean war with the Parthians, since the river Euphrates marked the boundary between Rome and Parthia during John's day. Perhaps, the Nero *Redivivus*

Hence, John switches his attention from the four angels to an army—a vast number of mounted troops—starting in Revelation 9:16. John hears their number as 20,000 times 10,000, which comes out to two hundred million, a vast number indeed (9:16). John also sees the cavalry (9:17–19). They wear breastplates that are fiery red, hyacinth blue, and sulfur yellow, which matches in color the fire, smoke, and sulfur that come out of the horses' mouth to kill people.[69] The horses are devilish looking, with heads that are like the lions' and with tails that are like the serpents' heads. John's description of the cavalry invites comparison with the locust army of the fifth trumpet, but in a much more intensified manner.

Amid all the horror, John is careful to let his readers know that those who belong to God will be protected from the plagues of the sixth trumpet that will kill a third of mankind. First of all, the release of the four angels occurs at the command of a voice from the four horns of the golden altar that is before God (9:13–14). If this is not the voice of God himself, then some other heavenly being is speaking on behalf of God. Either way, the plagues of the sixth trumpet can only happen when God allows it. Second, John tells that the four angels had been prepared for the hour, the day, the month, and the year (9:15). This must mean that God is sovereign and that he is the one in control of the judgment of the sixth trumpet. Third, John had made clear in Revelation 8:13 that the three woes, namely fifth through seventh trumpet, are directed to those who dwell on the earth (τοὺς κατοικοῦντας ἐπὶ τῆς γῆς). This group called "those who dwell on the earth" consistently refers to those who do not worship God but worship the beast in Revelation (13:8, 12, 14).[70] The study of the phrase or something similar confirms that these earth dwellers are the objects of Jesus's hour of trial (3:10) and of God's judgment (6:10; 8;13), that they rejoice over the destruction of the church and of the saints (11:10), that they fornicate with the evil woman Babylon (17:2), and that their names are not written in the Lamb's book of life (13:8; 17:8). They are thus the people of the beast, and the sixth trumpet judgment is directed at them, not at the people of God.

---

myth was also recalled, for the myth claimed that Nero will one day come back to destroy Rome with the Parthians. In any case, something being done at Euphrates is not good news for John's audience.

69. Smalley, *Revelation*, 239.
70. Bauckham, *Climax*, 239–41.

But John tells something peculiar in the closing verses of the sixth trumpet vision (9:20–21). Using a vice list, he lists sinful actions that the rest of mankind, those earth dwellers who were not killed by the plagues of the sixth trumpet (hence, the other two-third that survived), did not repent of. At this point, John's readers are confused and conflicted. God's judgment upon the earth dwellers is severe and has become worse especially through the fifth and the sixth trumpets. With the sixth trumpet, a third of mankind will be killed, an event they will all witness. God's judgment is certainly something to be terrified of if one is not a believer, and the petrified reaction of the people of the world in hiding themselves from God's wrath is something that is expected (6:15–17). But they still do not repent after experiencing God's judgment. This is most certainly peculiar.

John's first vice list in Revelation seems to hold the answer. The first vice in this list is idolatry. John says that the rest of mankind did not repent of the works of their hands, with the result that (ἵνα) they did not give up worshipping demons, that is (καί), idols of gold, silver, bronze, stone, and wood, which are not able to see, hear, or walk (9:20).[71] Thus, the earth dwellers do not repent because they choose, with their own hands, to worship something other than the one true God. John describes this in further detail in Revelation 13. The two beasts of Satan deceive and hold sway the people of the world to worship the first beast and to persecute those who do not. At the same time, the people choose to follow the beast and to receive its mark. This suggests that the earth dwellers are so enamored by Satan and what he can give, that they do not give up worship of demons even as they experience God's judgment.

The second to fifth vices are all found in 9:21. Since the verb μετανοέω occurs twice, once in 9:20 to cover the first vice and again in 9:21 to cover the second through fifth vices, it is likely that John wanted to distinguish the first vice with the rest. The first vice is a violation against worship of one true God and the second to fifth vices are violations against other people.[72] Just as those who worship God and Christ exhibit righteous deeds (cf. 14:13; 19:8), those who worship the beast

---

71. The ἵνα clause indicates result, namely that the result of the earth dwellers' works of hands is idol worship. Cf. Mathewson, *Revelation*, 128. The καί connecting the words "demons" and "idols" is not being taken as coordinate, but explanatory. Either way, Scripture understands idol worship as the worship of demons (cf. Deut 32:16–17; Lev 17:7; Matt 4:9–10; 1 Cor 10:19–21).

72. Fanning, *Revelation*, 306.

exhibit moral offenses (cf. 16:11; 18:6). These moral offenses, in turn, are captured in John's vice lists.

The second item in the first vice list is murder (φόνος). In Revelation, the earth dwellers especially kill God's people (cf. 2:13; 6:11; 11:2, 7–10; 13:7; 17:6). The third vice is sorcery (φάρμακον). Whereas Revelation's vice lists contain similar moral offenses to that of the Old Testament ethical teachings (cf. Decalogue, Exod 20:13–17) and of Christ's teachings (Matt 15:19; Mk 7:21–22; cf. Rom 1:29–31), a novel feature is the addition of sorcery.[73] Sorcery or magic is associated with idolatry and refers to practices that make one gain influence over other humans.[74] In Revelation, Babylon is denounced by God due to her deception of people via her sorcery (18:23), and it is apparent that God would do so, for the source of the power for magic or sorcery does not stem from God, but from other things.[75] The fourth vice is sexual immorality (πορνεία). While this may refer literally to unsanctioned sexual conduct, it could also be used metaphorically in denoting unfaithfulness to God as a result of idolatry.[76] The fifth vice is theft (κλέμμα). In the Gospel of John, Jesus compared himself with thieves who only come to steal and to destroy (Jn 10:10), and it may be that the fifth vice in Revelation 9:21 could denote spiritual destruction caused by the earth dwellers as they persecute and sway the believers from following Christ faithfully, as well as literal theft.

What is important to note here is the fact that the second through fifth vices are all connected with the first vice, idolatry. The earth dwellers follow the beast and the worship of idols, which beget moral offenses of every kind.[77] This is what John wants to communicate with his first vice

---

73. Related word φαρμακός appears in Revelation's two other vice lists (21:8; 22:15), and the feminine noun φαρμακεία appears in connection with Babylon the great (18:23).

74. Aune, *Revelation 6–16*, 544–45; Hoskins, *Revelation*, 179–80. For further information on sorcery and magic, see Thomas, *Magical Motifs*.

75. Thomas, *Magical Motifs*, 44.

76. Robinson argues that πορνεία in the vice list of Rev 9:20–21 should be understood literally as unsanctioned sexual conduct, since the other items in the vice list are to be understood literally and since John has already listed idolatry first in the list. The metaphorical meaning of πορνεία is idolatry, and it would be redundant to list idolatry twice in the vice list, if indeed πορνεία refers metaphorically to idolatry as well. Robinson, "Sexual Immorality Language," 162. However, as Robinson himself notes, πορνεία and its cognates frequently refer to spiritual fornication in Revelation, and it may be too quick to dismiss the metaphorical usage in Rev 9:21. At the very least, πορνεία in 9:21 could be emphasizing the unfaithfulness aspect that arises because of idolatry.

77. Putting the first vice of idolatry aside, John has listed four other vices in his

list in 9:20–21. The people of the world do not repent even in the midst of God's judgments, because they follow the beast and choose to commit sin. If the four bound angels at Euphrates who were released are evil, fallen angels, then God is simply using their character of treachery to fulfill his purpose, since these fallen angels are so quick to turn their back on their own people of the beast. Fanning has put it well:

> Satan's demons are all too happy to visit mayhem even on their own human "followers" if given the chance. The New Testament teaches that those who turn away from God become darkened in their understanding of what is really at stake in their lives. At some point in this sinful derangement, they come to believe that allegiance to Satan and his evil—in whatever deceptive form it presents itself to them—would be to their advantage. What a shock when they belatedly see what he and his minions are like! What a shock to find that the "choices" for sin they felt free to make have turned around and made them who they are (i.e., people trapped in false worship and its attendant moral enslavements, vv. 20–21).[78]

Whether the four angels and the mounted troops are fallen angels or not, the fact of the matter is that the earth dwellers have chosen idolatry and sin, and they will not repent because they have been enslaved by their choice even if it kills them. John's first vice list shows the horror of choosing evil and what is really at stake in making that choice. It functions to cause the readers to see the truth of evil, to turn away from it, and to make sure they continue faithfully in following the good: Christ and his ways.

Vice List 2: Revelation 21:8

The second vice list occurs in the opening of John's vision of the new creation. To understand the purpose of this vice list, it is important to look at what comes right before John's vision of the new creation. In Revelation 20:11–15, John tells of the last task that Christ performs at his second coming just prior to the eternal state, which is the great white throne

---

first vice list of Revelation. Number four in Revelation signifies entire world, and it could very well be that he listed four other vices after idolatry to signify moral offenses of every kind that people commit, of which the four other vices are representatives of.

78. Fanning, *Revelation*, 307.

judgment.[79] John sees Christ seated upon a great white throne and the earth and sky fleeing away from his presence (20:11). No matter how one may understand the fleeing of the earth and sky, it clearly suggests that those facing judgment will have no place to hide but will have to face the judge directly.[80] So John sees all the dead standing before the throne (20:12). That the dead refers to all who died without faith in Christ is clear from John's explanation that they were judged and were thrown into the lake of fire because their names were not found in the book of life (20:13–15).[81] Even Death and Hades, the realm of evil, are thrown into the lake of fire (20:14), signifying that there is now no place Satan and his henchmen can take foothold, and also anyone whose name is not written in the book of life (20:15).

Then John begins his vision of the new creation as he sees the new heaven and new earth starting with Revelation 21:1. He also sees the New Jerusalem coming down from God (21:2), with the eternal promise that God will now and forever dwell with his people and that there will no

---

79. This writer understands the one on the great white throne to be the Lamb. It is possible that it is God who is on the throne, since John does not specify who is sitting on it and since it was God who was seated on the throne in Rev 4:2. However, the Gospels picture Jesus to take on an active role at the last judgment (Matt 7:22–23; 10:32–33; 25:31–46; Mk 8:38; Jn 5:22–30). See Beasley-Murray, *Revelation*, 299. The Gospel of John especially claims that Jesus has received the authority to judge from God. In Revelation, the seal, trumpet, and bowl judgments all stem from the Lamb (cf. Rev 6:1), and since John has been depicting the second coming of Jesus starting from Rev 19:11 without an explicit hint that he is changing topics, it is likely that the great white throne judgment is also performed by Christ the returned king. In any case, John may be intentionally ambiguous as to the identity of the one seated on the great white throne, because he thinks both God and the Lamb are involved in the last judgment. After all, John does mention that the throne in New Jerusalem is "the throne of God and of the Lamb" (22:1).

80. Hoskins, *Revelation*, 414–15.

81. This writer understands the dead in Rev 20:11–15 to be comprised solely of the unbelievers. As this study has argued, all saints come to life (the first resurrection) during the millennium (20:4), whereas the rest of the dead (the unbelievers) do not until the end of the millennium (20:5). This means that by the time of the great white throne judgment which takes place after the millennium, only the unbelievers have not come to life. They will come to life for the great white throne judgment and be judged to the lake of fire. Nonetheless, there are others who understand the dead in 20:11–15 to be comprised of both the saints and the unbelievers. They argue that Daniel 12:1–2 is being alluded to in Rev 20:11–15. Since Daniel 12 envisions those whose names are written in the book to go to everlasting life and others to everlasting contempt, John is also envisioning this as being fulfilled in Rev 20:11–15. Thus, Rev 20:12 refers to the saints being judged to everlasting life, while 20:13–15 refer to the unbelievers being judged to everlasting contempt. For an example of a scholar who argues this position, see Osborne, *Revelation*, 721–22.

more be any suffering, for the former things have passed away (21:3–4). As if this promise is not enough, God himself speaks to John: "Behold, I make all things new" (21:5). God also tells John to write what he says down, because these words are trustworthy and true. The act of writing something down gives the writing the notion that it is final and concrete, especially since the words are the true and trustworthy words of God himself. These important words of assurance are captured in Revelation 21:6–8, of which the last verse is the vice list under examination.

The words that God commands John to write down are thus. First is the expression, "They are done" (γέγοναν). This expression signals the fulfillment of the new creation, which Christ made possible for those who believe when he said on the cross, "It is finished" (Jn 19:30).[82] Second is God's title, namely the Alpha and the Omega, the beginning and the end. This title proclaims the eternality of God and the truth that he is the sovereign creator and lord of all history, which in turn is a fitting title as God brings the former creation to a close and begins the new one in Revelation 21.[83] Third and fourth are declarations of promise. God declares that he will give to the thirsty from the spring of the water of life without payment (21:6). To those who are spiritually thirsty for God, God promises that he will freely give the water of life, meaning that he will provide all that is necessary for life in the new creation (cf. 22:1, 17).[84] God also declares that the one who conquers will have this inheritance and that God will be his God and he will be God's son (21:7). As this study has shown, the one who conquers refers to God's true people who faithfully persevere and submit fealty to God, and God promises that the new creation will be theirs and that God will also remain faithful to them with a perfect and eternal covenantal relationship.[85]

---

82. Beale, *Revelation*, 1055; Sweet, *Revelation*, 299.

83. Bauckham, *Theology*, 27.

84. Fanning observes that Isa 49:10 is being alluded here. The picture is that of God as a shepherd who feeds his sheep and leads them by springs of water, ensuring every necessity the sheep needs. Fanning, *Revelation*, 535 fn. 31. Revelation 7:16–17 also have this imagery, but there it is the Lamb who is the shepherd and who will guide God's people to springs of living water. See also, Jn 4:14 and 7:37–38.

85. Dempsey, "Revelation 21:1–8," 402. The expression "I will be his God and he will be my son" recalls the covenant God has made with Israel (Exod 6:7). Thomas and Macchia further argue that the expression recalls the Davidic covenant (2 Sam 7:14). Thomas and Macchia, *Revelation*, 369. In any case, Thomas and Macchia are correct in understanding that the covenant formula implies an intimate relationship that is far greater than anything anticipated. Thomas and Macchia, *Revelation*, 370.

In the midst of this splendid vision and the promise of blessing that far surpasses anything on the earth, God seems to change his tone as he wants John to write down a vice list. The list contains types of people who will not inherit the things of the new creation, but who will have a share in the lake of fire, the second death (21:8). When compared to Revelation's first vice list, the catalogue is similar. Both contain sins or sinful acts that describe the people of the beast. A major difference is that, in the first vice list, John tells of violations the people did not repent of, whereas in the second vice list, there is no mention of repentance. This is expected, for the second vice list occurs during the vision of the new creation when the opportunity for repentance is already past. In Revelation, people who commit such violations are the people of the beast, and they are all judged along with the unholy trinity to the lake of fire prior to the advent of new creation (19:20; 20:10, 11–15). The people of God do not partake in the second death, which is the lake of fire, but in the first resurrection (20:4–6). Yet God suddenly seems to speak as if there is still a threat of the second death in the new creation to his people.

It may be significant that this second vice list in Revelation contains a catalogue of sinners, whereas the first vice list contained a catalogue of sins. By providing a list of sinners rather than a list of sins, the effect is that such sinful behaviors become uncomfortably personal to those who commit them, while a list of sins would place some distance between such behaviors and the people.[86] Thus, John's readers, as they suddenly hear about the kinds of people who will not receive the inheritance of the new creation, would be stunned, especially if they have committed the very acts God is describing. The vice list hence functions to pressure and to warn the readers that, if they do not repent but continue to entertain the ways of the beast, they may not inherit the blessings of the new creation when the time comes. It is not that there is still a threat of second death in the new creation; it is a way of rhetorical reminder that God's people must remain faithful in the present no matter the cost.

This must be why the cowardly (δειλός) and the faithless (ἄπιστος) are listed at the front of the vice list. Boring is correct in understanding that this is not a traditional list; John has modified it to fit the occasion.[87] The two fronted items, namely the cowardly and the faithless, occur only here in Revelation and refer to those who compromise the Christian faith

---

86. Aune, "Lists, Ethical," 671.
87. Boring, *Revelation*, 217.

under pressure.⁸⁸ They are apparently the opposite kind of people from those mentioned in 21:7, namely those who conquer. The latter kind will inherit the new creation, whereas the former will not. The last item on the list is liars (ψευδής) of every kind. Genuine people of God stand and persevere for the truth, but if one does not, one is proving oneself to be a liar. The rest of the items in the vice list of 21:8, while they are standard characteristics of the followers of the beast in Revelation, could in the context of Revelation 21 likewise refer to the apostate Christians.⁸⁹ God, in turn, is declaring that if one cowers away from the truth, one is surrendering to sin and will join the unbelieving world in the lake of fire.

Therefore, the second vice list functions to warn the readers that if they do not persevere and stay faithful, they will not inherit the blessings of the new creation. By defecting, they prove themselves to be cowards and liars, properly belonging with the unbelieving world, and will have a share in the lake of fire. One thereby has a choice to make. One can "conquer" and inherit the new creation, or one can "cower" and inherit eternal damnation. The stark warning of the second vice list is effective both as a threat and as an encouragement.⁹⁰

Vice List 3: Revelation 21:27

The third vice list occurs towards the end of John's vision of the New Jerusalem (21:9—22:5). Revelation 22:1–5 describe the ultimate blessing of the New Jerusalem, namely the water of life and the tree of life, and one could argue that the actual description of the New Jerusalem ends

---

88. Hoskins, *Revelation*, 436; Mounce, *Revelation*, 386; Smalley, *Revelation*, 543.

89. Osborne, *Revelation*, 741–42; Smalley, *Revelation*, 543.

90. To be clear, this writer believes that genuine believers will always persevere and stay faithful. Those who cower away will be ones who were not real believers to begin with. But why then does John provide such warning to believers if they will not defect? Simply put, the warning functions for the genuine believers to persevere all the more. Believers can and do entertain sin even though they will not ultimately continue in sin. The warning will cause these believers to repent quickly. Furthermore, people do give stark warnings to their children about disciplining them if they continue their bad behavior even though the parents do not really intend on following through with the disciplinary acts. This is done to cause the children to behave correctly. The vice list functions in a similar way. It is not that God will actually take away the inheritance of the new creation from genuine believers if they cower. They cannot cower if they are genuine. The warning is made so that they will persevere all the more in light of what will happen to the unbelievers. This observation is relevant for all the other vice lists in Revelation as well.

with 21:27, precisely the verse where the third vice list is found. As noted earlier, the third vice list is not a vice list proper. It contains two vices and one virtue, and although it is not a vice list proper, it still is an ethical catalogue, and this study shall take the opportunity to examine its function in its context.

Starting in 21:9, John has been describing the grandeur of the Lamb's bride, the New Jerusalem. John has intentionally made his vision of the New Jerusalem to begin from the outside looking in, so that his readers can imaginatively follow the vision as visitors who see the city from afar, then right in front of it, and finally enter through its gates. First, John watches the holy city coming down from God from afar on a great, high mountain (21:9-10). John claims that the city has the glory of God, and its radiance is like the most precious jewel (21:11). This picks up the biblical concept of God's Shekinah presence among his people that was especially felt at the temple (Exod 24:15-16; 40:34-35; 1 Kgs 8:10-12; Isa 6:1-4; Ezek 43:5; Rev 15:8) now being eternally fulfilled with the coming of the New Jerusalem (Rev 21:11, 23).[91] The holy city is majestic precisely because it will be the place God's presence among his people will be perfect for all time.

Second, John observes the city's great and high wall with its twelve gates and twelve foundations (21:12-14). Rissi is correct in noting John's curious interest on the city's wall, since Ezekiel 40-48, which Revelation's depiction of the New Jerusalem comes from, do not focus on the wall and since its purpose in providing defense against enemies is obsolete, for there will not be any enemies in the new creation and for its gates are said to remain open continually (cf. 21:25).[92] The wall, thus, likely stresses the eternal invulnerability of the city and symbolizes the boundary between the insiders and the outsiders, with the insiders being the true people of God (the names of the twelve tribes of Israel and of the twelve apostles are inscribed on the gates and on the foundations respectively).[93] Third, John measures the city, highlighting the fact that the city is a perfect cube (21:15-17; cf. Ezek 40:5—42:20; 45:1-5; 48:8-13; Zech 2:1-2). The holy of holies in the earthly temple, which was the place of God's holy presence, was a cube (1 Kgs 6:20), and John's measurements of the New

---

91. Osborne, *Revelation*, 749.
92. Rissi, *The Future*, 67.
93. Rissi, *The Future*, 67. See also, du Rand, "The New Jerusalem," 294.

Jerusalem communicates that it is in fact a city-temple, a perfect place of God's holy presence on a cosmic scale.[94]

Fourth, John now seems to have moved in closer to examine the city as he notices the precious jewels that make the wall and its foundations and gates (Rev 21:18–21). Indeed, he seems to stand right in front of one of the gates, as he can peek inside to see that the street of the city is made of special kind of pure gold (21:21). The jewel motif certainly expresses the glory, purity, beauty, and preciousness of New Jerusalem.[95] Bauckham further notes that the jewel motif recalls the garden of Eden and the temple, as the list of jewels are stones found in Eden (cf. Gen 2:11–12; Ezek 28:13) and on the breastplate of the high priest (cf. Exod 28:17–20).[96] This means that the New Jerusalem is being presented as the ultimate fulfillment of Eden and the temple; it is a paradisical city-temple that surpasses all that represented the presence and the glory of God.[97]

Fifth, the vision zooms in even further as John seems to be now inside the city and notices another peculiar feature of the city: no temple (Rev 21:22–23)! The city needs no temple, for God and the Lamb both dwell personally in the city. The city itself will be the true temple where God and the Lamb are directly and perfectly present. Hence, the radiant glory of God and of the Lamb will light up the city.

Thus, John's vision of the New Jerusalem is carefully constructed to bring out the ultimate splendor of the city. It is a superb case of an ekphrasis, a technique of vivid description that invites participation from the readers and evokes intended emotions.[98] As the readers get involved in John's journey of the holy city, looking at it first from afar and then moving closer to it, finally arriving inside, their imagination is stirred, and their emotions aroused due to the grandiose nature of the city. On top of portraying his vision *spatially* for the readers to follow, John also communicates his vision *perspectivally*. He describes the New Jerusalem in various perspectives, including architecture (21:12–21), temple/religious (21:22–23), political (21:24–27), and creational (22:1–5).[99] In doing so,

---

94. Beale, *Revelation*, 1073; Paul, *Revelation*, 351.
95. Lee, *The New Jerusalem*, 285.
96. Bauckham, *Theology*, 133–34.
97. Du Rand, "The New Jerusalem," 295.
98. On the technique of ekphrasis, see Webb, *Ekphrasis*. See also, Bartsch and Elsner, "Introduction," i–vi; Stewart, "Ekphrasis," 227–40.
99. Du Rand, "The New Jerusalem," 294–98.

the readers are persuaded that this holy city is unlike any city they have encountered in this world. It is a city par excellence.

Indeed so, because it is a city where God is personally present in all his glory, as John emphasizes time and time again in the vision of the New Jerusalem. God's radiant glory that fills the New Jerusalem will also be the standard of life in the new creation (21:24). John moreover states that the nations will bring their glory into God's holy city through the city's open gates that will not be shut (21:24-26). This probably means that God's true people who shall be in the new creation will bring praises worthy of the glory of God into New Jerusalem.[100]

In the midst of such a surreal vision of the New Jerusalem, John abruptly provides a vice list (21:27). Until now in his description of the holy city, John's words have been absolutely positive. Yet, as if he does not want his readers to forget, John gives them a dose of spiritual reality so that they may reorient themselves. He states that nothing unclean (κοινός) will ever enter New Jerusalem, nor anyone who does what is detestable (βδέλυγμα) or false (ψεῦδος), but only those who are written in the book of life of the Lamb. Then the vision of the New Jerusalem

---

100. There are several issues raised regarding Rev 21:24-26. First, who are the nations and the kings of the earth mentioned in 21:24? Since the nations and the kings of the earth are references to people who are allied with the beast (6:15; 11:9, 18; 14:8; 16:14; 17:2, 15; 18:3), and since only the believers live in the new creation, some argue that the nations and the kings of the earth in 21:24 are those who were once allied with the beast but have repented and became believers. For instance, Bauckham, *Climax*, 313-16; Caird, *Revelation*, 279; McNicol, *Conversion of the Nations*. Some on the other hand argue that this is not likely, for the nations and the kings of the earth were killed by Christ in 19:15-21 and in 20:7-10. Rather, the nations and the kings of the earth in 21:24 refer to the true people of God who have been purchased from every nation (5:9; 7:9) and who will rule with Christ as kings forever (22:5). For instance, Hoskins, *Revelation*, 452; Kiddle, *Revelation*, 439; Mathewson, *New Heaven and New Earth*, 170; Smalley, *Revelation*, 559. In any case, the nations and the kings of the earth in 21:24 are true believers of the Lamb, irrespective of when they came to faith.

Second, what are the glory and honor the nations and the kings of the earth bring into New Jerusalem in 21:24-26? Are they material wealth? This is hardly thinkable considering the grandiose nature of the holy city. Wealth accumulation does not seem to be necessary in the New Jerusalem. Hence, some think that the glory and honor here refer to God's holy people themselves. The people are the glory and honor worthy to be brought to God. For instance, Smalley, *Revelation*, 558. Others think that the glory and honor are the praises of God's people in fulfillment of Isaiah 60:5-11 (cf. Rev 4:11; 5:12-14; 14:2-3). For instance, Beale, *Revelation*, 1095; Fekkes, *Isaiah*, 272; Hoskins, *Revelation*, 454; Mathewson, *New Heaven and New Earth*, 167-8. Whatever the exact nature of the glory and honor brought into New Jerusalem may be, they are certainly something good and worthy to be offered to God.

resumes, concluding on the pinnacle of blessing of the new creation, the water of life and the tree of life (22:1-5).

On the surface, the vice list in 21:27 seems redundant, as was the case with the list in 21:8. The words, "unclean," "detestable," and "false," describe the people of the beast (cf. 16:13; 17:4; 18:2; 21:8), but they will not be in the new creation.[101] Only the people of God will be present in the new creation. One of the reasons why the gates of New Jerusalem will be open all day is because there will be no more threat from opposing forces (cf. 21:25). But there must be a reason behind as to why John nonetheless mentions people who will not be around in the new heaven and the new earth.

The answer is that John is using the vice list as a warning for his readers. In the midst of describing the grandiose nature of the New Jerusalem, John has also emphasized the holiness of the city in contrast to the impurity of Babylon (cf. 18:4-5; 21:2, 10).[102] In doing so, John alludes especially to the first half of Isaiah 52:1.[103] The latter half of Isaiah 52:1 is captured in Revelation 21:27, the vice list under examination.[104] Isaiah 52:1 foretells of the rise of Jerusalem the holy city, to which the unclean may not come in. This works as a counterpart to Isaiah 52:11 (cf. Isa 48:20) where God's call to depart from Babylon is made, which Revelation uses to call the readers to come out of Babylon the great harlot (Rev 18:4).[105] The focus in these two verses in Isaiah 52 is holiness. God's people must be holy and so must depart Babylon; God's city must be holy and so must depart the unclean.

John's prohibition in Revelation 21:27 communicates the same message. The absolute holiness of the New Jerusalem means that the people who are deemed worthy to enter there must also be absolutely holy.

---

101. The descriptions, "detestable" and "false," already appeared in the vice list of 21:8. There, John stated that the sinners' portion is not the new creation but second death, which is the lake of fire. The sinners, also could be called the people of the beast, have already been judged to the lake of fire in 20:11-15, which in turn means that they are not present in the new creation. Only the people of God will be in the new creation. The description, "unclean" (κοινός), occurs only at 21:27 in Revelation, but has the same sense as ἀκάθαρτος that is used to describe the beast and the things of the beast in Revelation (cf. 16:13; 17:4; 18:2). So Fanning, *Revelation*, 546 fn. 86.

102. Mathewson, *New Heaven and New Earth*, 177.

103. So Beale, *Revelation*, 1044; Fekkes, *Isaiah*, 280; Osborne, *Revelation*, 731. Isaiah 65 and Ezekiel 40-48 also serve as major backgrounds to Revelation's vision of the New Jerusalem.

104. Mathewson, *New Heaven and New Earth*, 177.

105. Mathewson, *New Heaven and New Earth*, 177.

However, whereas the message of holiness in Isaiah 52:1 functions more as an encouragement for God's people to stay holy and to stay hopeful for the day when Jerusalem will rise again, Revelation 21:27 functions more as a warning. Nothing unclean will ever enter the New Jerusalem, nor anyone who does what is detestable or false. So, God's people better stay clean and do what is holy and true, or they will not enter the holy city.

Interestingly, John provides a virtue after he lists two vices in 21:27. The virtue stands opposite to the two vices and describes the only type of people who can enter New Jerusalem, namely those who are written in the book of life of the Lamb. Since these are the only people who can enter the holy city, they must be the only people Revelation understands as holy. In Revelation, those who are written in the book of life are described as those who conquer (3:5), who do not worship the beast (13:8; 17:8), and who are not thrown into the lake of fire (20:15). The latter two descriptions are obvious, the first not so clear. However, this study has already shown that conquering in Revelation has to do with being covered by the blood of the Lamb and with staying faithful in obedience, despite sufferings and even death (cf. 12:11).[106] In effect, John is claiming that to enter New Jerusalem, one must be holy, and being holy has to do with trusting Jesus's work on the cross and with being faithful to God and to the Lamb in obedience no matter the cost.

Therefore, the vice list in 21:27 serves to warn the readers that they must stay holy to be deemed worthy to partake in the blessings of New Jerusalem. God's people must not be unclean, detestable, or false like the people of the beast, but must be holy as those who are written in the book of life. To be holy is to stay loyal to God no matter what the beast may bring. If they persevere in faith and in loyalty in the present, God will grant them the blessings of New Jerusalem in the new creation. If they fall away and side with the beast, they may not enter God's holy city. In this way, the vice list in 21:27 bolsters John's main purpose in writing the book of Revelation: fidelity to God.

Vice List 4: Revelation 22:15

The final vice list in Revelation works similar to the one in 21:27. The list specifies those who will not be able to enter New Jerusalem but will remain outside. Again, this must not literally mean that there will be

---

106. See chapter 2 of this study regarding what it means to conquer in Revelation.

unbelievers living in the new creation outside of the holy city but serves to differentiate those who are worthy from those who are unworthy. The final list occurs near the end of Revelation and is the only list in Revelation that appears alongside a macarism (22:14–15). Since the context where the final macarism and vice list appear has already been looked at, this section will focus on how this final vice list is functioning in comparison with the third vice list.

The first item in the final vice list is dogs (κύων). As it was the case with the first and the second vice lists, this first item is likely put intentionally by John. This is also the only instance of the word κύων appearing in Revelation. When looking at the context of Revelation, the usage of this word must be figurative, for John is concerned with what types of people will and will not be in the new creation, not with literal animals. Moreover, κύων takes on a negative sense in 22:15, as it appears in a vice list.

This is in keeping with the usage of the word elsewhere in the Bible. In Deuteronomy 23:18 (MT 23:19), κύων (כלב in Hebrew) is used to refer to a male prostitute.[107] Other places in the Old Testament, κύων is frequently used to refer to reviled animals (cf. Exod 11:7; 22:31; 1 Sam 17:43; 24:14; 2 Sam 3:8; 9:8; 16:9; 1 Kgs 14:11; 16:4; 21:19, 23–24; 22:38; 2 Kgs 8:13; 9:10, 36; Job 30:1; Ps 22:16, 20; 59:6, 14; 68:23; Prov 26:11, 17; Eccl 9:4; Isa 56:10–11; 66:3; Jer 15:3).[108] More importantly, in most of these cases where κύων is used, the context has to do with unworthiness/impurity and worthiness/purity.

In the New Testament, κύων is also used in the contexts of holiness and worthiness.[109] Jesus himself teaches that dogs are not to receive what is holy (Matt 7:6) and that Lazarus who was associated with dogs actually goes to heaven in a reversal of fortunes (Lk 16:21). Apostle Paul calls the Judaizers who do evil in the church dogs and separates them from the true people of God (Phil 3:2). Likewise, Apostle Peter, as he discusses the false teachers' sins, those who had known the way of righteousness but have since turned away from the truth and went back to the way of

---

107. *HALOT*, s.v. "כלב."

108. Idan Breier has examined ANE literature regarding the image dogs had in the lands of the Bible. He also notes the prominence of negative image dogs had in the ANE, thereby representing the miserable, pathetic person. Breier, "'Who Is This Dog?,'" 47–62.

109. The same is true for the word κυνάριον in Matt 15:26–27 and Mk 7:27–28.

corruption, uses a wisdom saying (a true proverb) and equates them with dogs who return to their own vomit (2 Pet 2:22; cf. Prov 26:11).[110]

It is thereby apt that John would use the word κύων in Revelation 22:15, for the context here also has to do with specifying who is worthy or unworthy to enter God's holy city. Those who are clean or holy will enter, but those who are "dogs," meaning those who are unclean and sinful, will not enter, as it was the case with the vice list in 21:27. Furthermore, as noted above, it may be significant that both Paul and Peter connect false teachers with dogs (so does Ignatius in *Eph* 7:1). John also mentions false teachers who were ravaging the churches in Revelation 2:2, 6, 9, 14–15, 20–24; 3:9, and it is possible that these false teachers were on John's mind as he wrote 22:15.[111] The false teachers, together with the people of the beast, will be outside the New Jerusalem, for they are sinful, unclean, and ultimately unworthy.

The next items on John's vice list in 22:15 have appeared in all of John's other proper vice lists (9:20–21; 21:8), except for 21:27.[112] Sorcerers, the sexually immoral, murders, idolaters, and all who love and do falsehood consistently describe the people of the beast in Revelation. This is fitting, for these characteristics are also who the unholy trinity and Babylon are and what they do. As such, it is no surprise that they will not be present in the New Jerusalem.

Thus, John, as he closes the book of Revelation, reminds his readers one last time on who will be victorious in receiving the eternal blessing of the New Jerusalem and who will be losing out, as to encourage them to choose the proper side. It is thereby not coincidental that the last macarism and the last vice list occur together. It may also be that the last macarism and vice list (22:14–15) unpack and conclude the ethical list of 21:27. There are indeed two ethical lists within the vision of the New

---

110. In the extrabiblical literature, *Didache* 9:5 utilizes Christ's teaching regarding not giving dogs what is holy (Matt 7:6) in prohibiting the unbelievers from partaking the Eucharist. In *Eph* 7:1, Ignatius calls the false teachers who carry the name of Jesus Christ in a wicked manner and who acts in a manner unworthy of God dogs from whom God's people must flee. Here the context in which κύων is used has to do with worthiness and holiness.

111. Robinson thinks the dogs likely refer specifically to the Jewish false teachers in the churches. Robinson, "Sexual Immorality Language," 170. However, this writer understands the term more broadly as a reference to all people who are unclean and unworthy.

112. Hoskins argues, "Idolatry shows up in all of Revelation's vice lists, because it is one of the main sins or abominations that the harlot engages in and entices the world to engage in as well." Hoskins, "Another Possible Interpretation," 93.

Jerusalem, namely at 21:27 and 22:14–15. As it has been noted, the vice list of 21:27 is not a vice list proper. It is an ethical list nonetheless as it contains two vices and one virtue. On the other hand, virtually all scholars agree that the list of 22:15 is a vice list proper and that it is the only instance in Revelation where a vice list occurs together with a macarism. It may very well be that John wanted to concretize what he stated in 21:27 with a proper macarism and a proper vice list.

So John's ethical list in 21:27 began with vices and ended with a virtue; John's ethical list in 22:14–15 begins with a virtue proper and ends with vices proper. The virtue in 21:27 stated that those whose names are written in the book of life will enter New Jerusalem. The macarism in 22:14 unpacks this truth further by stating that blessed are the ones who wash their robes, for these are the ones who will have access not only to New Jerusalem, but also to the tree of life, which is the focal point of blessing found inside New Jerusalem. It follows then that those whose names are written in the book of life are also the ones who wash their robes, since only these people will be able to enter God's holy city. More importantly, this study has analyzed what having one's name written in the book of life and washing one's robes entail, and both are connected to the notion of conquering. In Revelation, the believers conquer by the blood of the Lamb and by staying faithful to God. Therefore, both virtues in 21:27 and 22:14 emphasize loyalty to God as a prerequisite to the entrance of New Jerusalem.

The vice list in 22:15 also unpacks the two vices found in 21:27. The two vices in 21:27 stated that the unclean and the ones who do what is detestable and false will never enter New Jerusalem. The vice list in 22:15 clarifies this by giving a stock characteristic of the people of the beast, substantiating that the unclean, detestable, and false are indeed the people of the beast. John also fronts his vice list in 22:15 with a word that captures brilliantly who these unclean, detestable, and false people are, namely the "dog," which would include those false teachers in the churches. In doing so, John encourages and warns his readers at the same time that they must not be like the people of the beast and that they must not follow their beastly ways. They must also shun the false teachers within the churches who entice people to follow Satan rather than Christ. Indeed, God's people must stay holy and faithful no matter what in this world, and they will be granted access to the ultimate blessing of the New Jerusalem in the new creation.

Conclusion: Vice Lists as a Whole

The four vice lists in Revelation all describe the people of the beast. In effect, the lists succinctly capture sins or sinful actions John's readers must avoid in order to be true people of God. The first list in 9:20–21 is the only instance that occurs outside of John's vision of the eschaton. By showing the deplorable reason why the people of the world do not repent from their beastly ways of living even in the midst of God's stern judgments, namely their choice in following the beast in idolatry, John warns his readers of the snare of choosing evil rather than God. The second list (21:8) occurs at the end of the vision of the new heaven and new earth (21:1–8). John gives the second list right after describing the blessed state of the new creation, which stuns his readers since these listed sinners should not be in the new creation. In doing so, John pressures his readers, especially the ones who might be committing those same sins he describes, to stop them and instead to faithfully persevere in order to receive the inheritance of the new creation.

The third list (21:27) occurs towards the end of the vision of the New Jerusalem (21:9—22:5). While not a vice list proper, this ethical list nonetheless describes who will not be able to enter God's holy city and who will. The fourth list (22:15) also states who will be able to enter New Jerusalem and who will not and unpacks the third list in detail. As it turns out, the third and fourth lists together show that only God's holy people will enter the city whereas the unclean people of the beast will not. This warns and encourages John's readers to stay faithful and holy before God in the present as to make sure they inherit the ultimate blessing of the New Jerusalem.

John's use of the vice lists in Revelation clearly show concern for paraenesis, namely warning and encouragement for the audience to continue in the true way of life. The lists are also placed strategically by John to effectively promote paraenesis. It is also significant that at least three of his vice lists (second to fourth lists) are connected with the notion of conquering. Revelation defines conquering as staying faithful to God and his commands, and John emphasizes repeatedly that it is those who conquer who will inherit eternal life. In this way, the vice lists lend support to John's purpose in writing Revelation, which is to strengthen loyalty to God on part of the readers.

SUMMARY AND CONCLUSION

The seven macarisms, together with the four vice lists, are placed intentionally by John throughout Revelation to promote faithfulness and fidelity to God. The macarisms emphasize the notion of obedience, reward for those who stay faithful, becoming worthy to possess the reward, and the imminent fulfillment of God's promises. Similarly, the vice lists emphasize the importance of shunning evil, not following the ways of the beast, and staying holy and faithful in order to inherit the blessings of the new creation. The macarisms and vice lists evidence that John is not solely concerned with eschatology but also with ethics. This world follows what John determines as vices. Yet, God's people must follow the virtue of God's ways, and thus conquering, they will be granted the right of eternal life. This, in short, is the message of macarisms and vice lists in Revelation.

CHAPTER 7

Conclusion

THIS STUDY HAS EXAMINED the three major wisdom motifs that occur in the book of Revelation in order to ascertain their function and their contribution to the overall purpose of the book. To conclude, this chapter will first bring together the findings of the previous chapters in summary and synthesis. It will end with providing implications for future study and for the church today.

SUMMARY AND SYNTHESIS

Chapters 2 and 3 of this study dealt with the four instances of the word σοφία in Revelation. The first two instances of σοφία show that true wisdom belongs only to the Lamb and to God. In Revelation 5:12, wisdom is first attributed to the Lamb by the heavenly cohort. The message of the throne room vision of Revelation 4–5 where the word σοφία occurs for the first time, in turn, becomes relevant for understanding John's purpose in attributing wisdom to the Lamb. The message is one of assurance, namely that God and the Lamb are in absolute control of all things. The throne room vision then focuses upon the fact that only the Lamb can take the sealed scroll and open its contents due to his worthiness and his conquering (5:5, 9). Since God and the Lamb are in absolute control of all matters, it necessarily follows that they are the ones who know and who determine what true worthiness and conquering life entail.

As this study has shown, the emphasis on the worthiness of the Lamb's conquering means that there is a redefinition of what victorious life involves. True victorious life is not through might, but through faithful obedience even to the point of death just like Christ. This is what makes the Lamb worthy, and the people of God must understand that, if they are to be worthy before God, they also need to stay faithful in obedience to God and to the Lamb. Further, the fact that wisdom is attributed to the Lamb based on his worthiness of sacrifice show that true wise living rests on the example of Christ's faithfulness to God. In fact, the throne room vision itself functions as a disclosure of wisdom. Yet, by intentionally attributing wisdom to the Lamb, John shows that true wisdom has the Lamb at the center and that he defines what true wisdom entails. This wisdom has been disclosed to John's readers and they must align their lives with it. The Lamb is the one who has true wisdom, and with this true wisdom, he will execute judgment accordingly. He shall discern each person's path of allegiance and shall see who is worthy and who is not. By presenting Christ as one who has true wisdom and true conquering life in Revelation 4–5, John sets down proper standards of Christian living before his main visions get underway.

The second instance of σοφία is in 7:12. It occurs in the midst of another throne room vision in which the innumerable multitude is added to the picture along with the other heaven cohort already introduced in Revelation 4–5. The throne room vision of Revelation 7 is, in effect, another instance of the disclosure of wisdom. This time, σοφία is attributed to God by the heavenly worshippers, which shows that true divine wisdom is also defined by God who is on the throne. Revelation 7 is the book's first interlude which John uses to communicate an important message, namely that God's people shall be protected from God's judgments which the Lamb executes and shall be eternally secure before God. John wants his readers to know that God has wisdom and thus knows who shall appear before him at the time of the end. God, in his wisdom, has accomplished his redemptive work through the faithful obedience of the Lamb. God knows who belong to him, and he will protect those who are worthy and will secure the fate of those whose lives have been redefined in the footsteps of their master, the Lamb.

In this way, John places the first two instances of σοφία strategically within two significant throne room visions (Rev 4–5; 7) to communicate an important truth, namely that true wisdom belongs to God and the Lamb and that this wisdom has now been disclosed to the readers of Revelation. This true wisdom is intricately tied to Christ's act of sacrifice, which is an act done in full obedience to the Father. Christ is thus worthy and can claim that he has conquered. In turn, Christ has shown what true

CONCLUSION 229

wise and victorious living entails, and if God's people stay faithful and loyal in obedience no matter the cost just like Christ, then the wise Father shall claim them also to be worthy and shall secure their eternal fate.

The last two instances of σοφία are also placed strategically by John and are intended to show that God's people must live wisely as they utilize true σοφία in recognizing the deceptive reality of the beast. The third σοφία occurs in 13:18 as John calls his readers to exercise σοφία in understanding the beast's number. John shows in Revelation 13 that the beast is hard at work in imitating Christ and in deceiving the people of the world into following it and ultimately Satan. Those who do not worship the beast are to be slain (13:15) and those who do not take the mark of the beast are not able to buy or sell things (13:16–17). This surmounts to an inevitable conflict. If people follow the beast and take its mark, they submit their fidelity to the beast and can enjoy the rights afforded by the beast, especially economic rights. If people do not submit their fidelity to the beast, they will be persecuted. God's people who supposedly submit their fidelity to God alone have an unavoidable choice to make in the midst of the pressure to defect. But John wants his readers to exercise wisdom in understanding the beast's number, which shows that the beast and its kingdom, no matter how much it claims to be greater than God, is in truth far inferior to God and his kingdom. God's wise people must not be deceived but must stay faithful in perseverance (13:10; 14:12–13), fully knowing that the day of reaping is coming (14:14–20).

The fourth instance of σοφία is in 17:9, another important passage where John calls his readers to understand the reality of the beast and of Babylon the harlot. Babylon, the great city of the beast, is presented as an evil woman who seduces the people of the world into fornication and who persecutes God's people. She looks ravishing and powerful, but John wants his readers to exercise wisdom in seeing through the deception. The mystery of the beast is that its rule is very short and that its end will be ironically futile and unimpressive. Babylon the harlot will also meet the same ironic end and will be completely destroyed when God's judgment comes. Wise believers must realize this truth and must remain faithful to God rather than allying themselves with Babylon (18:4–8).

Therefore, the last two instances of σοφία especially call the readers to exercise divine wisdom to see the true reality of the beast and of its kingdom. The beast may seem powerful in this world as it deceives people into following it via the appeals to power and to success. Yet those with wisdom should be able to see past the deception and realize that the beast's kingdom can never compare with the grandeur of God's kingdom and that it only has a little time left, which, once it runs out, will mean its complete destruction. In knowing this, God's people must not align themselves with the beast's kingdom but must "come out" of Babylon (18:4) and must stay loyal to God until the end.

Chapters 4 and 5 of this study analyzed the two-women motif utilized by John in Revelation. Chapter 4 first examined the two-women topos that occurs outside of Revelation in extrabiblical and biblical literatures. It was found that the two-women topos was used frequently in sapiential literatures, and the two-women topos was defined as a sapiential motif in which two ethical choices are represented by two women or two camps of women—one good and the other evil—contrasted to bring about the author's intended exhortation to embrace the correct one and to forsake the other. Chapter 5 then dealt with the four women figures in Revelation in light of the two-women motif. Unlike Rossing who understands Revelation as anti-imperial polemic and who thus only examines Babylon and the bride, this study advocated that Revelation deep down has a polemic that is anti-Satan or anti-beast. This meant that all four women figures of Revelation (Jezebel of Rev 2, the radiant woman of Rev 12, Babylon of Rev 17-18, and the bride of Rev 21-22) are relevant and should be examined according to the two-women topos.

As it turns out, Babylon is clearly depicted by John as an evil woman figure of the two-women topos. As the evil woman, she has an amazing ability in seducing and deceiving people into fornication, a feature quite akin to the evil woman of Proverbs 1-9. John also focuses on Babylon's complete demise and not so much on the demise of those who associate with her, which differs from other works that utilize the topos. This makes John's ethical warning not to follow her way of folly even more effective. John has an eternal view in mind, and following Babylon is to participate in her sins which reaps eternal consequences. Only lament from God's judgment awaits those who choose her.

On the other hand, the bride of the Lamb is depicted as a virtuous woman. She is described as wearing fine linen, "bright" and "pure" (19:8), which is a stock description for the good woman of the two-women topos. Furthermore, John has cleverly combined the biblical nuptial imagery of God's people as the bride with virtuous woman imagery of the two-women topos, in order to exhort his readers not only to strive to choose the right woman, but also to become the right woman themselves by righteous deeds (cf. 19:8). By going further than the typical two-women topos in this way, John's call for his readers to remain faithful to God in obedience becomes even more compelling. In any event, using the two-women topos, John has deliberately presented the bride as the counterpart to Babylon, so to communicate that the audience must shun Babylon ("come out"; 18:4) but must choose the bride ("come"; 22:17).

Furthermore, Jezebel of Thyatira and the radiant woman also represent the evil woman and the good woman figures of the two-women respectively. Jezebel of Thyatira has many affinities with Babylon the great harlot. She is a false prophetess and a sorcerer (2:20; cf. 2 Kgs 9:22) just like Babylon (Rev 18:23). Jezebel is also described as a woman who teaches and seduces people to commit harlotry (2:20), which are also actions associated with Babylon (18:23), as well as the second beast (13:14; 19:20) and Satan (12:9; 20:3, 8, 10). She is destroyed by Christ in the end after an opportunity for repentance was exhausted, a fitting end for an evil woman figure of the two-women topos. Jezebel can be thus considered an embodiment, a local manifestation of the evil woman figure of the topos who was wreaking havoc in the Thyatiran church, whom Revelation presents as a female figure the rest of the church at Thyatira did well by not choosing to follow.

This "rest" of the church at Thyatira who did not associate with Jezebel and who gets commended by Christ (2:24–26) has a sure connection with the "rest" of the offspring of the radiant woman (12:17). These "remnants" are described with actions befitting of the faithful believers (cf. 1:9; 2:13; 3:11; 14:12; 19:10; 20:4; 22:9), which in turn suggests that they are true believers who are loyal to God and to the Lamb. This also means that the radiant woman of Revelation 12 is a virtuous woman figure of the two-women topos, since she is the opposite female figure to Jezebel. The radiant woman's appearance, which is one of pure brightness, is a stock image of the virtuous woman of the two-women topos and thus confirms the above observation. As such, Revelation 12 shows that the radiant woman stands in a relationship of enmity with the dragon. She can also be compared with Babylon and with Jezebel in terms of contrast, as well as the bride in terms of resemblance.

In fact, all four women of Revelation share points of contact with one another, whether they be similarities or dissimilarities, and this must be deliberate on the part of the author. Jezebel and Babylon are described in terms of the evil woman figure of the two-women topos and share affinities with one another. Their relationship shows that the threat of the evil woman is real and is evermore present to God's people. The radiant woman and the bride are described in terms of the virtuous woman figure of the topos and share affinities with one another. Their relationship shows that choosing to follow the virtuous woman is an ongoing decision that God's people must continually make in the present despite the threat. Moreover, Jezebel and Babylon stand in contrast with the radiant woman and the bride in Revelation. The former two seduce people with good promises in this life which come to an end just like them; the latter two appeal to people with true promises that are eternal despite hardships in this life. John, using the two-women topos, effectively entreats his readers to make the right choice in Revelation.

Chapter 6 of this study analyzed the seven macarisms and the four ethical lists in Revelation. Macarisms one and six (1:3; 22:7) function to authenticate John's message and to encourage his readers not only to read his message carefully, but also to keep the things written in it precisely in obedience. This means that one must not only obey the specific commands given in Revelation, but also that one must shape one's life in accordance with the message of the book, which is really in loyalty to God and to the Lamb. The second macarism (14:13) functions to assure John's readers that as they stay faithful to God despite what the beast's kingdom may bring, even death by martyrdom, they are "in the Lord," which is truly all that matters. The third macarism (16:15) functions to shift the readers' attention from the violence of the unholy trinity to Christ's second coming, thus urging their preparedness in staying faithful and in perseverance. The fourth macarism (19:9) functions to instill hope on the audience who stay faithful to God that they will gain the honor of getting invited to the messianic banquet which symbolizes perfect communion between the Lamb and his people. The fifth macarism (20:6) promotes the first resurrection that God's people shall gain when Christ comes back, as opposed to the second death that the unbelievers are destined toward, thereby motivating the believers with the upcoming blissful state of the resurrection. The seventh macarism (22:14) encourages the believers one last time to persevere in faithful obedience using the ultimate blessing of the new creation, the tree of life and the right to enter God's holy city. As such, all seven macarisms function to motivate the believers to remain faithful to God in order to participate in the blessings of eternal life.

The first vice list (9:20–21) occurs during the vision of the sixth trumpet and lists sinful actions that the earth dwellers did not repent of. John tells that the people do not repent even with the severity of God's judgment because they choose to worship the beast rather than God, and this causes the readers to see the ugly side of evil and to turn away from it. The second vice list (21:8) occurs during the vision of the new creation and lists sinners who will not inherit the blessings of the new creation. The list is intended to give a more personal discomfort and to warn John's readers that if they continue in the ways of the beast, if they do not persevere and stay faithful to God but cower, they may not inherit the new creation. The third vice list (21:27) is not a vice list proper but is an ethical list nonetheless consisting of two vices and one virtue. It occurs near the end of otherwise perfectly fantastic vision of the New Jerusalem, to give the readers a dose of spiritual reality that they must stay holy in order to participate in the blessings of New Jerusalem. The fourth vice list (22:15) occurs alongside the final macarism (22:14) to remind the readers one last time on who will have the right to the blessings of New Jerusalem and who will not. The fourth vice list also likely unpacks and concretizes the ethical list in 21:27. The combined effect of the vice lists is paraenesis, namely, to encourage the readers to shun the things listed in the lists and to continue the proper way of life which is in fidelity to God.

Therefore, the three major wisdom motifs in Revelation are utilized by John as rhetorical devices to further exhort his readers to persevere in faithfulness and in loyalty to God and to the Lamb. First, John uses the word σοφία strategically to promote the truth that only the Lamb and God possess genuine wisdom, and that believers can exercise this divine wisdom in seeing the deceptive nature of the beast's kingdom as to not be fooled in following it blindly. Second, John uses the two-women topos to shape the four women in Revelation, two evil and two virtuous, to persuade his readers with a familiar ethical choice: following the evil women will lead to death and destruction but following the virtuous women will lead to life and salvation. In doing so, John connects the two evil women with the beast, while the two virtuous women relate to the Lamb. Third, John uses macarisms and vice lists throughout Revelation to show which type of people are blessed for eternal life and which are not, with the effect of warning and encouragement to his readers to be the right type.

As John's use of the wisdom motifs and their functions show, John is very much interested in his readers behaving with the right kind of ethics. This ethics is closely connected with persevering in faithfulness and in obedience to God. John understands a certain drama of conflict between God's kingdom and the beast's kingdom playing out currently in this world, and he also understands that there is an end coming with the sure return of Christ the king. In light of this, he wants his readers to stay loyal to God despite what temptations or persecutions the beast's kingdom may bring. In turn, John's concern for right behavior as expected of God's people evidences that Revelation is not solely about prophesying about the future or about portraying what is wrong in the current world in apocalyptic terms as a way of escape. Revelation yields strong ethical responsibilities on part of its readers, responsibilities that must not be shoved aside. Surely, blessed is the one who reads and who keeps John's words of prophecy, for eternal life depends on it.

POSSIBILITIES FOR FUTURE RESEARCH

As this study concludes, it is fitting to propose several areas for further research. First, although this study highlighted some connections between Revelation and the book of Proverbs, the examination was only partial. There are undoubtedly more instances in Revelation where Proverbs is used or alluded to. A notable difficulty to the study of the use of Proverbs in Revelation, however, is the inherent subjectivity involved in determining the likelihood of allusions. Although challenging, if one can navigate the issue of subjectivism fairly, Revelation studies will significantly benefit from this research.

Second, apart from the two-women topos, this study primarily focused on the text of Revelation in analyzing the use of wisdom motifs. It would now be beneficial to examine how Revelation compares to other Jewish apocalyptic literature in its use of these motifs. Understanding how Revelation is similar or dissimilar to other apocalypses will aid in better understanding the text of Revelation and the world behind this text. In fact, both Revelation studies and Jewish apocalyptic studies will mutually benefit from this endeavor.

Third, while research on Revelation's ethics is in existence, it is scarce to find research on Revelation's ethics in connection with ethics from the other Johannine corpus. This is, first, because scholars do not understand Revelation to be written by John the apostle and because they believe Revelation to be a distinct work, apart from the other works alleged to be written by John. However, it is this author's belief that the Johannine corpus (Gospel of John, 1–3 John, and Revelation) was all written by John the apostle. It will thus be worthwhile to research further on how Revelation's ethics can complement ethics from the other Johannine corpus and vice versa. It will also be worthwhile to see John's employment of wisdom motifs in other Johannine literatures in terms of their function and in conjunction with Revelation.

IMPLICATIONS FOR THE CHURCH TODAY

Revelation's ethics does not simply have a bearing on John's original readers, but it is this author's understanding that it has implications for all time. The church today has had an inordinate focus on Revelation's eschatology, especially on how to interpret its apocalyptic symbols and its times. On the opposite side, the church likewise has had a disproportionate focus on Revelation's backgrounds, especially on what it meant for the original audience. While both focuses are important and are needed, the unfortunate side effect has been the depreciation of Revelation's ethics for the church today. This must be remedied, for Revelation's ethics has eternal consequences.

First, the church must preach and teach Revelation's robust ethics. The sermons on Revelation in the churches tend to revolve around Revelation 1–5, especially chapters 2–3 on the letters to the seven churches, and not much is being preached on chapters 6 and beyond. This is in a way expected, since John's strange visions with peculiar apocalyptic symbols have not fully begun yet in chapters 1–5, which makes the first few chapters easier to handle and to preach from than the rest of the chapters of Revelation. But John is resolute in that the church must keep *all of* his prophecy contained in Revelation (1:3; 22:7, 9, 18–19; cf. 3:3). To truly keep all of John's prophecy, it requires knowing not only the explicit and implicit commands scattered throughout the book, but also the worldviews, behaviors, and patterns of life and of faith John is promoting in the book as a whole. This means that the church cannot ignore what John speaks about in the latter chapters of Revelation but must teach them. This also means that the academia must invest and produce research that can meaningfully and effectively communicate Revelation's theology and ethics in its entirety to the church. To be sure, there is a lot of research on Revelation that cater to the academia, but a perennial question that remains is on how to distill that information so that it can speak clearly to the laity who are already confused and unsure due to the maze of interpretations that exist out there. Perhaps focusing on Revelation's worldviews and ethics that any believer can apply irrespective of one's eschatology and interpretative methods may help remedy the gap and aid in truly keeping all of John's prophecy on part of the believers.

Second, as the church teaches Revelation, it must be adamant in communicating that if one loves the ways of this world, one is following the beast. This is the worldview of Revelation. One either worships God or one worships the beast. There is no in-between. Satan, knowing that his short time is coming to an end, actively uses his partners to persecute God's people and to tempt the world into following its ways, even those in the church, since the cross (see esp. Rev 12–13; 17–18). The beast's influence over the world is powerful, and if one is not careful, it will be very easy to be swallowed up and to entertain the beast's ways. Believers must remember that even John marveled at the beast's city (17:6) and must not presume that it will be simple to resist the devil. They must stay awake and continue to check their ways, whether their ways look more like the ways of the beast or the ways of the Lamb. The communication of the seriousness of this responsibility rests upon the church to instill to its members.

Third, in continuation of the second point above, one of the best means for the church to teach its members about the ways of the beast and of the Lamb can be through examining the macarisms and the vice lists in Revelation. As this study has shown, the macarisms and the vice lists are ethical catalogues of what is acceptable and what is not, and in the case of Revelation, what God specifies as worthy or unworthy for God's new creation. The characteristics of the faithful believers whom God sees as worthy and the characteristics of the people of the beast whom God sees as unworthy are well captured in these ethical catalogues and reminding them firmly to the laity will cause them to strive to be those worthy people destined for eternal life. The church must not shy away but must take Revelation's warning from the vice lists seriously, for if one who professes to be a believer continuously follows the ways of the beast as listed in the vice lists, one may not be a true believer and thereby may not enter New Jerusalem.

Fourth, not only should the church warn its members, but it must also encourage them to be faithful in obedience to God in all areas of their lives, especially finance. Revelation is clear that one of the best methods the beast uses to seduce people is wealth (13:17). Babylon, the beast's city, also uses the seduction of wealth to lure people to follow the beast and its ways (see esp. Rev 18). John wants God's people to use wisdom to see past the deception of seduction and persevere in staying faithful to the

Lamb no matter the cost. The church today must heed John's calling for faithfulness and, instead of giving in, the church must conquer Satan by the blood of the Lamb and by the word of their testimony (12:11; cf. 3:21; 15:2). Encouragement for persevering and conquering, not surviving and evading, must be real goal of the church.

Bibliography

Adekambi, Moïse Adeniran. "Babylone, La Ville à Plusieurs Symbolismes. Une Lecture Exégétique de Ap 18." In *"New Heaven and New Earth" (Rev 21:1) Relevance of the Book of Revelation for the Church in Africa*, edited by Jean-Bosco Matand Bulembat, 103–19. Kinshasa: Association Panafricaine des Exégètes Catholiques, 2004.

Agharanya, Obioma Melak Alemayehu Tsegaw. "Connections between Wisdom Motifs in Proverbs 1–9 and the Three Angels' Messages of Revelation 14:6–12." *Journal of Biblical Theology* 5 (2022) 83–102.

Ahn, Keun-Jo. "A Rhetorical and Theological Study on the Personified Woman Wisdom in the Book of Proverbs." *KJOTS* 79 (2021) 131–65.

Allen, Garrick V. "Zechariah's Horse Visions and Angelic Intermediaries: Translation, Allusion, and Transmission in Early Judaism." *CBQ* 79 (2017) 222–39.

Auberlen, Carl A. *The Prophecies of Daniel and the Revelations of St. John Viewed in Their Mutual Relation*. Translated by A. Saphir. Edinburgh: T&T Clark, 1856.

Aune, David E. "The Apocalypse of John and the Problem of Genre." *Semeia* 36 (1986) 65–96.

———. "Intertextuality and the Genre of the Apocalypse." In *Society of Biblical Literature 1991 Seminar Papers*. SBL Seminar Paper Series 30, edited by Eugene H. Lovering, Jr., 142–60. Atlanta: Scholars, 1991.

———. "Lists, Ethical." In *The New Interpreter's Dictionary of the Bible*. Vol. 3, edited by Katharine Doob Sakenfeld, 670–72. Nashville: Abingdon, 2008.

———. *The New Testament in Its Literary Environment*. Library of Early Christianity 8. Philadelphia: Westminster, 1987.

———. *Revelation 1–5*. Word Biblical Commentary, vol. 52a. Dallas: Word, 1997.

———. *Revelation 6–16*. Word Biblical Commentary, vol. 52b. Nashville: Thomas Nelson, 1998.

———. *Revelation 17–22*. Word Biblical Commentary, vol. 52c. Nashville: Thomas Nelson, 1999.

Baines, Matthew C. "The Identity and Fate of the Kings of the Earth in the Book of Revelation." *RTR* 75 (2016) 73–88.

Bandy, Alan S. *The Prophetic Lawsuit in the Book of Revelation*. New Testament Monographs 29. Sheffield: Sheffield Phoenix, 2010.

Barnard, Leslie William trans. *St. Justin Martyr: The First and Second Apologies*. Ancient Christian Writers 56. New York: Paulist, 1997.

Barr, David L. "Beyond Genre: The Expectation of Apocalypse." In *The Reality of Apocalypse: Rhetoric and Politics in the Book of Revelation*. SBL Symposium Series 39, edited by David L. Barr, 71–89. Atlanta: SBL, 2006.

Barr, James. "Jewish Apocalyptic in Recent Scholarly Study." *BJRL* 58 (1975) 9–35.

Barton, John. "Ethics in Apocalyptic." In *Revealed Wisdom: Studies in Apocalyptic in Honour of Christopher Rowland*. Ancient Judaism and Early Christianity 88, edited by John Ashton, 37–51. Leiden: Brill, 2014.

Bartsch, Shadi and Jaś Elsner. "Introduction: Eight Ways of Looking at an Ekphrasis." *Classical Philology* 102 (2007) i–vi.

Bauckham, Richard. "Approaching the Apocalypse." In *Decide for Peace: Evangelicals and the Bomb*, edited by Dana Mills-Powell, 88–98. Basingstoke: Marshall Pickering, 1986.

———. "The Book of Revelation as a Christian War Scroll." *Neotestamentica* 22 (1988) 17–40.

———. *The Climax of Prophecy: Studies in the Book of Revelation*. Edinburgh: T&T Clark, 1993.

———. "The Economic Critique of Rome in Revelation 18." In *Images of Empire*. JSOT Supplement Series 122, edited by Loveday Alexander, 47–90. Sheffield: JSOT, 1991.

———. "The Eschatological Earthquake in the Apocalypse of John." *NovT* 19 (1977) 224–33.

———. *Gospel of Glory: Major Themes in Johannine Theology*. Grand Rapids: Baker, 2015.

———. *Jesus and the Eyewitnesses: The Gospels as Eyewitness Testimony*. 2nd ed. Grand Rapids: Eerdmans, 2017.

———. "The List of the Tribes in Revelation 7 Again." *JSNT* 42 (1991) 99–115.

———. "Revelation." In *The Oxford Bible Commentary*, edited by John Barton and John Muddiman, 1287–1306. Oxford: Oxford University Press, 2001.

———. "Synoptic Parousia Parables Again." *NTS* 29 (1983) 129–34.

———. *The Theology of the Book of Revelation*. New Testament Theology. New York: Cambridge University Press, 1993.

Baughan, Elizabeth P. "Anatolian Funerary *Klinai*: Tradition and Identity." PhD diss., University of California, Berkeley, 2004. ProQuest Dissertations & Theses Global.

Beale, G. K. *The Book of Revelation*. The New International Greek Testament Commentary. Grand Rapids: Eerdmans, 1999.

———. "The Danielic Background for Revelation 13:18 and 17:9." *Tyndale Bulletin* 31 (1980) 163–70.

———. *Handbook on the New Testament Use of the Old Testament: Exegesis and Interpretation*. Grand Rapids: Baker, 2012.

———. *John's Use of the Old Testament in Revelation*. Journal for the Study of the New Testament Supplement Series 166. Sheffield: Sheffield Academic, 1998.

———. *The Use of Daniel in Jewish Apocalyptic Literature and in the Revelation of St. John*. Eugene, OR: Wipf and Stock, 1984.

———. "The Use of the Old Testament in the Apocalypse." *Southwestern Journal of Theology* 64 (2021) 127–45.

Beale, G. K. and D. A. Carson, eds. *Commentary on the New Testament Use of the Old Testament*. Grand Rapids: Baker Academic, 2007.

Beale, G. K. and Benjamin L. Gladd. *Hidden but Now Revealed: A Biblical Theology of Mystery*. Downers Grove: IVP Academic, 2014.

Beasley-Murray, G. R. *The Book of Revelation*. New Century Bible. Grand Rapids: Eerdmans, 1981.

Beckwith, Isbon T. *The Apocalypse of John: Studies in Introduction with a Critical and Exegetical Commentary*. New York: The Macmillan Company, 1919.

Begrich, Joachim. *Studien zu Deuterojesaja*. Theologische Bücherei 20. München: Kaiser, 1963.

Bengel, Johann Albrecht. *Die Offenbarung des Johannes*. Ernst Franz Metzingen: Württ, 1975.

Betz, Hans Dieter. *The Sermon on the Mount: A Commentary on the Sermon on the Mount, including the Sermon on the Plain (Matthew 5:3–7:27 and Luke 6:20–49)*. Edited by Adela Yarbro Collins. Hermeneia. Minneapolis: Augsburg, 1995.

Bieder, Werner. "Die sieben Seligpreisungen in der Offenbarung des Johannes." *Theologische Zeitschrift* 10 (1954) 13–30.

Biguzzi, Giancarlo. "A Figurative and Narrative Language: Grammar of Revelation." *Novum Testamentum* 45 (2003) 382–402.

Black, C. Clifton. "Rhetorical Criticism." In *Hearing the New Testament: Strategies for Interpretation*, edited by Joel B. Green, 166–88. 2nd ed. Grand Rapids: Eerdmans, 2010.

Blackwell, Ben C., John K. Goodrich, and Jason Maston, eds. *Paul and the Apocalyptic Imagination*. Minneapolis: Fortress, 2016.

——— eds. *Reading Revelation in Context: John's Apocalypse and Second Temple Judaism*. Grand Rapids: Zondervan Academic, 2019.

Blount, Brian K. *Revelation: A Commentary*. The New Testament Library. Louisville: Westminster John Knox, 2009.

Bodner, Keith and Brent A. Strawn. "Solomon and 666 (Revelation 13.18)." *NTS* 66 (2020) 299–312.

Bohak, Gideon. "Greek-Hebrew Gematrias in 3 Baruch and in Revelation." *JSP* (1990) 119–21.

Boismard, Marie Emile. "'L'Apocalypse', ou 'Les Apocalypses' de S. Jean." *Revue Biblique* 56 (1949) 507–41.

Boring, M. Eugene. *Revelation*. Interpretation. Louisville: Westminster John Knox, 2011.

Bousset, Wilhelm. *Die Offenbarung Johannis*. Göttingen: Vandenhoeck & Ruprecht, 1906.

———. *Die Religion des Judentums im späthellenistischen Zeitalter*, edited by H. Gressmann. 4th ed. Tübingen: Mohr Siebeck, 1966.

Bovon, François. "Names and Numbers in Early Christianity." *NTS* 47 (2001) 267–88.

Boxall, Ian. *Christ in the Book of Revelation*. Biblical Studies from the Catholic Biblical Association of America 5. New York: Paulist, 2021.

———. *The Revelation of Saint John*. Black's New Testament Commentary. Peabody, MA: Hendrickson, 2009.

Breier, Idan. "'Who Is This Dog?': The Negative Image of Canines in the Lands of the Bible," *ANES* 54 (2017) 47–62.

Brenner, Athalya. *The Israelite Woman: Social Role and Literary Type in Biblical Narrative*. Sheffield: Journal for the Study of the Old Testament, 1985.

Briggs, Robert A. *Jewish Temple Imagery in the Book of Revelation*. Studies in Biblical Literature 10. New York: Peter Lang, 1999.

Brown, Ian R. "The Two Witnesses of Revelation 11:1-13: Arguments, Issues of Interpretation, and a Way Forward." PhD diss., Andrews University, 2016. ProQuest Dissertations & Theses Global.

Bruns, J. Edgar. "The Contrasted Women of Apocalypse 12 and 17." *CBQ* 26 (1964) 459-63.

Buchanan, George Wesley. *The Book of Revelation: Its Introduction and Prophecy*. The Mellen Biblical Commentary: New Testament Series, vol. 22. Lewiston: Mellen Biblical, 1993.

Burnet, Régis and Pierre-Édouard Detal. "Armageddon: A History of the Location of the End of Time." *Journal of the Bible and Its Reception* 10 (2023) 193-219.

Butler, Josh. "The Politics of Worship: Revelation 4 as Theopolitical Encounter." *Cultural Encounters* 5 (2009) 7-23.

Caird, G. B. *A Commentary on the Revelation of St. John the Divine*. New York: Harper & Row, 1966.

Callahan, Allen D. "Apocalypse as Critique of Political Economy: Some Notes on Revelation 18." *Horizons in Biblical Theology* 21 (1999) 46-65.

Carey, Greg. *Elusive Apocalypse: Reading Authority in the Revelation of John*. Macon: Mercer University Press, 1999.

Carmignac, Jean. "Qu'est-ce Que L'Apocalyptique?: Son Emploi a Qumrân." *Revue de Qumran* 10 (1979) 3-33.

Carter, Warren. "Accommodating 'Jezebel' and Withdrawing John: Negotiating Empire in Revelation Then and Now." *Interpretation* 63 (2009) 32-47.

Charles, J. Daryl. "An Apocalyptic Tribute to the Lamb (Rev 5:1-14)." *JETS* 34 (1991) 461-73.

Charles, R. H. *A Critical and Exegetical Commentary on the Revelation of St. John with Introduction, Notes, and Indices also the Greek Text and English Translation*. 2 vols. International Critical Commentary. Edinburgh: T&T Clark, 1920.

———. *Religious Development between the Old and the New Testaments*. Home University Library of Modern Knowledge 94. London: Oxford University Press, 1914.

Cheung, P. W. "The Mystery of Revelation 17:5 and 7: A Typological Entrance." *Jian Dao* 18 (2002) 1-19.

Cicero. *De Officiis*. Translated by Walter Miller. LCL 30. New York: Macmillan, 1913.

Clement of Alexandria. *Christ the Educator*. Translated by Simon P. Wood. The Fathers of the Church 23. New York: Fathers of the Church, 1954.

Clifford, Richard J. "Isaiah 55: Invitation to a Feast." In *The Word of the Lord Shall Go Forth: Essays in Honor of David Noel Freedman in Celebration of His Sixtieth Birthday*. American Schools of Oriental Research 1, edited by Carol L. Meyers and M. O'Connor, 27-35. Winona Lake, IN: Eisenbrauns, 1983.

Collins, John J., ed. *Apocalypse: The Morphology of a Genre*. Semeia 14. Missoula, MT: Scholars, 1979.

———. *The Apocalyptic Imagination: An Introduction to Jewish Apocalyptic Literature*. 3rd ed. Grand Rapids: Eerdmans, 2016.

———. "The Court-Tales in Daniel and the Development of Apocalyptic." *JBL* 94 (1975) 218-34.

———. *Daniel*. Hermeneia. Minneapolis: Fortress, 1993.

———. *Daniel with an Introduction to Apocalyptic Literature*. The Forms of the Old Testament Literature 20. Grand Rapids: Eerdmans, 1984.
———. "The Genre Apocalypse Reconsidered." *Zeitschrift für antikes Christentum* 20 (2016) 21–40.
———. "Introduction: Towards the Morphology of a Genre." *Semeia* 14 (1979) 1–20.
———. *Jewish Wisdom in the Hellenistic Age*. The Old Testament Library. Louisville: Westminster John Knox, 1997.
———. *Seers, Sibyls and Sages in Hellenistic-Roman Judaism*. Leiden: Brill, 2001.
———. "Social Ethics in Apocalyptic Perspective: The Case of the Epistle of Enoch." *Biblical Research* 64 (2019) 25–41.
———. "Was the Dead Sea Sect an Apocalyptic Movement?." In *Archaeology and History in the Dead Sea Scrolls: The New York University Conference in Memory of Yigael Yadin*. JSPSup 8, edited by Lawrence H. Schiffman, 25–51. Sheffield: JSOT, 1990.
Conzelmann, Hans. *1 Corinthians: A Commentary on the First Epistle to the Corinthians*. Translated by James W. Leitch. Hermeneia. Philadelphia: Fortress, 1975.
Coogan, Michael D., ed. *The New Oxford Annotated Apocrypha*. 4th ed. New York: Oxford University Press, 2010.
Cotterell, Peter and Max Turner. *Linguistics & Biblical Interpretation*. Downers Grove: InterVarsity, 1989.
Coughenour, Robert A. "Enoch and Wisdom: A Study of Wisdom Elements in the Book of Enoch." PhD diss., Case Western Reserve University, 1972. ProQuest Dissertations & Theses Global.
Court, John M. *Myth and History in the Book of Revelation*. Atlanta: John Knox, 1979.
Crawford, Sidnie White. "Lady Wisdom and Dame Folly at Qumran." *DSD* 5 (1998) 355–66.
Crenshaw, James L. "Method in Determining Wisdom Influence upon 'Historical' Literature." *JBL* 88 (1969) 129–42.
———. *Old Testament Wisdom: An Introduction*. 3rd ed. Louisville: Westminster John Knox, 2010.
———., ed. *Studies in Ancient Israelite Wisdom*. Library of Biblical Studies. New York: Ktav Pub. House, 1976.
———. "Wisdom." In *Old Testament Form Criticism*, edited by John H. Hayes, 225–64. San Antonio: Trinity University Press, 1974.
Cruz, Virgil P. "The Beatitudes of the Apocalypse: Eschatology and Ethics." In *Perspectives on Christology: Essays in Honor of Paul K. Jewett*, edited by M. Shuster and R. Muller, 269–83. Grand Rapids: Zondervan, 1991.
Dearman, J. Andrew. *The Book of Hosea*. NICOT. Grand Rapids: Eerdmans, 2010.
Decker, Timothy L. "Faithfulness to Christ as Covenant Fidelity: The Pastoral Purpose behind the Old Testament Allusions in the Seven Messages of Revelation 2–3." *Andrews University Seminary Studies* 55 (2017) 165–93.
Decock, Paul B. "The Scriptures in the Book of Revelation." *Neotestamentica* 33 (1999) 373–410.
Deere, Donald S. "Whose Faith/Loyalty in Revelation 2:13 and 14:12?." *The Bible Translator* 38 (1987) 328–30.
Dempsey, Carol J. "Revelation 21:1–8." *Interpretation* 65 (2011) 400–2.
deSilva, David A. *Seeing Things John's Way: The Rhetoric of the Book of Revelation*. Louisville: Westminster John Knox, 2009.

———. "The Strategic Arousal of Emotion in John's Visions of Roman Imperialism: A Rhetorical-Critical Investigation of Revelation 4–22." *Neotestamentica* 42 (2008) 1–34.

Devine, R. "The Virgin Followers of the Lamb." *Scripture* 16 (1964) 1–5.

De Waal, Kayle B. "The Two Witnesses and the Land Beast in the Book of Revelation." *AUSS* 53 (2015) 159–74.

Dio Chrysostom. *Discourses 1–11*. Translated by J. W. Cohoon. LCL 257. Cambridge, MA: Harvard University Press, 1932.

Dudreck, Matthew A. "The Use of Jeremiah in the Book of Revelation." PhD diss., Westminster Theological Seminary, 2018. ProQuest Dissertations & Theses Global.

Duff, Paul Brooks. *Who Rides the Beast? Prophetic Rivalry and the Rhetoric of Crisis in the Churches of the Apocalypse*. New York: Oxford University Press, 2001.

Du Rand, Jan A. "The New Jerusalem as Pinnacle of Salvation: Text (Rev 21:1–22:5) and Intertext." *Neotestamentica* 38 (2004) 275–302.

Du Toit, Sean. "Ethical Lists in 1 Peter." *JGRChJ* 18 (2022) 59–91.

Dyer, Charles H. "The Identity of Babylon in Revelation 17–18, Part 1." *Bibliotheca Sacra* 144 (1987) 305–16.

———. "The Identity of Babylon in Revelation 17–18, Part 2." *Bibliotheca Sacra* 144 (1987) 433–49.

Easton, Burton Scott. "New Testament Ethical Lists." *JBL* 51 (1932) 1–12.

Ehrman, Bart D., ed. *The Apostolic Fathers*. Vol. 2. LCL 25. Cambridge, MA: Harvard University Press, 2003.

Elliott, Susan M. "Who Is Addressed in Revelation 18:6–7?." *BR* 40 (1995) 98–113.

Escaffre, Bernadette. "Un signe sur le front: d'Ézéchiel à l'Apocalypse." *La Maison-Dieu* 262 (2010) 9–24.

Eurell, John-Christian. "Reconsidering the John of Revelation." *Novum Testamentum* 63 (2021) 505–18.

Fanning, Buist M. *Revelation*. Zondervan Exegetical Commentary on the New Testament. Grand Rapids: Zondervan Academic, 2020.

Farrer, Austin. *The Revelation of St. John the Divine*. Oxford: Clarendon, 1964.

Fee, Gordon D. *Revelation: A New Covenant Commentary*. New Covenant Commentary 18. Eugene, OR: Cascade, 2011.

Fekkes, Jan. "'His Bride Has Prepared Herself': Revelation 19–21 and Isaian Nuptial Imagery." *JBL* 109 (1990) 269–87.

———. *Isaiah and Prophetic Traditions in the Book of Revelation: Visionary Antecedents and Their Development*. JSNT Supplement Series 93. Sheffield: JSOT, 1994.

Fensham, F. Charles. "The Marriage Metaphor in Hosea for the Covenant Relationship between the Lord and His People (Hos 1:2–9)." *Journal of Northwest Semitic Languages* 12 (1984) 71–78.

Feuillet, André. *The Apocalypse*. Translated by Thomas E. Crane. Staten Island, NY: Alba House, 1964.

———. "Les 144,000 Israélites Marqués d'un Sceau." *NovT* 9 (1967) 191–224.

Finitsis, Antonios. *Visions and Eschatology: A Socio-Historical Analysis of Zechariah 1–6*. London: Bloomsbury, 2013.

Fiorenza, Elisabeth Schüssler. *The Book of Revelation: Justice and Judgment*. 2nd ed. Minneapolis: Fortress, 1998.

———. "The Followers of the Lamb: Visionary Rhetoric and Social-Political Situation." *Semeia* 36 (1986) 123–46.

———. "The Phenomenon of Early Christian Apocalyptic. Some Reflections on Method." In *Apocalypticism in the Mediterranean World and the Near East: Proceedings of the International Colloquium on Apocalypticism, Uppsala, August 12-17, 1979*, edited by David Hellholm, 295–316. Tübingen: Mohr, 1983.

———. *Revelation: Vision of a Just World*. Proclamation Commentaries. Minneapolis: Fortress, 1991.

Fishbane, Michael. "The Well of Living Water: A Biblical Motif and Its Ancient Transformations." In *Sha'arei Talmon: Studies in the Bible, Qumran, and the Ancient Near East Presented to Shemaryahu Talmon*, edited by Michael Fishbane and Emanuel Tov, 3–16. Winona Lake, IN: Eisenbrauns, 1992.

Fitzgerald, John T. and L. Michael White. *The Tabula of Cebes*. Graeco-Roman Religion Series 7. Chico, CA: Scholars, 1983.

Fletcher, Michelle. "Flesh for Franken-Whore: Reading Babylon's Body in Revelation 17." In *The Body in Biblical, Christian and Jewish Texts*. Library of Second Temple Studies 85, edited by Joan E. Taylor, 144–64. London: Bloomsbury, 2014.

Ford, J. Massyngberde. *Revelation: Introduction, Translation and Commentary*. The Anchor Bible. Garden City, NY: Doubleday, 1975.

Forti, Tova. "The *Isha Zara* in Proverbs 1–9: Allegory and Allegorization." *Hebrew Studies* 48 (2007) 89–100.

Fox, Michael V. "Ideas of Wisdom in Proverbs 1–9." *JBL* 116 (1997) 613–33.

———. *Proverbs 1–9: A New Translation with Introduction and Commentary*. The Anchor Bible 18A. New York: Doubleday, 2000.

Frey, Jörg. "Erwägungen zum Verhältnis der Johannesapokalypse zu den übrigen Schriften im Corpus Johanneum." In *Die johanneische Frage*. Wissenschaftliche Untersuchungen zum Neuen Testament 67, 326–429. Tübingen: J. C. B. Mohr, 1993.

Frey, Jörg, James A. Kelhoffer, and Franz Tóth, eds. *Die Johannesapokalypse: Kontexte-Konzepte-Rezeption*. Wissenschaftliche Untersuchungen zum Neuen Testament 287. Tübingen: Mohr Siebeck, 2012.

Friesen, Steven J. *Imperial Cults and the Apocalypse of John: Reading Revelation in the Ruins*. Oxford: Oxford University Press, 2001.

Frilingos, Christopher A. *Spectacles of Empire: Monsters, Martyrs, and the Book of Revelation*. Philadelphia: University of Pennsylvania Press, 2004.

Gage, Warren. "St. John's Vision of the Heavenly City." PhD diss., University of Dallas, 2001. ProQuest Dissertations & Theses Global.

Gammie, John G. "Paraenetic Literature: Toward the Morphology of a Secondary Genre." *Semeia* 50 (1990) 41–77.

García Martínez, Florentino and Eibert J.C. Tigchelaar, eds. *The Dead Sea Scrolls: Study Edition*. 2 vols. Leiden: Brill, 1997.

Giblin, Charles H. *The Book of Revelation*. Good News Studies 34. Collegeville: The Liturgical Press, 1991.

———. "Revelation 11:1–13: Its Form, Function, and Contextual Integration." *New Testament Studies* 30 (1984) 433–39.

Giesen, Heinz. *Die Offenbarung des Johannes*. Regensburg: Friedrich Pustet, 1997.

Glabach, Wilfried. *Reclaiming the Book of Revelation: A Suggestion of New Readings in the Local Church*. New York: Peter Lang, 2007.

Gladd, Benjamin L. *Revealing the Mysterion: The Use of Mystery in Daniel and Second Temple Judaism with Its Bearing on First Corinthians*. Beihefte zur Zeitschrift für die neutestamentliche Wissenschaft und die Kunde der älteren Kirche 160. Berlin: Walter de Gruyter, 2008.

Glancy, Jennifer A., and Stephen D. Moore. "How Typical a Roman Prostitute Is Revelation's 'Great Whore'?" *JBL* 130 (2011) 551–69.

Goff, Matthew. "Wisdom and Apocalypticism." In *The Oxford Handbook of Apocalyptic Literature*, edited by John J. Collins, 52–68. Oxford: Oxford University Press, 2014.

Gregory, Peter F. "Its End Is Destruction: Babylon the Great in the Book of Revelation." *CTQ* 73 (2009) 137–53.

Grimm, Carl Ludwig Wilibald. *A Greek-English Lexicon of the New Testament*. Translated by Joseph Henry Thayer. New York: Harper, 1885.

Gumerlock, Francis X. "Nero Antichrist: Patristic Evidence for the Use of Nero's Naming in Calculating the Number of the Beast (Rev 13:18)." *WTJ* 68 (2006) 347–60.

Gundry, Robert H. "The New Jerusalem: People as Place, Not Place for People." *Novum Testamentum* 29 (1987) 254–64.

Han, Chul Heum. "Suffering and Resistance in the Apocalypse: A Cultural Studies Approach to Apocalyptic Crisis." PhD diss., Vanderbilt University, 2014. ProQuest Dissertations & Theses Global.

Hanson, Paul D. "Apocalypticism." In *IDBSup*, edited by Keith Crim, 27–34. Nashville: Abingdon, 1976.

———. *The Dawn of Apocalyptic*. Philadelphia: Fortress, 1975.

———. "Prolegomena to the Study of Jewish Apocalyptic." In *Magnalia Dei, the Mighty Acts of God: Essays on the Bible and Archaeology in Memory of G. Ernest Wright*, edited by Frank Moore Cross, Werner E. Lemke, and Patrick D. Miller, Jr., 389–413. Garden City, NY: Doubleday, 1976.

Harker, Ryan D. "Intertextuality, Apocalypticism, and Covenant: The Rhetorical Force of the New Jerusalem in Rev 21:9—22:5." *Horizons in Biblical Theology* 38 (2016) 45–73.

Harland, Philip A. *Associations, Synagogues, and Congregations: Claiming a Place in Ancient Mediterranean Society*. Minneapolis: Fortress, 2003.

———. "Honouring the Emperor or Assailing the Beast: Participation in Civic Life among Associations (Jewish, Christian and Other) in Asia Minor and the Apocalypse of John." *Journal for the Study of the New Testament* 77 (2000) 99–121.

Harmon, A. M., trans. *Lucian*. Vol. 3. LCL 130. London: William Heinemann, 1921.

Harrington, Daniel J. *Wisdom Texts from Qumran*. London: Routledge, 1996.

Hartman, Lars. *Prophecy Interpreted: The Formation of Some Jewish Apocalyptic Texts and of the Eschatological Discourse Mark 13 Par*. Translated by Neil Tomkinson. Coniectanea Biblica New Testament Series 1. Lund: CWK Gleerup, 1966.

Hartopo, Yohanes Adrie. "The Marriage of the Lamb: The Background and Function of the Marriage Imagery in the Book of Revelation." PhD diss., Westminster Theological Seminary, 2005. ProQuest Dissertations & Theses Global.

Hatfield, Stephen G. "The Rhetorical Function of Selected Vice/Virtue Lists in the Letters of Paul." PhD diss., Southwestern Baptist Theological Seminary, 1987.

Hays, Richard B. *Echoes of Scripture in the Letters of Paul*. New Haven: Yale University Press, 1989.

Hayward, Robert. *The Targum of Jeremiah: Translation, with a Critical Introduction, Apparatus and Notes.* The Aramaic Bible 12. Collegeville, MN: Michael Glazier, 1987.
Heister, Chantel R. "Jezebel's Punishment in Revelation 2: Research and Trends." *CBR* 20 (2022) 186–99.
Hellholm, David, ed. *Apocalypticism in the Mediterranean World and the Near East: Proceedings of the International Colloquium on Apocalypticism, Uppsala, August 12–17, 1979.* Tübingen: J. C. B. Mohr, 1983.
———. "The Problem of Apocalyptic Genre and the Apocalypse of John." *Semeia* 36 (1986) 13–64.
Hemer, Colin J. *The Letters to the Seven Churches of Asia in Their Local Setting.* The Biblical Resource Series. Grand Rapids: Eerdmans, 2001.
Hendricksen, William. *More than Conquerors: An Interpretation of the Book of Revelation.* London: Tyndale, 1962; reprint, Grand Rapids: Baker, 1982.
Hengstenberg, Ernst Wilhelm. *The Revelation of St John: Expounded for Those Who Search the Scriptures.* Vol. 2. Translated by Patrick Fairbairn. New York: Robert Carter and Brothers, 1853.
Hölscher, Gustav. "Die Entstehung des Buches Daniel." *ThStKr* 92 (1919) 113–38.
Horsley, Richard. *Revolt of the Scribes: Resistance and Apocalyptic Origins.* Minneapolis: Fortress, 2010.
———. *Scribes, Visionaries, and the Politics of Second Temple Judea.* Louisville, KY: Westminster John Knox, 2007.
Hort, F. J. A. *The Apocalypse of St John I–III: The Greek Text with Introduction, Commentary, and Additional Notes.* London: Macmillan, 1908.
Hoskins, Paul M. "Another Possible Interpretation of the Seven Heads of the Beast and the Eighth King (Rev 17:9–11)." *BBR* 30 (2020) 86–102.
———. *The Book of Revelation: A Theological and Exegetical Commentary.* Charleston: ChristoDoulos, 2017.
———. "Priesthood in the Book of Revelation." *The Southern Baptist Journal of Theology* 22 (2018) 101–17.
Howard-Brook, Wes and Anthony Gwyther. *Unveiling Empire: Reading Revelation Then and Now.* Maryknoll, NY: Orbis, 1999.
Huber, Lynn R. "The City-Women Babylon and New Jerusalem in Revelation." In *The Oxford Handbook of the Book of Revelation,* edited by Craig R. Koester, 307–24. Oxford: Oxford University Press, 2020.
———. *Like a Bride Adorned: Reading Metaphor in John's Apocalypse.* Emory Studies in Early Christianity. New York: T&T Clark International, 2007.
Hughes, Philip Edgcumbe. *The Book of the Revelation.* Grand Rapids: Eerdmans, 1990.
———. "The First Resurrection: Another Interpretation." *WTJ* 39 (1977) 315–18.
Humphrey, Edith McEwan. *The Ladies and the Cities: Transformation and Apocalyptic Identity in Joseph and Aseneth, 4 Ezra, the Apocalypse and the Shepherd of Hermas.* JSPSup 17. Sheffield: Sheffield Academic, 1995.
Hylen, Susan E. "The Power and Problem of Revelation 18: The Rhetorical Function of Gender." In *Pregnant Passion: Gender, Sex, and Violence in the Bible.* SBL Semeia Studies 44, edited by Cheryl A. Kirk-Duggan, 205–19. Atlanta: SBL, 2003.
Isbell, Barbara Ann. "The Past Is Yet to Come: Exodus Typology in the Apocalypse." PhD diss., Southwestern Baptist Theological Seminary, 2013. ProQuest Dissertations & Theses Global.

Istrate, Daniel. "Sealing the Slaves of God: Revelation 7 in the Stream of Biblical-Christological Interpretation." PhD diss., Westminster Theological Seminary, 2014. ProQuest Dissertations & Theses Global.
Italicus, Silius. *Punica*. Vol. 2. Translated by J. D. Duff. LCL 278. Cambridge, MA: Harvard University Press, 1934.
Jauhiainen, Marko. *The Use of Zechariah in Revelation*. Wissenschaftliche Untersuchungen zum Neuen Testament 199. Tübingen: Mohr Siebeck, 2005.
Johnson, Dennis E. *Triumph of the Lamb: A Commentary on Revelation*. Phillipsburg, NJ: P&R Publishing, 2001.
Johnson, E. Elizabeth. *The Function of Apocalyptic and Wisdom Traditions in Romans 9–11*. SBL Dissertation Series 109. Atlanta: Scholars, 1989.
Johnson, Timothy. "Apocalypticism, Apocalyptic Literature." In *Dictionary of the Old Testament Prophets*, edited by Mark J. Boda and J. Gordon McConville. Downers Grove: IVP Academic, 2012.
———. "From Where Should Apocalyptic Be Found?: The Book of Job as Key to von Rad's Theory." In *Riddles and Revelations: Explorations into the Relationship between Wisdom and Prophecy in the Hebrew Bible*. Library of Hebrew Bible/Old Testament Studies 634, edited by Mark J. Boda, Russell L. Meek, and William R. Osborne, 215–32. London: T&T Clark, 2018.
Jones, Daryl L. "An Examination of the Function and Significance of the Seventh Seal, Seventh Trumpet, and Seventh Bowl Towards a Sequential Interpretation of the Twenty-One Judgments in the Book of Revelation." PhD diss., Southwestern Baptist Theological Seminary, 2022. ProQuest Dissertations & Theses Global.
Keener, Craig S. *Revelation*. The NIV Application Commentary. Grand Rapids: Zondervan, 2000.
Keil, B., ed. *Orationes XVII–LIII Continens*. Vol. 2 of Aelii Aristidis Smyrnaei Quae Supersunt Omnia. Berlin: Apud Weidmannos, 1898.
Kiddle, Martin. *The Revelation of St. John*. The Moffatt New Testament Commentary. London: Hodder and Stoughton, 1963.
Kistemaker, Simon. "The Temple in the Apocalypse." *JETS* 43 (2000) 433–41.
Klassen, William. "Vengeance in the Apocalypse of John." *CBQ* (1966) 300–11.
Klauck, Hans-Josef. "Do They Never Come Back? *Nero Redivivus* and the Apocalypse of John." *CBQ* 63 (2001) 683–98.
Kline, Meredith G. "Double Trouble." *JETS* 32 (1989) 171–79.
———. "The First Resurrection." *WTJ* 37 (1975) 366–75.
———. "The First Resurrection: A Reaffirmation." *WTJ* 39 (1976) 110–19.
Klingbeil, Gerald A. "'Eating' and 'Drinking' in the Book of Revelation: A Study of New Testament Thought and Theology." *Journal of the Adventist Theological Society* 16 (2005) 75–92.
Knibb, M. A. "The Book of Enoch in the Light of the Qumran Wisdom Literature." In *Wisdom and Apocalypticism in the Dead Sea Scrolls and in the Biblical Tradition*. Biobliotheca Ephemeridum Theologicarum Lovaniensium 168, edited by F. Garcia Martinez, 193–210. Leuven: Leuven University Press, 2003.
Koch, Klaus. *The Rediscovery of Apocalyptic: A Polemical Work on a Neglected Area of Biblical Studies and Its Damaging Effects on Theology and Philosophy*. Studies in Biblical Theology 22. Naperville: A. R. Allenson, 1972.

Koch, Michael. *Drachenkampf und Sonnenfrau: Zur Funktion des Mythischen in der Johannesapokalypse am Beispiel von Apk 12*. Wissenschaftliche Untersuchungen zum Neuen Testament 184. Tübingen: Mohr Siebeck, 2004.
Koester, Craig R. "The Number of the Beast in Revelation 13 in Light of Papyri, Graffiti, and Inscriptions." *JECH* 6 (2016) 1–21.
———. *Revelation and the End of All Things*. Grand Rapids: Eerdmans, 2001.
———. *Revelation: A New Translation with Introduction and Commentary*. The Anchor Yale Bible. New Haven: Yale University Press, 2014.
König, Judith. "The 'Great Whore' of Babylon (Rev 17) as a Non-Survivor of Sexual Abuse." *Religions* 13 (2022) 1–12.
Kowalski, Beate. "Martyrdom and Resurrection in the Revelation to John." *AUSS* 41 (2003) 55–64.
Kraft, Heinrich. *Die Offenbarung des Johannes*. Handbuch zum Neuen Testament. Vol. 16a. Tübingen: Mohr Siebeck, 1974.
Kraybill, J. Nelson. *Imperial Cult and Commerce in John's Apocalypse*. JSNTSup 132. Sheffield: Sheffield Academic, 1996.
Kuykendall, Michael. "An Expanded Role for the Spirit in the Book of Revelation." *JETS* 64 (2021) 527–44.
Kynes, Will. "The 'Wisdom Literature' Category: An Obituary." *JTS* 69 (2018) 1–24.
Ladd, George Eldon. *A Commentary on the Revelation of John*. Grand Rapids: Eerdmans, 1972.
Lee, Michelle V. "A Call to Martyrdom: Function as Method and Message in Revelation." *Novum Testamentum* 40 (1998) 164–94.
Lee, Pilchan. *The New Jerusalem in the Book of Revelation: A Study of Revelation 21–22 in the Light of Its Background in Jewish Tradition*. WUNT 129. Tübingen: Mohr Siebeck, 2001.
Lemche, Niels Peter. "From Prophetism to Apocalyptic: Fragments of an Article." In *In the Last Days: On Jewish and Christian Apocalyptic and Its Period*, edited by Knud Jeppesen, Kirsten Nielsen, and Bent Rosendal, 98–103. Aarhus: Aarhus University Press, 1994.
Lenski, R. C. H. *The Interpretation of St. John's Revelation*. Minneapolis: Augsburg, 1963.
Leong, Siang-Nuan. "Windows to the Polemics against the So-Called Jews and Jezebel in Revelation: Insights from Historical and Co(n)textual Analysis." PhD diss., University of Edinburgh, 2009. ProQuest Dissertations & Theses Global.
Lindijer, Coert H. "Die Jungrauen in der Offenbarung des Johannes xiv." In *Studies in John Presented to J. N. Sevenster*. Novum Testamentum Supplements 24, edited by W. C. van Unnik, 124–42. Leiden: Brill, 1970.
Loader, William. *The Pseudepigrapha on Sexuality: Attitudes towards Sexuality in Apocalypses, Testaments, Legends, Wisdom, and Related Literature*. Vol. 4, *Attitudes towards Sexuality in Judaism and Christianity*. Grand Rapids: Eerdmans, 2011.
Lohmeyer, Ernst. *Die Offenbarung des Johannes*. Handbuch zum Neuen Testament 16. Tübingen: J. C. B. Mohr, 1953.
Lohse, Eduard. *Die Offenbarung des Johannes*. Göttingen: Vandenhoeck & Ruprecht, 1983.
Loisy, Alfred. *L'apocalypse de Jean*. Paris: Émile Nourry, 1923.
López, René A. "Does the Vice List in 1 Corinthians 6:9–10 Describe Believers or Unbelievers?" *Bibliotheca Sacra* 164 (2007) 59–73.
———. "Paul's Vice List in Ephesians 5:3–5." *Bibliotheca Sacra* 169 (2012) 203–18.

———. "Paul's Vice List in Galatians 5:19–21." *Bibliotheca Sacra* 169 (2012) 48–67.

———. "A Study of Pauline Passages with Vice Lists." *Bibliotheca Sacra* 168 (2011) 301–16.

———. "Vice Lists in Non-Pauline Sources." *Bibliotheca Sacra* 168 (2011) 178–95.

———. "Views on Paul's Vice Lists and Inheriting the Kingdom." *Bibliotheca Sacra* 168 (2011) 81–97.

Louw, Johannes P., and Eugene A. Nida, eds. *Greek-English Lexicon of the New Testament Based on Semantic Domains*. New York: United Bible Societies, 1988–89.

Lunceford, Joe. *Parody and Counterimaging in the Apocalypse*. Eugene, OR: Wipf & Stock, 2009.

Lund, Nils Wilhelm. *Studies in the Book of Revelation*. Chicago: Covenant, 1955.

MacLeod, David J. "The Adoration of God the Redeemer: An Exposition of Revelation 5:8–14." *Bibliotheca Sacra* 164 (2007) 454–71.

———. "The Lion Who Is a Lamb: An Exposition of Revelation 5:1–7." *Bibliotheca Sacra* 164 (2007) 323–40.

Maier, Gerhard. *Die Offenbarung des Johannes: Kapitel 1–11*. Historich-Theologische Auslegung. Witten: SCM R. Brockhaus, 2009.

———. *Die Offenbarung des Johannes: Kapitel 12–22*. Historich-Theologische Auslegung. Witten: SCM R. Brockhaus, 2012.

Malina, Bruce J. *The New Jerusalem in the Revelation of John: The City as Symbol of Life with God*. Zacchaeus Studies: New Testament. Collegeville, MN: The Liturgical, 2000.

Mangina, Joseph L. *Revelation*. Brazos Theological Commentary on the Bible. Grand Rapids: Brazos, 2010.

Marshall, John W. *Parables of War: Reading John's Jewish Apocalypse*. Studies in Christianity and Judaism 10. Waterloo, ON: Wilfred Laurier University Press, 2001.

Mathews, Mark D. *Riches, Poverty, and the Faithful: Perspectives on Wealth in the Second Temple Period and the Apocalypse of John*. Society for New Testament Studies 154. Cambridge: Cambridge University Press, 2013.

Mathewson, David L. "Isaiah in Revelation." In *Isaiah in the New Testament*. New Testament and the Scriptures of Israel, edited by Steve Moyise and Maarten J. J. Menken, 189–210. New York: T&T Clark, 2005.

———. "New Exodus as a Background for 'The Sea Was No More' in Revelation 21:1C." *TrinJ* 24 (2003) 243–58.

———. *A New Heaven and a New Earth: The Meaning and Function of the Old Testament in Revelation 21.1–22.5*. JSNTSup 238. New York: Sheffield Academic, 2003.

———. *Revelation: A Handbook on the Greek Text*. Baylor Handbook on the Greek New Testament. Waco, TX: Baylor University Press, 2016.

———. "Verbal Aspect in the Apocalypse of John: An Analysis of Revelation 5." *Novum Testamentum* 50 (2008) 58–77.

Maximus of Tyre. *The Philosophical Orations*. Translated by M. B. Trapp. Oxford: Clarendon, 1997.

May, David M. "Counting Kings (Revelation 17:10): A Novel Approach from Roman Imperial Coinage." *Review and Expositor* 114 (2017) 239–46.

McEleney, Neil J. "The Vice Lists of the Pastoral Epistles." *CBQ* 36 (1974) 203–19.

McNicol, Allan J. *The Conversion of the Nations in Revelation.* Library of New Testament Studies 438. New York: T&T Clark, 2011.
Michaels, J. Ramsey. "The First Resurrection: A Response." *WTJ* 39 (1976) 100–9.
———. *Interpreting the Book of Revelation.* Guides to New Testament Exegesis 6. Grand Rapids: Baker, 1992.
———. *Revelation.* The IVP New Testament Commentary Series. Downers Grove: IVP Academic, 1997.
Middleton, Paul. *The Violence of the Lamb: Martyrs as Agents of Divine Judgment in the Book of Revelation.* Library of New Testament Studies 586. New York: T&T Clark, 2018.
Miguéns, Manuel. "Los 'Reyes' de Apc 17, 9ss." *Estudios Bíblicos* 32 (1973) 5–24.
Miller, Kevin E. "The Nuptial Eschatology of Revelation 19–22." *CBQ* 60 (1998) 301–18.
Miller, Jr., Patrick D., Paul D. Hanson, and S. Dean McBride, eds. *Ancient Israelite Religion.* Philadelphia: Fortress, 1987.
Minear, Paul S. *I Saw a New Earth: An Introduction to the Visions of the Apocalypse.* Washington: Corpus, 1968.
———. "Ontology and Ecclesiology in the Apocalypse." *New Testament Studies* 12 (1966) 89–105.
———. "The Wounded Beast." *JBL* 72 (1953) 93–101.
Moeller, Henry R. "Wisdom Motifs and John's Gospel." *Bulletin of the Evangelical Theological Society* 6 (1963) 92–99.
Mollett, Margaret. "Telescopic Reiteration: How Ralph Korner Left Behind a Linear Reading of the Visionary Content in the Apocalypse." *Religion & Theology* 21 (2014) 401–20.
Moloney, Francis J. "Tracing a Literary Structure in the Book of Revelation." *CBQ* 84 (2022) 642–59.
Moo, Jonathan. "The Sea That Is No More: Rev 21:1 and the Function of Sea Imagery in the Apocalypse of John." *Novum Testamentum* 51 (2009) 148–67.
Morales, Jon. *Christ, Shepherd of the Nations: The Nations as Narrative Character and Audience in John's Apocalypse.* Library of New Testament Studies 577. New York: T&T Clark, 2018.
Morray-Jones, C. R. A. "The Opening of Heaven in the Book of Job." In *Revealed Wisdom: Studies in Apocalyptic in Honour of Christopher Rowland.* Ancient Judaism and Early Christianity 88, edited by John Ashton, 10–36. Leiden: Brill, 2014.
Morris, Leon. *The Book of Revelation: An Introduction and Commentary.* 2nd ed. The Tyndale New Testament Commentaries. Grand Rapids: Eerdmans, 1987.
Morton, Russell. "Glory to God and to the Lamb: John's Use of Jewish and Hellenistic/Roman Themes in Formatting His Theology in Revelation 4–5." *JSNT* 83 (2001) 89–109.
Mounce, Robert H. *The Book of Revelation.* Rev. ed. NICNT. Grand Rapids: Eerdmans, 1997.
Moyise, Steve. *The Old Testament in the Book of Revelation.* Journal for the Study of the New Testament Supplement Series 115. New York: Bloomsbury, 1995.
Muirhead, I. A. "The Bride of Christ." *Scottish Journal of Theology* 5 (1952) 175–87.
Müller, Hans-Peter. "Mantische Weisheit und Apokalyptik." In *Congress Volume Uppsala 1971.* Supplements to Vetus Testamentum 22, edited by G. W. Anderson, P. A. H. De Boer, G. R. Castellino, et al, 268–93. Leiden: Brill, 1972.

Müller, Ulrich B. *Die Offenbarung des Johannes.* Würzburg: Gütersloher Verlagshaus, 1984.

Nagy, József. "'I Will Come Like a Thief' (Rev 3:3, 16:15)." *Studia Universitatis Babeș-Bolyai, Theologia Reformata Transylvanica* 68 (2023) 7–25.

Nakhro, Mazie. "The Manner of Worship according to the Book of Revelation." *Bibliotheca Sacra* 158 (2001) 165–80.

———. "The Meaning of Worship according to the Book of Revelation." *Bibliotheca Sacra* 158 (2001) 75–85.

———. "The Worship of God in the Apocalypse: Its Function for the Corporate Worship of the Church." PhD diss., Dallas Theological Seminary, 2000. ProQuest Dissertations & Theses Global.

Nickelsburg, George W. E. and James C. VanderKam. *1 Enoch: The Hermeneia Translation.* Minneapolis: Fortress, 2012.

Nwachukwu, Oliver O. *Beyond Vengeance and Protest: A Reflection on the Macarisms in Revelation.* Studies in Biblical Literature 71. New York: Peter Lang, 2005.

O'Kane, Martin. "Wisdom Influence in First Isaiah." *Proceedings of the Irish Biblical Association* 14 (1991) 64–78.

Osborne, Grant R. *The Hermeneutical Spiral: A Comprehensive Introduction to Biblical Interpretation.* 2nd ed. Downers Grove: IVP Academic, 2006.

———. *Revelation.* Baker Exegetical Commentary on the New Testament. Grand Rapids: Baker, 2002.

Oswalt, John N. *The Book of Isaiah: Chapters 40–66.* NICOT. Grand Rapids: Eerdmans, 1998.

Parrott, Shannon. "Apparel Oft Proclaims the (Jerusale)man: The Priority of Dress and Formation of the Subject in Isaiah 61:10–62:5." Paper presented at the annual meeting of the Society of Biblical Literature, virtual meeting, November 30, 2020.

Passaro, Angelo, Giuseppe Bellia, and John J. Collins, eds. *The Book of Wisdom in Modern Research: Studies on Tradition, Redaction, and Theology.* Deuterocanonical and Cognate Literature Yearbook 2005. Berlin: Walter de Gruyter, 2005.

Pate, C. Marvin, ed. *Four Views on The Book of Revelation.* Counterpoints. Grand Rapids: Zondervan, 1998.

Patrick, Dale and Allen Scult. *Rhetoric and Biblical Interpretation.* JSOTSup 82. Sheffield: The Almond, 1990.

Pattemore, Stephen. *The People of God in the Apocalypse: Discourse, Structure, and Exegesis.* Society for New Testament Studies 128. Cambridge: Cambridge University Press, 2004.

Patterson, Paige. *Revelation.* The New American Commentary. Nashville: B&H, 2012.

Patterson, Richard D. "Singing the New Song: An Examination of Psalms 33, 96, 98, and 149." *Bibliotheca Sacra* 164 (2007) 416–34.

Paul, Ian. "The Book of Revelation: Image, Symbol and Metaphor." In *Studies in the Book of Revelation,* edited by Steve Moyise, 131–47. New York: T&T Clark, 2001.

———. *Revelation: An Introduction and Commentary.* Tyndale New Testament Commentaries. Downers Grove: IVP Academic, 2018.

Paulien, Jon. "Elusive Allusions: The Problematic Use of the OT in Revelation." *Biblical Research* 33 (1988) 37–53.

Perdue, Leo G., Bernard Brandon Scott, and William Johnston Wiseman, eds. *In Search of Wisdom: Essays in Memory of John G. Gammie.* Louisville: Westminster/John Knox, 1993.

Perdue, Leo G. *Reconstructing Old Testament Theology: After the Collapse of History*. Overtures to Biblical Theology. Minneapolis: Fortress, 2005.
——. *Wisdom & Creation: The Theology of Wisdom Literature*. Nashville: Abingdon, 1994.
Peters, Olutola K. *The Mandate of the Church in the Apocalypse of John*. Studies in Biblical Literature 77. New York: Peter Lang, 2005.
Philo. *Philo in Ten Volumes*. Vol. 2. Translated by F. H. Colson and G. H. Whitaker. LCL 227. Cambridge, MA: Harvard University Press, 1958.
——. *Philo in Ten Volumes*. Vol. 4. Translated by F. H. Colson and G. H. Whitaker. LCL 261. Cambridge, MA: Harvard University Press, 1958.
——. *Philo in Ten Volumes*. Vol. 5. Translated by F. H. Colson and G. H. Whitaker. LCL 275. Cambridge, MA: Harvard University Press, 1958.
Philostratus. *The Life of Apollonius of Tyana: Books 5–8*. Vol. 2. Translated by Christopher P. Jones. LCL 17. Cambridge, MA: Harvard University Press, 2005.
Pieters, Albertus. *The Lamb, the Woman and the Dragon: An Exposition of the Revelation of St. John*. 2nd ed. Grand Rapids: Church, 1946.
Pillay, Miranda N. "Reading Revelation 18: A South African Theo-Ethical Feminist Perspective in a Context of Violence against Women." *Neotestamentica* 53 (2019) 421–36.
Pippin, Tina. *Apocalyptic Bodies: The Biblical End of the World in Text and Image*. London: Routledge, 1999.
——. *Death and Desire: The Rhetoric of Gender in the Apocalypse of John*. Louisville, KY: Westminster/John Knox, 1992.
——. "Jezebel Re-Vamped." *Semeia* 69 (1995) 221–33.
——. "Wisdom and Apocalyptic in the Apocalypse of John: Desiring Sophia." In *In Search of Wisdom: Essays in Memory of John G. Gammie*, edited by Leo G. Perdue, Bernard Brandon Scott, and William Johnston, 285–95. Louisville: Westminster/John Knox, 1993.
Podeszwa, Paweł. "Doksologie Apokalipsy jako Model Modlitwy Uwielbienia." *Verbum Vitae* 22 (2012) 155–84.
Pollard, Leslie N. "The Function of Λοιπος in the Letter to Thyatira." *AUSS* 46 (2008) 45–63.
Pope, Martin H. "Number." In *The Interpreter's Dictionary of the Bible*, 561–67. Nashville: Abingdon, 1962.
Portier-Young, Anathea E. *Apocalypse against Empire: Theologies of Resistance in Early Judaism*. Grand Rapids: Eerdmans, 2011.
Prigent, Pierre. *L'Apocalypse de Saint Jean*. Commentaire du Nouveau Testament XIV. Lausanne, Paris: Delachaux & Niestlé, 1981.
——. "Au temps de l'Apocalypse, 2. Le culte impérial au Ier siècle en Asie Mineure." *Revue d'histoire et de philosophie religieuses* 55 (1975) 215–35.
——. *Commentary on the Apocalypse of St. John*. Translated by Wendy Pradels. Tübingen: Mohr Siebeck, 2001.
Provan, Iain. "Foul Spirits, Fornication, and Finance: Revelation 18 from an Old Testament Perspective." *Journal for the Study of the New Testament* 64 (1996) 81–100.
Puech, Émile. "4Q525 et les péricopes des Béatitudes en Ben Sira et Matthieu." *Revue Biblique* 98 (1991) 80–106.

Quick, Laura. "The Hidden Body as Literary Strategy in *4QWiles of the Wicked Woman* (4Q184)." *DSD* 27 (2020) 234–56.
Rainbow, Paul A. *Johannine Theology: The Gospel, the Epistles, and the Apocalypse.* Downers Grove: InterVarsity, 2014.
Ramsay, W. M. *The Letters to the Seven Churches of Asia and Their Place in the Plan of the Apocalypse.* Grand Rapids: Baker, 1963.
Räpple, Eva Maria. *The Metaphor of the City in the Apocalypse of John.* Studies in Biblical Literature 67. New York: Peter Lang, 2004.
Razafiarivony, Davidson. "Is the Woman of Revelation 17 the Same Woman of Revelation 12?." *JBT* 6 (2023) 134–49.
Resseguie, James L. *Revelation Unsealed: A Narrative Critical Approach to John's Apocalypse.* Boston: Brill, 1998.
Reynolds, Benjamin E. "Jewish Apocalyptic Tradition's Shaping of New Testament Thought." Paper presented at the Wisdom and Apocalypticism Program Unit during the annual meeting of the Society of Biblical Literature, November 19, 2018.
Reynolds, Benjamin E. and Loren T. Stuckenbruck, eds. *The Jewish Apocalyptic Tradition and the Shaping of New Testament Thought.* Minneapolis: Fortress, 2017.
Richard, Pablo. *Apocalypse: A People's Commentary on the Book of Revelation.* Maryknoll, NY: Orbis, 1995.
Riley, William. "Who is the Woman of Revelation 12?." *PIBA* 18 (1995) 15–39.
Rissi, Mathias. *The Future of the World: An Exegetical Study of Revelation 19.11–22.15.* Studies in Biblical Theology 23. Naperville, IL: A. R. Allenson, 1972.
———. *Time and History: A Study on the Revelation.* Translated by Gordon C. Winsor. Richmond: John Knox, 1966.
Robinson, Adam D. "An Interpretation of the Sexual Immorality Language in the Book of Revelation." PhD diss., Southwestern Baptist Theological Seminary, 2019. ProQuest Dissertations & Theses Global.
Robinson, J. A. T. *Jesus and His Coming: The Emergence of a Doctrine.* London: SCM, 1957.
Roloff, Jürgen. *Die Offenbarung des Johannes.* Zürcher Bibelkommentare. Zürich: Theologischer Verlag, 1984.
Rosenberg, Eliza. "'When Mr. Lamb Took Ms. Jerusalem to Be His Loftily Wedded Wife:' Marriage, Slave-Trading, and Violent Justice in Revelation 17–22." PhD diss., McGill University, 2015. ProQuest Dissertations & Theses Global.
Rossing, Barbara R. *The Choice between Two Cities: Whore, Bride, and Empire in the Apocalypse.* Harvard Theological Studies 48. Harrisburg, PA: Trinity Press International, 1999.
Rowland, Christopher. *The Open Heaven: A Study of Apocalyptic in Judaism and Early Christianity.* New York: Crossroad, 1982.
Rowley, H. H. *The Relevance of Apocalyptic: A Study of Jewish and Christian Apocalypses from Daniel to the Revelation.* Rev. ed. New York: Association, 1963.
Royalty, Jr., Robert M. *The Streets of Heaven: The Ideology of Wealth in the Apocalypse of John.* Macon, GA: Mercer University Press, 1998.
Ruiz, Jean-Pierre. "The Apocalypse of John and Contemporary Roman Catholic Liturgy." *Worship* 68 (1994) 482–504.

———. *Ezekiel in the Apocalypse: The Transformation of Prophetic Language in Revelation 16,17 – 19,10*. European University Studies 23. New York: Peter Lang, 1989.

Sæbø, Magne. "Old Testament Apocalyptic in Its Relation to Prophecy and Wisdom: The View of Gerhard von Rad Reconsidered." In *In the Last Days: On Jewish and Christian Apocalyptic and Its Period*, edited by Knud Jeppesen, Kirsten Nielsen, and Bent Rosendal, 78–91. Aarhus: Aarhus University Press, 1994.

Sappington, Thomas J. "The Factor of Function in Defining Jewish Apocalyptic Literature." *JSP* 12 (1994) 83–123.

Satake, Akira. *Die Offenbarung des Johannes*. Göttingen: Vandenhoeck & Ruprecht, 2008.

Schedtler, Justin Jeffcoat. "Mother of Gods, Mother of Harlots: The Image of the Mother Goddess behind the Depiction of the 'Whore of Babylon' in Revelation 17." *Novum Testamentum* 59 (2017) 52–70.

———. "Praising Christ the King: Royal Discourse and Ideology in Revelation 5." *Novum Testamentum* 60 (2018) 162–82.

Schmidt, Johann M. *Die jüdische Apokalyptik: Die Geschichte ihrer Erforschung von den Anfängen bis zu den Textfunden von Qumran*. 2nd ed. Neukirchen-Vluyn: Neukirchener Verlag, 1969.

Schmidt, Josef. "Νους und Σοφια in Offb 17." *Novum Testamentum* 46 (2004) 164–89.

Schreiner, Thomas R. *The Joy of Hearing: A Theology of the Book of Revelation*. NTT 1. Wheaton: Crossway, 2021.

Seal, David R. "A Performance-Critical Analysis of Revelation 1:5B–8." *Bibliotheca Sacra* 175 (2018) 215–27.

Selvidge, Marla J. "Powerful and Powerless Women in the Apocalypse." *Neotestamentica* 26 (1992) 157–67.

Shupak, Nili. "Female Imagery in Proverbs 1–9 in the Light of Egyptian Sources." *Vetus Testamentum* 61 (2011) 310–23.

Siew, Antoninus King Wai. *The War between the Two Beasts and the Two Witnesses: A Chiastic Reading of Revelation 11.1–14.5*. LNTS 283. New York: T&T Clark, 2005.

Skehan, Patrick W. "The Acrostic Poem in Sirach 51:13–30." *The Harvard Theological Review* 64 (1971) 387–400.

Smalley, Stephen S. *The Revelation to John: A Commentary on the Greek Text of the Apocalypse*. Downers Grove: IVP, 2005.

Smith, Christopher R. "The Portrayal of the Church as the New Israel in the Names and Order of the Tribes in Revelation 7.5–8." *JSNT* 39 (1990) 111–18.

———. "The Tribes of Revelation 7 and the Literary Competence of John the Seer." *JETS* 38 (1995) 213–18.

Smolarz, Sebastian R. *Covenant and the Metaphor of Divine Marriage in Biblical Thought: A Study with Special Reference to the Book of Revelation*. Eugene, OR: Wipf & Stock, 2011.

Sneed, Mark. "Is the 'Wisdom Tradition' a Tradition?." *CBQ* 73 (2011) 50–71.

———, ed. *Was There a Wisdom Tradition?: New Prospects in Israelite Wisdom Studies*. Ancient Israel and Its Literature 23. Atlanta: SBL, 2015.

Spatafora, Andrea. *From the Temple of God to God as the Temple: A Biblical Theological Study of the Temple in the Book of Revelation*. Tesi Gregoriana Serie Teologia 27. Rome: Gregorian University Press, 1997.

Sperou, Mark and Kevin Mitchell, eds. "Vice and Virtue Lists of the New Testament." North Clackamas Bible Community. Last modified March 1, 2014. https://bcresources.net/2200000-nts-frg12-lit-frm-vv-lists-nt-art-bcrx/.

Stanley, John E. "The New Creation as a People and City in Revelation 21:1–22:5: An Alternative to Despair." *The Asbury Theological Journal* 60 (2005) 25–38.

Stefanovic, Ranko. *Revelation of Jesus Christ: Commentary on the Book of Revelation*. Berrien Springs, MI: Andrews University Press, 2002.

Stewart, Alexander E. "Ekphrasis, Fear, and Motivation in the Apocalypse of John." *Bulletin for Biblical Research* 27 (2017) 227–40.

———. "The Future of Israel, Early Christian Hermeneutics, and the Apocalypse of John." *JETS* 61 (2018) 563–75.

———. "Soteriology as Motivation in the Apocalypse of John." PhD diss., Southeastern Baptist Theological Seminary, 2012. ProQuest Dissertations & Theses Global.

Stewart, Alexander E. and Alan S. Bandy, eds. *The Apocalypse of John among Its Critics: Questions and Controversies*. Studies in Scripture and Biblical Theology. Bellingham, WA: Lexam Academic, 2023.

Stone, Michael E. "Lists of Revealed Things in the Apocalyptic Literature." In *Magnalia Dei, the Mighty Acts of God: Essays on the Bible and Archaeology in Memory of G. Ernest Wright*, edited by Frank Moore Cross, Werner E. Lemke, and Patrick D. Miller, Jr., 414–52. Garden City, NY: Doubleday, 1976.

Streete, G. C. *The Strange Woman: Power and Sex in the Bible*. Louisville: Westminster John Knox, 1997.

Stubblefield, Benjamin S. "The Function of the Church in Warfare in the Book of Revelation." PhD diss., The Southern Baptist Theological Seminary, 2012. ProQuest Dissertations & Theses Global.

Stuckenbruck, Loren T. "The Book of Revelation as a Disclosure of Wisdom." In *The Jewish Apocalyptic Tradition and the Shaping of New Testament Thought*, edited by Benjamin E. Reynolds and Loren T. Stuckenbruck, 347–59. Minneapolis: Fortress, 2017.

———. "Early Enochic Tradition and the Restoration of Humanity: The Function and Significance of *1 Enoch* 10." In *Judah between East and West: The Transition from Persian to Greek Rule (ca. 400–200 BCE)*. Library of Second Temple Studies 75, edited by Lester L. Grabbe and Oded Lipschits, 225–41. New York: T&T Clark, 2011.

———. "Revelation 4–5: Divided Worship or One Vision?." *Stone-Campbell Journal* 14 (2011) 235–48.

Sweet, J. P. M. *Revelation*. Westminster Pelican Commentaries. Philadelphia: Westminster, 1979.

Swete, Henry Barclay. *The Apocalypse of St John: The Greek Text with Introduction Notes and Indices*. 3rd ed. London: Macmillan, 1911.

Tabb, Brian J. *All Things New: Revelation as Canonical Capstone*. NSBT 48. Downers Grove: IVP, 2019.

Tan, Nancy Nam-Hoon. "Where Is Foreign Wisdom to Be Found in Septuagint Proverbs?." *CBQ* 70 (2008) 699–708.

Telfer, Charles Kelly. "Gerhard von Rad (1901–1971): A Reluctant Modernist's Approach to Wisdom Literature." *Unio cum Christo* 5 (2019) 191–205.

Thomas, John Christopher and Frank D. Macchia. *Revelation*. The Two Horizons New Testament Commentary. Grand Rapids: Eerdmans, 2016.

Thomas, Robert L. *Revelation 1–7: An Exegetical Commentary*. Chicago: Moody, 1992.
———. *Revelation 8–22: An Exegetical Commentary*. Chicago: Moody, 1995.
Thomas, Rodney Lawrence. *Magical Motifs in the Book of Revelation*. Library of New Testament Studies 416. New York: T&T Clark, 2010.
Thompson, Leonard L. *The Book of Revelation: Apocalypse and Empire*. Oxford: Oxford University Press, 1990.
Tigchelaar, Eibert J. C. "Lady Folly and Her House in Three Qumran Manuscripts: On the Relation between 4Q525 15, 5Q16, and 4Q184 1." *Revue de Qumran* 23 (2008) 371–81.
———. *Prophets of Old and the Day of the End: Zechariah, the Book of Watchers and Apocalyptic*. OTS 35. Leiden: Brill, 1996.
Tiller, Patrick A. "The Rich and Poor in James: An Apocalyptic Ethic." In *Conflicted Boundaries in Wisdom and Apocalypticism*. SBL Symposium Series 35, edited by Benjamin G. Wright III and Lawrence M. Wills, 169–79. Atlanta: SBL, 2005.
Tonstad, Sigve. "Appraising the Myth of *Nero Redivivus* in the Interpretation of Revelation." *AUSS* 46 (2008) 175–99.
Torrance, Thomas F. *The Apocalypse Today*. Grand Rapids: Eerdmans, 1959.
Trax, Kenneth. "Happy Reading: Textual Self-Consciousness and Human Flourishing in the Macarisms of Lk 11.28, *Gos. Thom.* 79.2, and Rev 1.3." *JSNT* 45 (2023) 304–29.
Trible, Phyllis. "Wisdom Builds a Poem: The Architecture of Proverbs 1:20–33." *JBL* 94 (1975) 509–18.
Tull, Patricia K. "Rhetorical Criticism and Intertextuality." In *To Each Its Own Meaning: An Introduction to Biblical Criticisms and Their Application*, edited by Steven L. McKenzie and Stephen R. Haynes, 156–80. Louisville: Westminster John Knox, 1999.
Uusimäki, Elisa. "'Happy Is the Person to Whom She Has Been Given': The Continuum of Wisdom and Torah in *4QSapiential Admonitions B* (4Q185) and *4QBeatitudes* (4Q525)." *Revue de Qumran* 26 (2014) 345–59.
———. *Turning Proverbs towards Torah: An Analysis of 4Q525*. Studies on the Texts of the Desert of Judah 117. Leiden: Brill, 2016.
Valdez, Adylson. "El número 666 y las doce tribus de Israel." *RevistB* 68 (2006) 191–214.
Vanhoozer, Kevin J. *Is There a Meaning in This Text?: The Bible, the Reader, and the Morality of Literary Knowledge*. Grand Rapids: Zondervan, 1998.
Vanhoye, Albert. "L'utilisation du livre d'Ézéchiel dans l'Apocalypse." *Biblica* 43 (1962) 436–76.
Van Leeuwen, Raymond C. "Liminality and Worldview in Proverbs 1–9." *Semeia* 50 (1990) 111–44.
Vermes, Geza. *The Complete Dead Sea Scrolls in English*. Rev. ed. London: Penguin, 2011.
Vogelgesang, Jeffrey M. "The Interpretation of Ezekiel in the Book of Revelation." PhD diss., Harvard University, 1985. ProQuest Dissertations & Theses Global.
Von Rad, Gerhard. *The Theology of Israel's Historical Traditions*. Vol. 1 of Old Testament Theology. Translated by D. M. G. Stalker. London: Oliver and Boyd, 1962.
———. *The Theology of Israel's Prophetic Traditions*. Vol. 2 of Old Testament Theology. Translated by D. M. G. Stalker. London: Oliver and Boyd, 1965.
———. *Die Theologie der prophetischen Überlieferungen Israels*. Vol. 2 of Theologie des Alten Testaments. 4th ed. Munich: Kaiser Verlag, 1965.

———. *Weisheit in Israel*. Neukirchen-Vluyn: Neukirchener Verlag, 1970.
———. *Wisdom in Israel*. Translated by James D. Martin. Nashville: Abingdon, 1972.
Vos, Louis A. *The Synoptic Traditions in the Apocalypse*. Kampen: J. H. Kok, 1965.
Waltke, Bruce K. *The Book of Proverbs: Chapters 1–15*. NICOT. Grand Rapids: Eerdmans, 2004.
Walvoord, John F. *Revelation*. Revised and Edited by Philip L. Rawley and Mark Hitchcock. The John Walvoord Prophecy Commentaries. Chicago: Moody, 2011.
———. *The Revelation of Jesus Christ*. Chicago: Moody, 1966.
Waymeyer, Matt. "The First Resurrection in Revelation 20." *MSJ* 27 (2016) 3–32.
Webb, Ruth. *Ekphrasis, Imagination and Persuasion in Ancient Rhetorical Theory and Practice*. Burlington, VT: Ashgate, 2009.
Weeks, Stuart. *An Introduction to the Study of Wisdom Literature*. T&T Clark Approaches to Biblical Studies. New York: T&T Clark, 2010.
Weima, Jeffrey A. D. *The Sermons to the Seven Churches of Revelation: A Commentary and Guide*. Grand Rapids: Baker, 2021.
Wettstein, J. J. *Novum Testamentum Graecum*. Vol. 2. Amsterdam: Ex officina Dommeriana, 1751.
Whybray, R. N. *The Book of Proverbs: A Survey of Modern Study*. History of Biblical Interpretation Series 1. Leiden: Brill, 1995.
———. *The Intellectual Tradition in the Old Testament*. Beiheft zur Zeitschrift für die alttestamentliche Wissenschaft 135. Berlin: De Gruyter, 1974.
Wibbing, Siegfried. *Die Tugend- und Lasterkataloge im Neuen Testament: und ihre Traditionsgeschichte unter besonderer Berücksichtigung der Qumran-Texte*. BZNW 25. Berlin: Töpelmann, 1959.
Wilder, Amos N. "Rhetoric of Ancient and Modern Apocalyptic." *Interpretation* 25 (1971) 436–53.
Williamson, Peter S. *Revelation*. CCSS. Grand Rapids: Baker, 2015.
Wilson, J. Christian. "The Problem of the Domitianic Date of Revelation." *NTS* 39 (1993) 587–605.
Winkle, Ross E. "Another Look at the List of Tribes in Revelation 7." *AUSS* 27 (1989) 53–67.
Witherington III, Ben. *Revelation*. NCBC. New York: Cambridge University Press, 2003.
Wright, N. T. *The Resurrection of the Son of God*. Vol. 3, *Christian Origins and the Question of God*. Minneapolis: Fortress, 2003.
———. *Revelation for Everyone*. Louisville: Westminster John Knox, 2011.
Wright III, Benjamin G. and Lawrence M. Wills, eds. *Conflicted Boundaries in Wisdom and Apocalypticism*. SBL Symposium Series 35. Atlanta: SBL, 2005.
Xenophon. *Memorabilia. Oeconomicus. Symposium. Apology*. Translated by E. C. Marchant and O. J. Todd. LCL 168. Cambridge, MA: Harvard University Press, 2013.
Yarbro Collins, Adela. "Apocalypse Now: The State of Apocalyptic Studies Near the End of the First Decade of the Twenty-First Century." *The Harvard Theological Review* 104 (2011) 447–57.
———. *The Combat Myth in the Book of Revelation*. Missoula, MT: Scholars, 1976.
———. *Cosmology and Eschatology in Jewish and Christian Apocalypticism*. Leiden: Brill, 1996.

———. *Crisis and Catharsis: The Power of the Apocalypse.* Philadelphia: Westminster, 1984.

———. "Feminine Symbolism in the Book of Revelation." *Biblical Interpretation* 1 (1993) 20–33.

———. "Introduction: Early Christian Apocalypticism." *Semeia* 36 (1986) 1–12.

———. "Numerical Symbolism in Jewish and Early Christian Apocalyptic Literature." In *Aufstieg und Niedergang der römischen Welt.* 21.2:1221–87.

———. "The Political Perspective of the Revelation to John." *JBL* 96 (1977) 241–56.

———. "Revelation 18: Taunt-song or Dirge?" In *L'Apocalypse johannique et l'Apocalyptique dans le Nouveau Testament.* BETL 53, edited by J. Lambrecht, 185–204. Louvain: Leuven University Press, 1980.

——— ed. *Early Christian Apocalypticism: Genre and Social Setting.* Semeia 36. Decatur, GA: Society of Biblical Literature, 1986.

——— ed. *New Perspectives on the Book of Revelation.* Bibliotheca Ephemeridum Theologicarum Lovaniensium 291. Leuven: Peeters, 2017.

Yee, Gale A. "'I Have Perfumed My Bed with Myrrh': The Foreign Woman (*'iššâ zārâ*) in Proverbs 1–9." *JSOT* 43 (1989) 53–68.

Zahn, Theodor. *Die Offenbarung des Johannes.* Wuppertal: Broackhaus, 1986.

Zimmerman, Ruben. "Nuptial Imagery in the Revelation of John." *Biblica* 84 (2003) 153–83.

www.ingramcontent.com/pod-product-compliance
Lightning Source LLC
Chambersburg PA
CBHW050344230426
43663CB00010B/1984